Feminist Theory in Practice and Process

Feminist Theory in Practice and Process

Edited by
Micheline R. Malson
Jean F. O'Barr
Sarah Westphal-Wihl
and Mary Wyer

The University of Chicago Press
Chicago and London

The essays in this volume originally appeared in various issues of SIGNS: JOURNAL OF WOMEN IN CULTURE AND SOCIETY. Acknowledgment of the original publication date can be found on the first page of each essay.

The University of Chicago Press, Chicago 60637
The University of Chicago Press, Ltd., London
 Published 1989
Printed in the United States of America
93 92 91 90 89 5 4 3 2 1

Library of Congress Cataloging-in-Publication Data
Feminist theory in practice and process/edited by Micheline R. Malson . . . [et al.].
p. cm.
"Essays . . . originally appeared in various issues of Signs: journal of women in culture and society"—T.p. verso.
Includes bibliographies and index.
ISBN 0-226-50293-7 : $30.00 (est.). — ISBN 0-226-50294-5 (pbk.) : $14.95 (est.)
1. Feminism—Philosophy. I. Malson, Micheline R. II. Signs.
HQ1206.F455 1989 305.4'2'01—dc19 88-33986
CIP

The paper used in this publication meets the minimum requirements of American National Standard for Information Sciences—Permanence of Paper for Printed Library Materials, ANSI Z39.48-1984. ∞ ™

CONTENTS

ACKNOWLEDGEMENTS

Our thanks to Sandra Harding and Nancy Miller for critically helpful comments on an earlier draft of the introduction. Special thanks go to the students we teach, those who challenge us to replace our daily habits of thought with new understandings.

INTRODUCTION

There is change afoot. The fourteen essays collected herein capture a moment of transition, a shift in our scholarship, from the necessarily continuing task of examining the categories and constructs that confine us toward a self-reflective reeducation of ourselves. It is not that the angry theory of the 1970s has been supplanted: the anger remains, just as the reasons for it remain. Nor have we found a single construct or explanation to define our experiences—like social archaeologists who have found their prize. We can say that feminist theory is alive and well, informed by and informing a postmodern world. From Sandra Harding's careful outline of some of the dilemmas within feminist theoretical work to Mary Hawkesworth's rejection of the intellectual angst of postmodernism, the readings in this collection promise to "release the imagination of what could be."[1]

Perhaps the greatest change marked by these essays is the shift away from an undifferentiated concept of woman. The perspectives of Black women, in particular, confirm the observation that "once essential and universal man dissolves, so does his hidden companion, woman" (Harding, 17). And from this dissolution comes the understanding that "whatever we have found useful from the perspective of the social experience of Western, bourgeois, heterosexual white women is especially suspect when we begin our analyses with the social experiences of any other women" (Harding, 16). So, for instance, just as one of the first acts in the development of a feminist theory was to reject the standpoint and experiences of white men as normative, so, too, one of the first acts in developing Black feminist theory has been to reject the perspectives of white women as normative, focusing instead on the concrete everyday experiences of Black women as the basis for theory making. Once these steps have been taken, feminists can begin to document and

[1] Sheila Rowbotham, Lynne Segal, and Hilary Wainwright, *Beyond the Fragments: Feminism and the Making of Socialism* (Boston: Alyson Publications, 1981), 147.

interpret those experiences through a lens unclouded by preconceived notions of what constitutes women's experiences. In this way, Black feminist theory points toward a scholarship that actively dissolves universalizing notions about women.[2]

At the same time, there is a new complexity in feminist thinking about the subjectivity of the individual woman. This development has reintroduced the first person into feminist scholarship. As one *Signs* editorial put it, "We are our own subject matter as, and because, women or Woman is our subject matter; we live and think and write within the gender constructs about which we think and on which we work. The narrative 'I' of the woman may break the subject/object dichotomy that distinguishes the individual from the general."[3]

Another aspect of the new subjectivity can be seen in the emergence of "the concept of a multiple, shifting, and often self-contradictory identity, a subject that is not divided in, but rather at odds with, language."[4] Two scholars from India, Zakia Pathak and Rajeswari Sunder Rajan, incorporate this development into their essay—first in their account of competing religious and cultural values surrounding one woman's story, and then in their attempt to retrieve the "I" of that woman, Shahbano, whose individual identity is subsumed by a hegemonic discourse about "protecting" women. " 'Shahbano' " describes the events and controversies surrounding the passage of the Muslim Women (Protection of Rights in Divorce) Act of 1986. By contesting a lower court's token award for support, a seventy-three-year-old Muslim (whose husband divorced her after forty years of marriage) became the ground upon which India debated religious, legal, and political priorities. Shahbano's practical need for a sustaining income was subsumed under the "discourse of protection" that dominated the ensuing public debate. Though

[2] Some early, and more recent, contributions to this effort include Joyce Ladner, *Tomorrow's Tomorrow: The Black Woman* (Garden City: Anchor Books/Doubleday, 1971), 1–14; Bonnie Thornton Dill, "The Dialectics of Black Womanhood," *Signs: Journal of Women in Culture and Society* 4, no. 3 (Spring 1979): 543–55, and her "Race, Class, and Gender: Prospects for an All Inclusive Sisterhood," *Feminist Studies* 9, no. 1 (Spring 1983): 131–50; Janice Porter Gump, "Reality and Myths: Employment and Sex Role Ideology in Black Women," in *The Psychology of Women: Future Directions in Research*, ed. Julia Sherman and Florence Denmark (New York: Psychological Dimensions, 1978), 351–80; and Phyllis Palmer, "White Women/ Black Women: The Dualism of Female Identity and Experience in the U.S.," *Feminist Studies* 9, no. 1 (Spring 1983): 151–70; and Dorothy Smith, "Women's Perspectives as a Radical Critique of Sociology," *Feminist Methodology* (Bloomington: Indiana University Press, 1987), 84–96.

[3] Editorial, *Signs* 12, no. 4 (Summer 1987): 619–20, esp. 620.

[4] Teresa de Lauretis, "Feminist Studies/Critical Studies: Issues, Terms, and Contexts," in *Feminist Studies/Critical Studies*, ed. Teresa de Lauretis (Bloomington: Indiana University Press, 1986), 9.

the Supreme Court overturned the earlier judgment and awarded Shahbano a more favorable settlement, six months later she attempted to quell the controversy by rejecting the judgment as contrary to Islamic teachings. Pathak and Rajan catalog the debates that continue to rage between and among Muslims, Hindus, progressives and fundamentalists, the government and the courts; and they describe a woman who became a " 'subject-effect,' that is, a consciousness that comes into being in response to and through the investments of a hegemonic or dominant consciousness" (263). The search for an understanding of Shahbano, the individual woman, becomes a search for the moment at which representations of women's experiences are displaced by the discourse of phallocentric privilege.

These new developments—one involving women as a multiple concept and one involving the multiplicity of the individual woman's subjectivity—have required that feminist theoretical constructs assume less and question more about our own theory making. Our critique of totalizing systems in the male tradition, with their "worship of rationality and that circular, academic, analytic thinking,"[5] has taught us to be deeply suspicious of totalizing feminisms as well. The essays herein disprove the notion of a single feminist theory, or even the possibility in the near future that the many strands in feminist theory will be woven into a single fabric. Rather, several contributors directly and eloquently argue that multiplicity must be embedded within the concept of theory itself.

Thus feminist monism has been replaced by "conversation," as Elizabeth Young-Bruehl explains it, "a constant interconnecting of all sorts of representations of our experience . . . as we hear ourselves and others and reflexively interpret ourselves in and through novel conjunctions or conversational moments" (44). You will see the interconnections as you read through the essays: a concern with identity politics, the historical and collective construction of subjectivity, the self-determination of women of color, to name but a few. These concepts have little in common with the academic nouveau. Rather, they affirm the insight of the editors of a previous theory reader from *Signs, Feminist Theory: A Critique of Ideology*, who maintained that women's experience—in one sense ungraspable, but also a human construct—should be the direct focus of feminist theory.[6]

[5] Audre Lorde, *Sister Outsider: Essays and Speeches* (Trumansburg, N.Y.: Crossing Press, 1984).

[6] Nannerl O. Keohane and Barbara C. Gelpi, "Foreword," to *Feminist Theory: A Critique of Ideology*, ed. Nannerl O. Keohane, Michelle Z. Rosaldo, and Barbara C. Gelpi (Chicago: University of Chicago Press, 1981), vii.

This introduction was born of a conversation among the editors of *Feminist Theory in Practice and Process* as we tried to name and formulate our mutually held conviction that these essays together constitute a benchmark in feminist theory. These essays are prefigurative in the sense shared by Sheila Rowbotham and Julia Kristeva, and explored by Thomas Foster's essay, since they open "the possibility of transforming present conditions by bringing to light elements or potentialities that have been repressed and excluded" (Foster, 247). We see not only the future promise of feminist theory as a prefigurative practice, but also how insights might be carried from the past into present understandings. As represented here, feminists seem to have adopted a notion of theory that rejects a discourse of elite empowerment, formulating instead an understanding of theory as a process, a constellation of ideas reconfigured and reconfiguring within a myriad of feminist practices. What follows is a tentative and necessarily partial outline of ideas that have come to the fore since the 1981 publication of *Feminist Theory: A Critique of Ideology.*

Complicating gender

The concept of gender has been one of the most powerful contributions of feminist theory and analysis. By the early 1970s, feminists in the social sciences and the humanities had developed the insight that the behaviors that mark masculinity and femininity are socially constructed, neither innate nor determined once and for all by a biological substratum. The explosion in feminist scholarship across the disciplines in the years since has established gender as a category of analysis, a method for bringing a new, critical, and feminist perspective to the traditional disciplines, and a keystone in the new project called women's studies. With this new approach we have been able not only to identify the bias and error in androcentric knowledge systems but also to begin to question their unexpressed assumptions and tacit ideologies. Now, more than a decade later, feminists have begun to question the assumptions embedded in our own, most productive insight.

The process of thinking about how we think about gender has complicated feminist theory to the point that the dichotomy between sex and gender which afforded the major insight that gender is a social construct has now become problematical. The dichotomy—or rather the thinking in terms of dichotomy—itself seems rooted in androcentric bias. The distinction that was once useful may, in effect, replicate other dichotomies—nature/culture, emotion/reason, female/male—that feminist theory long ago rejected as ideological mystifications of social arrangements that did not serve women's interests. Scholars have documented the hierarchical implications of dualistic thinking in androcentric thought systems; must feminists repeat the mistake?

Jane Flax opens her article by proposing that feminists focus instead on gender as a varying and mutable social relation. By placing gender relations near the center of feminist inquiry, Flax attempts to name that which makes feminist theory specifically feminist. "The fundamental purpose of feminist theory is to analyze how we think, or do not think, or avoid thinking about gender. Obviously, then, to understand the goals of feminist theory we must consider its central subject—gender" (Flax, 56–57). Teresa de Lauretis has also affirmed the centrality of gender for feminist theory: "The female subject is always constructed and defined in gender, starting from gender."[7] As a relation, gender is never independent of other social systems.

Yet gender *relations*, as they are experienced by any individual, are not fixed and immutable. Instead, they are part of the larger category of social relations. Once this is acknowledged and understood, it becomes apparent and acceptable that gender relations are not monolithic but are based on the myriad of social relations that may exist in any society. Social relations imply a positionality that occurs in historical as well as social time, within various (and varying) political and economic contexts that result in a range of interpersonal interactions. An understanding of Black American women's experience of gender, for instance, must be based on the particularities of Black American social and historical experiences, as well as on an individual woman's relationships with Black men, white men, and white women. "Gender relations thus have no fixed essence: they vary both within and over time" (Flax, 54). Or, as de Lauretis puts it, "The female subject is en-gendered across multiple representations of class, race, language, and social relations."[8]

The theoretical advance in thinking about gender as a system of human relations is that this way of thinking both affirms the inseparability of gender and other social relations, such as those involving class, race, or religion, and opens the concept of gender to historical and cultural differentiation. As a result, we can no longer assume a universal determinate of the social construction of gender.

[7] de Lauretis, 14.

[8] Ibid.

Raising consciousness

In *Feminist Theory: A Critique of Ideology,* Catherine A. MacKinnon made a statement that has been quoted and echoed on many subsequent occasions: "Feminist method is consciousness raising: the collective critical reconstitution of the meaning of women's social experience, as women live through it. . . . This method stands inside its own determinations in order to uncover them."[9] A key aspect of MacKinnon's definition is that consciousness and consciousness raising are not only reactive but also explanatory. Consciousness is a collective process that both comprehends social structures and acts upon them. Consciousness raising is the process that mediates between our inner and outer worlds.

Linda Alcoff develops the collective and political aspects of consciousness raising in her feminist theory of subjectivity. Her approach has two parts: a concept of the subject as positionality and a concept of identity politics. The former posits the historical and personal experiences of women as the reference points from which to begin theorizing about our subjectivity. Thus consciousness, as an individual and collective process, is the starting point for feminist theories of the subject; not, as in other theories, essentializing biological or psychological factors, and not external discursive formations that tend to totalize language or textuality. Thus, by beginning with women's experiences feminists hope to escape creating overly deterministic constructs and instead to encourage notions of subjectivity that recognize a mutable historical position. The idea that gender relations construct subjectivity is "an interpretation of our history within a particular discursive constellation, a history in which we are both subjects of and subjected to social construction" (Alcoff, 321). Or, restating this idea in terms of individual agency, Alcoff writes, "All women can (and do) think about, criticize and alter discourse [thus] subjectivity can be reconstructed through the process of reflective practice" (315). Reflective practice, both active and reactive—a concept that conveys important aspects of what others have called consciousness raising—shows how subjectivity is "imbued with race, class, and gender without being subjected to an overdetermination that erases agency" (315).

The idea that consciousness is a strategy (rather than a static state of being) opens the way to a new concept of identity politics. Alcoff begins her discussion with reference to the Combahee River Collective's "A Black Feminist Statement," adding that identity pol-

[9] Catharine A. MacKinnon, "Feminism, Marxism, Method, and the State," in Keohane, Rosaldo, and Gelpi, eds., 1–30, esp. 29.

itics "can be readily intuited by people of mixed races and cultures who have had to choose in some sense their identity" (322).[10] This changes the emphasis from the notion that one's identity is a limiting construction enforced from without to the idea that identity can be a departure point for political action and a decisive rejoinder to the generic human thesis. "As Jewish people can choose to assert their Jewishness, so Black men, women of all races, and other members of more immediately recognizable oppressed groups can practice identity politics by choosing their . . . political point of departure" (322). Consciousness, identity, choice—all are components of a feminist political practice.

Deborah King engages the concepts of identity politics and positionality from the perspective of a Black scholar. She proposes the idea of multiple consciousness, giving it a decisive theoretical formulation. King bases her argument on a lucid historical and sociological account of the multiple exclusions experienced by Black women. She argues that the subject position of Black women can be understood only by abandoning the totalizing analytic constructs of race, class, and gender and replacing them with an understanding of Black women as independent subjects who practice a multiple consciousness and maintain a multifaceted ideological stance. This formulation announces that we do not simply "raise consciousness" but rather that we constantly juggle our various social and psychological identities as we make decisions about the strength and directions of our resistance to multiple oppressions. One challenge for feminist theory, then, is to recognize the myriad forms of Black women's race, gender, and class politics and to envision theories that encompass these lived realities and concrete practices.

Yet another relationship between consciousness and theory making is described by Carol Cohn in her article, "Sex and Death in the Rational World of Defense Intellectuals." It is her "fidelity to parameters of dissonance within and between assumptions of patriarchal discourses" (Harding, 20) that enables her to explain how technostrategic language represents a body of truth to its speakers that exists independently of any other known truth or knowledge. Thus, defense intellectuals can dismiss human suffering and death as irrelevant to their theoretical calculations about the survival rates of nuclear weapons. Cohn describes the shift in her own consciousness during the course of her research, from "feminist spy in the house of death" to competent speaker of a discourse that converts, distorts, and denies all that she values. She realizes with dismay

[10] "The Combahee River Collective Statement," in *Home Girls: A Black Feminist Anthology,* ed. Barbara Smith (New York: Kitchen Table, 1983), 272–82.

that she has forgotten her most pressing convictions, and yet it is precisely the dissonance between these worlds that has informed her analysis. As Harding puts it, "As feminists we need to cherish certain kinds of intellectual, political, and psychic discomforts," since alienated consciousness, bifurcated consciousness, oppositional consciousness, or multiple consciousness can function at the level of theory making as well as at the level of skepticism and rebellion (20).

Engaging contradictions

In her article that appeared in the first *Signs* theory reader, "Archimedes and the Paradox of Feminist Criticism," Myra Jehlen wrote that "there are many ways of dealing with contradictions . . . of which only one is to try to resolve them. Another way amounts to joining a contradiction—engaging it not so much for the purpose of overcoming it as to tap its energy."[11] Engaging a contradiction in order to tap its energy is one way to describe the methodology developed by many of the authors in this collection. The contradictions are those produced within feminist theory itself. They include the contradictions between feminist successor science and feminist postmodernism, between our critique and our embeddedness in the social processes we are trying to critique; between nominalist and essentialist theories of gender, between Kristeva's first and second feminist generations, between the disparate issues of the knower and the known. The energy is personal, political, and transformational.

In his introduction to an essay on Marilynne Robinson's novel *Housekeeping,* Thomas Foster explains that in Marxist analysis, contradiction has the political function of indicating a conflict of interests, an effect of exploitation. Kristeva, he says, departs from traditional Marxism to reconceptualize contradiction so that difference is not reduced to opposition, exclusion, and hierarchic arrangement.[12] Many of the essays in this collection occupy the horizon of hopeful hypothesis that constitutes Kristeva's third generation, showing how feminist theory can, in fact, must embrace seemingly contradictory tendencies—that by doing so we fruitfully complicate feminist political consciousness and strategies. The modifier "seem-

[11] Myra Jehlen, "Archimedes and the Paradox of Feminist Criticism," in Keohane, Rosaldo, and Gelpi, eds., 189–216, esp. 200.

[12] Julia Kristeva, "Women's Time," in Keohane, Rosaldo, and Gelpi, eds., 31–54.

ingly" does not deny that these contradictions are painfully real in our present social reality. Rather, it preserves the possibility that what must now be called a contradiction in feminist theory in fact only seems so from within the discourses and limiting ideologies we now inhabit. Thus Harding observes that feminist theory, and individual feminists, embrace with seeming ease concepts that are diametrically opposed in nonfeminist discourse (25). This ease suggests that feminist theorizing is an extemporal attempt to find ways to talk about our practices.

For instance, while feminist theory questions the epistemological assumptions behind dualistic thinking, it can at the same time retain the sex/gender dichotomy as a highly context-specific concept. Thus, it could become politically expeditious to recognize a special bond between biological mothers and their children in the wake of the baby M controversy. Susan Suleiman sees such a stance as a necessary affirmation of mothers who are asked to choose between being defined principally in relation to their children and being denied the relationship altogether. And yet, feminist theory, in general, can continue to insist on maintaining a strict differentiation between sex and gender, precisely in order to ensure that motherhood does not have to be a choice between unreasonable options.

Engaging the contradictions in feminist theory has two strategic benefits for the present. First, it resists the representation of feminism as a "coherent and available image" in nonfeminist discourses, for "the image of feminism as a coherent ideology, a set of dogmas and rules of conduct repressive to some and oppressive to others, has currency inside as well as outside, the discursive boundaries of feminism."[13] In other words, since feminism can too easily be contained and dismissed as another dogmatic monism, contradictions promise a process that includes theoretical flexibility. Second, by engaging contradictions we can pursue a logic of concrete demands for women in the sphere of policy making, while rejecting essentialist thinking that would see women's interests as both homogeneous and fixed for all time. Alcoff's two-stranded theory of subjectivity is a clear formulation of how such a course is possible. For example, a political program of demands in the name of women—based on a consciousness of gender identity as a point of political departure—can coexist with our problematizing of essentialist concepts like "woman's needs" (Alcoff, 317).

[13] de Lauretis, 15.

Transforming experience

Many of the essays in this collection examine literary and/or autobiographical representations of women's experiences. They are a diverse lot; they do not share methodological approaches or ideological premises; they do not share themes or emphases. They do not even, for the most part, share secondary references. Nonetheless, without any intention to do so, they express in common a determination to end the distortions that have so shaped women's lives and their relations with one another. As Celie says in Alice Walker's *The Color Purple*, "I felt sorry for mama. Trying to believe his story kilt her."[14] They share this ground through a focus on what Christine Froula calls "the breaking of women's forbidden stories into literary history—an event that reverberates far beyond their heroes' individual histories to reshape our sense of our cultural past and its possible future directions" (141).

The salvaging of women's experiences through women's texts—so that fiction becomes a location for theoretical expression—enables us to remember a feminist future by retrieving those elements of women's experiences that have been neglected, repressed, or suppressed.[15] Feminist fiction and feminist theory have, in the past decade and one-half, been closely intertwined, but not in the hierarchical way that would award theory some privileged angle of vision, or, alternatively, see fiction as a substitute for theory. Rather, these essays confirm connections already implied by Adrienne Rich and Audre Lorde (among others), connections that show feminist theory and women's writing in a conversation that suspends interpretive oppositions like textuality versus representation, or French feminist versus North American feminist theory, or theory versus practice.

Leslie Adelson, for example, shows how a short story by the West German author Anne Duden colludes with the distorting influences of white privilege even while it exposes the violence of sexual domination. The story is about the violent silencing of a white German woman by a gang of Black American GIs. Yet the author's affirmation of blackness as "negative opposition" accompanies a racist premise in the description of Blacks. "The cross-cultural specificity of racial conflict in this particular context is very clearly not woven into the texture of the story" (180). As a result,

[14] Alice Walker, *The Color Purple* (New York: Harcourt Brace Jovanovich, 1982), 15.

[15] The concept of remembering the future is evoked by Christa Wolf in her *The Quest for Christa T*, trans. Christopher Middleton (London: Virago, 1982).

the question of the writer's position vis-à-vis racism is unanswerable. Adelson's own positionality is the theoretical lever that attempts to displace the uncritical reception of this story by many West German feminists.

Patricia Williams's autobiographical essay, "On Being the Object of Property," resonates with connections to feminist theory and shows that this theorizing emerges at its best when it is based in the particulars of women's experiences. This is a deeply personal account, and yet Williams offers up to her readers a self woven from threads of many lives. Perhaps because she genuinely shares (rather than claims) insights, her reflections refuse the exclusivity of categories. She offers her readers a series of snapshots through which she and her communities emerge as cohabitating housemates. She breathes life into the feminist theoretical notion of "positional perspective" by embracing her experiences as the granddaughter of slaves, a woman, a writer, and a lawyer, as her location(s) for constructing personal, political, and textual meaning.

One of the critical pitfalls of claiming too close a relationship between women's writing and feminist theory, however, is that it is not clear that the process of writing itself is unmediated by the tacit assumptions and ideologies that historically have privileged the male author. As Marilyn Farwell points out, lesbian experience, when placed at the center of the creative process, exposes the heterosexist underpinnings of literary production. Farwell catalogs the historical and contemporary co-optation of the act of writing—an act that has been defined as essentially masculinist—and reclaims the literary imagination through the highly charged political territory of lesbian consciousness. She proposes that we imagine the text as an expression of the affirmation of self in community with others—to begin a remaking of our culture's monolithic and symbolic representation of women with the understanding that the author and reader together engage in a relationship of primary intensity between and among women.

Naming the politics of theory

In thinking about why Black feminists have not rushed to create abstract theories, Barbara Christian has said that Black feminists are likely to be cautious about pronouncing a theory that might well be misunderstood as a totalizing statement about all women of color. Then she added, "This is not to say we are not theorizing. Certainly our literature is an indication of the ways in which our theorizing, of necessity, is based on our multiplicity of experiences."[16] The multidisciplinary qualities that have become characteristic of feminist research seem also to have created an intellectual climate that values multimodal interpretation. Though the essays collected here speak across disciplines as diverse as literary studies, philosophy, political science, and sociology, they still engage in a single, yet not homogenizing, conversation about women's experiences. This could happen because feminist scholarship, as Chandra Mohanty says, "is not the mere production of knowledge about a certain subject. It is a directly political and discursive practice in that it is purposeful and ideological. It is best seen as a mode of intervention into particular hegemonic discourses (for example, traditional anthropology, sociology, literary criticism, etc.); it is a political praxis which counters and resists the totalizing imperative of age-old 'legitimate' and 'scientific' bodies of knowledge."[17]

Feminist theory, then, is a framework from which to discuss the directions and strategies that formulate our prefigurative practices in the multidisciplinary recovery of women's experiences. Such an enterprise necessarily requires a negotiating of the rugged territory of transdisciplinary theory making. The editors of *Feminist Theory: A Critique of Ideology* put it this way: "Feminist theory reconsiders historical, economic, religious, biological, artistic, and anthropological constructs and explanations. It brings to consciousness facets of our experience as women that have hitherto escaped attention because they have not been part of, and may even have contradicted, predominant theoretical accounts of human life. For to conceive our women's lives as actual often modifies or fractures the constructs that left those lives out of account."[18]

Many of the authors in this collection struggle with the idea that theory must somehow embed within itself a consciousness of its own limitations. Their concerns tend to focus on the inadequacy of theoretical statement to explode boundaries to new thought and not on the inadequacies of those who develop theory. It could be the case (at least the question is still up for debate) that we cannot even begin to operate outside that which contains and constrains our thinking about our womanselves until these boundaries become obvious. What exactly are the dimensions of the boundaries? How do they constrain our choices? When and how have the boundaries been transgressed? What are the various ways in which women

[16] Barbara Christian, "The Race for Theory," *Feminist Studies* 14, no. 1 (Spring 1988): 67–79, esp. 76.

[17] Chandra Talpade Mohanty, "Under Western Eyes: Feminist Scholarship and Colonial Discourses," *Boundary 2*, 12, no. 3 (1984): 333–58, esp. 334.

[18] Keohane and Gelpi (n. 6 above), vii.

mediate the force of the boundaries? Mary Hawkesworth suggests a way to think about answering these questions in her notion of the politics of knowledge and her challenge to those who would abandon "facts" as they have abandoned the search for master theory. She argues for a reconceptualization of rationality and rejects the totalizing (and political) concept of reason as essentially masculinist. In maintaining that human rationality is an ever-expansive and irreducibly plural concept, she gives us a partial listing of its many dimensions: perception, intuition, conceptualization, inference, representation, reflection, imagination, remembrance, conjecture, argumentation, justification, contemplation, ratiocination, speculation, meditation, validation, deliberation.

What this suggests for the process of feminist theorizing is that we can claim all of the resources of our prefigurative practices within an expanded concept of the rational construction of human knowledge. We can structure an understanding of the patterns of women's lives through theories that reject totalities and embrace temporalities as enriching and empowering opportunities for new insight. We cannot argue away the daily realities of the radical inequalities that are based on sexual preference, race, class, culture, region, or religion (it is a long list), generated and perpetuated by and for the hegemonic power of white male privilege. We can be sure that our ability to effect social transformation will be doubted, by ourselves and by others, but the essays herein offer a collective affirmation of an intention to proceed with our pattern making undaunted.

THE INSTABILITY OF THE ANALYTICAL CATEGORIES OF FEMINIST THEORY

SANDRA HARDING

Feminist theory began by trying to extend and reinterpret the categories of various theoretical discourses so that women's activities and social relations could become analytically visible within the traditions of intellectual discourse.[1] If women's natures and activities are as fully social as are men's, then our theoretical discourses should reveal women's lives with just as much clarity and detail as we presume the traditional approaches reveal men's lives. We had thought that we could make the categories and concepts of the traditional approaches objective or Archimedean where they were not already.

As we all have come to understand, these attempts revealed that neither women's activities nor gender relations (both inter- and intra-

[1] My thinking about these issues has been greatly improved by the comments of Margaret Andersen and the anonymous reviewers for *Signs: Journal of Women in Culture and Society*, as well as by discussions over the last several years with many of the feminist science critics cited in this paper. I am grateful for support for this research and the larger project of which it is a part provided by the National Science Foundation, a Mina Shaughnessy Fellowship from the Fund for the Improvement of Post-Secondary Education, University of Delaware Faculty Research Grants, and a Mellon Fellowship at the Wellesley Center for Research on Women. For the larger project, see *The Science Question in Feminism* (Ithaca, N.Y.: Cornell University Press, 1986).

This essay originally appeared in *Signs*, vol. 11, no. 4, Summer 1986.

gender relations) can be added to these theoretical discourses without distorting the discourses and our subject matters. The problem here is not a simple one, because liberal political theory and its empiricist epistemology, Marxism, critical theory, psychoanalysis, functionalism, structuralism, deconstructionism, hermeneutics, and the other theoretical frameworks we have explored both do and do not apply to women and to gender relations. On the one hand, we have been able to use aspects or components of each of these discourses to illuminate our subject matters. We have stretched the intended domains of these theories, reinterpreted their central claims, or borrowed their concepts and categories to make visible women's lives and feminist views of gender relations. After our labors, these theories often do not much resemble what their nonfeminist creators and users had in mind, to put the point mildly. (Think of the many creative uses to which feminists have put Marxist or psychoanalytic concepts and categories; of how subversive these revised theories are of fundamental tendencies in Marxism and Freudianism.) On the other hand, it has never been women's experiences that have provided the grounding for any of the theories from which we borrow. It is not women's experiences that have generated the problems these theories attempt to resolve, nor have women's experiences served as the test of the adequacy of these theories. When we begin inquiries with women's experiences instead of men's, we quickly encounter phenomena (such as emotional labor or the positive aspects of "relational" personality structures) that were made invisible by the concepts and categories of these theories. The recognition of such phenomena undermines the legitimacy of the central analytical structures of these theories, leading us to wonder if we are not continuing to distort women's and men's lives by our extensions and reinterpretations. Moreover, the very fact that we borrow from these theories often has the unfortunate consequence of diverting our energies into endless disputes with the nonfeminist defenders of these theories: we end up speaking not to other women but to patriarchs.

Furthermore, once we understand the destructively mythical character of the essential and universal "man" which was the subject and paradigmatic object of nonfeminist theories, so too do we begin to doubt the usefulness of analysis that has essential, universal woman as its subject or object—as its thinker or the object of its thought. We have come to understand that whatever we have found useful from the perspective of the social experience of Western, bourgeois, heterosexual, white women is especially suspect when we begin our analyses with the social experiences of any other women. The patriarchal theories we try to extend and reinterpret were created to explain not men's experience but only the experience of those men who are Western, bourgeois, white, and heterosexual. Feminist theorists also come primarily from these categories—not through conspiracy but through the historically common pattern that it is people in these categories who have had the time and resources to theorize, and who—among women—can be heard at all. In trying to develop theories that provide the one, true (feminist) story of human experience, feminism risks replicating in theory and public policy the tendency in the patriarchal theories to police thought by assuming that only the problems of *some* women are human problems and that solutions for them are the only reasonable ones. Feminism has played an important role in showing that there are not now and never have been any generic "men" at all—only gendered men and women. Once essential and universal man dissolves, so does his hidden companion, woman. We have, instead, myriads of women living in elaborate historical complexes of class, race, and culture.

I want to talk here about some challenges for theorizing itself at this moment in history, and, in particular, for feminist theorizings. Each has to do with how to use our theories actively to transform ourselves and our social relations, while we and our theories—the agents and visions of reconstruction—are themselves under transformation. Consider, for instance, the way in which we focus on some particular inadequate sexist or earlier feminist analysis and show its shortcomings—often with brilliance and eloquence. In doing so, we speak from the assumptions of some other discourse feminism has adopted or invented. These assumptions always include the belief that we can, in principle, construct or arrive at the perspective from which nature and social life can be seen as they really are. After all, we argue that sexist (or earlier feminist) analyses are wrong, inadequate, or distorting—not that they are equal in scientific or rational grounding to our criticisms.

However, we sometimes claim that theorizing itself is suspiciously patriarchal, for it assumes separations between the knower and the known, subject and object, and the possibility of some powerful transcendental, Archimedean standpoint from which nature and social life fall into what we think is their proper perspective. We fear replicating—to the detriment of women whose experiences have not yet been fully voiced within feminist theory—what we perceive as a patriarchal association between knowledge and power.[2] Our ability to detect androcentrism in traditional analyses has escalated from finding it in the content of knowledge claims to locating it in the forms and goals of traditional knowledge seeking. The voice making *this* proposal is itself super-Archimedean, speaking from some "higher" plane, such that Archimedes' followers in contemporary intellectual life are

[2] See, e.g., Maria C. Lugones and Elizabeth V. Spelman, "Have We Got a Theory for You! Feminist Theory, Cultural Imperialism and the Demand for 'the Women's Voice,'" *Hypatia: A Journal of Feminist Philosophy* (special issue of *Women's Studies International Forum*) 6, no. 6 (1983): 573–82; many of the selections in *New French Feminisms*, ed. Elaine Marks and Isabelle de Courtivron (New York: Schocken Books, 1981); Jane Flax, "Gender as a Social Problem: In and For Feminist Theory" *American Studies/Amerika Studien* (June 1986); Donna Haraway, "A Manifesto for Cyborgs: Science, Technology, and Socialist Feminism in the 1980's," *Socialist Review* 80 (1983): 65–107.

heard as simply part of the inevitable flux and imperfectly understood flow of human history. (And this is true even when the voice marks its own historical particularity, its femininity.) When it is unreflective, this kind of postmodernism—a kind of absolute relativism—itself takes a definitive stand from yet further outside the political and intellectual needs that guide our day-to-day thinking and social practices. In reaction we wonder how we can not want to say *the way things really are* to "our rulers" as well as to ourselves, in order to voice opposition to the silences and lies emanating from the patriarchal discourses and our own partially brainwashed consciousnesses. On the other hand, there is good reason to agree with a feminist postmodernist suspicion of the relationship between accepted definitions of "reality" and socially legitimated power.

How then are we to construct adequate feminist theory, or even *theories*—whether postmodern or not? Where are we to find the analytical concepts and categories that are free of the patriarchal flaws? What are the analytical categories for the absent, the invisible, the silenced that do not simply replicate in mirror-image fashion the distorting and mystifying categories and projects of the dominant discourses? Again, there are two ways to look at this situation. On the one hand, we can use the liberal powers of reason and the will, shaped by the insights gained through engaging in continuing political struggles, to piece what we see before our eyes in contemporary social life and history into a clear and coherent conceptual form, borrowing from one androcentric discourse here, another one there, patching in between in innovative and often illuminating ways, and revising our theoretical frameworks week by week as we continue to detect yet further androcentrisms in the concepts and categories we are using. We can then worry about the instability of the analytical categories and the lack of a persisting framework from which we continue to build our accounts. (After all, there should be some progress toward a "normal" discourse in our explanations if we are to create a coherent guide to understanding and action.) On the other hand, we can learn how to embrace the instability of the analytical categories; to find in the instability itself the desired theoretical reflection of certain aspects of the political reality in which we live and think; to use these instabilities as a resource for our thinking and practices. No "normal science" for us![3] I recommend we take the second course, an uncomfortable goal, for the following reason.

The social life that is our object of study and within which our analytical categories are formed and tested is in exuberant transformation.[4] Reason,

[3] See Thomas S. Kuhn, *The Structure of Scientific Revolutions* (Chicago: University of Chicago Press, 1970). "Normal science" was Kuhn's term for a "mature science," one where conceptual and methodological assumptions are shared by the inquirers in a field.

[4] Perhaps it has always been. But the emergence of "state patriarchy" from the "husband patriarchy" of the first half of the century, the rising of people of color from colonized

will power, reconsidering the material—even political struggle—will not slow these changes in ways over which our feminisms should rejoice. It would be a delusion for feminism to arrive at a master theory, at a "normal science" paradigm with conceptual and methodological assumptions that we presume all feminists accept. Feminist analytical categories *should* be unstable—consistent and coherent theories in an unstable and incoherent world are obstacles to both our understanding and our social practices.

We need to learn how to see our theorizing projects as illuminating "riffing" between and over the beats of patriarchal theories, rather than as rewriting the tunes of any particular one (Marxism, psychoanalysis, empiricism, hermeneutics, deconstructionism, to name a few) so that it perfectly expresses *what we think at the moment we want to say*. The problem is that we do not know and should not know just what we want to say about a number of conceptual choices with which we are presented—except that the choices themselves create no-win dilemmas for our feminisms.

In the field in which I have been working—feminist challenges to science and epistemology—this situation makes the present moment an exciting one in which to live and think, but a difficult one in which to conceptualize a definitive overview. That is, the arguments between those of us who are criticizing science and epistemology are unresolvable within the frameworks in which we have been posing them. We need to begin seeing these disputes not as a process of naming issues to be resolved but instead as opportunities to come up with better problems than those with which we started. The destabilization of thought often has advanced understanding more effectively than restabilizations, and the feminist criticisms of science point to a particularly fruitful arena in which the categories of Western thought need destabilization. Though these criticisms began by raising what appeared to be politically contentious but theoretically innocuous questions about discrimination against women in the social structure of science, misuses of technology, and androcentric bias in the social sciences and biology, they have quickly escalated into ones that question the most fundamental assumptions of modern, Western thought. They therefore implicitly challenge the theoretical constructs within which the original questions were formulated and might be answered.

Feminisms are totalizing theories. Because women and gender relations are everywhere, the subject matters of feminist theories are not containable within any single disciplinary framework or any set of them. "The scientific worldview" has also taken itself to be a totalizing theory—anything and everything worth understanding can be explained or inter-

---

subjugations, and the ongoing shifts in international capitalism all insure that this moment, at any rate, is one of exuberant transformation. See Ann Ferguson, "Patriarchy, Sexual Identity, and the Sexual Revolution," *Signs: Journal of Women in Culture and Society* 7, no. 1 (1981): 158–99, for discussion of the shifts in forms of patriarchy.

preted within the assumptions of modern science. Of course there is another world—the world of emotions, feelings, political values, of the individual and collective unconscious, of social and historical particularity explored in novels, drama, poetry, music, and art, and the world within which we all live most of our waking and dreaming hours under constant threat of its increasing reorganization by scientific rationality.[5] One of the projects of feminist theorists is to reveal the relationships between these two worlds—how each shapes and informs the other. In examining feminist criticisms of science, then, we must consider all that science does not, the reasons for these exclusions, how these shape science precisely through their absences—both acknowledged and unacknowledged.

Instead of fidelity to the assumption that coherent theory is a desirable end in itself and the only reliable guide to action, we can take as our standard fidelity to *parameters* of dissonance within and between assumptions of patriarchal discourses. This approach to theorizing captures what some take to be a distinctively women's emphasis on contextual thinking and decision making and on the processes necessary for gaining understanding in a world not of our own making—that is, a world that does not encourage us to fantasize about how we could order reality into the forms we desire.[6] It locates the ways in which a valuably "alienated consciousness," "bifurcated consciousness," "oppositional consciousness" might function at the level of active theory making—as well as at the level of skepticism and rebellion. We need to be able to cherish certain kinds of intellectual, political, and psychic discomforts, to see as inappropriate and even self-defeating certains kinds of clear solutions to the problems we have been posing.

"Bad science" or "science as usual"?

Are sexist assumptions in substantive scientific research the result of "bad science" or simply "science as usual"? The first alternative offers hopes of reforming the kind of science we have; the second appears to deny this possibility.

It is clear that feminist criticisms of the natural and social sciences have

[5] Milan Kundera, in the article "The Novel and Europe" (*New York Review of Books*, vol. 31, no. 12 [July 19, 1984]), asks if it is an accident that the novel and the hegemony of scientific rationality arose simultaneously.

[6] This emphasis is expressed in different ways by Sara Ruddick, "Maternal Thinking," *Feminist Studies* 6, no. 2 (Summer 1980): 342–67; Carol Gilligan, *In a Different Voice: Psychological Theory and Women's Development* (Cambridge, Mass.: Harvard University Press, 1982); Dorothy Smith, "Women's Perspective as a Radical Critique of Sociology," *Sociological Inquiry* 44, no. 1 (1974): 7–13; and "A Sociology for Women," in *The Prism of Sex: Essays in the Sociology of Knowledge*, ed. J. Sherman and E. T. Beck (Madison: University of Wisconsin Press, 1979).

identified and described science badly practiced—that is, science distorted by masculine bias in problematics, theories, concepts, methods of inquiry, observations, and interpretations of results of research.[7] There are facts of the matter, these critics claim, but androcentric science cannot locate them. By identifying and eliminating masculine bias through more rigorous adherence to scientific methods, we can get an objective, de-gendered (and in that sense, value-free) picture of nature and social life. Feminist inquiry represents not a substitution of one gender loyalty for the other—one subjectivism for another—but the transcendence of gender which thereby increases objectivity.

In this argument, we use empiricist epistemology because its ends are the same as ours: objective, value-neutral results of research. This feminist empiricism argues that sexism and androcentrism are social biases. Movements for social liberation "make it possible for people to see the world in an enlarged perspective because they remove the covers and blinders that obscure knowledge and observation."[8] Thus the women's movement creates the opportunity for such an enlarged perspective—just as did the bourgeois revolution of the fifteenth to seventeenth centuries, the proletarian revolution of the nineteenth century, and the revolutions overthrowing European and U.S. colonialism in recent decades. Furthermore, the women's movement creates more women scientists and more feminist scientists (men as well as women), who are more likely than nonfeminist men to notice androcentric bias.

Feminist empiricism offers a powerful explanation—though a misleading one—for the greater empirical adequacy of so much of feminist research. It has the virtue of answering the question of how a political movement such as feminism could be contributing to the growth of objective scientific knowledge. In making this argument, however, we avert our eyes from the fact that this appeal to empiricism in fact subverts empiricism in three ways. (1) For empiricism, the social identity of the observer is supposed to be irrelevant to the quality of research results. Feminist empiricism argues that women (or feminists, men and women) as a group are more likely to produce unbiased, objective results of inquiry than are men (or nonfeminists) as a group. (2) We claim that a key origin of

[7] See, e.g., the *Signs* review essays in the social sciences, and the papers in Brighton Women and Science Group, *Alice through the Microscope* (London: Virago Press, 1980); Ruth Hubbard, M. S. Henifin, and Barbara Fried, eds., *Biological Woman: The Convenient Myth* (Cambridge, Mass.: Schenkman Publishing Co., 1982); Marian Lowe and Ruth Hubbard, eds., *Woman's Nature: Rationalizations of Inequality* (New York: Pergamon Press, 1983); Ethel Tobach and Betty Rosoff, eds., *Genes and Gender I, II, III, IV* (New York: Gordian Press, 1978, 1979, 1981, 1984) (Hubbard and Lowe are the guest editors for vol. 2 in the series, subtitled *Pitfalls in Research on Sex and Gender*); Ruth Bleier, *Science and Gender: A Critique of Biology and Its Theories on Women* (New York: Pergamon Press, 1984).

[8] Marcia Millman and Rosabeth Moss Kanter, "Editorial Introduction," in *Another Voice: Feminist Perspectives on Social Life and Social Science* (New York: Anchor Books, 1975), vii.

androcentric bias lies in the selection of problems for inquiry and in the definition of what is problematic about them. Empiricism insists that its methodological norms are meant to apply only to the context of justification and not to the context of discovery where problematics are identified and defined. Hence we have shown the inadequacy, the impotence, of scientific methods to achieve their goals. (3) We often point out that it is exactly following the logical and sociological norms of inquiry which results in androcentric results of research—appealing to the already existing (Western, bourgeois, homophobic, white, sexist) scientific community for confirmation of the results of research; generalizing to all humans from observations only of males. Our empiricist criticisms of "bad science" in fact subvert the very understandings of science they are meant to reinforce.

These problems suggest that the most fundamental categories of scientific thought are male biased. Many of the critics of "bad science" also make this second criticism though it undercuts the assumptions of the first.[9] Here they point to historians' descriptions of how sexual politics have shaped science, and science, in turn, has played a significant role in advancing sexual politics. Each has provided a moral and political resource for the other.[10] Furthermore, they show that "pure science"—inquiry immune from the technological and social needs of the larger culture—exists only in the unreflective mental life of some individual scientists and in the rhetoric of science apologists. That is, one does not have to impugn the motives of individual physicists, chemists, or sociologists in order to make a convinc-

[9] This tension between the two kinds of criticisms is pointed out by Helen Longino and Ruth Doell, "Body, Bias and Behavior: A Comparative Analysis of Reasoning in Two Areas of Biological Science," *Signs* 9, no. 2 (1983): 206–27; and by Donna Haraway, "In the Beginning Was the Word: The Genesis of Biological Theory," *Signs* 6, no. 3 (1981): 469–81. Longino and Doell think "feminists do not have to choose between correcting bad science or rejecting the entire scientific enterprise" (208) and that "only by developing a more comprehensive understanding of the operation of male bias in science, as distinct from its existence, can we move beyond these two perspectives in our search for remedies" (207). Longino and Doell's analysis is helpful indeed in creating this understanding, but since they do not come to grips with the criticisms of "science as usual," my remedy parts from theirs. Haraway does not propose a solution to the dilemma.

[10] See, e.g., Elizabeth Fee, "Nineteenth Century Craniology: The Study of the Female Skull," *Bulletin of the History of Medicine* 53, no. 3 (1979): 415–33; Susan Griffin, *Woman and Nature: The Roaring inside Her* (New York: Harper & Row, 1978); Diana Long Hall, "Biology, Sex Hormones and Sexism in the 1920's," *Philosophical Forum* 5 (1973–74): 81–96; Donna Haraway, "Animal Sociology and a Natural Economy of the Body Politic, Parts 1, 2," *Signs* 4, no. 1 (1978): 21–60; Ruth Hubbard, "Have Only Men Evolved?" in Hubbard, Henifin, and Fried, eds. (n. 7 above); L. J. Jordanova, "Natural Facts: A Historical Perspective on Science and Sexuality," in *Nature, Culture and Gender*, ed. Carol MacCormack and Marilyn Strathern (New York: Cambridge University Press, 1980); Carolyn Merchant, *The Death of Nature: Women, Ecology and the Scientific Revolution* (New York: Harper & Row, 1980); Evelyn Fox Keller, *Reflections on Gender and Science* (New Haven, Conn.: Yale University Press, 1985).

ing case that the scientific enterprise is structurally and symbolically part and parcel of the value systems of those cultures that maintain it. This argument poses difficulties for us, nonetheless, since if the very concepts of nature, of dispassionate, value-free, objective inquiry, and of transcendental knowledge are androcentric, white, bourgeois, and Western, then no amount of more rigorous adherence to scientific method will eliminate such bias, for the methods themselves reproduce the perspectives generated by these hierarchies and thus distort our understandings.

While these new understandings of the history of science and sexuality expand our understanding immensely, they do not tell us whether a science apparently so inextricably intertwined with the history of sexual politics can be pried loose to serve more inclusive human ends—or whether it is strategically worthwhile to try to do so. Is history destiny? Would the complete elimination of androcentrisms from science leave no science at all? But isn't it important to try to degender science as much as we can in a world where scientific claims are *the* model of knowledge? How can we afford to choose between redeeming science or dismissing it altogether when neither choice is in our best interest?

Successor science or postmodernism

The dilemma that arises in criticisms of "bad science" and of "science as usual" reappears at a metalevel in feminist theory's conflicting tendencies toward postmodernism and what I shall call the feminist successor science projects. Feminist empiricism explains (albeit subversively) the achievements of feminist inquiry—of that purported contradiction in terms: a politicized scientific inquiry—by appeal to the familiar empiricist assumptions. In contrast, the feminist standpoint epistemologies articulate an understanding of scientific knowledge seeking that replaces, as successor to, the Enlightenment vision captured by empiricism.[11] Both the standpoint and postmodern tendencies within feminist theory place feminism in an uneasy and ambivalent relationship to patriarchal discourses and proj-

[11] Important formulations of the epistemology for a feminist "successor science" have been provided by Jane Flax, "Political Philosophy and the Patriarchal Unconscious: A Psychoanalytic Perspective on Epistemology and Metaphysics," in *Discovering Reality: Feminist Perspectives on Epistemology, Metaphysics, Methodology and Philosophy of Science*, ed. Sandra Harding and Merrill B. Hintikka (Dordrecht: D. Reidel Publishing Co., 1983); Nancy Hartsock, "The Feminist Standpoint: Developing the Ground for a Specifically Feminist Historical Materialism," in Harding and Hintikka, eds., and chap. 10 of *Money, Sex and Power* (Boston: Northeastern University Press, 1983); Hilary Rose, "Hand, Brain and Heart: A Feminist Epistemology for the Natural Sciences," *Signs* 9, no. 1 (1983): 73–90, and "Is a Feminist Science Possible?" (paper presented at MIT, Cambridge, Massachusetts, 1984); D. Smith, "Women's Perspective as a Radical Critique of Sociology," and "A Sociology for Women" (both in n. 6 above).

ects (just as did feminist empiricism). There are good reasons to think of both as imperfect and converging tendencies toward a postmodernist reality, but there are also good reasons to nourish the tendencies in each which conflict.

The feminist standpoint epistemologies use for feminist ends the Marxist vision in which science can reflect "the way the world is" and contribute to human emancipation. Feminist research claims in the natural and social sciences do appear to be truer to the world, and thus more objective than the sexist claims they replace. They provide an understanding of nature and social life that transcends gender loyalties and does not substitute one gender-loyal understanding for another. Furthermore, these feminist appeals to truth and objectivity trust that reason will play a role in the eventual triumph of feminism, that feminism correctly will be perceived as more than a power politic—though it is that, too. The successor science tendencies aim to provide more complete, less false, less distorting, less defensive, less perverse, less rationalizing understandings of the natural and social worlds.

This is already a radical project, for the Enlightenment vision explicitly denied that women possessed the reason and powers of dispassionate, objective observation required by scientific thinking. Women could be objects of (masculine) reason and observation but never the subjects, never the reflecting and universalizing human minds. Only men were in fact envisioned as ideal knowers, for only men (of the appropriate class, race, and culture) possessed the innate capacities for socially transcendant observation and reason. The ends and purposes of such a science turned out to be far from emancipatory for anyone.

Marxism reformulated this Enlightenment vision so that the proletariat, guided by Marxist theory and by class struggle, became the ideal knowers, the group capable of using observation and reason to grasp the true form of social relations, including our relations with nature.[12] This Marxist successor to bourgeois science was, like its predecessor, to provide one social group—here, the proletariat—with the knowledge and power to lead the rest of the species toward emancipation. Marxism's epistemology is grounded in a theory of labor rather than a theory of innate (masculine) faculties; so just as not all human faculties are equal in the bourgeois version, here not all labor is equal. It was through struggle in the workplace that the proletariat would generate knowledge. In neither socialist practice nor Marxist theory were any women ever conceptualized as fundamentally defined by their relation to the means of production, regardless of their

[12] Friedrich Engels, "Socialism: Utopian and Scientific," in *The Marx and Engels Reader*, ed. R. Tucker (New York: W. W. Norton & Co., 1972); George Lukács, "Reification and the Consciousness of the Proletariat," *History and Class Consciousness* (Cambridge, Mass.: MIT Press, 1968).

work force participation. They were never thought of as full-fledged members of the proletariat who could reason and thus know how the world is constructed. Women's distinctive reproductive labor, emotional labor, "mediating" labor thus disappeared within the conceptual framework of Marxist theory, leaving women invisible as a class or social group of agents of knowledge. (Other forms of nonwage or nonindustrial labor similarly disappeared from the center of this conceptual scheme, mystifying the knowing available to slaves and colonized peoples.)

This standpoint tendency in feminist epistemology is grounded in a successor theory of labor or, rather, of distinctively human activity, and seeks to substitute women or feminists (the accounts differ) for the proletariat as the potentially ideal agents of knowledge. Men's (sexists') perceptions of themselves, others, nature, and the relations between all three are characteristically not only partial but also perverse.[13] Men's characteristic social experience, like that of the bourgeoisie, hides from them the politically imposed nature of the social relations they see as natural. Dominant patterns in Western thought justify women's subjugation as necessary for the progress of culture, and men's partial and perverse views as uniquely and admirably human. Women are able to use political struggle and analysis to provide a less partial, less defensive, less perverse understanding of human social relations—including our relations with nature. The standpoint theorists argue that this analysis, not feminist empiricism, accounts for the achievements of feminist theory and research because it is politically engaged theory and research from the perspective of the social experience of the subjugated sex/gender.

The second line of thought, one that can be found within many of these very same writings, expresses a profound skepticism toward the Enlightenment vision of the power of "the" human mind to reflect perfectly a readymade world that is out there for the reflecting. Many feminists share a rejection of the value of the forms of rationality, of dispassionate objectivity, of the Archimedean perspective, which were to be the means to knowledge. Here they are ambivalently related to such other skeptics of modernism as Nietzsche, Wittgenstein, Derrida, Foucault, Lacan, Feyerabend, Rorty, Gadamer, and the discourses of semiotics, psychoanalysis, structuralism, and deconstructionism.[14] What is striking is how the succes-

[13] Hartsock, especially, discusses the perversity of the androcentric vision (n. 11 above). I shall subsequently refer to the men vs. women dichotomy since that is the way most of these standpoint theorists put the issue. However, I think these categories are inadequate even for the standpoint projects: it is feminists vs. nonfeminists (sexists) we should be discussing here.

[14] Jane Flax discusses this postmodern strain in feminist theory in "Gender as a Social Problem: In and For Feminist Theory" (n. 2 above) and cites these as among the key skeptics of modernism: Friedrich Nietzsche, *On the Genealogy of Morals* (New York: Vintage, 1969), and *Beyond Good and Evil* (New York: Vintage, 1966); Jacques Derrida, *L'écriture et la Difference* (Paris: Editions du Seuil, 1967); Michel Foucault, *The Order of Things* (New York:

sor science idea and the postmodern skepticism of science are both embraced by these theorists, though the concepts are diametrically opposed in the nonfeminist discourses.[15]

From the perspective of this postmodern tendency in feminist thinking, the feminist successor science project can appear still too firmly rooted in distinctively masculine modes of being in the world. As one theorist puts the issue, "Perhaps 'reality' can have 'a' structure only from the falsely universalizing perspective of the master. That is, only to the extent that one person or group can dominate the whole, can 'reality' appear to be governed by one set of rules or be constituted by one privileged set of social relations."[16] How can feminism radically redefine the relationship between knowledge and power if it creates yet another epistemology, yet another set of rules for the policing of thought?

However, this postmodern project can appear viciously utopian from the perspective of the successor science tendency.[17] It seems to challenge the legitimacy of trying to describe the way the world is from a distinctively feminist perspective. It can appear of a piece with masculine and bourgeois desire to justify one's activities by denying one's social, embodied location in history; to attempt to transcend one's objective location in politics by appeal to a *mea culpa*, all-understanding, bird's-eye view (the transcendental ego in naturalistic garb) of the frailty of mere humans. That is, in its uneasy affiliation with nonfeminist postmodernism, the feminist postmodernist tendency appears to support an inappropriate relativist stance by the subjugated groups, one that conflicts with feminism's perception that the realities of sexual politics in our world demand engaged political struggle. It appears to support an equally regressive relativism for those mildly

---

Vintage, 1973), and *The Archaeology of Knowledge* (New York: Harper & Row, 1972); Jacques Lacan, *Speech and Language in Psychoanalysis* (Baltimore: Johns Hopkins University Press, 1968), and *The Four Fundamental Concepts of Psychoanalysis* (New York: W. W. Norton & Co., 1973); Paul Feyerabend, *Against Method* (New York: Schocken Books, 1975); Richard Rorty, *Philosophy and the Mirror of Nature* (Princeton, N.J.: Princeton University Press, 1979); Hans-Georg Gadamer, *Philosophical Hermeneutics* (Berkeley: University of California Press, 1976); Ludwig Wittgenstein, *On Certainty* (New York: Harper & Row, 1972), and *Philosophical Investigations* (New York: Macmillan Publishing Co., 1970). See also Jean-François Lyotard, *The Postmodern Condition: A Report on Knowledge*, trans. G. Bennington and B. Massumi (Minneapolis: University of Minnesota Press, 1984).

[15] However, different weight is given to one or the other tendency by each theorist. Nevertheless, all are explicitly aware of the tension in their own work between the two kinds of criticisms of modern, Western epistemology. It is another project to explain how each attempts to resolve this tension. See Harding (n. 1 above) for further discussion of these theorists' work.

[16] Flax, "Gender as a Social Problem" (n. 2 above), 17.

[17] Flax appears to be unaware of this problem. Engels distinguishes utopian and scientific socialisms (n. 12 above).

estranged members of the subjugating groups with doubts about the legitimacy of their own objective privilege and power (see list above of nonfeminist skeptics of modernism). It is worth keeping in mind that the articulation of relativism as an intellectual position emerges historically only as an attempt to dissolve challenges to the legitimacy of purportedly universal beliefs and ways of life. It is an objective problem, or a solution to a problem, only *from the perspective of the dominating groups*. Reality may indeed appear to have many different structures from the perspectives of our different locations in social relations, but some of those appearances are ideologies in the strong sense of the term: they are not only false and "interested" beliefs but also ones that are used to structure social relations for the rest of us. For subjugated groups, a relativist stance expresses a false consciousness. It accepts the dominant group's insistence that their right to hold distorted views (and, of course, to make policy for all of us on the basis of those views) is intellectually legitimate.

Are not the policing of thought in the service of political power and the retreat to purportedly politically innocent, relativistic, mere interpretations of the world the two sides of the Enlightenment and bourgeois coin to which feminism is opposed? Is it not true—as these theorists all argue in different ways—that men's and women's different kinds of interactions with nature and social life (different "labor") provide women with distinctive and privileged scientific and epistemological standpoints? How can feminism afford to give up a successor science project if it is to empower all women in a world where socially legitimated knowledge and the political power associated with it are firmly lodged in white, Western, bourgeois, compulsorily heterosexual, men's hands? Yet how can we give up our distrust of the historic links between this legitimated knowledge and political power?

One way to see these two tendencies in feminist theory is as converging approaches to a postmodernist world—a world that will not exist until both (conflicting) tendencies achieve their goals. From this perspective, at its best postmodernism envisions epistemology in a world where thought does not need policing. It recognizes the existence today of far less than the ideal speech situation, but disregards (or fails to acknowledge) the political struggles necessary to bring about change. The standpoint tendency attempts to move us toward that ideal world by legitimating and empowering the "subjugated knowledges" of women, without which that postmodern epistemological situation cannot come into existence. It fails nonetheless to challenge the modernist intimacies between knowledge and power, or the legitimacy of assuming there can be a single, feminist story of reality. Whether or not this is a useful way to see the relationship between the two tendencies, I am arguing that we must resist the temptation to explain away the problems each addresses and to choose one to the exclusion of the other.

The feminist standpoint and other "others"

Feminist successor science projects stand in an uneasy relation to other emancipatory epistemologies insofar as the former seek to ground a uniquely legitimate and distinctive science and epistemology on the shared characteristics of women's activity. Hilary Rose locates these grounds in the way women's labor unifies mental, manual, and caring labor. Nancy Hartsock focuses on the deeper opposition to the dualities of mental versus manual labor to be found in women's daily, concrete activities both in domestic life and wage labor. Jane Flax identifies the relatively more reciprocal sense of self women bring to all their activities. She suggests that the small gap between men's and women's concepts of self, others, and nature prefigures the possible larger gap between the defensively dualistic knowledge characteristic of male-dominant social orders and the relational and contextual knowledge possible in a future society of "reciprocal selves." Dorothy Smith argues that women's social labor is concrete rather than abstract, that it cannot be articulated to either administrative forms of ruling or the categories of social science, and that it has been socially invisible—combining to create a valuably alienated and bifurcated consciousness in women.[18] However, other emancipatory perspectives claim as resources for their politics and epistemologies similar aspects of their own activity.

On the one hand, of course, feminism is right to identify women and men as classes in opposition at this moment in history. Everywhere in the world we find these two classes, and virtually everywhere the men subjugate the women in one way or another.[19] Furthermore, even male feminists receive benefits from an institutionalized sexism they actively struggle to eliminate. Objectively, no individual men can succeed in renouncing sexist privilege any more than individual whites can succeed in renouncing racist privilege—the benefits of gender and race accrue regardless of the wishes of the individuals who bear them. Gender, like race and class, is not a voluntarily disposable individual characteristic. After all, fundamentally our feminisms address the extraction and transfer of social benefits from women to men *as groups* of humans, on a worldwide scale. Thus the standpoint theorists, in identifying the common aspects of women's social experience cross-culturally, contribute something important to our work.

On the other hand, the distinctive characteristics of women's activities that Rose, Hartsock, Flax, and Smith identify for our culture are probably to be found also in the labor and social experience of other subjugated

[18] Flax (n. 11 above); Hartsock (both items cited in n. 11 above); Rose (n. 11 above); Smith (n. 6 above).

[19] "Virtually everywhere" to give the benefit of the doubt to anthropologists' claims about "egalitarian cultures." See, e.g., Eleanor Leacock, *Myths of Male Dominance* (New York: Monthly Review Press, 1981).

groups. There are suggestions in the literature on Native Americans, Africans, and Asians that what feminists call feminine versus masculine personalities, ontologies, ethics, epistemologies, and worldviews may be what these other liberation movements call non-Western versus Western personalities and worldviews.[20] Thus, should there not also be Native American, African, and Asian sciences and epistemologies, based on the distinctive historical and social experience of these peoples? Would not such successor sciences and epistemologies provide similar analyses to those of the standpoint theorists? (I set aside the crucial and fatal complication for this way of thinking—the facts that one-half of these peoples are women and that most women are not Western.) On what grounds would the feminist sciences and epistemologies be superior to these others? What is and should be the relationship of the feminist projects to these other emancipatory knowledge-seeking projects?

It is a vast overgeneralization to presume that all Africans, let alone all colonized peoples, share distinctive personalities, ontologies, ethics, epistemologies, or worldviews. But is it any worse than the presumption that there are commonalities to be detected in *all women's* social experiences or worldviews? Let us note that we are thinking here about perspectives as inclusive as those referred to in such phrases as the "feudal worldview," the "modern worldview," or the "scientific worldview." Moreover, we women also claim an identity we were taught to despise;[21] around the globe we insist on the importance of our social experience as *women*, not just as gender-invisible members of class, race, or cultural groups. Similarly, Third World peoples claim their colonized social experience as the grounding for a shared identity and as a common source of alternative understandings. Why is it not reasonable to explore how the experience of colonization itself shapes personalities and worldviews? How can white Western women insist on the legitimacy of what we think we share with all women and not acknowledge the equal legitimacy of what colonized peoples think they share with each other? In short, we cannot resolve this problem for the feminist standpoint by insisting on the cultural particularity of indi-

[20] Russell Means, "Fighting Words on the Future of the Earth," *Mother Jones* (December 1980): 167; Vernon Dixon, "World Views and Research Methodology," in *African Philosophy: Assumptions and Paradigms for Research on Black Persons*, ed. L. M. King, V. Dixon, and W. W. Nobles (Los Angeles: Fanon Center Publication, Charles R. Drew Postgraduate Medical School, 1976) (but see also Paulin Hountondji, *African Philosophy: Myth and Reality* [Bloomington: Indiana University Press, 1983]); Joseph Needham, "History and Human Values: A Chinese Perspective for World Science and Technology," in *Ideology of/in the Natural Sciences*, ed. Hilary Rose and Steven Rose (Boston: Schenkman Publishing Co., 1979). I have discussed this situation more fully in "The Curious Coincidence of African and Feminine Moralities," in *Women and Moral Theory*, ed. Diana Meyers and Eva Kittay (Totowa, N.J.: Rowman & Allenheld, 1986), and in chap. 7 of Harding (n. 1 above).

[21] Michele Cliff, *Claiming an Identity They Taught Me to Despise* (Watertown, Mass.: Persephone Press, 1980).

viduals in other cultures while at the same time arguing for the gender similarities of women cross-culturally.

One resolution of this dilemma for the standpoint tendency would be to say that feminist science and epistemology will be valuable in their own right alongside and as a part of these other possible sciences and epistemologies—not superior to them. With this strategy we have relinquished the totalizing, "master theory" character of our theory making which is at least an implicit goal of much feminist theorizing, and we have broken away from the Marxist assumptions that informed the feminist successor science projects. This response to the issue has managed to retain the categories of feminist theory (unstable though they be) and simply set them alongside the categories of the theory making of other subjugated groups. Instead of the "dual systems" theory with which socialist feminists wrestle,[22] this response gives us multisystems theory. Of course, it leaves bifurcated (and perhaps even more finely divided) the identities of all except ruling-class white Western women. There is a fundamental incoherence in this way of thinking about the grounds for feminist approaches to knowledge.

Another solution would be to renounce the goal of unity around shared social experiences in favor of solidarity around those goals that can be shared.[23] From this perspective, each standpoint epistemology—feminist, Third World, gay, working class—names the historical conditions producing the political and conceptual oppositions to be overcome but does not thereby generate universal concepts and political goals. Because gender is also a class and racial category in cultures stratified by class and race as well as by gender, no particular women's experience can uniquely generate the groundings for the visions and politics that will emancipate us from gender hierarchy. A variety of social groups are currently struggling against the hegemony of the Western, white, bourgeois, homophobic androcentric worldview and the politics it both generates and justifies. Our internal racial, sexual, and class struggles, and the differences in our cultural histories which define for us who we are as social beings, prevent our federating around our shared goals. It is history that will resolve or dissolve this problem, not our analytic efforts. Nevertheless, white, Western, bourgeois feminists should attend to the need for a more active theoretical and political struggle against our own racism, classism, and cultural centrism as forces that insure the continued subjugation of women around the world.

[22] Iris Young, "Beyond the Unhappy Marriage: A Critique of the Dual Systems Theory," in *Women and Revolution*, ed. L. Sargent (Boston: South End Press, 1981).

[23] See Bell Hooks, *Feminist Theory from Margin to Center* (Boston: South End Press, 1983), esp. chap. 4; and Haraway, "A Manifesto for Cyborgs" (n. 2 above).

Culture versus nature and gender versus sex

Historians and anthropologists show that the way contemporary Western society draws the borders between culture and nature is clearly both modern and culture bound.[24] The culture versus nature dichotomy reappears in complex and ambiguous ways in a number of other oppositions central to modern, Western thinking: reason versus the passions and emotions; objectivity versus subjectivity; mind versus the body and physical matter; abstract versus concrete; public versus private—to name a few. In our culture, and in science, masculinity is identified with culture and femininity with nature in all of these dichotomies. In each case, the latter is perceived as an immensely powerful threat that will rise up and overwhelm the former unless the former exerts severe controls over the latter.

This series of associated dualisms has been one of the primary targets of feminist criticisms of the conceptual scheme of modern science. It is less often recognized, however, how the dualism reappears in feminist thinking about gender, sex, or the sex/gender system. In preceding sections, I have talked about eliminating gender as if the social could be cleanly separated from the biological aspects of our sexual identities, practices, and desires. In feminist discourses, this mode of conceptualizing sexuality is clearly an advance over the biological determinist assumption that gender differences simply follow from sex differences. Since biological determinism is alive and flourishing in sociobiology, endocrinology, ethology, anthropology and, indeed, most nonfeminist discourses, I do not want to devalue the powerful analytical strategy of insisting on a clean separation between the known (and knowable) effects of biology and of culture. Nevertheless, a very different picture of sexual identities, practices, and desires emerges from recent research in biology, history, anthropology, and psychology.[25] Surprisingly, it could also be called biological determinism, though what is determined on this account is the plasticity rather than the rigidity of sexual identity, practice, and desire. Our species is doomed to freedom from biological constraints in these respects, as existentialists would put the issue.

The problem for feminist theory and practice here is twofold. In the first place, we stress that humans are *embodied* creatures—not Cartesian minds that happen to be located in biological matter in motion. Female embodiment is different from male embodiment. Therefore we want to know the implications for social relations and intellectual life of that differ-

[24] See esp. the responses to Sherry Ortner's "Is Female to Male as Nature Is to Culture?" (in *Woman, Culture and Society*, ed. M. Z. Rosaldo and L. Lamphere [Stanford, Calif.: Stanford University Press, 1974]) in MacCormack and Strathern, eds. (n. 10 above).

[25] See references cited in nn. 7, 10 above.

ent embodiment. Menstruation, vaginal penetration, lesbian sexual practices, birthing, nursing, and menopause are bodily experiences men cannot have. Contemporary feminism does not embrace the goal of treating women "just like men" in public policy. Se we need to articulate what these differences are. However, we fear that doing so feeds into sexual biological determinism (consider the problems we have had articulating a feminist perspective on premenstrual syndrome and work-related reproductive hazards in ways that do not victimize women). The problem is compounded when it is racial differences between women we want to articulate.[26] How can we choose between maintaining that our biological differences ought to be recognized by public policy and insisting that biology is not destiny for either women or men?

In the second place, we have trouble conceptualizing the fact that the culture versus nature dichotomy and its siblings are not simply figments of thought to be packed up in the attic of outmoded ideas. The tendency toward this kind of dualism is an ideology in the strongest sense of the term, and such tendencies cannot be shucked off by mental hygiene and will power alone. The culture/nature dichotomy structures public policy, institutional and individual social practices, the organization of the disciplines (the social vs. the natural sciences), indeed the very way we see the world around us. Consequently, until our dualistic practices are changed (divisions of social experience into mental vs. manual, into abstract vs. concrete, into emotional vs. emotion denying), we are forced to think and exist within the very dichotomizing we criticize. Perhaps we can shift the assumption that the natural is hard to change and that the cultural is more easily changed, as we see ecological disasters and medical technologies on the one hand, and the history of sexism, classism, and racism on the other.[27] Nonetheless, we should continue insisting on the distinction between culture and nature, between gender and sex (especially in the face of biological determinist backlash), even as we analytically and experientially notice how inextricably they are intertwined in individuals and in cultures. These dichotomies are empirically false, but we cannot afford to dismiss them as irrelevant as long as they structure our lives and our consciousnesses.

Science as craft: Anachronism or resource?

Traditional philosophies of science assume an anachronistic image of the inquirer as a socially isolated genius, selecting problems to pursue, formu-

[26] Inez Smith Reid, "Science, Politics, and Race," *Signs* 1, no. 2 (1975): 397–422.

[27] Janice G. Raymond makes this point in "Transsexualism: An Issue of Sex-Role Stereotyping," in Tobach and Rosoff, eds., vol. 2 (n. 7 above).

lating hypotheses, devising methods to test the hypotheses, gathering observations, and interpreting the results of inquiry. The reality of most scientific research today is quite different, for these craft modes of producing scientific knowledge were replaced by industrialized modes in the nineteenth century for the natural sciences, and by the mid-twentieth century for the vast majority of social science research. Consequently, philosophy of science's rules and norms for individual knowledge seekers are irrelevant to the conduct of, and understanding of, most of contemporary science, as a number of science critics have pointed out.[28]

However, it is precisely in areas of inquiry that remain organized in craft ways where the most interesting feminist research has appeared.[29] Perhaps all of the most revolutionary claims have emerged from research situations where individual feminists (or small groups of them) identify a problematic phenomenon, hypothesize a tentative explanation, design and carry out evidence gathering, and then interpret the results of this research. In contrast, when the conception and execution of research are performed by different social groups of persons, as is the case in the vast majority of mainstream natural science and much social science research, the activity of conceptualizing the research is frequently performed by a privileged group and the activity of executing the research by a subjugated group. This situation insures that the conceptualizers will be able to avoid challenges to the adequacy of their concepts, categories, methods, and interpretations of the results of research.

This kind of analysis reinforces the standpoint theorists' argument that a prescriptive theory of knowledge—an epistemology—should be based on a theory of labor or human activity, not on a theory of innate faculties as empiricist epistemology assumes. In fact, the feminist epistemologies mentioned above are all grounded in a distinctive theory of human activity, and in one that gains support from an examination of the preconditions for the emergence of modern science in the fifteenth to seventeenth centuries. Feminists point to the unification of mental, manual, and emotional labor in women's work which provides women with a potentially more comprehensive understanding of nature and social life. As women increasingly are drawn into and seek men's work—from law and policy-making to medicine and scientific inquiry—our labor and social experience violate the traditional distinctions between men's and women's work, thus permitting women's ways of understanding reality to begin to shape public understandings. Similarly, it was a violation of the feudal division of labor that

[28] Jerome Ravetz, *Scientific Knowledge and Its Social Problems* (New York: Oxford University Press, 1971); Rose and Rose, eds. (n. 20 above); Rita Arditti, Pat Brennan, Steve Cafrak, eds., *Science and Liberation* (Boston: South End Press, 1980).

[29] Hilary Rose in particular has pointed this out in "Hand, Brain and Heart," and in "Is a Feminist Science Possible?" (n. 11 above). Perhaps all new research paradigms must be established through craft activity, as Kuhn argued.

made possible the unity of mental and manual labor necessary to create science's new experimental method.[30]

Traditional philosophy of science's prescriptive image of the scientific inquirer, as craftsman, then, is irrelevant as a model for the activity that occupies the vast majority of scientific workers today. This image instead reflects the practices of the very few scientifically trained workers who are engaged in the construction of new research models. However, since the scientific worldview that feminism criticizes was constructed to explain the activity, results, and goals of the *craft labor* that constituted science in an earlier period, and since contemporary feminist craft inquiry has produced some of the most valuable new conceptualizations, it looks like we need to think more carefully about which aspects of the scientific worldview to reject and retain. Perhaps the mainstream enterprise of today is not scientific at all in the original sense of the term! Can it be that feminism and similarly estranged inquiries are the true offspring of Copernicus, Galileo, and Newton? Can this be true while at the same time these offspring undermine the epistemology that Hume, Locke, Descartes, and Kant developed to explain the birth of modern science? Once again, we are led to what I propose should be regarded as fruitful ambivalence toward the science we have. We should cultivate both "separatist" craft-structured inquiry *and* infuse the industrially structured sciences with feminist values and goals.

These are some of the central conceptual instabilities that emerge in considering the feminist criticism of science. Several of them arise in feminist theorizing more generally. I have been arguing that we cannot resolve these dilemmas in the terms in which we have been posing them and that instead we should learn how to regard the instabilities themselves as valuable resources. If we can learn how to use them, we can match Archimedes' greatest achievement—his inventiveness in creating a new kind of theorizing.

Department of Philosophy
University of Delaware

[30] Edgar Zilsel, "The Sociological Roots of Science," *American Journal of Sociology* 47, no. 4 (1942): 545–60.

THE EDUCATION OF WOMEN AS PHILOSOPHERS

ELISABETH YOUNG-BRUEHL

It is unfortunate that, for reasons of personal and cultural habit, when we think about ourselves as askers of questions, thinkers, or, using the generic title, as philosophers, lovers of wisdom, we think of ourselves as selves. That is, we think: *I* am thinking—first person singular, one person solitary, an interiority, a mental machine.

Of course, it is fortunate that we—women—ever do think of ourselves as thinking; and in this light, the matter of *how* we do so seems secondary. For there is a great deal in our personal and cultural histories suggesting that thinking is not our province, not our privilege, not even our possibility. So great, indeed, is the weight of prejudice about women's abilities and achievements as thinkers that we often look to the lives of thoughtful women with questions not about how they thought of their thinking but with questions about how they thought at all, how they managed *not* to be as this great weight of prejudice prescribed.

Biographies of women often have about them an air of amazement. They are infused—particularly when they are written by women—with an

The title and topic for this essay were suggested by the sesquicentennial committee at Mount Holyoke College, where it was delivered as a lecture in October 1985 to celebrate the college's sesquicentennial. My thanks for their comments on an earlier draft to the members of the Mount Holyoke Project on Gender in Context.

This essay originally appeared in *Signs*, vol. 12, no. 2, Winter 1987.

exclamation: She did it! Institutions for the education of women originate—even when they are circumscribed by visions of educated women as ideal helpmeets for educated men—from the imperative form of the same impulse: You can do it! Despite everything and almost everyone outside, here you can do it! In most stories of exemplary women who have managed to do what was not expected of them, and in most stories of institutions that have tried to make the exception more of a rule, the focus is on sources of support. In every exemplary woman's drama, there will be a cast—usually a very limited cast—of encouragers, and in every institution's story there will be exemplary leaders who encourage a cast of encouragers.

Because women find it no easy matter to think at all, they are more inclined to be aware of (even if not openly acknowledging of) their supporters than men, who, after all, are supposed to be able by nature to set up in the thinking business as solitary entrepreneurs. For women—I want to argue—the supportive others are always there, and always there *in thinking*.

Thinking, we usually assume, goes on in our heads. It involves a control center that produces thoughts. Thoughts, then, flow forth like a stream unless somehow blocked or distracted. That is, we have perceptions passively or actively received, and ideas innate or acquired, which are all by some ruling mental fabricator or organizer fixed for flow into languages of various sorts that allow us to express ourselves. Thoughts are made or crafted or commandeered. Simple.

I want to question this notion, this enthralling picture, of thinking as a kind of mental organizing of mental material or mental troops; but since I want to question also what this picture means for women, for women who are trying to think, I want to raise my question contextually. So let me continue for a few minutes like a manifesto.

We live as women in a revolutionary era for women: it is a time of nothing less than the first concerted effort by women to question and change definitions of our sex and gender—our femaleness and femininity, our proper place and purpose—that have been proposed, with variations, throughout the history of patriarchies. We live in and with a mass movement that has grown in the post–World War II period from an aspiration to a reality; from a vision particular to a segment of the Western intelligentsia to an achievement known to and contributed to by people all over the world. The feminist movement is truly an Internationale for the first time in history.

It is certainly obvious that, as a movement hoping to secure socioeconomic and political equality for women, the feminist movement is still in its infancy. The changes in women's statuses that it has brought about are everywhere insecurely instituted and under constant threat—in bedrooms, at breakfast tables, in marketplaces, clinics, courts, and political forums—from those who resist change, wish to roll it back, and even sometimes from those who are working for it.

But I think that it is reasonable to claim that although the movement has miles to go in the matter of rights, it has already made a revolution by adding to the query, What do women want? the question, How and by whom have women's wants been determined? It is one thing, for example, when a psychological study is conducted to try to assess differences between women and men, and quite another when the assumptions—the perceptual and conceptual biases—that shape such a study are themselves the object of study.

I do not consider this example to be isolated or academic. The shift it exemplifies is crucial and, I think, novel, even though it is certainly the case that, throughout the history of women's struggles for emancipation, analysts of the female condition have understood that prejudice predetermines and perpetuates institutions of inequality as much as institutions of inequality reflect and confirm prejudice; that habits of thought organize social relations as much as social relations organize habits of thought. Proclamists of emancipation have also understood that lasting change requires both reform of our ways of ordering our lives in all spheres and intellectual critique. The classics of the feminist movement have won their positions as perennials because their addresses to institutionalized inequality have been combined with studies of prejudice.

But what is new in the postwar era is that the institutions and intellectual disciplines that shape the form and content of education—by which I do not mean simply schooling—are being critically reshaped. Studies of prejudice are no longer reported by voices in the wilderness; they are broadcast in the metropli of consciousness, in educational settings of all sorts. "The whole pyramid of discrimination," as Juliet Mitchell has written, "rests on solid extra-economic foundation—education."

When intellectual critique is reflexive and self-critical, that is, when it both questions *and* questions how its questions have been and are being posed, then intellectual critique is truly philosophical. What is going on now, as the feminist movement's critique reaches into the root systems of prejudice against women, is the education of women as philosophers. But when I say this "as philosophers" I mean not as professional philosophers or even as heiresses to traditional philosophical inquiry. What I do mean will take me a little while to say.

* * *

Within our European tradition, philosophizing began in an era of cultural ferment. All around the Mediterranean Sea, peoples who had lived in relative isolation encountered each other as traders and soldiers, adventurers and empire builders. Among the sixth-century B.C.E. Hellenes settled on the Ionian coast, at the edge of an empire (the Persian) being swept with a fervor called Zoroastrianism, there lived thinkers now known collectively as the pre-Socratics. These men began to ask whether the world in all its rich diversity is not really made up of one primal stuff, or moved by one regnant power, or ruled on one principle. At the same time, among the Israelites (settled uncertainly in their Promised Land), prophets and priests, heirs of Moses, wrote texts declaring that one God created the world and rules over it. In both of these traditions, for all their differences, the ruler was conceived as the orderer, the world-mind.

Many and diverse are the ways in which the search for a *monos*, a one, transcendent or imminent, has taken place since this foundational era of our history. Each renewal of the search has summoned up the original search reflexively, asking whether and how the monisms of the founders were true. Is the one Anaxagoras's *Nous* (Mind)? Heraclitus's *Logos*, Parmenides' Being? Is it Plato's Good? or Aristotle's telic Unmoved Mover? Is the one God the God of the Jews? or the Christians? or perhaps even the Ahura-Mazda of the Zoroastrians?

In another period of great cultural ferment and contact among peoples—peoples not just of the Mediterranean but of the then circumnavigated globe—there grew up alongside this reflexive questioning that had been the impulse of many renaissances other forms of reflexivity. In the European era known as the Enlightenment, people began to question how the *human* mind conducts its philosophical and religious searches. Are all the monisms, so seemingly diverse, mere variations of a single Truth? A Truth for Man? Could it be that all the different monisms are themselves manifestations of one universal human Mind?

These were the questions of Enlightenment cosmopolitanism, but there were also questions in the Enlightenment that marked a second new form of reflexivity, quite different from the cosmopolitan one that ushered in mental monism. Is it possible that people's minds, rather than being fitted for knowing the single Truth and hindered from such knowledge only by local differences of customs and languages, are and always have been destined to know only themselves? Do minds know only the walls of their prisons—the walls of diverse, historically determined prisons? Perhaps (so this form of questioning went) human beings are condemned to mind-bound truths and forever precluded from any Truth with a capital *T*. These questions were focused on the nature of mental activity, as were the cosmopolitan questions; but they did not reach beyond mental activity to a monistic Mind of Man. On the contrary, they opened the way for notions of cultural diversity, mental relativism—the basic ingredients of what might be called the intellectual French Revolution.

This second form of Enlightenment reflexivity is apparent in many kinds of nineteenth-century studies of what we today call "difference":

anthropological studies of "primitive" non-European peoples; sociological studies of nonaristocratic peoples of various classes; historical studies of nonvictorious peoples suppressed in the triumph of European civilization; philosophical inquiries into the history of ideas, *Geistesgeschichte*, including suppressed ideas. But it is certainly the case that before Marx and Freud were heeded, most of these studies contained more or less explicit assumptions about the evolutionary truth of the predominating modes of civilization—that is, they acknowledged the different but then measured it by the standard of the successful, the ideal mind: given time, evolution will reinstate the Truth.

Feminist writers participated in this great upheaval and expansion of horizon, but often quite ambiguously. The ambiguity of their critiques centered in their attitudes toward reason. From the time of Mary Wollstonecraft until the time of Simone de Beauvoir, feminists noted that women do not think as men do—that their minds are not male minds, educated like male minds. Women, it was understood, have been kept in economic, social, and political conditions that deprived them of the rationality of men. Mary Wollstonecraft and Simone de Beauvoir both—in the eighteenth century and in the twentieth century—lamented that women have been kept from rationality and from the transcendent capacities of reason. One of the key aspirations of feminism, to put the matter in other words, was to free women from their circumscribed mental worlds and let them enter into male rationality, participate in it as equals.

To this aspiration, postwar feminism has addressed probing questions about whether it is not, in effect, a reinstatement or reaffirmation of the monistic Enlightenment ideals, one Mind of Man or one evolutionarily ideal mind. Recent feminists have said—to speak baldly—why emulate male rationality? Male rationality, after all, has been supplying reasons—for centuries—for the oppression of women; why emulate it? Male rationality has judged women's mental abilities—as well as their physical abilities—inferior; why emulate it? This questioning is coordinated to an inquiry that Jane Martin has summarized well in her *Reclaiming a Conversation:* "Since the early 1970s, research has documented the ways in which such intellectual disciplines as history and psychology, literature and the fine arts, sociology and biology are biased according to sex. This work has revealed that on at least three counts the disciplines fall short of the ideal of epistemological equality for women: they exclude women from their subject matter, distort the female according to the male image of her, and deny value to characteristics the society considers feminine." The phrase "epistemological equality" does not mean equal participation in male rationality; it means equal acknowledgment for male and female minds, lives, and histories.

The first level of critique launched by feminists from Wollstonecraft to de Beauvoir against the prejudice that women cannot think was launched against the prejudice itself. Once this critique had cleared a space, and once women in large numbers had begun to speak and act in public on "the woman question," its sequel came. Questions were raised, are being raised, about how thinking or reason is thought about. Do the predominant modes of thinking about thinking exclude or suppress not just groups of people but types of activity—that might or might not be specific to those excluded groups? Maybe the definitions of thinking laid down by men—so this critique suggests—exclude what women do. Thus the old feminist question has been re-posed: Do men and women think differently? And the answer to it is: yes. Sometimes now the answer is: yes, and furthermore, women's thinking is *better*. But at any rate, the message of this critique is clear: no longer are women or their thinking to be judged by the standards of male rationality.

When I spoke earlier of the feminist movement's critique reaching to the roots of prejudice and the consequent education of women as philosophers, I did not mean—as must now be obvious—as philosophers in the monistic tradition. I meant as continuers and radicalizers of the reflexive critical mode that has slowly brought the monistic tradition into question. But before I try to continue the story of what this questioning means for women, I want to consider one further crucial intellectual obstacle that the feminist movement's critique has met and tried to overcome. If, as I have claimed, the Mind or Reason has been at the center of religious and philosophical monism, how did women's alleged inferiority come to be associated with her anatomy?

There are many ways to approach this question. Let me choose just one—the broadly historical—as an example. Ever since the Enlightenment, there have been speculations that the era in which Greek philosophy and the Israelite and Zoroastrian religions were born was an era of transition in the eastern Mediterranean from matriarchal to patriarchal societies, from Earth Goddess religions to religions in which male deities or a male deity dominated. Recently, this speculation has intensified and been supported with archaeological evidence and reinterpretations of literary evidence. If this transition did take place, then monistic thought can be seen as male intellectualization triumphant, in the sense that as men placed themselves in rulership over women, they placed the mind in rulership over the body. That is, women became defined by and associated with the body that the mind ruled. Monism, to put the same point differently, involves suppression: for the one to rule, it must rule something other, which is conceived as nonmental—either animally all-body or ethereally extramental, whorish, or saintly.

Such a broad historical speculation is not, in any strict sense, provable, any more than are corollary psychoanalytic speculations about why men began to dominate women and to dominate rationally their own bodies, to regulate their erotic pleasures. The importance of such speculations has been and is that they have helped establish a distinction that is central to feminist critique: the distinction between sex and gender, or between anatomical differences and differences of socialization, education, and political power. Anatomical differences are, so this distinction implies, perennially matters of fact, but, as facts, they are never without valuative interpretation or manipulation; they are never contextless.

The distinction between sex and gender was crucial to Simone de Beauvoir's work. It was she who gave the postwar feminist movement its orienting maxim: Women are not born, but made. But the issue of anatomical difference has not disappeared from the theoretical scene; indeed, it haunts it. Again and again, either in a sexist mode (like contemporary sociobiology) or in a woman-affirming mode, these differences have been brought back as the essential ones and as the sources of mental differences. Women, that is, have been said to have genetic endowments or brain lateralizations productive of mental differences, or an essential, timeless "corporeal ground" (in Adrienne Rich's phrase) productive of mental differences. In the current phase of feminism, each and every way that anatomical difference has been evaluated or "genderized" is up for questioning: do the evaluations reflect or transcend the old forms of male/female, mind/body hierarchical dualisms? Simone de Beauvoir's own version of the mind/body dualism has been rigorously criticized, particularly insofar as she thought that women, to be free, to be rational, ought to transcend their reproductive capacity and not have children, or insofar as she thought that women who accepted themselves as women, as anatomically female, would desire only other women.

Let me put this development more generally. It has been widely acknowledged that accepting the male/female, mind/body dualisms in a merely reformative spirit, that is, either by reversing the values of the dualisms and elevating female over male and body over mind, or by attributing to females the mind power of males at the expense of their bodies, means foreclosing a deep critique of those dualisms.

When I say that the feminist movement's critique has brought about the education—the beginning of the education—of women as philosophers, I mean that we all, regardless of the terms we use, struggle at this philosophical bedrock. Twentieth-century philosophy, in its most radical modes, has been struggling in a crisis known as "the end of metaphysics." And that means the end of enthrallment by tradition-long metaphysical forms of thought such as the dualistic forms I noted. But what we can see in the last decade is the beginning of a merger of philosophical questioning and feminist questioning. That is, we can also see the very beginning of the education of philosophers as feminists.

Now that the pluralistic reflexive critical tendency within the European tradition and the feminist critique have begun to relate to each other explicitly, many developments are possible. Once the framing dualisms of the tradition are grasped as part of the problem—and we, as critics, are aware that our own critiques are historically bound up with, intertwined with, the very foundational thought forms we wish to criticize—the reconstruction of our history and the envisioning of future possibilities become very rich, complex projects. With what thought forms are you criticizing inherited thought forms?—this is the omnipresent question. It could produce a mire of methodologism and it could produce new feminist factions, but I do not think these are the likely outcomes.

When inherited thought forms are grasped as enthrallments of the imagination, *all* of their ingredients are up for critique. And I think this job will prove too compelling to be reduced to battles over method or to permit rigidification of theoretical and practical experimentation. And, besides, once the European tradition has ceased to enthrall our minds, it and its particularities—the differences of moments within it, the efforts at rebellion or nonconformity it has been laced with—become newly interesting, and so do all of the traditions which it is *not*; in time and space, we can hope that the feminist inquiry will become more global, more comparative, more concrete, more subtle. Minds and bodies, not the mind and the body; men and women, not the male and the female; masculinities and femininities, not the masculine and the feminine; sexualities and genderizations—the plurals will come forward, and the past will be viewed as a resource, not just as a tragedy. We will see, as Adrienne Rich once wrote, "the damage that was done and the treasures that prevail."

* * *

It is in this context, or with this hope, that I want to return to the statement with which I began. When we think of ourselves as thinkers, we tend to think of ourselves as selves, I said, as first person singulars, solitaries, interiorities, mental machines.

In our own period of great cultural ferment and contact among diverse peoples—in the period of world wars and, since the Second World War, worldwide shared sense of planetary peril—both the mental monism of the Enlightenment and the mental pluralism of the Enlightenment with its monistic evolutionary bias have been under question. What is at philosophical issue are images of the mind in which one part or function predominates, either structurally or evolutionarily, and (ideally) produces one kind of thought, one kind of truth, one form of rationality.

Within the Western tradition, the critical assault upon such images has come, I think, not just from philosophy proper but from the practice of psychoanalysis. And these two critiques have gained strength from various forms of sociopolitical critique of what Foucault has called "totalizing discourse" that show the exclusionary import of such images; that show how they exclude non-European modes of thought, classes and races not educated in and for rationalism, and, finally, women whose thinking is derided as feminine, irrational.

Let me focus my attention for a moment on the psychoanalytic critical strand. Even though Freud's metapsychological formulations were indebted to, embedded in, traditional divisions of the mind into hierarchically arranged parts as well as to traditional notions of one mental function maturing over time into natural dominance over others, his key insights all point to a new venue. The mind or psyche has structures, but these are in constant interaction; id, ego, and superego are not separate faculties or compartments; they are definable only in dynamic relation to each other. And unconscious, preconscious, and conscious are not like steps going up, each to be left behind as the next is achieved. Our mental processes are, to speak simply, conversational. We are not solitary when we think; we are full of voices.

These voices are representations of both our drives or instincts and their worldly encounters, from the first ones in our parents' care to the most recent, from the early ones with objects and words to the later ones with ranges of others and with our cultural heritage in all its many forms. These voices represent in us all we have desired and all desires we have desired to have or not to have; they represent all the linkages and severances we have made among our desires and all the interpretations of our desiring with which we order ourselves, setting and resetting, repeating and extending, boundaries on the confusing and never entirely lost initial boundarilessness of our natalities. Reason does not rule over instinctual desires in this conception; desires are the reason for reason and reason is the reasoning of desires. Reason without desire is empty, as desire without reason is blind. Even when the two are in tension, in conflict, neither wins.

Freud distinguished between primary unconscious or unarticulated mental processes to which we have very little access and secondary mental processes, conscious processes to which we do have access or of which we are self-conscious. The latter include differentiating, connecting, and categorizing of things, events, words, and also what we generally call thinking. There is, obviously, a dualistic conception here, but primary and secondary processes are not rigidly distinct or hierarchically related in structural or evolutionary terms. Freud made it quite clear that if conscious secondary organizing processes become severed from the primary processes of the unconscious and the desirous id, they are in danger of running unhealthily empty or being actually ruled by the severed-off processes, just as an adulthood, if it is built too firmly upon repressed childhood instincts, is in danger of running into depression, paralysis, or distortion of thinking. Freud himself valued scientific thinking as the most advanced and valuable form of secondary-process thinking, but he was keenly aware that the conversation of primary and secondary processes in, for example, poetry is responsible for poetry's universality and power, just as he was aware that a clinician listens not to secondary-process mentation but to the complex conversation of processes that is free associational speech.

The value of the idea that our mental life with others and with ourselves is conversational—that it is a constant interconnecting of all sorts of representations of our experience and also potentially an extension of our experience as we hear ourselves and others and reflexively interpret ourselves in and through novel conjunctions or conversational moments—the value of this idea is that, if we take this idea seriously, *live* this idea richly, we cannot become what I have called mental monists. And the corollary to this impossibility is that we cannot become prescriptivists of the mental realm.

By these claims I mean several things. First, we cannot assert that any one form or process of mental life is to be cultivated to the exclusion of others or that any one structuring of mental life is absolutely superior. Second, we cannot hope to organize the social world in order to structure the conversation of mental processes, including the conflictual conversations, for our mental life does not reflect directly or reproduce unmediatedly the social world—it is not in any simple way causally related to the social world.

* * *

Let me say what these statements imply by returning to the monistic tradition, which, I said, has been questioned within philosophy and by feminist inquiry into the roots of prejudice. Throughout the Western philosophical tradition, since the time of the pre-Socratics, Plato, and Aristotle, we can observe a tendency to establish corollations between images of the mind and ideal images of social-political organization. Plato, for example, asserted that the mind has three parts—reason, spirit, and appetites—and that the ideal *polis* should have three classes—philosopher-kings, guardians, and artisans or laborers. Aristotle asserted that the mind matures over time so that reason actualizes its potential to rule over the irrational parts of the mind, and that city-state organization, analogously, matures over time so that it grows closer to the ideal of a naturally superior male class ruling over inferior men, youths, and, at the bottom of the hierarchy, reasonless women and slaves. In the developed Christian tradition, the mind is ruled by a divine part—the *lumen naturale*—as the creation is ruled by God, and as the state should ideally, by divine right, be ruled by kings. Many variations on these notions have existed, some of which seem to come from introjections into the mind of idealized political arrangements, and some of which seem to be projections of analyses of the mind into visions of ideal political arrangements. At any rate, the philosophical *esprit de systeme* has the effect that images are constructed that protect the hegemony of a part of the mind and also legitimate a mentally superior ruling class or person. Mental monism and legitimations of political domination have mutually supported one another.

With respect to this habit of construction, the idea of our minds as conversations poses two challenges. First, it refuses the hierarchical tendency in the habitual constructions by insisting that all mental structures and processes have their importances relationally but not in relations of, so to speak, unrotating authoritarian rulership. The idea of our minds as conversations is, to use sociopolitical terms, radically democratic, antiauthoritarian; and thus it is no surprise that it should percolate in the philosophical tradition at a moment when radical democracy is an ideal and when forms of authoritarianism have been more cruel than at any other time in history. The image of our minds as conversations is, I think, crucial to progressivism in political theory: it implies that mental and political democracies can be mutually supporting, in accord with the traditional constructing technique but not in accord with the traditional constructions.

But, second, the idea of minds as conversations refuses the homology between mind and sociopolitical organization by insisting that the primary processes of the unconscious do not directly reflect or recapitulate any existing sociopolitical relations and cannot be the basis for envisioning any such sociopolitical relations. Unless you believe that there is such a thing as a collective unconscious, there is no homologue in the sociopolitical sphere for the unconscious and primary processes (though there are certainly processes awaiting an adequate group psychology). And what this means is that the individual lives and the particularities of individual internal conversations of people will always defy political theoretical constructions, even democratic ones, that are prescriptive.

It seems to me that some contemporary feminist visions are continuations of the long habit of constructing idealized sociopolitical forms as corollaries to images of the mind—and vice versa. For example, among those feminists who advocate for the future some form of matriarchy or some form of lesbian nation as the means for overthrowing or separating from patriarchy, there is an assumption that "natural" female thinking or feminine mental virtues are superior and should dominate over male rationality. Thus emotionality, intuition, maternal or nurturing thinking, or even the "primary narcissism" of mother-daughter (or woman-woman) bonds should rule in mental matriarchy, or mental gynarchy. The tradition of corollating mental images and political images is simply turned upside down.

This kind of upside-down construction has been criticized by other feminists, and their main critical approach has been psychoanalysis, because it points to what is left out of such a reversal: the conversation of primary and secondary processes, and, specifically, any appreciation of how the Freudian "discovery" of the unconscious asks us to respect the irreducible differences among us. But the entire habit of construction, I think, also needs philosophical critique, and the education of women as philosophers is the way to such a critique.

Psychoanalytic attention to the conversation of mental process and the general philosophical critique of mental monism that I have been noting as emergent have in common their skepticism toward any form of what Jacqueline Rose has called "utopianism of the psyche." The common caution about such utopianism asks that inversions of traditional habits not replace traditional habits as one ruling group replaces another in a political revolution that stops short of a cultural revolution, a critique of rulership, a change of attitude toward rulership. But even on the level of cultural revolution, this common caution asks that we not assume that social or political changes—for example, changes in the structure of the nuclear family, which is one of the primary locuses for the transmission of patriarchy—imply changes in peoples' psychic structures in any *direct* way. If shared parenting, one of the most frequently advocated social goals, is seen as the way to break up a social syndrome of the reproduction of mothering (in Nancy Chodorow's phrase) and to bring about the autonomy which too much embeddedness in relationship has kept unavailable to women, then this common caution asks that advocates of shared parenting not neglect processes of the psyche that may very well go on in *any* kind of parenting. It does not seem possible, for example, for there to be child rearing without unconscious communication between rearer (male or female) and child, a conversation that would not be conflict free even among angels. This is so (in psychoanalytic terms) both because all children *need* parenting and because we all have in us a plurality of psychic purposes—id purposes, ego purposes, superego purposes—that will conflict to some degree even in the healthiest of us as we outgrow our childhood instinctuality. And it is also so because parents bring their own purposes—often their own narcissistic loves—to the raising of their children. Autonomy is always a struggle—though there is certainly every reason to work toward making it a struggle worth waging.

* * *

Let me try to indicate what these reflections on "psychopolitical" constructions imply by beginning again in a different key. The simplest way in which mental monism as a prescriptive ideal translates into our everyday life is apparent, I think, in the goal to which we are so often urged to direct ourselves: we are to seek an "identity."

It seems to me that the quest for identity is particularly strong—in our Western societies at least—among women. It is the self-imposed equivalent of what social rites of passages traditionally have been for males: entrance ways into adulthood, into manhood in the sexual sense, into extra-familial love and work. It marks the need for individuation and autonomy in female terms: the need for definition achieved rather than accepted, chosen rather than enforced, made rather than born. Identity has become, for many women, the personal translation of emancipation: the political *made* personal, not suffered like a decree or a fate.

Our need for identity is our need not to be dictated to, dominated—not to be, as Simone de Beauvoir expressed it, always the Other, to others or to ourselves. The quest for this identity is in many ways laudable in sociopolitical terms. But it seems to me that it can also run contrary to—or involve suppression of—our internal conversations, and especially the unwelcome conflicts in them and the archaic voices in them that are kept (as D. W. Winnicott once put it) "in a state of uncommunication." To put this matter another way: identity—unity, cohesion—at the price of further repression or denial is an achievement awaiting an explosion. It can be a form of mental monism consciously chosen but nonetheless itself exclusionary.

These remarks about prescriptivism could be understood as implying a critique of feminism's sociopolitical emancipatory goals; but I want to make it as clear as I can that this is not what I intend. What I am trying to suggest is that all of the voices or purposes that are our minds must be heard in order for us to achieve not *an* identity but a more communicative form of life—the possibility of conversational reconciling, both in ourselves and with others. This, I take it, is the psychotherapeutic hope: making the unconscious or id voices conscious does not mean eliminating them; it means becoming reconciled to them and allowing them many other ends, a plurality which may include the ends of social and political revolution and which certainly will include the goal of thinking in many modalities. As Anna Freud once put this hope (in an unpublished letter): "What we are actually trying to do in education and in therapy is to sort out the individual's purposes and to make room for ego (reality) and superego (morality) purposes where the individual had felt hopelessly under the sway of id (instinctual) purposes."

The education of women as philosophers that I have been describing and invoking is an educational and therapeutic hope phrased as a conversation with a tradition at the moment of its internal crisis: the unsilencing of its suppressed voices and the breakup of its inhibiting monistic formations. From it will come support for thinking in the very processes that thinking traditionally has been said to transcend, or over which thinking has been said to rule.

* * *

At the beginning of this reflection I claimed that, because women find it no easy matter to think at all, given the weight of prejudice against them as thinkers, they are much more aware of (even if not openly acknowledging of) their supporters, those who have encouraged them to do what so much in our tradition holds they cannot or should not do: think. The supportive others, I said, are always there *in our thinking*.

What I meant by this claim is that the exemplary women who have in the past done what was not expected of them have never been entirely absent from our memories or the historical record. Women's history and biography writing are projects to make this heritage more richly and widely known and to recover the parts of it that have been neglected or distorted—often distorted by the kinds of mental habits I have been discussing. These are projects for redressing injustice and for giving our history a foundation that prevents future injustices. But I also meant that we all have in us voices that are supportive. We all have, for example, the voices of our own initial curiosities about the world and about the so-called facts of life, our first efforts at explaining to ourselves such perplexing matters as the origins of ourselves or the origins of our younger siblings. The education of male and female children as "good" children in narrow and often sexist terms, which it is the business of higher education to question, usually consists of dulling this curiosity with moral or rational strictures, not allowing it to meet freely with the "ego (reality) and superego (morality) purposes" that connect us to ourselves and to others. But the original curiosity remains—even if, under the worst circumstance, the curiosity is tyrannizing because distorted or denied. And it can remain as the primary-process spur to and contribution to all future intellectual activity.

Between prohibitions upon childhood questioning and denigrations of women's thinking, there is an obvious link: the assertion of adult power over children and the assertion, by individuals or in the general cultural discourse, of power over women are both forms of obedience training. This link is, I think, what makes the link between psychoanalysis and philosophy so important for our later lives. But between the exemplary women who inhabit our memories and imaginations, and our own curious childhood selves there is also, I think, a link: we turn to exemplary intellectual women with our still-active early desires to know, as well as with our later resurgences of this desire in different forms, including those forms that we have come to feel are obstructed because we are female. We internalize exemplary men and women, and we need "ego ideals" of both sexes, but it is women who were marginalized and continued thinking with whom we associate our own marginalized desires to know.

* * *

The culturally transmitted thought forms and habits of construction I have been examining are the intellectual manifestations of obstacles that have deep roots—in our culture and in ourselves. Both restoration of women's voices suppressed in the history of the cultural discourses and restoration of the pluralities of voices inside us that have been threatened with monism in our upbringings and in our encounters with the cultural discourses require analysis of those thought forms and habits of construction. Higher education for women is the outward and visible sign that this analysis is under way, that a cultural revolution is advancing. The inward and spiritual grace of this revolution will take longer—for it is a deeper matter. I have tried to suggest that the education of women as philosophers is the framing of its guiding questions.

College of Letters
Wesleyan University

POSTMODERNISM AND GENDER RELATIONS IN FEMINIST THEORY

JANE FLAX

> As the thought of the world, [philosophy] appears only when actuality is already there cut and dried after its process of formation has been completed. . . . When philosophy paints its grey in grey, then has a shape of life grown old. By philosophy's grey in grey it cannot be rejuvenated but only understood. The owl of Minerva spreads its wings only with the falling of the dusk. [G. W. F. HEGEL, preface to *Philosophy of Right*]

It seems increasingly probable that Western culture is in the middle of a fundamental transformation: a "shape of life" is growing old. In retrospect, this transformation may be as radical (but as gradual) as the shift from a medieval to a modern society. Accordingly, this moment in the history of the West is pervaded by profound yet little-comprehended change, uncertainty, and ambivalence. This transitional state makes certain forms of

This paper has been through many transformations. It was originally written for presentation at the annual meeting of the German Association for American Studies, June 1984, Berlin. Travel to Germany was made possible by a grant from the Volkswagen Foundation. An earlier version of this paper, entitled "Gender as a Problem: In and for Feminist Theory," will appear in the German journal, *Amerikastudien/American Studies*. I have been fortunate to have many attentive readers of this paper whose influences undoubtedly improved it, including Gisela Bock, Sandra Harding, Mervat Hatem, Phyllis Palmer, and Barrie Thorne.

This essay originally appeared in *Signs*, vol. 12, no. 4, Summer 1987.

thought possible and necessary, and it excludes others. It generates problems that some philosophies seem to acknowledge and confront better than others.

I think there are currently three kinds of thinking that best present (and represent) our own time "apprehended in thought": psychoanalysis, feminist theory, and postmodern philosophy. These ways of thinking reflect and are partially constituted by Enlightenment beliefs still prevalent in Western (especially American) culture. At the same time they offer ideas and insights that are only possible because of the breakdown of Enlightenment beliefs under the cumulative pressure of historical events such as the invention of the atomic bomb, the Holocaust, and the war in Vietnam.[1]

Each of these ways of thinking takes as its object of investigation at least one facet of what has become most problematic in our transitional state: how to understand and (re-)constitute the self, gender, knowledge, social relations, and culture without resorting to linear, teleological, hierarchical, holistic, or binary ways of thinking and being.

My focus here will be mainly on one of these modes of thinking: feminist theory. I will consider what it could be and reflect upon the goals, logics, and problematics of feminist theorizing as it has been practiced in the past fifteen years in the West. I will also place such theorizing within the social and philosophical contexts of which it is both a part and a critique.

I do not mean to claim that feminist theory is a unified or homogeneous discourse. Nonetheless, despite the lively and intense controversies among persons who identify themselves as practitioners concerning the subject matter, appropriate methodologies, and desirable outcome of feminist theorizing, it is possible to identify at least some of our underlying goals, purposes, and constituting objects.

A fundamental goal of feminist theory is (and ought to be) to analyze gender relations: how gender relations are constituted and experienced and how we think or, equally important, do not think about them.[2] The study of gender relations includes but is not limited to what are often

[1] For a more extended discussion of these claims, see my forthcoming work "Freud's Children? Psychoanalysis and Feminism in the Postmodern West."

[2] Representative examples of feminist theories include Barbara Smith, ed., *Home Girls: A Black Feminist Anthology* (New York: Kitchen Table: Women of Color Press, 1983); Cherríe Moraga and Gloria Anzaldúa, eds., *This Bridge Called My Back* (Watertown, Mass.: Persephone Press, 1981); Elizabeth Abel, Marianne Hirsch, and Elizabeth Langland, *The Voyage In: Fictions of Female Development* (Hanover, N.H., and London: University Press of New England, 1983); Zillah R. Eisenstein, ed., *Capitalist Patriarchy and the Case for Socialist Feminism* (New York: Monthly Review Press, 1979); Annette Kuhn and Ann Marie Wolpe, eds., *Feminism and Materialism* (Boston: Routledge & Kegan Paul, 1978); Hunter College Women's Studies Collective, *Women's Realities, Women's Choices* (New York: Oxford University Press, 1983); Elaine Marks and Isabelle de Courtivron, eds., *New French Feminisms* (New York: Schocken Books, 1981); Joyce Trebilcot, ed., *Mothering: Essays in Feminist Theory* (Totowa, N.J.: Rowman & Allanheld, 1984); Sherry B. Ortner and Harriet

considered the distinctively feminist issues: the situation of women and the analysis of male domination. Feminist theory includes an (at least implicit) prescriptive element as well. By studying gender we hope to gain a critical distance on existing gender arrangements. This critical distance can help clear a space in which reevaluating and altering our existing gender arrangements may become more possible.

Feminist theory by itself cannot clear such a space. Without feminist political actions theories remain inadequate and ineffectual. However, I have come to believe that the further development of feminist theory (and hence a better understanding of gender) also depends upon locating our theorizing within and drawing more self-consciously upon the wider philosophic contexts of which it is both a part and a critique. In other words, we need to think more about how we think about gender relations or any other social relations and about how other modes of thinking can help or hinder us in the development of our own discourses. In this paper, I will be moving back and forth between thinking about gender relations and thinking about how I am thinking—or could think—about them.

Metatheory: Thinking about thinking

Feminist theory seems to me to belong within two, more inclusive, categories with which it has special affinity: the analysis of social relations and postmodern philosophy.[3] Gender relations enter into and are constituent

---

Whitehead, eds., *Sexual Meanings: The Cultural Construction of Gender and Sexuality* (New York: Cambridge University Press, 1981); Nancy C. M. Hartsock, *Money, Sex, and Power* (New York: Longman, Inc., 1983); Ann Snitow, Christine Stansell and Sharon Thompson, eds., *The Powers of Desire: The Politics of Sexuality* (New York: Monthly Review Press, 1983); Sandra Harding and Merrill B. Hintikka, eds., *Discovering Reality: Feminist Perspectives on Epistemology, Metaphysics, Methodology, and Philosophy of Science* (Boston: D. Reidel Publishing Co., 1983); Carol C. Gould, *Beyond Domination: New Perspectives on Women and Philosophy* (Totowa, N.J.: Rowman & Allanheld, 1984); Alison M. Jaggar, *Feminist Politics and Human Nature* (Totowa, N.J.: Rowman & Allanheld, 1983); Isaac D. Balbus, *Marxism and Domination* (Princeton, N.J.: Princeton University Press, 1982).

[3] Sources for and practitioners of postmodernism include Friedrich Nietzsche, *On the Genealogy of Morals* (New York: Vintage, 1969) and *Beyond Good and Evil* (New York: Vintage, 1966); Jacques Derrida, *L'écriture et la difference* (Paris: Editions du Seuil, 1967); Michel Foucault, *Language, Counter-Memory, Practice* (Ithaca, N.Y.: Cornell University Press, 1977); Jacques Lacan, *Speech and Language in Psychoanalysis* (Baltimore: Johns Hopkins University Press, 1968), and *The Four Fundamental Concepts of Psychoanalysis* (New York: W. W. Norton & Co., 1973); Richard Rorty, *Philosophy and the Mirror of Nature* (Princeton, N.J.: Princeton University Press, 1979); Paul Feyerabend, *Against Method* (New York: Schocken Books, 1975); Ludwig Wittgenstein, *On Certainty* (New York: Harper & Row, 1972), and *Philosophical Investigations* (New York: Macmillan Publishing Co., 1970); Julia Kristeva, "Women's Time," *Signs: Journal of Women in Culture and Society* 7, no. 1 (Autumn 1981): 13–35; and Jean-François Lyotard, *The Postmodern Condition* (Minneapolis: University of Minnesota Press, 1984).

elements in every aspect of human experience. In turn, the experience of gender relations for any person and the structure of gender as a social category are shaped by the interactions of gender relations and other social relations such as class and race. Gender relations thus have no fixed essence; they vary both within and over time.

As a type of postmodern philosophy, feminist theory reveals and contributes to the growing uncertainty within Western intellectual circles about the appropriate grounding and methods for explaining and/or interpreting human experience. Contemporary feminists join other postmodern philosophers in raising important metatheoretical questions about the possible nature and status of theorizing itself. Given the increasingly fluid and confused status of Western self-understandings, it is not even clear what would constitute the basis for satisfactory answers to commonly agreed upon questions within feminist (or other forms of social) theory.

Postmodern discourses are all "deconstructive" in that they seek to distance us from and make us skeptical about beliefs concerning truth, knowledge, power, the self, and language that are often taken for granted within and serve as legitimation for contemporary Western culture.

Postmodern philosophers seek to throw into radical doubt beliefs still prevalent in (especially American) culture but derived from the Enlightenment, such as:

1. The existence of a stable, coherent self. Distinctive properties of this Enlightenment self include a form of reason capable of privileged insight into its own processes and into the "laws of nature."

2. Reason and its "science"—philosophy—can provide an objective, reliable, and universal foundation for knowledge.

3. The knowledge acquired from the right use of reason will be "True"—for example, such knowledge will represent something real and unchanging (universal) about our minds and/or the structure of the natural world.

4. Reason itself has transcendental and universal qualities. It exists independently of the self's contingent existence (e.g., bodily, historical, and social experiences do not affect reason's structure or its capacity to produce atemporal knowledge).

5. There are complex connections between reason, autonomy, and freedom. All claims to truth and rightful authority are to be submitted to the tribunal of reason. Freedom consists in obedience to laws that conform to the necessary results of the right use of reason. (The rules that are right for me as a rational being will necessarily be right for all other such beings.) In obeying such laws, I am obeying my own best transhistorical part (reason) and hence am exercising my own autonomy and ratifying my existence as a free being. In such acts, I escape a determined or merely contingent existence.

6. By grounding claims to authority in reason, the conflicts between

truth, knowledge, and power can be overcome. Truth can serve power without distortion; in turn, by utilizing knowledge in the service of power both freedom and progress will be assured. Knowledge can be both neutral (e.g., grounded in universal reason, not particular "interests") and also socially beneficial.

7. Science, as the exemplar of the right use of reason, is also the paradigm for all true knowledge. Science is neutral in its methods and contents but socially beneficial in its results. Through its process of discovery we can utilize the "laws of nature" for the benefit of society. However, in order for science to progress, scientists must be free to follow the rules of reason rather than pander to the "interests" arising from outside rational discourse.

8. Language is in some sense transparent. Just as the right use of reason can result in knowledge that represents the real, so, too, language is merely the medium in and through which such representation occurs. There is a correspondence between "word" and "thing" (as between a correct truth claim and the real). Objects are not linguistically (or socially) constructed, they are merely *made present* to consciousness by naming and the right use of language.

The relation of feminist theorizing to the postmodern project of deconstruction is necessarily ambivalent. Enlightenment philosophers such as Kant did not intend to include women within the population of those capable of attaining freedom from traditional forms of authority. Nonetheless, it is not unreasonable for persons who have been defined as incapable of self-emancipation to insist that concepts such as the autonomy of reason, objective truth, and beneficial progress through scientific discovery ought to include and be applicable to the capacities and experiences of women as well as men. It is also appealing, for those who have been excluded, to believe that reason will triumph—that those who proclaim such ideas as objectivity will respond to rational arguments. If there is no objective basis for distinguishing between true and false beliefs, then it seems that power alone will determine the outcome of competing truth claims. This is a frightening prospect to those who lack (or are oppressed by) the power of others.

Nevertheless, despite an understandable attraction to the (apparently) logical, orderly world of the Enlightenment, feminist theory more properly belongs in the terrain of postmodern philosophy. Feminist notions of the self, knowledge, and truth are too contradictory to those of the Enlightenment to be contained within its categories. The way(s) to feminist future(s) cannot lie in reviving or appropriating Enlightenment concepts of the person or knowledge.[4]

[4] In "The Instability of the Analytical Categories of Feminist Theory," *Signs* 11, no. 4 (Summer 1986): 645–64, Sandra Harding discusses the ambivalent attraction of feminist

Feminist theorists enter into and echo postmodernist discourses as we have begun to deconstruct notions of reason, knowledge, or the self and to reveal the effects of the gender arrangements that lay beneath their "neutral" and universalizing facades.[5] Some feminist theorists, for example, have begun to sense that the motto of Enlightenment, "*sapere aude*—'Have courage to use your own reason,'"[6] rests in part upon a deeply gender-rooted sense of self and self-deception. The notion that reason is divorced from "merely contingent" existence still predominates in contemporary Western thought and now appears to mask the embeddedness and dependence of the self upon social relations, as well as the partiality and historical specificity of this self's existence. What Kant's self calls its "own" reason and the methods by which reason's contents become present or "self-evident," it now appears, are no freer from empirical contingency than is the so-called phenomenal self.[7]

In fact, feminists, like other postmodernists, have begun to suspect that all such transcendental claims reflect and reify the experience of a few persons—mostly white, Western males. These transhistoric claims seem plausible to us in part because they reflect important aspects of the experience of those who dominate our social world.

A feminist problematic

This excursus into metatheory has now returned us to the opening of my paper—that the fundamental purpose of feminist theory is to analyze how we think, or do not think, or avoid thinking about gender. Obviously, then,

---

theorizing to both sorts of discourse. She insists that feminist theorists should live with the ambivalence and retain both discourses for political and philosophical reasons. However, I think her argument rests in part on a too uncritical appropriation of a key Enlightenment equation of knowing, naming, and emancipation.

[5] Examples of such work include Alice A. Jardine, *Gynesis: Configurations of Woman and Modernity* (Ithaca, N.Y.: Cornell University Press, 1985); Donna Haraway, "A Manifesto for Cyborgs: Science, Technology, and Socialist Feminism in the 1980s," *Socialist Review* 80 (1983): 65–107; Kristeva; Kathy E. Ferguson, *The Feminist Case against Bureaucracy* (Philadelphia: Temple University Press, 1984); and Luce Irigaray, *Speculum of the Other Woman* (Ithaca, N.Y.: Cornell University Press, 1985).

[6] Immanuel Kant, "What Is Enlightenment?" in *Foundations of the Metaphysics of Morals* (Indianapolis: Bobbs-Merrill Co., 1959), 85.

[7] For critiques of the mind (reason)/body split, see Naomi Scheman, "Individualism and the Objects of Psychology," in Harding and Hintikka, eds.; Susan Bordo, "The Cartesian Masculinization of Thought," *Signs* 11, no. 3 (Spring 1986): 439–56; Nancy C. M. Hartsock, "The Feminist Standpoint: Developing the Ground for a Specifically Feminist Historical Materialism," in Harding and Hintikka, eds.; Caroline Whitbeck, "Afterword to the 'Maternal Instinct,'" in Trebilcot, ed.; and Dorothy Smith, "A Sociology for Women," in *The Prison of Sex: Essays in the Sociology of Knowledge*, ed. J. Sherman and E. T. Beck (Madison: University of Wisconsin Press, 1979).

to understand the goals of feminist theory we must consider its central subject—gender.

Here, however, we immediately plunge into a complicated and controversial morass. For among feminist theorists there is by no means consensus on such (apparently) elementary questions as: What is gender? How is it related to anatomical sexual differences? How are gender relations constituted and sustained (in one person's lifetime and more generally as a social experience over time)? How do gender relations relate to other sorts of social relations such as class or race? Do gender relations have a history (or many)? What causes gender relations to change over time? What are the relationships between gender relations, sexuality, and a sense of individual identity? What are the relationships between heterosexuality, homosexuality, and gender relations? Are there only two genders? What are the relationships between forms of male dominance and gender relations? Could/would gender relations wither away in egalitarian societies? Is there anything distinctively male or female in modes of thought and social relations? If there is, are these distinctions innate and/or socially constituted? Are gendered distinctions socially useful and/or necessary? If so, what are the consequences for the feminist goal of attaining gender justice?[8]

Confronted with such a bewildering set of questions, it is easy to overlook the fact that a fundamental transformation in social theory has occurred. The single most important advance in feminist theory is that the existence of gender relations has been problematized. Gender can no longer be treated as a simple, natural fact. The assumption that gender relations are natural, we can now see, arose from two coinciding circumstances: the unexamined identification and confusion of (anatomical) sexual differences with gender relations, and the absence of active feminist movements. I will return to a consideration of the connections between gender relations and biology later in the paper.

Contemporary feminist movements are in part rooted in transformations in social experience that challenge widely shared categories of social meaning and explanation. In the United States, such transformations include changes in the structure of the economy, the family, the place of the United States in the world system, the declining authority of previously powerful social institutions, and the emergence of political groups that have increasingly more divergent ideas and demands concerning justice, equality, social legislation, and the proper role of the state. In such a "decentered" and unstable universe it seems plausible to question one of the most natural facets of human existence—gender relations. On the other

[8] These questions are suggested by Judith Stacey, "The New Conservative Feminism," *Feminist Studies* 9, no. 3 (Fall 1983): 559–83; and Nancy Chodorow, "Gender, Relation, and Difference in Psychoanalytic Perspective," in *The Future of Difference*, ed. Hester Eisenstein and Alice Jardine (1980; reprint, New Brunswick, N.J.: Rutgers University Press, 1985).

hand, such instability also makes old modes of social relations more attractive. The new right and Ronald Reagan both call upon and reflect a desire to go back to a time when people and countries were in their "proper" place. The conflicts around gender arrangements become both the locus for and symbols of anxieties about all sorts of social-political ideas, only some of which are actually rooted primarily in gender relations.[9]

The coexistence of such social transformations and movements makes possible an increasingly radical and social, self-conscious questioning of previously unexamined "facts" and "explanations." Thus, feminist theory, like all other forms of theory (including gender-biased ones), is dependent upon and reflects a certain set of social experiences. Whether, to what extent, and why feminist theory can be "better" than the gender-biased theories it critiques are questions that vex many writers.[10] In considering such questions feminist theorists invariably enter the epistemological terrain shared in part with other postmodern philosophies. Hence, I wish to bracket these questions for now in order to consider more closely a fundamental category and object of investigation of feminist theory—gender relations.

Thinking in relations

"Gender relations" is a category meant to capture a complex set of social relations, to refer to a changing set of historically variable social processes. Gender, both as an analytic category and a social process, is relational. That is, gender relations are complex and unstable processes (or temporary "totalities" in the language of dialectics) constituted by and through interrelated parts. These parts are interdependent, that is, each part can have no meaning or existence without the others.

Gender relations are differentiated and (so far) asymmetric divisions and attributions of human traits and capacities. Through gender relations two types of persons are created: man and woman. Man and woman are posited as exclusionary categories. One can be only one gender, never the

[9] On the appeal of new right ideology to women, see Stacey.

[10] Harding discusses these problems in detail. See n. 4 above. See also Sandra Harding, "Is Gender a Variable in Conceptions of Rationality? A Survey of Issues," in Gould (n. 2 above), and "Why Has the Sex/Gender System Become Visible Only Now?" in Harding and Hintikka, eds.; and Jaggar (n. 2 above), 353–94. Since within modern Western cultures science is the model for knowledge and is simultaneously neutral/objective yet socially useful/powerful (or destructive), much epistemological inquiry has focused on the nature and structure of science. Compare Hilary Rose, "Hand, Brain, and Heart: A Feminist Epistemology for the Natural Sciences," *Signs* 9, no. 1 (Autumn 1983): 73–90; and Helen Longino and Ruth Doell, "Body, Bias, and Behavior: A Comparative Analysis of Reasoning in Two Areas of Biological Science," *Signs* 9, no. 2 (Winter 1983): 206–27.

other or both. The actual content of being a man or woman and the rigidity of the categories themselves are highly variable across cultures and time. Nevertheless, gender relations so far as we have been able to understand them have been (more or less) relations of domination. That is, gender relations have been (more) defined and (imperfectly) controlled by one of their interrelated aspects—the man.

These relations of domination and the existence of gender relations themselves have been concealed in a variety of ways, including defining women as a "question" or the "sex" or the "other"[11] and men as the universal (or at least without gender). In a wide variety of cultures and discourses, men tend to be seen as free from or as not determined by gender relations. Thus, for example, academics do not explicitly study the psychology of men or men's history. Male academics do not worry about how being men may distort their intellectual work, while women who study gender relations are considered suspect (of triviality, if not bias). Only recently have scholars begun to consider the possibility that there may be at least three histories in every culture—"his," "hers," and "ours." "His" and "ours" are generally assumed to be equivalents, although in contemporary work there might be some recognition of the existence of that deviant—woman (e.g., women's history).[12] However, it is still rare for scholars to search for the pervasive effects of gender relations on all aspects of a culture in the way that they feel obligated to investigate the impact of relations of power or the organization of production.

To the extent that feminist discourse defines its problematic as "woman," it, too, ironically privileges the man as unproblematic or exempted from determination by gender relations. From the perspective of social relations, men and women are both prisoners of gender, although in highly differentiated but interrelated ways. That men appear to be and (in many cases) are the wardens, or at least the trustees within a social whole, should not blind us to the extent to which they, too, are governed by the rules of gender. (This is not to deny that it matters a great deal—to individual men, to the women and children sometimes connected to them, and to those concerned about justice—where men as well as women are distributed within social hierarchies.)[13]

[11] For example, the Marxist treatments of the "woman question" from Engels onward, or existentialist, or Lacanian treatment of woman as the "other" to man.

[12] On this point, see Joan Kelly, "The Doubled Vision of Feminist Theory," *Feminist Studies* 6, no. 2 (Summer 1979): 216–27; and also Judith Stacey and Barrie Thorne, "The Missing Feminist Revolution in Sociology," *Social Problems* 32, no. 4 (April 1985): 301–16.

[13] Compare Phyllis Marynick Palmer, "White Women/Black Women: The Dualism of Female Identity and Experience in the United States," *Feminist Studies* 9, no. 1 (Spring 1983): 151–70.

Feminist theorizing and deconstruction

The study of gender relations entails at least two levels of analysis: of gender as a thought construct or category that helps us to make sense out of particular social worlds and histories; and of gender as a social relation that enters into and partially constitutes all other social relations and activities. As a practical social relation, gender can be understood only by close examination of the meanings of "male" and "female" and the consequences of being assigned to one or the other gender within concrete social practices.

Obviously, such meanings and practices will vary by culture, age, class, race, and time. We cannot presume a priori that in any particular culture there will be a single determinant or cause of gender relations, much less that we can tell beforehand what this cause (or these causes) might be. Feminist theorists have offered a variety of interesting causal explanations including the "sex/gender system," the organization of production or sexual division of labor, child-rearing practices, and processes of signification or language. These all provide useful hypotheses for the concrete study of gender relations in particular societies, but each explanatory scheme also seems to me to be deeply flawed, inadequate, and overly deterministic.

For example, Gayle Rubin locates the origin of gender systems in the "transformation of raw biological sex into gender."[14] However, Rubin's distinction between sex and gender rests in turn upon a series of oppositions that I find very problematic, including the opposition of "raw biological sexuality" and the social. This opposition reflects the idea predominant in the work of Freud, Lacan, and others that a person is driven by impulses and needs that are invariant and invariably asocial. This split between culture and "natural" sexuality may in fact be rooted in and reflect gender arrangements.

As I have argued elsewhere,[15] Freud's drive theory reflects in part an unconscious motive: to deny and repress aspects of infantile experience which are relational (e.g., the child's dependence upon and connectedness with its earliest caregiver, who is almost always a woman). Hence, in utilizing Freud's concepts we must pay attention to what they conceal as well as reveal, especially the unacknowledged influences of anxieties about gender on his supposedly gender-neutral concepts (such as drive theory).

Socialist feminists locate the fundamental cause of gender arrange-

[14] This is Gayle Rubin's claim in "The Traffic in Women: Notes on the 'Political Economy' of Sex," in *Toward an Anthropology of Women*, ed. Rayna Rapp Reiter (New York: Monthly Review Press, 1975).

[15] I develop this argument in "Psychoanalysis as Deconstruction and Myth: On Gender, Narcissism and Modernity's Discontents," in *The Crisis of Modernity: Recent Theories of Culture in the United States and West Germany*, ed. Kurt Shell (Boulder, Colo.: Westview Press, 1986).

ments in the organization of production or the sexual division of labor. However, this explanatory system also incorporates the historical and philosophical flaws of Marxist analysis. As Balbus convincingly argues,[16] Marxists (including socialist feminists) uncritically apply the categories Marx derived from his description of a particular form of the production of commodities to all areas of human life at all historical periods. Socialist feminists replicate this privileging of production and the division of labor with the concomitant assumptions concerning the centrality of labor itself. Labor is still seen as the essence of history and human being. Such conceptions distort life in capitalist society and surely are not appropriate to all other cultures.[17]

An example of the problems that follow from this uncritical appropriation of Marxist concepts can be found in the attempts by socialist feminists to "widen" the concept of production to include most forms of human activity. These arguments avoid an essential question: why "widen" the concept of production instead of dislodging it or any other singularly central concept from such authoritative power?

This question becomes more urgent when it appears that, despite the best efforts of socialist feminists, the Marxist concepts of labor and production invariably exclude or distort many kinds of activity, including those traditionally performed by women. Pregnancy and child rearing or relations between family members more generally cannot be comprehended merely as "property relations in action."[18] Sexuality cannot be understood as an "exchange" of physical energy, with a "surplus" (potentially) flowing to an "exploiter."[19] Such concepts also ignore or obscure the existence and activities of other persons as well—children—for whom at least a part of their formative experiences has nothing to do with production.

However, the structure of child-rearing practices also cannot serve as *the* root of gender relations. Among the many problems with this approach is that it cannot explain why women have the primary responsibility for

[16] See Balbus (n. 2 above), chap. 1, for a further development of these arguments. Despite Balbus's critique of Marx, he still seems to be under Marx's spell on a metatheoretical level when he tries to locate a root of all domination—child-rearing practices. I have also discussed the inadequacy of Marxist theories in "Do Feminists Need Marxism?" in *Building Feminist Theory*, ed. Quest Staff (New York: Longman, Inc., 1981), and "The Family in Contemporary Feminist Thought: A Critical Review," in Jean Bethke Elshtain, ed., *The Family in Political Thought* (Amherst: University of Massachusetts Press, 1982), 232–39.

[17] Marx may replicate rather than deconstruct the capitalist mentality in his emphasis on the centrality of production. Compare Albert O. Hirschman, *The Passions and the Interests* (Princeton, N.J.: Princeton University Press, 1977) for a very interesting discussion of the historical emergence and construction of specifically *capitalist* mentality.

[18] Annette Kuhn, "Structures of Patriarchy and Capital in the Family," in Kuhn and Wolpe, eds. (n. 2 above), 53.

[19] Ann Ferguson, "Conceiving Motherhood and Sexuality: A Feminist Materialist Approach," in Trebilcot (n. 2 above), 156–58.

child rearing; it can explain only some of the consequences of this fact. In other words, the child-rearing practices taken as causal already presuppose the very social relations we are trying to understand: a gender-based division of human activities and hence the existence of socially constructed sets of gender arrangements and the (peculiar and in need of explanation) salience of gender itself.

The emphasis that (especially) French feminists place on the centrality of language (e.g., chains of signification, signs, and symbols) to the construction of gender also seems problematic.[20] A problem with thinking about (or only in terms of) texts, signs, or signification is that they tend to take on a life of their own or become the world, as in the claim that nothing exists outside of a text; everything is a comment upon or a displacement of another text, as if the modal human activity is literary criticism (or writing).

Such an approach obscures the projection of its own activity onto the world and denies the existence of the variety of concrete social practices that enter into and are reflected in the constitution of language itself (e.g., ways of life constitute language and texts as much as language constitutes ways of life). This lack of attention to concrete social relations (including the distribution of power) results, as in Lacan's work, in the obscuring of relations of domination. Such relations (including gender arrangements) then tend to acquire an aura of inevitability and become equated with language or culture (the "law of the father") as such.

Much of French (including feminist) writing also seems to assume a radical (even ontological rather than socially constructed) disjunction between sign/mind/male/world and body/nature/female.[21] The prescription of some French feminists for the recovery (or reconstitution?) of female experience—"writing from the body"—seems incoherent given this sort of (Cartesian) disjunction. Since "the body" is presocial and prelinguistic, what could it say?

All of these social practices posited as explanations for gender arrangements may be more or less important, interrelated, or themselves partially constituted in and through gender relations depending upon context. As in any form of social analysis, the study of gender relations will necessarily reflect the social practices it attempts to understand. There cannot, nor should we expect there to be, a feminist equivalent to (a falsely universaliz-

[20] The theories of French feminists vary, of course. I am focusing on a predominant and influential approach within the variations. For further discussion of French feminisms, see the essays in *Signs*, vol. 7, no. 1 (Autumn 1981) and *Feminist Studies*, vol. 7, no. 2 (Summer 1981).

[21] Domna Stanton, in "Difference on Trial: A Critique of the Maternal Metaphor in Cixous, Irigaray, and Kristeva," in *The Poetics of Gender*, ed. Nancy Miller (New York: Columbia University Press, 1986), discusses the ontological and essentialist aspects of these writers' work.

ing) Marxism; indeed, the epistemologies of feminism undercut all such claims, including feminist ones.[22]

It is on the metatheoretical level that postmodern philosophies of knowledge can contribute to a more accurate self-understanding of the nature of our theorizing. We cannot simultaneously claim (1) that the mind, the self, and knowledge are socially constituted and that what we can know depends upon our social practices and contexts *and* (2) that feminist theory can uncover the Truth of the whole once and for all. Such an absolute truth (e.g., the explanation for all gender arrangements at all times is *X* . . .) would require the existence of an "Archimedes point" outside of the whole and beyond our embeddedness in it from which we could see (and represent) the whole. What we see and report would also have to be untransformed by the activities of perception and of reporting our vision in language. The object seen (social whole or gender arrangement) would have to be apprehended by an empty (ahistoric) mind and perfectly transcribed by/into a transparent language. The possibility of each of these conditions existing has been rendered extremely doubtful by the deconstructions of postmodern philosophers.

Furthermore, the work of Foucault (among others) should sensitize us to the interconnections between knowledge claims (especially to the claim of absolute or neutral knowledge) and power. Our own search for an "Archimedes point" may conceal and obscure our entanglement in an "episteme" in which truth claims may take only certain forms and not others.[23] Any episteme requires the suppression of discourses that threaten to differ with or undermine the authority of the dominant one. Hence within feminist theory a search for a defining theme of the whole or a feminist viewpoint may require the suppression of the important and discomforting voices of persons with experiences unlike our own. The suppression of these voices seems to be a necessary condition for the (apparent) authority, coherence, and universality of our own.

Thus, the very search for a root or cause of gender relations (or more narrowly, male domination) may partially reflect a mode of thinking that is itself grounded in particular forms of gender (and/or other) relations in which domination is present. Perhaps reality can have "a" structure only

[22] Catherine MacKinnon, in "Feminism, Marxism, Method, and the State: An Agenda for Theory," *Signs* 7, no. 3 (Spring 1982): 515–44, seems to miss this basic point when she makes claims such as: "The defining theme of the whole is the male pursuit of control over women's sexuality—men not as individuals nor as biological beings, but as a gender group characterized by maleness as socially constructed, of which this pursuit is definitive" (532). On the problem of the "Archimedes point," see Myra Jehlen, "Archimedes and the Paradox of Feminist Criticism," *Signs* 6, no. 4 (Summer 1981): 575–601.

[23] Compare Michel Foucault, *Power/Knowledge*, ed. Colin Gordon (New York: Random House, 1981).

from the falsely universalizing perspective of the dominant group. That is, only to the extent that one person or group can dominate the whole, will reality appear to be governed by one set of rules or be constituted by one privileged set of social relations. Criteria of theory construction such as parsimony or simplicity may be attained only by the suppression or denial of the experiences of the "other(s)."

The natural barrier

Thus, in order for gender relations to be useful as a category of social analysis we must be as socially and self-critical as possible about the meanings usually attributed to those relations and the ways we think about them. Otherwise, we run the risk of replicating the very social relations we are attempting to understand. We have to be able to investigate both the social and philosophical barriers to our comprehension of gender relations.

One important barrier to our comprehension of gender relations has been the difficulty of understanding the relationship between gender and "sex." In this context, sex means the anatomical differences between male and female. Historically (at least since Aristotle), these anatomical differences have been assigned to the class of "natural facts" of biology. In turn, biology has been equated with the pre- or nonsocial. Gender relations then become conceptualized as if they are constituted by two opposite terms or distinct types of being—man and woman. Since man and woman seem to be opposites or fundamentally distinct types of being, gender cannot be relational. If gender is as natural and as intrinsically a part of us as the genitals we are born with, it follows that it would be foolish (or even harmful) to attempt either to change gender arrangements or not to take them into account as a delimitation on human activities.

Even though a major focus of feminist theory has been to "denaturalize" gender, feminists as well as nonfeminists seem to have trouble thinking through the meanings we assign to and the uses we make of the concept "natural."[24] What after all, is the "natural" in the context of the human world?[25] There are many aspects of our embodiedness or biology that we

[24] But see the work of Evelyn Fox Keller on the gendered character of our views of the "natural world," especially her essays "Gender and Science," in Harding and Hintikka, eds., and "Cognitive Repression in Physics," *American Journal of Physics* 47 (1979): 718–21.

[25] In *Public Man, Private Woman*, Jean Bethke Elshtain provides an instructive instance of how allegedly natural properties (of infants) can be used to limit what a "reflective feminist" ought to think. In Elshtain's recent writings it becomes (once again) the responsibility of *women* to rescue children from an otherwise instrumental and uncaring world. Elshtain evidently believes that psychoanalytical theory is exempt from the context-dependent hermeneutics she believes characterize all other kinds of knowledge about social relations. She utilizes psychoanalytic theory as a warrant for absolute or foundational claims about the nature

might see as given limits to human action which Western medicine and science do not hesitate to challenge. For example, few Westerners would refuse to be vaccinated against diseases that our bodies are naturally susceptible to, although in some cultures such actions would be seen as violating the natural order. The tendency of Western science is to "disenchant" the natural world.[26] More and more the "natural" ceases to exist as the opposite of the "cultural" or social. Nature becomes the object and product of human action; it loses its independent existence. Ironically, the more such disenchantment proceeds, the more humans seem to need something that remains outside our powers of transformation. Until recently one such exempt area seemed to be anatomical differences between males and females.[27] Thus in order to "save" nature (from ourselves) many people in the contemporary West equate sex/biology/nature/gender and oppose these to the cultural/social/human. Concepts of gender then become complex metaphors for ambivalences about human action in, on, and as part of the natural world.

But in turn the use of gender as a metaphor for such ambivalences blocks further investigation of them. For the social articulation of these equations is not really in the form I stated above but, rather, sex/biology/nature/woman:cultural/social/man. In the contemporary West, women become the last refuge from not only the "heartless" world but also an increasingly mechanized and fabricated one as well.[28] What remains masked in these modes of thought is the possibility that our concepts of biology/nature are rooted in social relations; they do not merely reflect the given structure of reality itself.

Thus, in order to understand gender as a social relation, feminist theorists need to deconstruct further the meanings we attach to biology/sex/gender/nature. This process of deconstruction is far from complete and certainly is not easy. Initially, some feminists thought we could merely separate the terms "sex" and "gender." As we became more sensitive to the social histories of concepts, it became clear that such an (apparent) disjunc-

---

of "real human needs" or "the most basic human relationships" and then bases political conclusions on these "natural" facts. See Jean Bethke Elshtain, *Public Man, Private Woman* (Princeton, N.J.: Princeton University Press, 1981), 314, 331.

[26] See Max Weber, "Science as a Vocation," in *From Max Weber*, ed. H. H. Gerth and C. Wright Mills (New York: Oxford University Press, 1958); and Max Horkheimer and Theodor W. Adorno, *Dialectic of Enlightenment* (New York: Herder & Herder, 1972).

[27] I say "until recently" because of developments in medicine such as "sex change" operations and new methods of conception and fertilization of embryos.

[28] As in the work of Christopher Lasch, *Haven in a Heartless World* (New York: Basic Books, 1977). Lasch's work is basically a repetition of the ideas stated earlier by members of the "Frankfurt School," especially Horkheimer and Adorno. See, e.g., the essay, "The Family," in *Aspects of Sociology*, Frankfurt Institute for Social Research (Boston: Beacon Press, 1972).

tion, while politically necessary, rested upon problematic and culture-specific oppositions, for example, the one between "nature" and "culture" or "body" and "mind." As some feminists began to rethink these "oppositions," new questions emerged: does anatomy (body) have no relation to mind? What difference does it make in the constitution of my social experiences that I have a specifically female body?

Despite the increasing complexity of our questions, most feminists would still insist that gender relations are not (or are not only) equivalent to or a consequence of anatomy. Everyone will agree that there are anatomical differences between men and women. These anatomical differences seem to be primarily located in or are the consequence of the differentiated contributions men and women make to a common biological necessity—the physical reproduction of our species.

However, the mere existence of such anatomical differentiation is a descriptive fact, one of many observations we might make about the physical characteristics of humans. Part of the problem in deconstruction of the meaning of biology/sex/gender/nature is that sex/gender has been one of the few areas in which (usually female) embodiment can be discussed at all in (nonscientific) Western discourses. There are many other aspects of our embodiedness that seem equally remarkable and interesting, for example, the incredible complexity of the structure and functioning of our brains, the extreme and relatively prolonged physical helplessness of the human neonate as compared to that of other (even related) species, or the fact that every one of us will die.

It is also the case that physically male and female humans resemble each other in many more ways than we differ. Our similarities are even more striking if we compare humans to (say) toads or trees. So why ought the anatomical differences between male and female humans assume such significance in our sense of our selves as persons? Why ought such complex human social meanings and structures be based on or justified by a relatively narrow range of anatomical differences?

One possible answer to these questions is that the anatomical differences between males and females are connected to and are partially a consequence of one of the most important functions of the species—its physical reproduction. Thus, we might argue, because reproduction is such an important aspect of our species life, characteristics associated with it will be much more salient to us than, say, hair color or height.

Another possible answer to these questions might be that in order for humans physically to reproduce the species, we have to have sexual intercourse. Our anatomical differences make possible (and necessary for physical reproduction) a certain fitting together of distinctively male and female organs. For some humans this "fitting together" is also highly desirable and pleasurable. Hence our anatomical differences seem to be inextricably connected to (and in some sense, even causative of) sexuality.

Thus, there seems to be a complex of relations that have associated, given meanings: penis or clitoris, vagina, and breasts (read distinctively male or female bodies), sexuality (read reproduction—birth and babies), sense of self as a distinct, differentiated gender—as either (and only) a male or female person (read gender relations as a "natural" exclusionary category). That is, we believe there are only two types of humans, and each of us can be only one of them.

A problem with all these apparently obvious associations is that they may assume precisely what requires explanation—that is, gender relations. We live in a world in which gender is a constituting social relation and in which gender is also a relation of domination. Therefore, both men's and women's understanding of anatomy, biology, embodiedness, sexuality, and reproduction is partially rooted in, reflects, and must justify (or challenge) preexisting gender relations. In turn, the existence of gender relations helps us to order and understand the facts of human existence. In other words, gender can become a metaphor for biology just as biology can become a metaphor for gender.

Prisoners of gender: Dilemmas in feminist theory

The apparent connections between gender relations and such important aspects of human existence as birth, reproduction, and sexuality make possible both a conflating of the natural and the social *and* an overly radical distinction between the two. In modern Western culture and sometimes even in feminist theories, "natural" and "social" become conflated in our understanding of "woman." In nonfeminist and some feminist writings about men a radical disjunction is frequently made between the "natural" and the "social." Women often stand for/symbolize the body, "difference," the concrete. These qualities are also said by some feminist as well as nonfeminist writers to suffuse/define the activities most associated with women: nurturing, mothering, taking care of and being in relation with others, "preserving."[29] Women's minds are also often seen as reflecting the qualities of our stereotypically female activities and bodies. Even feminists sometimes say women reason and/or write differently and have different interests and motives than men.[30] Men are said to have more interest in utilizing the power of abstract reason (mind), to want mastery over nature (including bodies), and to be aggressive and militaristic.

[29] Compare Sara Ruddick's essays, "Maternal Thinking," and "Preservative Love and Military Destruction: Some Reflections on Mothering and Peace," both in Trebilcot, ed. (n. 2 above).

[30] On women's "difference," see the essays in Eisenstein and Jardine, eds. (n. 8 above); and Marks and de Courtivron (n. 2 above); also Carol Gilligan, *In a Different Voice* (Cambridge, Mass.: Harvard University Press, 1982); and Stanton (n. 21 above).

The reemergence of such claims even among some feminists needs further analysis. Is this the beginning of a genuine transvaluation of values and/or a retreat into traditional gendered ways of understanding the world? In our attempts to correct arbitrary (and gendered) distinctions, feminists often end up reproducing them. Feminist discourse is full of contradictory and irreconcilable conceptions of the nature of our social relations, of men and women and the worth and character of stereotypically masculine and feminine activities. The positing of these conceptions such that only one perspective can be "correct" (or properly feminist) reveals, among other things, the embeddedness of feminist theory in the very social processes we are trying to critique and our need for more systematic and self-conscious theoretical practice.

As feminist theorizing is presently practiced, we seem to lose sight of the possibility that each of our conceptions of a practice (e.g., mothering) may capture an aspect of a very complex and contradictory set of social relations. Confronted with complex and changing relations, we try to reduce these to simple, unified, and undifferentiated wholes. We search for closure, or the right answer, or the "motor" of the history of male domination. The complexity of our questions and the variety of the approaches to them are taken by some feminists as well as nonfeminists as signs of weakness or failure to meet the strictures of preexisting theories rather than as symptoms of the permeability and pervasiveness of gender relations and the need for new sorts of theorizing.

Some of the reductive moves I have in mind include the constricting of "embodiedness" to a glorification of the distinctively female aspects of our anatomy.[31] This reduction precludes considering the many other ways in which we experience our embodiedness (e.g., nonsexual pleasures, or the processes of aging, or pain). It also replicates the equating of women with the body—as if men did not have bodies also! Alternatively, there is a tendency simply to deny or neglect the meaningfulness or significance of any bodily experience within both women's and men's lives or to reduce it to a subset of "relations of production" (or reproduction).

Within feminist discourse, women sometimes seem to become the sole "bearers" of both embodiedness and difference. Thus we see arguments for the necessity to preserve a gender-based division of labor as our last protection from a state power that is depersonalizing and atomizing.[32] In such arguments the family is posited as an intimate, affective realm of natural relations—of kinship ties, primarily between mothers, children, and female kin—and it is discussed in opposition to the impersonal realms of the state and work (the worlds of men). Alternatively, feminists some-

[31] As in, e.g., Hélène Cixous, "Sorties," in *The Newly Born Woman*, ed. Hélène Cixous and Catherine Clement (Ithaca, N.Y.: Cornell University Press, 1986).

[32] See for instance, Elshtain (n. 25 above), and Elshtain, ed. (n. 16 above), 7–30.

times simply deny that there are any significant differences between women and men and that insofar as such differences exist, women should become more like men (or engage in men's activities). Or, the family is understood only as the site of gender struggle and the "reproduction" of persons—a miniature political economy with its own division of labor, source of surplus (women's labor), and product (children and workers).[33] The complex fantasies and conflicting wishes and experiences women associate with family/home often remain unexpressed and unacknowledged. Lacking such self-analysis, feminists find it difficult to recognize some of the sources of our differences or to accept that we do not necessarily share the same past or share needs in the present.[34]

Female sexuality is sometimes reduced to an expression of male dominance, as when Catherine MacKinnon claims "gender socialization is the process through which women come to identify themselves as sexual beings, as beings that exist for men."[35] Among many other problems such a definition leaves unexplained how women could ever feel lust for other women and the wide variety of other sensual experiences women claim to have—for example, in masturbation, breast feeding, or playing with children. Alternatively, the "essence" of female sexuality is said to be rooted in the quasi-biological primal bonds between mother and daughter.[36]

For some theorists, our fantasy and internal worlds have expression only in symbols, not in actual social relations. For example, Iris Young claims that gender differentiation as a "category" refers only to "ideas, symbols and forms of consciousness."[37] In this view, fantasy, our inner worlds, and sexuality may structure intimate relations between women and men at home, but they are rarely seen as also entering into and shaping the structure of work and the state. Thus feminist theory recreates its own version of the public/private split. Alternatively, as in some radical feminist accounts, innate male drives, especially aggression and the need to domi-

[33] This seems to be the basic approach characteristic of socialist-feminist discussions of the family. See, e.g., the essays by A. Ferguson (n. 19 above); and Kuhn (n. 18 above).

[34] See, e.g., Barbara Smith's discussion of the meanings of "home" to her in the "Introduction" to *Home Girls* (n. 2 above). Smith's definition contrasts strongly with the confinement and exploitation some middle-class white women associate with "home." See, e.g., Michele Barrett and Mary McIntosh, *The Anti-social Family* (London: Verso, 1983); and Heidi I. Hartmann, "The Family as the Locus of Gender, Class, and Political Struggle: The Example of Housework," *Signs* 6, no. 3 (Spring 1981): 366–94.

[35] MacKinnon (n. 22 above), 531.

[36] This seems to be Adrienne Rich's argument in "Compulsory Heterosexuality and Lesbian Existence," *Signs* 5, no. 4 (Summer 1980): 631–60. See also Stanton (n. 21 above) on this point.

[37] Iris Young, "Is Male Gender Identity the Cause of Male Domination?" in Trebilcot, ed. (n. 2 above), 140. In this essay, Young replicates the split Juliet Mitchell posits in *Psychoanalysis and Feminism* (New York: Pantheon Books, 1974) between kinship/gender/superstructure and class/production/base.

nate others are posited as the motor that drives the substance and teleology of history.[38]

Feminist theorists have delineated many of the ways in which women's consciousness is shaped by mothering, but we often still see "fathering" as somehow extrinsic to men's and children's consciousness.[39] The importance of modes of child rearing to women's status and to women's and men's sense of self is emphasized in feminist theory; yet we still write social theory in which everyone is presumed to be an adult. For example, in two recent collections of feminist theory focusing on mothering and the family,[40] there is almost no discussion of children as human beings or mothering as a relation between persons. The modal "person" in feminist theory still appears to be a self-sufficient individual adult.

These difficulties in thinking have social as well as philosophical roots, including the existence of relations of domination and the psychological consequences of our current modes of child rearing. In order to sustain domination, the interrelation and interdependence of one group with another must be denied. Connections can be traced only so far before they begin to be politically dangerous. For example, few white feminists have explored how our understandings of gender relations, self, and theory are partially constituted in and through the experiences of living in a culture in which asymmetric race relations are a central organizing principle of society.[41]

Furthermore, just as our current gender arrangements create men who have difficulties in acknowledging relations between people and experiences, they produce women who have difficulties in acknowledging differences within relations. In either gender, these social relations produce a disposition to treat experience as all of one sort or another and to be intolerant of differences, ambiguity, and conflict.

The enterprise of feminist theory is fraught with temptations and pitfalls. Insofar as women have been part of all societies, our thinking cannot be free from culture-bound modes of self-understanding. We as well as men internalize the dominant gender's conceptions of masculinity

[38] As in Shulamith Firestone, *The Dialectic of Sex* (New York: Bantam Books, 1970); and MacKinnon (n. 22 above).

[39] On this point, see the essay by Nancy Chodorow and Susan Contratto, "The Fantasy of the Perfect Mother," in *Rethinking the Family*, ed. Barrie Thorne with Marilyn Yalom (New York: Longman, Inc., 1983).

[40] Trebilcot, ed. (n. 2 above); and Thorne and Yalom, eds.

[41] But see the dialogues between Gloria I. Joseph and Jill Lewis, *Common Differences: Conflicts in Black and White Feminist Perspectives* (New York: Doubleday & Co., 1981); and Marie L. Lugones and Elizabeth V. Spelman, "Have We Got a Theory for You," in *Women and Values*, ed. Marilyn Pearsall (Belmont, Calif.: Wadsworth Publishing Co., 1986); and Palmer (n. 13 above). Women of color have been insisting on this point for a long time. Compare the essays in B. Smith, ed. (n. 2 above); and Moraga and Anzaldúa, eds. (n. 2 above). See also Audre Lorde, *Sister Outsider* (Trumansburg, N.Y.: Crossing Press, 1984).

and femininity. Unless we see gender as a social relation, rather than as an opposition of inherently different beings, we will not be able to identify the varieties and limitations of different women's (or men's) powers and oppressions within particular societies. Feminist theorists are faced with a fourfold task. We need to (1) articulate feminist viewpoints of/within the social worlds in which we live; (2) think about how we are affected by these worlds; (3) consider the ways in which how we think about them may be implicated in existing power/knowledge relationships; and (4) imagine ways in which these worlds ought to/can be transformed.

Since within contemporary Western societies gender relations have been ones of domination, feminist theories should have a compensatory as well as a critical aspect. That is, we need to recover and explore the aspects of social relations that have been suppressed, unarticulated, or denied within dominant (male) viewpoints. We need to recover and write the histories of women and our activities into the accounts and stories that cultures tell about themselves. Yet, we also need to think about how so-called women's activities are partially constituted by and through their location within the web of social relations that make up any society. That is, we need to know how these activities are affected but also how they effect, or enable, or compensate for the consequences of men's activities, as well as their implication in class or race relations.

There should also be a transvaluation of values—a rethinking of our ideas about what is humanly excellent, worthy of praise, or moral. In such a transvaluation, we need to be careful not to assert merely the superiority of the opposite. For example, sometimes feminist theorists tend to oppose autonomy to being-in-relations. Such an opposition does not account for adult forms of being-in-relations that can be claustrophobic without autonomy—an autonomy that, without being-in-relations, can easily degenerate into mastery. Our upbringing as women in this culture often encourages us to deny the many subtle forms of aggression that intimate relations with others can evoke and entail. For example, much of the discussion of mothering and the distinctively female tends to avoid discussing women's anger and aggression—how we internalize them and express them, for example, in relation to children or our own internal selves.[42] Perhaps women are not any less aggressive than men; we may just express our aggression in different, culturally sanctioned (and partially disguised or denied) ways.

Since we live in a society in which men have more power than women, it makes sense to assume that what is considered to be more worthy of praise may be those qualities associated with men. As feminists, we have the right to suspect that even "praise" of the female may be (at least in part)

[42] Compare the descriptions of mothering in Trebilcot, ed. (n. 2 above); especially the essays by Whitbeck and Ruddick.

motivated by a wish to keep women in a restricted (and restrictive) place. Indeed, we need to search into all aspects of a society (the feminist critique included) for the expressions and consequences of relations of domination. We should insist that all such relations are social, that is, they are not the result of the differentiated possession of natural and unequal properties among types of persons.

However, in insisting upon the existence and power of such relations of domination, we should avoid seeing women/ourselves as totally innocent, passive beings. Such a view prevents us from seeing the areas of life in which women have had an effect, in which we are less determined by the will of the other(s), and in which some of us have and do exert power over others (e.g., the differential privileges of race, class, sexual preference, age, or location in the world system).

Any feminist standpoint will necessarily be partial. Thinking about women may illuminate some aspects of a society that have been previously suppressed within the dominant view. But none of us can speak for "woman" because no such person exists except within a specific set of (already gendered) relations—to "man" and to many concrete and different women.

Indeed, the notion of *a* feminist standpoint that is truer than previous (male) ones seems to rest upon many problematic and unexamined assumptions. These include an optimistic belief that people act rationally in their own interests and that reality has a structure that perfect reason (once perfected) can discover. Both of these assumptions in turn depend upon an uncritical appropriation of the Enlightenment ideas discussed earlier. Furthermore, the notion of such a standpoint also assumes that the oppressed are not in fundamental ways damaged by their social experience. On the contrary, this position assumes that the oppressed have a privileged (and not just different) relation and ability to comprehend a reality that is "out there" waiting for our representation. It also presupposes gendered social relations in which there is a category of beings who are fundamentally like each other by virtue of their sex—that is, it assumes the otherness men assign to women. Such a standpoint also assumes that women, unlike men, can be free of determination from their own participation in relations of domination such as those rooted in the social relations of race, class, or homophobia.[43]

I believe, on the contrary, that there is no force or reality "outside" our social relations and activity (e.g., history, reason, progress, science, some transcendental essence) that will rescue us from partiality and differences. Our lives and alliances belong with those who seek to further decenter the world—although we should reserve the right to be suspicious of their

[43] For contrary arguments, see Jaggar (n. 10 above); and also Hartsock, "The Feminist Standpoint" (n. 7 above).

motives and visions as well.[44] Feminist theories, like other forms of postmodernism, should encourage us to tolerate and interpret ambivalence, ambiguity, and multiplicity as well as to expose the roots of our needs for imposing order and structure no matter how arbitrary and oppressive these needs may be.

If we do our work well, "reality" will appear even more unstable, complex, and disorderly than it does now. In this sense, perhaps Freud was right when he declared that women are the enemies of civilization.[45]

Department of Political Science
Howard University

[44] I discuss the gender biases and inadequacies of postmodern philosophy in "Freud's Children" (n. 1 above). See also Naomi Schor, "Dreaming Dissymmetry: Barthes, Foucault, and Sexual Difference" (paper delivered to the Boston Area Colloquium on Feminist Theory, Northeastern University, Fall 1986).

[45] Sigmund Freud, *Civilization and Its Discontents* (New York: W. W. Norton & Co., 1961), 50–51.

MULTIPLE JEOPARDY, MULTIPLE CONSCIOUSNESS: THE CONTEXT OF A BLACK FEMINIST IDEOLOGY

DEBORAH K. KING

Black women have long recognized the special circumstances of our lives in the United States: the commonalities that we share with all women, as well as the bonds that connect us to the men of our race. We have also realized that the interactive oppressions that circumscribe our lives provide a distinctive context for black womanhood. For us, the notion of double jeopardy is not a new one. Near the end of the nineteenth century, Anna Julia Cooper, who was born a slave and later became an educator and earned a Ph.D., often spoke and wrote of the double enslavement of black women and of our being "confronted by both a woman question and a race problem."[1] In 1904, Mary Church Terrell, the first president of the National Association of Colored Women, wrote, "Not only are colored women . . . handicapped on account of their sex, but they are almost everywhere baffled and mocked because of their race. Not only because they are women, but because they are colored women."[2]

I am greatly indebted to Elsa B. Brown, Elaine Upton, Patricia Palmieri, Patricia Hill Collins, Dianne Pinderhughes, Rose Brewer, and *Signs'* referees for their thoughtful and critical comments on this paper.

[1] Gerda Lerner, ed., *Black Women in White America: A Documentary History* (New York: Vintage, 1973), 573.

[2] Mary Church Terrell, "The Progress of Colored Women," *Voice of the Negro* 1, no. 7 (July 1904): 292.

This essay originally appeared in *Signs*, vol. 14, no. 1, Autumn 1988.

The dual and systematic discriminations of racism and sexism remain pervasive, and, for many, class inequality compounds those oppressions. Yet, for as long as black women have known our numerous discriminations, we have also resisted those oppressions. Our day-to-day survival as well as our organized political actions have demonstrated the tenacity of our struggle against subordination. In the mid-nineteenth century, Sojourner Truth, an antislavery activist and women's rights advocate, repeatedly pronounced the strength and perseverance of black women.[3] More than one hundred years later, another black woman elaborated on Truth's theme. In addressing the National Association for the Advancement of Colored People (NAACP) Legal Defense Fund in 1971, Fannie Lou Hamer, the daughter of sharecroppers and a civil rights activist in Mississippi, commented on the special plight and role of black women over 350 years: "You know I work for the liberation of all people because when I liberate myself, I'm liberating other people . . . her [the white woman's] freedom is shackled in chains to mine, and she realizes for the first time that she is not free until I am free."[4] The necessity of addressing all oppressions is one of the hallmarks of black feminist thought.

The theoretical invisibility of black women

Among the first and perhaps most widely used approaches for understanding women's status in the United States has been the race-sex analogy. In essence, the model draws parallels between the systems and experiences of domination for blacks and those for women, and, as a result, it assumes that political mobilizations against racism and sexism are comparable. In 1860, Elizabeth Cady Stanton observed, "Prejudice against color, of which we hear so much, is no stronger than that against sex."[5] Scholars in various disciplines have drawn similar analogies between racism and sexism. Sociologist Helen Hacker and historian William Chafe have both noted

[3] See Lerner, ed., esp. 566–72; and Bert James Loewenberg and Ruth Bogin, eds., *Black Women in Nineteenth-Century American Life* (University Park: Pennsylvania State University Press, 1976), 234–42.

[4] See Lerner, ed., 609, 610, 611.

[5] Elizabeth Cady Stanton as quoted by William Chafe, *Women and Equality: Changing Patterns in American Culture* (New York: Oxford University Press, 1977), 44. Some eighty years after Stanton's observation, Swedish social psychologist Gunnar Myrdal, in an appendix to his *An American Dilemma: The Negro Problem and Modern Democracy* (New York: Harper & Row, 1962), also saw the woman problem as parallel to the Negro problem.

that unlike many ethnic groups, women and blacks possess ineradicable physical attributes that function "systematically and clearly to define from birth the possibilities to which members of a group might aspire."[6] In the first formal typology of the race-sex analogy, Helen Hacker identifies four additional dimensions on which the castelike status of blacks and women are similar: (1) ascribed attributes of emotionality, immaturity, and slyness; (2) rationalizations of status as conveyed in the notions of appropriate "place" and the contented subordinate; (3) accommodating and guileful behaviors; and (4) economic, legal, educational, and social discriminations.[7] Feminist theorists, including Simone de Beauvoir, Kate Millett, Mary Daly, and Shulamith Firestone have all drawn extensively on this analogy in their critiques of the patriarchy.[8]

This analogy has served as a powerful means of conveying an image of women's subordinate status, and of mobilizing women and men for political action. The social movements for racial equality in the United States, whether the abolitionist movement in the nineteenth century or the civil rights movement in the mid-twentieth century, were predecessors, catalysts, and prototypes for women's collective action. A significant segment of feminist activists came to recognize and understand their own oppression, as well as to develop important organizing skills through their participation in efforts for racial justice.[9] In sum, the race-sex correspondence has been used successfully because the race model was a well-established and effective pedagogical tool for both the theoretical conceptualization of and the political resistance to sexual inequality.

[6] Chafe, 77.

[7] Helen Hacker, "Women as a Minority Group," *Social Forces* 30 (1951): 60–69.

[8] For examples of feminist writings using the race-sex analogy or the master-slave model, see Simone de Beauvoir, *The Second Sex*, trans. and ed. H. M. Parshley (New York: Random House, 1974); Kate Millett, *Sexual Politics* (New York: Avon, 1969); Shulamith Firestone, *The Dialectics of Sex* (New York: Morrow, 1970); and Mary Daly, *Beyond God the Father: Toward a Philosophy of Women's Liberation* (Boston: Beacon, 1973).

[9] See Sara Evans, *Personal Politics: The Roots of Women's Liberation in the Civil Rights Movement and the New Left* (New York: Vintage, 1980); Catharine Stimpson, "Thy Neighbor's Wife, Thy Neighbor's Servants: Women's Liberation and Black Civil Rights," in *Woman in Sexist Society: Studies in Power and Powerlessness*, ed. Vivian Gornick and Barbara Moran (New York: Basic, 1971), 452–79; and Angela Davis, *Women, Race and Class* (New York: Random House, 1981). Recently, there has been some debate concerning precisely what lessons, if any, women learned from their participation in the abolitionist and civil rights movements. For an argument against the importance of race-oriented movements for feminist politics, see E. C. DuBois, *Feminism and Suffrage* (Ithaca, N.Y.: Cornell University Press, 1978).

We learn very little about black women from this analogy.[10] The experience of black women is apparently assumed, though never explicitly stated, to be synonymous with that of either black males or white females; and since the experiences of both are equivalent, a discussion of black women in particular is superfluous. It is mistakenly granted that either there is no difference in being black and female from being generically black (i.e., male) or generically female (i.e., white). The analogy obfuscates or denies what Chafe refers to as "the profound substantive differences" between blacks and women. The scope, both institutionally and culturally, and the intensity of the physical and psychological impact of racism is qualitatively different from that of sexism. The group experience of slavery and lynching for blacks, genocide for Native Americans, and military conquest for Mexican-Americans and Puerto Ricans is not substantively comparable to the physical abuse, social discrimination, and cultural denigration suffered by women. This is not to argue that those forms of racial oppressions are greater or more unjust but that the substantive differences need to be identified and to inform conceptualizations. Althea Smith and Abigail Stewart point out that "the assumption of parallelism led to research that masked the differences in these processes [i.e., racism, sexism, and their effects on self-image] for different groups."[11] A similar point has been forcefully made by bell hooks: "No other group in America has so had their identity socialized out of existence as have black women. We are rarely recognized as a group separate and distinct from black men, or a present part of the larger group 'women' in this culture. . . . When black people are talked about the focus tends to be on black men; and when women are talked about the focus tends to be on white women."[12] It is precisely those differences between blacks and women, between black men and black women,

[10] Other limitations have been noted by Linda LaRue, who contends that the analogy is an abstraction that falsely asserts a common oppression of blacks and women for rhetorical and propagandistic purposes ("The Black Movement and Women's Liberation," in *Female Psychology: The Emerging Self*, ed. Sue Cox [Chicago: Science Research Assoc., 1976]). In *Ain't I a Woman* (Boston: South End Press, 1981), bell hooks questions whether certain women, particularly those self-identified feminists who are white and middle class, are truly oppressed as opposed to being discriminated against. Stimpson bluntly declares that the race-sex analogy is exploitative and racist. See also Margaret A. Simons, "Racism and Feminism: A Schism in the Sisterhood," *Feminist Studies* 5 (1979): 384–401, for a critical review of this conceptual approach in feminist theorizing.

[11] Chafe, 76; Althea Smith and Abigail J. Stewart, "Approaches to Studying Racism and Sexism in Black Women's Lives," *Journal of Social Issues* 39 (1983): 1–15.

[12] hooks, *Ain't I a Woman*, 7.

between black women and white women that are crucial to understanding the nature of black womanhood.

The promise and limitations of double jeopardy

In 1972, Frances Beale, a founding member of the Women's Liberation Committee of the Student Nonviolent Coordinating Committee (SNCC) and, later, a member of the Third World Women's Alliance, introduced the term "double jeopardy" to describe the dual discriminations of racism and sexism that subjugate black women. Concerning black women, she wrote, "As blacks they suffer all the burdens of prejudice and mistreatment that fall on anyone with dark skin. As women they bear the additional burden of having to cope with white and black men."[13] Beale also astutely observed that the reality of dual discriminations often entailed economic disadvantage; unfortunately she did not incorporate that understanding into the conceptualization. Perhaps she viewed class status as a particular consequence of racism, rather than as an autonomous source of persecution; but such a preponderant majority of black women have endured the very lowest of wages and very poorest conditions of rural and urban poverty that some scholars have argued that economic class oppression must necessarily constitute a third jeopardy.[14] Still others have suggested that heterosexism or homophobia represents another significant oppression and should be included as a third or perhaps fourth jeopardy.[15] The triple jeopardy of racism, sexism, and classism is now widely accepted and used as the conceptualization of black women's status. However, while advancing our understanding beyond the erasure of black

[13] Frances Beale, "Double Jeopardy: To Be Black and Female," in *The Black Woman: An Anthology*, ed. Toni Cade (New York: New American Library, 1979), 90–100.

[14] See, e.g., Beverly Lindsay, "Minority Women in America: Black American, Native American, Chicana, and Asian American Women," in *The Study of Woman: Enlarging Perspectives of Social Reality*, ed. Eloise C. Synder (New York: Harper & Row, 1979), 318–63. She presents a paradigm wherein whiteness, maleness, and money are advantageous; a poor, black woman is triply disadvantaged. Lindsay argues that triple jeopardy, the interaction of sexism, racism, and economic oppression, is "the most realistic perspective for analyzing the position of black American women; and this perspective will serve as common linkage among the discussions of other minority women" (328).

[15] See Barbara Smith, ed., *Home Girls: A Black Feminist Anthology* (New York: Kitchen Table Press, 1983), esp. sec. 3; and Audre Lorde, "Scratching the Surface: Some Notes on Barriers to Women and Loving," *Black Scholar* 13 (Summer 1982): 20–24, and *Sister Outsider: Essays and Speeches* (Trumansberg, N.Y.: Crossing Press, 1984).

women within the confines of the race-sex analogy, it does not yet fully convey the dynamics of multiple forms of discrimination.

Unfortunately, most applications of the concepts of double and triple jeopardy have been overly simplistic in assuming that the relationships among the various discriminations are merely additive. These relationships are interpreted as equivalent to the mathematical equation, racism plus sexism plus classism equals triple jeopardy. In this instance, each discrimination has a single, direct, and independent effect on status, wherein the relative contribution of each is readily apparent. This simple incremental process does not represent the nature of black women's oppression but, rather, I would contend, leads to nonproductive assertions that one factor can and should supplant the other. For example, class oppression is the largest component of black women's subordinate status, therefore the exclusive focus should be on economics. Such assertions ignore the fact that racism, sexism, and classism constitute three, interdependent control systems. An interactive model, which I have termed multiple jeopardy, better captures those processes.[16]

The modifier "multiple" refers not only to several, simultaneous oppressions but to the multiplicative relationships among them as well. In other words, the equivalent formulation is racism multiplied by sexism multiplied by classism. The sexual exploitation of black women in slavery is a historical example. While black women workers suffered the same demanding physical labor and brutal punishments as black men, as females, we were also subject to forms of subjugation only applicable to women. Angela Davis, in *Women, Race and Class,* notes, "If the most violent punishments of men consisted in floggings and mutilations, women were flogged and mutilated, as well as raped."[17] At the same time, our reproductive and child-rearing activities served to enhance the quantity and quality of the "capital" of a slave economy. Our institutionalized exploitation as the concubines, mistresses, and sexual slaves of white males distinguished our experience from that of white females' sexual oppression because it could only have existed in relation to racist and classist forms of domination.

[16] For other attempts at nonadditive models, see Smith and Stewart; Elizabeth M. Almquist, "Untangling the Effects of Race and Sex: The Disadvantaged Status of Black Women," *Social Science Quarterly* 56 (1975): 129–42; Margaret L. Andersen, *Thinking about Women: Sociological and Feminist Perspectives* (New York: Macmillan, 1983). The term "ethnogender" is introduced in Vincent Jeffries and H. Edward Ransford, *Social Stratification: A Multiple Hierarchy Approach* (Boston: Allyn & Bacon, 1980); and Edward Ransford and Jon Miller, "Race, Sex, and Feminist Outlook," *American Sociological Review* 48 (1983): 46–59.

[17] Davis, *Women, Race and Class,* 7.

The importance of any one factor in explaining black women's circumstances thus varies depending on the particular aspect of our lives under consideration and the reference groups to whom we are compared. In some cases, race may be the more significant predictor of black women's status; in others, gender or class may be more influential. Table 1 presents the varied and conditional influence of race and gender and, presumably, of racism and sexism on socioeconomic and educational status. White males earn the highest median incomes, followed in decreasing order by black males, white females, and black females. The educational rankings are different. White males are again on top; but whites, males and females, have more years of schooling than black males and females. While gender is more critical in understanding black women's income ranking, race is more important in explaining their level of educational attainment. But in both examples, black females have the lowest status.

Table 2 shows a more complex relationship between race, gender, and class (here represented by educational attainment), and the influence of these variables on income. Overall, education is an important determinant of income, and despite race or gender, those with more education earn more money than those with less. Men earn more than women at the same level of education, and whites earn more than blacks at the same level of education. But among women, the relationship of education to income is confounded by race. Given our subordinate statuses as female and black, we might expect black women to receive the lowest incomes regardless of their educational attainment. However, the returns of postsecondary education, a college degree or higher, are greater for black females than for white females, while among those with less than a college degree, black females earn less than white females. A similar pattern is not found among males. In this three-way anal-

TABLE 1 **RACE AND GENDER INTERACTIVE EFFECTS ON SOCIOECONOMIC STATUS**

	Economic Status ($)	Educational Status (yrs.)
White males	16,467	12.7
Black males	9,448	12.2
White females	6,949	12.6
Black females	6,164	12.2

NOTE.—Income figures are 1984 median incomes for those fifteen years or older. Educational attainment is for 1984, median years of school completed.

SOURCE.—U.S. Department of Commerce, Bureau of the Census, *Statistical Abstract of the United States, 1987* (Washington, D.C.: Government Printing Office, 1987).

TABLE 2 **MULTIPLICATIVE EFFECTS OF RACE, GENDER, AND CLASS ON INCOME**

	Income ($)			
	White Males	**Black Males**	**White Females**	**Black Females**
Less than a high school diploma	9,525	6,823	3,961	3,618
4 years of high school	13,733	9,260	6,103	5,954
1–3 years of college	14,258	10,532	6,451	6,929
Bachelor's degree	19,783	14,131	9,134	10,692
5 or more years of post-baccalaureate education	23,143	18,970	12,980	14,537

NOTE.—Income is 1979 median income. Educational attainment is used as a measure of economic class.

SOURCE.—*Detailed Population Characteristics,* U.S. Summary, Sec. A, 1980 (Washington, D.C.: Government Printing Office, 1980).

ysis, black women are not consistently in the lowest status, evidence that the importance of the multiple discriminations of race, gender, and class is varied and complex.

In the interactive model, the relative significance of race, sex, or class in determining the conditions of black women's lives is neither fixed nor absolute but, rather, is dependent on the socio-historical context and the social phenomenon under consideration. These interactions also produce what to some appears a seemingly confounding set of social roles and political attitudes among black women. Sociologist Bonnie Thornton Dill has discussed the importance of scholars' recognizing, incorporating, and interpreting the complex variety of social roles that black women have performed in reaction to multiple jeopardies. She argues that the constellation of "attitudes, behaviors, and interpersonal relationships . . . were adaptations to a variety of factors, including the harsh realities of their environment, Afro-American cultural images of black womanhood, and the sometimes conflicting values and norms of the wider society."[18]

A black woman's survival depends on her ability to use all the economic, social, and cultural resources available to her from both the larger society and within her community. For example, black women historically have had to assume economically productive roles as well as retain domestic ones, and until recently our labor

[18] Bonnie Thornton Dill, "The Dialectics of Black Womanhood," *Signs: Journal of Women in Culture and Society* 4 (1979): 543–55, esp. 547. Smith and Stewart, 1, make a similar point.

force participation rate well exceeded that of white women.[19] Labor, whether unpaid and coerced (as under slavery) or paid and necessary employment, has been a distinctive characteristic of black women's social roles. It has earned us a small but significant degree of self-reliance and independence that has promoted egalitarian relations with black men and active influence within the black family and community.[20] But it also has had costs. For instance, black women have most often had to work in low status and low paying jobs since race and sex discrimination have historically limited our employment options. The legacy of the political economy of slavery under capitalism is the fact that employers, and not black women, still profit the most from black women's labor. And when black women become the primary or sole earners for households, researchers and public analysts interpret this self-sufficiency as pathology, as deviance, as a threat to black family life.[21] Yet, it is black women's well-documented facility to encompass seemingly contra-

[19] In slavery, there was 100 percent labor force participation by black women. In 1910, 34 percent were in the official labor force. In 1960, the figure was 40 percent, and by 1980, it was over 50 percent. Comparable figures for white women are 18 percent in 1890, 22 percent in 1910, 37 percent in 1960, and 51 percent in 1980. For a more detailed discussion, see Phyllis A. Wallace, *Black Women in the Labor Force* (Cambridge, Mass.: MIT Press, 1980).

[20] Angela Davis, "Reflections of the Black Woman's Role in the Community of Slaves," *Black Scholar* 3 (December 1971): 2–16, offers an enlightening discussion of the irony of independence out of subordination. See also Deborah Gray White, *Ar'n't I a Woman? Female Slaves in the Plantation South* (New York: Norton, 1985), for a more detailed analysis of the contradictions of the black female role in slavery. For a discussion of the role of black women in the family, see Robert Staples, *The Black Woman in America* (Chicago: Nelson Hall, 1973); Robert Hill, *The Strengths of Black Families* (New York: Emerson Hall, 1972); Herbert Guttman, *The Black Family in Slavery and Freedom, 1750 to 1925* (New York: Random House, 1976); Carol Stack, *All Our Kin: Strategies for Survival in a Black Community* (New York: Harper & Row, 1974); and Charles Willie, *A New Look at Black Families* (New York: General Hall, 1976). For a discussion of black women's community roles, see Bettina Aptheker, *Woman's Legacy: Essays on Race, Sex, and Class in American History* (Amherst: University of Massachusetts Press, 1982); Paula Giddings, *When and Where I Enter: The Impact of Black Women on Race and Sex in America* (New York: William Morrow, 1983); Lerner, ed. (n. 1 above); Sharon Harley and Rosalyn Terborg-Penn, eds., *The Afro-American Woman: Struggles and Images* (Port Washington, N.Y.: Kennikat Press, 1978); Linda Perkins, "The Impact of the 'Cult of True Womanhood' on the Education of Black Women," *Journal of Social Issues* 39 (1983): 17–28; and the special issue, "The Impact of Black Women in Education," *Journal of Negro Education* 51, no. 3 (Summer 1982).

[21] See Robert Staples, "The Myth of the Black Matriarchy," in his *The Black Family: Essays and Studies* (Belmont, Calif.: Wadsworth, 1971), and *The Black Woman in America*. Also see hooks, *Ain't I a Woman* (n. 10 above); and Cheryl T. Gilkes, "Black Women's Work as Deviance: Social Sources of Racial Antagonism within Contemporary Feminism," Working Paper no. 66 (Wellesley, Mass.: Wellesley

dictory role expectations of worker, homemaker, and mother that has contributed to the confusion in understanding black womanhood.[22] These competing demands (each requiring its own set of resistances to multiple forms of oppression) are a primary influence on the black woman's definition of her womanhood, and her relationships to the people around her. To reduce this complex of negotiations to an addition problem (racism + sexism = black women's experience) is to define the issues, and indeed black womanhood itself, within the structural terms developed by Europeans and especially white males to privilege their race and their sex unilaterally. Sojourner's declaration, "ain't I a woman?" directly refutes this sort of conceptualization of womanhood as one dimensional rather than dialectical.

Multiple jeopardy within the politics of liberation

In order to understand the concept of multiple jeopardy, it is necessary to look beyond the social structure and process of the dominant society that insidiously pervade even the movements for race, gender, and class liberation. Thus, the confrontations among blacks about sexism and classism, among women about racism and classism, and among the various economic classes about racism and sexism compose a second feature of the context of black feminist ideology. A formidable impediment in these battles is the "monist" approach of most liberation ideologies. In *Liberating Theory,* monism is described as a political claim "that one particular domination precipitates all really important oppressions. Whether Marxist, anarchist, nationalist, or feminist, these 'ideal types' argue that important social relations can all be reduced to the economy, state, culture, or gender."[23] For example, during the suffrage debates, it was routinely asserted that only one group might gain voting privileges—either blacks or women, that is black men or white women. For black women, the granting of suffrage to either group would still mean our disenfranchisement because of either our sex or our

---

College, Center for Research on Women, 1979). However, more recently Robert Staples has argued that black women who are too independent will be unable to find black mates and that black men are justified in their preference for a more traditionally feminine partner ("The Myth of Black Macho: A Response to Angry Black Feminists," *Black Scholar* 10 [March–April 1979]: 24–32).

[22] See White; and Jacqueline Jones, *Labor of Love, Labor of Sorrow: Black Women, Work and the Family, From Slavery to the Present* (New York: Basic, 1985).

[23] Michael Albert et al., *Liberating Theory* (Boston: South End Press, 1986), 6.

race. Faced with this dilemma, many black women and most black men believed that the extension of suffrage to black males was imperative in order to protect race interests in the historical period of postbellum America. But because political empowerment for black women would require that both blacks and women gained the right to vote, some of these same black women also lobbied strenuously for women's suffrage.[24]

The contemporary efforts of black women to achieve greater equal opportunity and status present similar dilemmas, whether in the areas of reproductive rights, electoral politics, or poverty. Our history of resistance to multiple jeopardies is replete with the fierce tensions, untenable ultimatums, and bitter compromises between nationalism, feminism, and class politics. In a curious twist of fate, we find ourselves marginal to both the movements for women's liberation and black liberation irrespective of our victimization under the dual discriminations of racism and sexism. A similar exclusion or secondary status typifies our role within class movements. Ironically, black women are often in conflict with the very same subordinate groups with which we share some interests. The groups in which we find logical allies on certain issues are the groups in which we may find opponents on others. To the extent that we have found ourselves confronting the exclusivity of monistic politics, we have had to manage ideologies and activities that did not address the dialectics of our lives. We are asked to decide with whom to ally, which interests to advance. Should black women's primary ideological and activist commitment be to race, sex, or class-based social movements? Can we afford to be monist? Can we afford not to be?

In the following consideration of the dialectics within each of three liberation movements, I hope to describe the tensions and priorities that influence the construction of a black feminist ideology. To the extent that any politic is monistic, the actual victims of racism, sexism, or classism may be absent from, invisible within, or seen as antagonistic to that politic. Thus, prejudicial attitudes and discriminatory actions may be overt, subtle, or covert; and they may have various manifestations through ideological statements, policies and strategies, and interpersonal relations. That is, black and/or poor women may be marginal to monistic feminism, women's concerns may be excluded from nationalistic activism, and indif-

[24] For further discussion of suffrage and racism, see Davis, *Women, Race and Class* (n. 9 above); Giddings; Harley and Terborg-Penn; and Barbara H. Andolsen, *"Daughters of Jefferson, Daughters of Bootblacks": Racism and American Feminism* (Macon, Ga.: Mercer University Press, 1986).

ference to race and gender may pervade class politics. This invisibility may be due to actual exclusion or benign neglect, while marginality is represented in tokenism, minimization, and devalued participation. Antagonism involves two subordinate groups whose actions and beliefs are placed in opposition as mutually detrimental. From this conceptual framework, the following discussion highlights the major aspects of multiple jeopardy within liberation politics.

Intraracial politics

Racial solidarity and race liberation have been and remain a fundamental concern for black Americans. Historically and currently, slavery, segregation, and institutional as well as individual discrimination have been formative experiences in most blacks' socialization and political outlook. The inerasable physical characteristics of race have long determined the status and opportunities of black women in the United States. Since race serves as a significant filter of what blacks perceive and how blacks are perceived, many black women have claimed that their racial identity is more salient than either their gender or class identity.[25] Diane Lewis, an anthropologist, has remarked that when racism is seen as the principal cause of their subordinate status, "their interests as blacks have taken precedence over their interests as women."[26] This political importance of race is evident for other reasons as well. Certainly, the chronological order of the social movements for racial, gender, and class justice in part explains the priority given to racial interests. In both the nineteenth and twentieth centuries, the abolition and civil rights movements predate women's suffrage and the women's movement. Similarly, collective efforts that addressed economic deprivation and exploitation, such as trade unionism beginning in the late 1800s, communist organizing in the 1920s and 1930s, and the anti-imperialist activism of the 1960s were preceded by or simultaneous with race-oriented movements. Considering the order of events, it is reasonable to expect that most black women would have made commitments to and investments in the race movements

[25] See Gloria Joseph and Jill Lewis, *Common Differences: Conflicts in Black and White Feminist Perspectives* (New York: Avon, 1981); Diane K. Lewis, "A Response to Inequality: Black Women, Racism, and Sexism," *Signs* 3 (1977): 339–61; and bell hooks, *Feminist Theory: From Margin to Center* (Boston: South End Press, 1984), for extended discussions of the dynamics of structural subordination to and social conflict with varying dominant racial and sexual groups.

[26] Lewis, 343.

such that they would not or could not easily abandon those for later movements.

Furthermore, through the necessity of confronting and surviving racial oppression, black women have assumed responsibilities atypical of those assigned to white women under Western patriarchy. Black women often held central and powerful leadership roles within the black community and within its liberation politics. We founded schools, operated social welfare services, sustained churches, organized collective work groups and unions, and even established banks and commercial enterprises. That is, we were the backbone of racial uplift, and we also played critical roles in the struggle for racial justice.[27] Harriet Tubman led slaves to freedom on the underground railroad; Ida Wells Barnett led the crusade against lynching; Fannie Lou Hamer and Ella Baker were guiding political spirits of the southern black efforts that gave birth to SNCC and the Mississippi Freedom Democratic Party; the "simple" act of Rosa Parks catapulted Martin Luther King to national prominence. Black women, therefore, did not experience sexism within the race movement in quite the ways that brought many white women to feminist consciousness within either civil rights or New Left politics.[28]

All together this history constitutes a powerful impetus toward a monistic race approach as the means of liberation for black women. Michelle Wallace concludes that black women simply lack a feminist consciousness as a matter of choice, out of ignorance, misguided beliefs, or an inability to recognize sexual domination both within and without the black community.[29] Since the 1800s, however, the writings of such prominent black women as Sojourner Truth, Maria Stewart, Anna Julia Cooper, Josephine St. Pierre Ruffin, Frances Watkins Harper, Pauli Murray, Frances Beale, Audre Lorde, and Angela Davis have described a broader view of black consciousness.[30] Even among those black women who expressed

[27] Giddings; Harley and Terborg-Penn; and Davis, "Reflections on the Black Woman's Role in the Community of Slaves."

[28] See Evans (n. 9 above); and Clayborne Carson, *In Struggle: SNCC and the Black Awakening of the 1960s* (Cambridge, Mass.: Harvard University Press, 1981).

[29] Michelle Wallace, *Black Macho and the Myth of the Superwoman* (New York: Dial, 1979). See also Linda C. Powell, "Black Macho and Black Feminism," in Smith, ed. (n. 15 above), 283–92, for a critique of Wallace's thesis.

[30] For statements by Truth, Stewart, Cooper, Ruffin, and Harper, see Loewenberg and Bogin, eds. (n. 3 above); and Lerner, ed. (n. 1 above); for Lorde, see Lorde (n. 15 above); for Davis, see Davis, *Women, Race and Class;* for Beale, see Frances Beale, "Double Jeopardy" (n. 13 above), and "Slave of a Slave No More: Black Women in the Struggle," *Black Scholar* 12, no. 6 (November/December 1981): 16–24; and for Murray, see Pauli Murray, "The Liberation of Black Women," in *Women: A Feminist Perspective*, ed. Jo Freeman (Palo Alto, Calif.: Mayfield, 1975), 351–63.

grave reservations about participating in the women's movement, most recognized sexism as a factor of their subordination in the larger society and acknowledged sexual politics among blacks. They could identify the sexual inequities that resulted in the images of black women as emasculating matriarchs; in the rates of sexual abuse and physical violence; and in black men assuming the visible leadership positions in many black social institutions, such as the church, the intelligentsia, and political organizations.[31] During the civil rights and black nationalist movements of the 1960s and 1970s, men quite effectively used the matriarchy issue to manipulate and coerce black women into maintaining exclusive commitments to racial interests and redefining and narrowing black women's roles and images in ways to fit a more traditional Western view of women. Black feminists Pauli Murray and Pauline Terrelonge Stone both agree that the debates over this issue became an ideological ploy to heighten guilt in black women over their supposed collusion with whites in the oppression of black men.[32] Consequently, these intraracial tensions worked against the public articulations of a feminist consciousness by most black women. Nevertheless, a point of concern and contention within the black community was how sexual inequalities might best be addressed, not whether they existed. A few black women responded by choosing monistic feminism, others sought a distinct black feminist activism. While many organized feminist efforts within race-oriented movements, some also adopted a strict nationalist view. Over time, there were also transformations of perspectives. For example, the black women of SNCC created within it a women's liberation group which later became an independent feminists-of-color organization, the Third World Women's Alliance, which is today the only surviving entity of SNCC.

The politics of race liberation have rarely been exclusively race-based. Because so many blacks historically have been economically

[31] Regarding the church, see Pauline Terrelonge Stone, "Feminist Consciousness and Black Women," in Freeman, ed., 575–88; Joseph and Lewis; Jacqueline Grant, "Black Women and the Church," in *But Some of Us Are Brave: Black Women's Studies*, ed. Gloria T. Hull et al. (Old Westbury, N.Y.: Feminist Press, 1982), 141–52; and Cheryl Townsend Gilkes, " 'Together and in Harness'; Women's Traditions in the Sanctified Church," *Signs* 10, no. 4 (Summer 1985): 678–99. Concerning politics, see LaRue (n. 10 above); Mae C. King, "The Politics of Sexual Stereotypes," *Black Scholar* 4 (March/April 1973): 12–22; and Manning Marable, *How Capitalism Underdeveloped Black America* (Boston: South End Press, 1983), esp. chap. 3. For a discussion of sexual victimization, see Barbara Smith, "Notes for Yet Another Paper on Black Feminism, or Will the Real Enemy Please Stand Up," *Conditions* 5 (1979): 123–27, as well as Joseph and Lewis. For a critique of the notion of the matriarch, see Stone; and Staples, "The Myth of the Black Matriarchy" (n. 21 above).

[32] See Murray; and Stone.

oppressed, race liberation has out of necessity become more pluralistic through its incorporation of economic interests. Whether civil rights or a nationalist activism, the approach to class injustice generally promotes greater economic opportunities and rewards within the existing capitalist order. At the turn of the century, for instance, the collective action known as racial uplift involved the efforts of educated, middle-class blacks to elevate the moral, physical, social, and economic conditions of lower income blacks. The National Association of Wage Earners was established in the 1920s by women like Nannie Burroughs, Maggie Wallace, and Mary McCleod Bethune to assist black female domestic and factory workers.[33]

The civil rights movement initially seemed to avoid the value-laden implications of this pattern of middle-class beneficence toward those with fewer economic resources. Both Aldon Morris, a sociologist, and Clayborne Carson, a historian, have written of the genuine grass roots orientation of the black southern strategy in the 1950s and early 1960s.[34] The majority of the participants were rural, poorly educated, and economically disadvantaged, but more important, these same individuals set the priorities and the strategies of the movement. The legacy was an affirmation of the strength of seemingly powerless people, and particularly of the black women who were among the principal organizers and supporters.[35]

Despite these auspicious beginnings, Cornell West, a black theologian, described the 1960s as a time when the interests of poor blacks were often betrayed.[36] Middle-class blacks were better able to take advantage of the relatively greater opportunities made possible through the race-oriented, legal liberalism of equal opportunity and affirmative action policies and electoral politics. Only such groups as the Nation of Islam and the League of Revolutionary Black Workers, like Marcus Garvey's United Negro Improvement Association earlier in this century, continued to represent the interests of working class and impoverished blacks. The contemporary controversy over class polarization in the black community is a consequence of the movement not effectively addressing the economic

[33] Evelyn Brooks Bennett, "Nannie Burroughs and the Education of Black Woman," in Harley and Terborg-Penn (n. 20 above), 97–108.

[34] Aldon Morris, *The Origins of the Civil Rights Movement: Black Communities Organizing for Change* (New York: Free Press, 1984); and Carson.

[35] See the recent publication by Jo Ann Gibson Robinson, *The Montgomery Bus Boycott and the Women Who Started It* (Knoxville: University of Tennessee Press, 1987).

[36] Cornell West, "The Paradox of the Afro-American Rebellion," in *The Sixties without Apology,* ed. Sohnya Sayres, Anders Stephanson, Stanley Aronowitz, Fredric Jameson (Minneapolis: University of Minnesota Press, 1984).

status of all blacks. Given the particularly precarious economic status of black women, this neglect and marginalization of class is especially problematic for them. The National Welfare Rights Organization, founded in 1967, was one of the few successful, though short-lived, efforts to address the class divisions. Only recently have race-focal groups, including the Urban League and the National Association for the Advancement of Colored People addressed the plight of impoverished black women.

Racial solidarity has been a fundamental element of black women's resistance to domination. However, the intraracial politics of gender and class have made a strictly nationalistic approach overly restrictive and incalculably detrimental to our prospects for full liberation. Given a social condition that is also compounded by other oppressions, black women have necessarily been concerned with affecting, at the very least, an amelioration of economic and gender discriminations. Consequently, some black women have sought an association with feminism as one alternative to the limitations of monistic race politics.

Politics among women

At one level, black women, other women of color, and white women, share many common contemporary concerns about their legal status and rights, encounters with discrimination, and sexual victimization. It is on these shared concerns that feminists have sought to forge a sense of sisterhood and to foster solidarity. This effort is manifest in a variety of ways, but the slogan, "sisterhood is powerful," best exemplifies the importance and the hoped for efficacy of such solidarity in the achievement of women's equality and liberation. For example, all-female restrictions for consciousness-raising sessions, intellectual and artistic programs and publications, organizations, businesses, and communities reflect this singular orientation; and lesbian feminist separatism represents the absolute ideological expression of the monistic tendencies in feminism.

Presumably, black women are included in this sisterhood, but, nonetheless, invisibility and marginality characterize much of our relationship to the women's movement. The assertion of commonality, indeed of the universality and primacy of female oppression, denies the other structured inequalities of race, class, religion, and nationality, as well as denying the diverse cultural heritages that affect the lives of many women. While contending that feminist consciousness and theory emerged from the personal, everyday reality of being female, the reality of millions of women was ignored. The phrase, "the personal is the political" not only reflects a phenomenological approach to women's liberation—that is, of women defining and constructing their own reality—but it has also come to describe the politics of imposing and privileging a few women's personal lives over all women's lives by assuming that these few could be prototypical. For black women, the personal is bound up in the problems peculiar to multiple jeopardies of race and class, not the singular one of sexual inequality. This has not necessarily meant that black women rejected feminism, but merely that they were not singlemindedly committed to the organizations and some of the agenda that have come to be called the women's movement, that is, the movement of white, often protestant, middle-class women.

Feminism has excluded and devalued black women, our experiences, and our interpretations of our own realities at the conceptual and ideological level. Black feminists and black women scholars have identified and critically examined other serious flaws in feminist theorizing. The assumption that the family is by definition patriarchal, the privileging of an individualistic worldview, and the advocacy of female separatism are often antithetical positions to many of the values and goals of black women and thus are hindrances to our association with feminism.[37] These theoretical blinders obscured the ability of certain feminists first to recognize the multifaceted nature of women's oppressions and then to envision theories that encompass those realities. As a consequence, monistic feminism's ability to foresee remedies that would neither abandon women to the other discriminations, including race and class, nor exacerbate those burdens is extremely limited. Without theories and concepts that represent the experiences of black women, the women's movement has and will be ineffectual in making ideological appeals that might mobilize such women. Often, in fact, this conceptual invisibility has led to the actual strategic neglect and physical exclusion or nonparticipation of black women. Most black women who have participated in any organizations or activities of the women's movement are keenly aware of the racial politics that anger, frustrate, and alienate us.

The case of the struggle for suffrage in the nineteenth century again is an instructive example of the complexity of multiple jeopardy and its politics. Initially, there was an alliance of blacks and

[37] Lorde, *Sister Outsider*, esp. 66–71; hooks, *Feminist Theory* (n. 25 above); Linda Burnham, "Has Poverty Been Feminized in Black America?" *Black Scholar* 16, no. 2 (March/April 1985): 14–24; Maria C. Lugones and Elizabeth V. Spelman, "Have We Got A Theory for You! Feminist Theory, Cultural Imperialism and the Demand for 'The Woman's Voice,' " *Women's Studies International Forum* 6, no. 6 (1983): 573–81.

women for universal suffrage. However, as the campaign ensued, opponents of universal suffrage, and of any extension of voting privileges, were successful in transforming the debate into one of whom should receive the vote—women or black males. Many prominent white suffragists, including Elizabeth Cady Stanton, Susan B. Anthony, and Carrie Chapman Catt abandoned the alliance and demanded a "women only" enfranchisement. The question of black women's suffrage should have been especially problematical for them. In fact, it was never seriously considered. More damning, however, were their politics of expediency. They cooperated with avowed racists in order to gain the southern vote and liberally used racial slurs and epithets arguing that white women's superior character and intellect made them more deserving of the right to vote than blacks, Native Americans, and Eastern European and Asian immigrants.

As Angela Davis observes in her examination of race and class in the early women's rights campaign, even the Seneca Falls Declaration "all but ignored the predicament of white working-class women, as it ignored the condition of black women in the South and North alike."[38] Barbara Andolsen, in one of the most comprehensive studies of racism in the woman suffrage movement observed: "[it] had a bold vision and noble principles . . . but this is a story of a vision betrayed. For the white women who led this movement came to trade upon their privilege as the daughters (sisters, wives, and mothers) of powerful white men in order to gain for themselves some share of the political power those men possessed. They did not adequately identify ways in which that political power would not be accessible to poor women, immigrant women, and black women."[39] Yet despite the blatant racism and class bias of the women's suffrage movement, black women, discouraged and betrayed, continued to work for their right to vote, both as blacks and as women, through their own suffrage organizations.

This history of racism in the early women's movement has been sustained by contemporary white feminists. Within organizations, most twentieth-century black women encounter myriad experiences that deny their reality. In some instances, it is the absence of materials, information, speeches, readings, or persons representing black women. When present at all, women of color are underrepresented and have marginal and subordinate roles. Recently, Paula Giddings has reported that the National Organization of Women (NOW) remains insensitive to such problematic issues

[38] Davis, *Women, Race and Class* (n. 9 above), 53–54.
[39] Andolsen (n. 24 above), 78.

as rape, abortion, sterilization, poverty, and unions. Women of color are rarely elected as officers or appointed to major positions, and NOW has actually encouraged minority women's chapters rather than the incorporation of their concerns into the "regular" chapters.[40] Lawyer and educator Mary Frances Berry, in her analysis of the politics of amending the constitution, has argued that one reason for the defeat of the Equal Rights Amendment was the failure of its proponents to campaign, educate, and mobilize the black community, and especially black women.[41]

Many white feminist activists have often assumed that their antisexism stance abolished that all racial prejudice or discriminatory behaviors. At best, this presumption is naive and reflects a serious ignorance of the pervasiveness of racism in this society. Many blacks, women and men alike, see such postures as arrogant, racist, and dangerous to their own interests. Diane Lewis concluded that the status of black women and our interests within the women's movement and its organizations essentially replicates our structurally subordinate position to white women in the larger society.[42] Different opportunity structures and life options make interracial alliances and feminist solidarity problematic. Conceptually invisible, interpersonally misunderstood and insulted, and strategically marginal, black women have found that much in the movement has denied important aspects of our history and experience. Yet, despite the critical obstacles and limitations, the imperatives of multiple jeopardy necessitate recognizing and resisting sexism.

Beyond the race politics in feminism, many black women share concerns of impoverished and working-class women about class politics. What has become mainstream feminism rests on traditional, liberal economic aspirations of equal employment opportunities for women. In practice, however, the emphasis is often on the professional careers of those women who are already economically privileged and college educated. It could be argued, for instance, that equal access to all types of vocational training and jobs may not be desirable as a necessary or primary goal. While it is true that men on average earn more than women, all men do not have equally attractive jobs in terms of working conditions, compensation and benefits, prestige, and mobility. Those male jobs may represent, at best, only a minimal improvement over the jobs of many working women. White feminist economic concerns have concentrated on

[40] Giddings (n. 20 above), 348.

[41] Mary Frances Berry, *Why ERA Failed: Politics, Women's Rights, and the Amending Process of the Constitution* (Bloomington: Indiana University Press, 1986).

[42] Lewis (n. 25 above).

primary sector employment, but these are not the positions that are most critical and accessible to lower- or no-income women. Referring to the equal opportunity approach, Karen Kollias points out that "the majority of nonwhite, lower- and working-class women don't have the power to utilize these benefits because their primary, objective economic conditions haven't changed."[43]

Class stratification becomes an insignificant issue if economic disadvantage is seen as only relevant for feminism to the extent that women are unequal vis-à-vis men. The difference between male and female incomes is dramatically less among blacks than among whites (see table 1), suggesting that sex alone is not the sole determinant of economic status. From a monist feminist perspective, class exploitation is not understood as an independent system of oppression. Consequently, broad class dynamics are not addressed in liberal and some radical feminisms. Marxist and socialist feminists have sought to correct this biased view of class.[44] While the Marxists attempted to incorporate a concern for gender within traditional Marxist analysis, socialist feminists tried to develop a nonmonist perspective of feminism that saw sexism and classism as co-equal oppressions. Ellen Willis concludes that within various feminisms there was limited politics beyond an assertion that class hierarchy was oppressive. A radical feminist, she observes that the consciousness-raising, personal politics approach did not effectively challenge the structural, political economy of class oppression. She concludes that as a consequence, "women were implicated in the class system and had real class interests, that women could oppress men on the basis of class, and that class differences among women could not be resolved within a feminist context alone."[45]

First, the memberships of these class-oriented groups remained mostly middle class. Economically disadvantaged women have not directly contributed to a feminist theoretical understanding of class dynamics or the development of programs and strategies. Black feminist and literary critic, bell hooks notes that "had poor women

[43] Karen Kollias, "Class Realities: Create a New Power Base," in *Building Feminist Theory: Essays from Quest*, ed. *Quest* staff (New York: Longman, 1981), 125–38, esp. 134.

[44] See Josephine Donovan, *Feminist Theory: The Intellectual Traditions of American Feminism* (New York: Ungar, 1985); and Lydia Sargent, ed., *Woman and Revolution: A Discussion of the Unhappy Marriage of Marxism and Feminism* (Boston: South End Press, 1981); and Zillah R. Eisenstein, ed., *Capitalist Patriarchy and the Case for Socialist Feminism* (New York: Monthly Review Press, 1979), for fuller discussions.

[45] Ellen Willis, "Radical Feminism and Feminist Radicalism," in Sayres et al., eds. (n. 36 above), 91–118, esp. 110–11.

set the agenda for feminist movement, they might have decided that class struggle would be a central feminist issue."[46] She further contends that class oppression has not become central among women liberationists because their "values, behaviors, and lifestyles continue to be shaped by privilege."[47] In a similar fashion, feminist and race politics have not informed or established ties between poor and working-class black and white women. Phyllis M. Palmer reasons that from the perspective of a poor black woman, white women individually may suffer wage discrimination because of their sex, but their relations to white males, the top income earners, as daughters and wives grants them a relatively better quality of material well-being. "Most white women do not *in reality* live on what they earn; they have access to the resources of white male income earners."[48] Rejecting what she views as the hollow efforts of "slumming" or nonhierarchical organizing, she observes that no serious strategies have been developed for convincing bourgeois women that class liberation is critical for women's liberation or for organizing with poor and working-class women.

This lack of attention to economic issues has significant implications for the participation of black women. Many of the differences of priorities between black and white women are related to class. Issues of welfare, hunger, poor housing, limited health care, and transportation are seldom seen as feminist interests and are rarely the subject of feminist social policies. As Brenda Eichelberger maintains, "the black woman's energy output is more often directed toward such basic survival issues, while the white woman's is more often aimed at fulfillment."[49] The economic concerns of women from lower-income backgrounds are relatively ignored and distorted in the contemporary women's movement. The feminist interpretation of the "feminization" of poverty is a case in point. While noting that some women, again middle class, have indeed experienced a recent drastic decline in life circumstances as a consequence of divorce, the feminization analysis has misrepresented many of the causes of female poverty. For example, most impoverished women have been poor throughout their lives as a consequence of their class position or of racial oppression. Linda Burnham writes that race and class are more significant causative factors in

[46] hooks, *Feminist Theory* (n. 25 above), 60–61.

[47] Ibid., 61.

[48] Phyllis Marynick Palmer, "White Women/Black Women: The Dualism of Female Identity and Experiences in the United States," *Feminist Studies* 91 (Spring 1983): 162.

[49] Brenda Eichelberger, "Voices on Black Feminism," *Quest: A Feminist Quarterly* 4 (1977): 16–28, esp. 16.

black women's impoverishment than is gender. In the thesis of the feminization of poverty, she contends, "The vulnerability of white women to impoverishment is overstated; the impoverishment of Black men is ignored or underestimated; and the fundamental basis in working-class exploitation for the continual regeneration of poverty is abandoned for a focus on gender."[50]

In summary, feminism's neglect, misunderstanding, or deemphasis of the politics of race and class have direct implications for the actions of black women in relationship to the movement. Often, our response has been to avoid participation in white female, middle-class dominated organizations and to withhold our support from policies that are not in our race and class interests. Nevertheless, just as the importance of race led many black women to commitments to racially based politics, and gender interests compelled our feminist efforts, economic injustices have brought many to consider class politics as a major avenue of liberation.

Class politics

Economic exploitation is the third societal jeopardy constraining the lives of black women. Historically, the three major movements to address the deprivations of class in the United States have been trade unionism and the anticapitalist politics of the 1930s and 1960s which are colloquially referred to as the Old and the New Left. Having their origins in responses to the degradations that accompanied urbanization and industrialization, labor unionists and leftists organized to address the problems of wage labor and economic stratification in a capitalistic society, including the excessive working hours in poor, unsafe conditions, low pay and limited job security, fluctuations in the labor demand, the decline in work satisfaction, the loss of worker autonomy, and poverty. Each movement, although monistic, possessed different objectives. Unionism was reformist in orientation, seeking to ameliorate the worst of the above conditions. In contrast, the socialist and communist ideologies of the Left were revolutionary in that they aspired to eradicate capitalism and ostensibly to establish a classless society.

Into the first quarter of this century, organized labor's approach to economic disadvantage held little promise for blacks or women, and thus no promise for black women. Samuel Gompers, the leading force of trade unionism and president of the American Federation of Labor (AFL, founded in 1886), believed that the best means of improving wages for Anglo males was to restrict the labor supply.

[50] Burnham (n. 37 above), 15.

His strategy was to advocate the return of women to the home and the banning of blacks and Asians from the unions. Although the AFL never formally adopted these restrictions at the national level, many local chapters did so through both formal rules and informal practices.[51] Trade unionists cultivated a cultural image of the worker as a married male who required a family wage to support a wife and children. Labor actively supported protective labor legislation, which effectively excluded women from the jobs that would provide them with sufficient incomes to support themselves and their families. These efforts against women were coupled with the exclusion of blacks, other racial minorities, and initially southern and eastern European immigrant males from the most economically rewarding labor in the unionized crafts and the closed shops. Blacks, in particular, were specifically denied union membership or else relegated to the unskilled, low paying jobs. Consequently, the denial of a family wage to black males exacerbated the circumstances of already economically distressed black families and individuals. In occupations where blacks were well represented, unionization often meant their forceable expulsion. Many of the race riots in the early 1900s were related to the tensions between black laborers and white laborers in competition for employment. So, an effective two-prong strategy for improving white men's income required the demand for a family wage and the restriction of labor competition from women and racial minorities.

In response to union discrimination, white women and black women and men organized. The Working Women's Association, formed in 1868, was one of the earlier attempts at synthesizing feminist and white female workers concerns; the Women's Trade Union League, established in 1903, allied white working- and middle-class women, while the International Ladies' Garment Workers' Union publicized the conditions of white working women,

[51] For discussion of women, employment, and the labor movement, see Diane Balser, *Sisterhood and Solidarity: Feminism and Labor in Modern Times* (Boston: South End Press, 1987); Carol Groneman and Mary Beth Norton, eds., *"To Toil the Livelong Day": America's Women at Work, 1780–1980* (Ithaca, N.Y.: Cornell University Press, 1987); Philip S. Foner, *Women and the American Labor Movement: From World War I to the Present* (New York: Free Press, 1980); Bettina Berch, *The Endless Day: The Political Economy of Women and Work* (New York: Harcourt Brace Jovanovich, 1982); and Mary Frank Fox and Sharlene Hesse-Biber, *Women at Work* (Palo Alto, Calif.: Mayfield, 1984). For blacks, see Marable (n. 31 above); Richard Polenberg, *One Nation Divisible: Class, Race, and Ethnicity in the United States since 1938* (New York: Penguin, 1980); Philip S. Foner, *Organized Labor and the Black Worker, 1619–1973* (New York: International Publishers, 1976); and Dorothy K. Newman et al., *Protest, Politics, and Prosperity; Black Americans and White Institutions, 1940–75* (New York: Pantheon, 1978).

demanded equal pay, demanded female representation in the national labor unions, formed female unions, and organized strikes.[52] Ironically, most of the women's trade union organizations as well as many socialist feminists supported protective legislation but with the mistaken belief that involving the state would ensure safer work environments and reasonable labor requirements for both women and men. However, an unintended consequence of this strategy was that many women's economic situations declined because protective legislation could be used to reinforce occupational segregation and thus limit women's wage earning opportunities.

As the wives and daughters of men who did not earn a family wage, black women's participation in the labor market was crucial to the survival of themselves and their families. Yet, black women benefited little from the unionization efforts among white women. First, they were disproportionately situated in those occupations least likely to be unionized, such as domestic and nonhousehold service and agricultural labor. In large industrial workplaces, they were segregated from white female workers, where the organizing took place, and were often pawns in the labor-management contests.[53] Second, white trade unionists failed actively to recruit black females and they often were denied membership because of their race. The protective legislation further hampered their opportunities by closing off numerous employment opportunities simply on the basis of sex. Black women wanted better paying jobs, but they often had to settle for the jobs that were considered too hazardous, dirty, or immoral for white women, and for which they were not fairly compensated. During the Depression, race-gender discrimination was so pervasive that employment in federal work-relief projects often was closed to them. Thus, significant numbers of black women were unemployed and/or underemployed and, therefore, untouched by union activism.

Despite their exclusion from the major unions, black women and men organized caucuses within predominantly white unions and formed their own unions, such as the Urban League's Negro Workers Councils, African Blood Brotherhood, Negro American Labor Council, National Negro Labor Council, and Dodge Revolutionary Union Movement (DRUM). A. Phillip Randolph, founder of the Brotherhood of Sleeping Car Porters, called for a march on Washington in the 1940s to demand the end of wage and job dis-

[52] See Balser for a detailed consideration of the contemporary union activities of women, especially their efforts to organize clerical and other pink collar workers.

[53] See Jones (n. 22 above); Giddings (n. 20 above); and Davis, *Women, Race and Class* (n. 9 above), for an examination of black women's work roles and labor activism.

crimination, the desegregation of schools and public accommodations, protection of immigrant workers, cessation of lynching, and the unionization of black women. During the Depression, trade unions and unemployed councils held demonstrations demanding immediate cash relief and unemployment compensation, as well as advocating race solidarity. For blacks in the first half of this century, class and race interests were often inseparable. Black women benefited indirectly from black men's labor activism, and they often supported those efforts by participating on picket lines, providing food and clothing for strikers and their families, and, most important, making financial contributions to the households from their own paid labor. Black women also engaged in labor organizing directly, both through existing predominantly white unions and through their own activism. Black domestics, tobacco workers, garment workers, and others organized strikes and fought for union representation.[54]

Not all unions and economic organizations excluded white women and black women and men. The Knights of Labor, established in 1886, the Industrial Workers of the World, created in 1905, and the Congress of Industrial Organizations, formed in 1938, are noted for encouraging the unionization of millions of black men and black and white women workers. But overall, the record of organized labor on issues of import to black women and men and white women has not been outstanding. Until 1971, the major unions opposed the Equal Rights Amendment; and today, many challenge affirmative action and comparable worth policies. The continued need for black and women's labor organizations suggest that the historic barriers remain to their full participation and rewards in unions. But, it is also important to recognize that the trade unionist approach has many limitations, and first among these is its focus on the individual worker. As a result, the broad issues of poverty and economic inequality are perceived as beyond the purview of most labor activism. While seeking to ameliorate the worst of industrial society, unionists seldom challenge the economic order of capitalism.

This challenge was left to the Socialist and Communist activists, but this radical critique of the political economy has never been a part of the political mainstream of the United States as it has in other nations. Nevertheless, a small but significant group of activists and intellectuals have advanced radicalism throughout this century.[55] The

[54] See Dolores Janiewski, "Seeking 'a New Day and a New Way': Black Women and Unions in the Southern Tobacco Industry"; and Elizabeth Clark-Lewis, " 'This Work Had a End': African-American Domestic Workers in Washington, D.C., 1910–1940," both in Groneman and Norton, eds.

[55] See Peter Clecak, *Radical Paradoxes: Dilemmas of the American Left: 1945–1970* (New York: Harper & Row, 1973), for an illuminating analysis of the Old and New Left.

political Left, in general, supported black women and men and white working women during the Progressive Era. In fact, leading intellectuals, including Emma Goldman, Margaret Sanger, Charlotte Perkins Gilman, Elizabeth Gurley Flynn, Langston Hughes, Paul Robeson, W. E. B. DuBois, and C. L. R. James saw socialism as the route for liberation. Two black women, Lucy Parsons and Claudia Jones, were among the early labor activists and Socialists of the Old Left. And even Angela Davis, who describes the important role of individual women within the Socialist and Communist parties during the first half of the twentieth century, does not offer us much insight into the general status of black women, besides noting the Socialist party's indifference to blacks, both males and females.[56]

But even within these efforts, there still were gaps in recognizing the needs of black women. In 1900, the Socialist party was founded and immediately began campaigning for women's suffrage and labor rights through its Woman's National Committee. Because it focused on the industrial proletariat, it paid no particular attention to blacks since they were mostly agricultural laborers. Consequently, the party also paid minimal attention to the black women who were not industrially employed. In contrast, members of the Communist party were actively involved in organizing industrial workers, sharecoppers, and the unemployed during the Depression and in championing racial as well as economic justice for blacks.[57] However, the Communist party remained relatively silent on various feminist concerns. Its vigorous defense of the Scottsboro boys and other victims of racial bigotry linked with its call for black self-determination initially attracted numerous blacks to the party in the 1930s and 1940s. Nevertheless, it became increasingly clear that the international Communist party was concerned with the liberation of blacks only as long as those efforts advanced its overall objective of aiding the revolutionary leadership of a European working class. Eventually, the collusion of the American Communist party with racism and sexism dissuaded many blacks and women of the advantages of Soviet-oriented communist activism.

The second surge of anticapitalism was an integral part of the so-called New Left of the 1960s. Sociologist Stanley Aronowitz has described the sixties' radicalism as the movements of a generation, which were not oriented around any particular class or race issue.[58] While this might characterize certain aspects of the radical critique

[56] Davis, *Women, Race and Class.*

[57] See Vincent Harding, *The Other American Revolution* (Los Angeles and Atlanta: University of California, Los Angeles, Center for Afro-American Studies, and Institute of the Black World, 1980), for discussion of blacks and communist organizing.

[58] Stanley Aronowitz, "When the New Left Was New," in Sayres et al., eds. (n. 36 above), 11–43.

of the liberal society, his interpretation does not account for the ideological and activist history that informed both the black and women's liberation efforts of that decade. In an analysis of the contradictions and dilemmas of the New Left, Peter Clecak described the era as one that lacked a vision of a new society beyond the negation of the present ills of poverty, racism, imperialism, and hegemony. Its apocalyptic perspectives on American society and utopian images of community were founded on a fundamental acceptance of capitalist notions of individualism, personal gain, and personal liberty.[59] By implication, much of the New Left lacked a basic, critical understanding of the dynamics of oppressions as group and systemic processes.

The disillusionment that characterized the New Left movement was compounded by the frustration of its failure to organize the urban poor and racial minorities. The free speech and antiwar activists, Students for a Democratic Society and the Weather Underground (i.e., the weathermen), mistakenly attempted to organize northern urban communities using SNCC's southern mobilization model. At another level, new leftists did not understand that most members of oppressed groups desired a piece of the American Dream, not its destruction. The efforts to create coalitions with civil rights and black nationalist groups were strained and defeated because of the conflicting objectives and tactics. The aims of civil rights groups were integrationist through nonviolent means; and while black militants advocated armed defense or even revolution and adopted a Maoist, anticapitalist program, their separatist orientation made black-white alliances almost impossible. Moreover, while the Left condemned the role of U.S. imperialism in Southeast Asia, it ignored the advance of Western, capitalist interests into the continent of Africa, especially South Africa.

At the same time, women active in the New Left became increasingly frustrated with the theoretical and strategic indifference to the woman question. The sexual politics within the movement subjected women to traditional gender role assignments, sexual manipulation, male leadership and domination, plus a concentration on an essentially male issue, the draft.[60] Once again, invisibility

[59] Clecak.

[60] Heidi Hartmann and Zillah Eisenstein provide theoretical critiques of monist Marxism as an adequate avenue for women's liberation. Both Lydia Sargent and Sara Evans detail the sexual politics on the Left (see Heidi Hartmann, "The Unhappy Marriage of Marxism and Feminism," in Sargent, ed. [n. 44 above]; Eisenstein, "Reform and/or Revolution: Toward a Unified Women's Movement," in Sargent, ed. [n. 44 above], 339–62; Sargent, "New Left Women and Men: The Honeymoon Is Over," in Sargent, ed. [n. 44 above], xi–xxxii; and Evans [n. 9 above]).

typifies the role of black women in New Left radical politics. Black women responded by incorporating class interests into their race and gender politics. In the founding documents of various black feminist organizations, scathing critiques of the political economy are a cornerstone of the analysis of domination. For example, the *Combahee River Collective Statement* pointedly declared that "the liberation of all oppressed peoples necessitates the destruction of the political-economic systems of capitalism and imperialism, as well as partriarchy. . . . We are not convinced, however, that a socialist revolution that is not also a feminist and anti-racism revolution will guarantee our liberation."[61] This excerpt clearly articulates an understanding of multiple jeopardy and its function in the dominant society and within liberation politics. Out of necessity, black women have addressed both narrow labor and broad economic concerns.

Political theorist Manning Marable has argued that progressive forces must uproot racism and patriarchy in their quest for a socialist democracy through a dedication to equality.[62] Yet a major limitation of both unionism and radical class politics is their monist formulations, wherein economics are exaggerated at the expense of understanding and confronting other oppressions such as racism and sexism. Despite the historical examples of black women and men and white women as union activists and socialists and the examples of the sporadic concern of organized labor and leftists with race and gender politics, class politics have not provided the solution to black women's domination because they continue to privilege class issues within a white male framework. Given the inability of any single agenda to address the intricate complex of racism, sexism, and classism in black women's lives, black women must develop a political ideology capable of interpreting and resisting that multiple jeopardy.

Multiple consciousness in black feminist ideology

Gloria Joseph and Jill Lewis have suggested that black women face a dilemma analogous to that of Siamese twins, each of whom have distinct and incompatible interests.[63] Black women cannot, they argue, be wholeheartedly committed and fully active in both the black liberation struggle and the women's liberation movement,

[61] See Combahee River Collective, *Combahee River Collective Statement: Black Feminist Organizing in the Seventies and Eighties* (New York: Kitchen Table Press, 1986), 12–13.

[62] Marable (n. 31 above).

[63] Joseph and Lewis (n. 25 above), 38.

because of sexual and racial politics within each respectively. The authors recognize the demands of multiple jeopardy politics and the detrimental effect of neglecting these dual commitments. But what they fail to consider are the multiple and creative ways in which black women address their interdependent concerns of racism, sexism, and classism.

Black women have been feminists since the early 1800s, but our exclusion from the white women's movement and its organizations has led many incorrectly to assume that we were not present in the (white) women's movement because we were not interested in resisting sexism both within and without the black community. What appears recently to be a change in black women's position, from studied indifference to disdain and curiosity to cautious affirmation of the women's movement, may be due to structural changes in relationships between blacks and whites that have made black women "more sensitive to the obstacles of sexism and to the relevance of the women's movement."[64] Black women's apparent greater sensitivity to sexism may be merely the bolder, public articulation of black feminist concerns that have existed for well over a century. In other words, black women did not just become feminists in the 1970s. We did, however, grant more salience to those concerns and become more willing to organize primarily on that basis, creating the Combahee River Collective, the National Black Feminist Organization, and Sapphire Sapphos. Some black women chose to participate in predominantly white, women's movement activities and organizations, while others elected to develop the scholarship and curriculum that became the foundation of black women's studies, while still others founded black feminist journals, presses, and political organizations.[65]

Several studies have considered the relevance of black women's diverse characteristics in understanding our political attitudes; these

[64] Lewis (n. 25 above), 341.

[65] For information on the development of black feminist scholarship and academic programs, see Patricia Bell Scott, "Selective Bibliography on Black Feminism" in Hull et al., eds. (n. 31 above); Black Studies/Women's Studies Faculty Development Project, "Black Studies/Women's Studies: An Overdue Partnership" (Women's Studies, University of Massachusetts—Amherst, mimeograph, 1983); Nancy Conklin et al., "The Culture of Southern Black Women: Approaches and Materials" (University: University of Alabama Archives of American Minority Cultures and Women's Studies Program, Project on the Culture of Southern Black Women, 1983); the premier issue of *Sage: A Scholarly Journal on Black Women* 1, no. 1 (Spring 1984); and the establishment of Kitchen Table: A Women of Color Press, New York. The Center for Research on Women at Memphis State University, the Women's Research and Resource Center at Spelman College, and the Minority Women's Program at Wellesley College are among the academic centers.

reports seem fairly inconsistent, if not contradictory.[66] The various findings do suggest that the conditions that bring black women to feminist consciousness are specific to our social and historical experiences. For black women, the circumstances of lower socioeconomic life may encourage political, and particularly feminist, consciousness.[67] This is in contrast to feminist as well as traditional political socialization literature that suggests that more liberal, that is, feminist, attitudes are associated with higher education attainment and class standing. Many of the conditions that middle-class, white feminists have found oppressive are perceived as privileges by black women, especially those with low incomes. For instance, the option not to work outside of the home is a luxury that historically has been denied most black women. The desire to struggle for this option can, in such a context, represent a feminist position, precisely because it constitutes an instance of greater liberty for certain women. It is also important to note, however, that the class differences among black women regarding our feminist consciousness are minimal. Black women's particular history thus is an essential ingredient in shaping our feminist concerns.

Certainly the multifaceted nature of black womanhood would meld diverse ideologies, from race liberation, class liberation, and women's liberation. The basis of our feminist ideology is rooted in our reality. To the extent that the adherents of any one ideology insist on separatist organizational forms, assert the fundamental nature of any one oppression, and demand total cognitive, affective, and behavioral commitment, that ideology and its practitioners exclude black women and the realities of our lives.

[66] See Andrew Cherlin and Pamela Waters, "Trends in United States Men's and Women's Sex-Role Attitudes: 1972–1978," *American Sociological Review* 46 (1981): 453–60. See also, Janice Gump, "Comparative Analysis of Black Women's and White Women's Sex-role Attitudes," *Journal of Consulting and Clinical Psychology* 43 (1975): 858–63; and Marjorie Hershey, "Racial Difference in Sex-Role Identities and Sex Stereotyping: Evidence against a Common Assumption," *Social Science Quarterly* 58 (1978): 583–96. For various opinion polls, see "The 1972 Virginia Slims American Women's Opinion Poll" and "The 1974 Virginia Slims American Women's Opinion Poll," conducted by the Roper Organization (Williamstown, Mass.: Roper Public Opinion Research Center, 1974). See Barbara Everitt Bryant, "American Women: Today and Tomorrow," National Commission on the Observance of International Women's Year (Washington, D.C.: Government Printing Office, March 1977). Gloria Steinem, "Exclusive Louis Harris Survey: How Women Live, Vote and Think," *Ms. Magazine* 13 (July 1984): 51–54.

[67] For analyses of the influence of socioeconomic class and race on feminist attitudes, see Willa Mae Hemmons, "The Women's Liberation Movement: Understanding Black Women's Attitudes," in *The Black Woman*, ed. LaFrances Rodgers-Rose (Beverly Hills, Calif.: Sage Publications, 1980), 285–99; and Ransford and Miller (n. 16 above).

A black feminist ideology, first and foremost, thus declares the visibility of black women. It acknowledges the fact that two innate and inerasable traits, being both black and female, constitute our special status in American society. Second, black feminism asserts self-determination as essential. Black women are empowered with the right to interpret our reality and define our objectives. While drawing on a rich tradition of struggle as blacks and as women, we continually establish and reestablish our own priorities. As black women, we decide for ourselves the relative salience of any and all identities and oppressions, and how and the extent to which those features inform our politics. Third, a black feminist ideology fundamentally challenges the interstructure of the oppressions of racism, sexism, and classism both in the dominant society and within movements for liberation. It is in confrontation with multiple jeopardy that black women define and sustain a multiple consciousness essential for our liberation, of which feminist consciousness is an integral part.

Finally, a black feminist ideology presumes an image of black women as powerful, independent subjects. By concentrating on our multiple oppressions, scholarly descriptions have confounded our ability to discover and appreciate the ways in which black women are not victims. Ideological and political choices cannot be assumed to be determined solely by the historical dynamics of racism, sexism, and classism in this society. Although the complexities and ambiguities that merge a consciousness of race, class, and gender oppressions make the emergence and praxis of a multivalent ideology problematical, they also make such a task more necessary if we are to work toward our liberation as blacks, as the economically exploited, and as women.

Department of Sociology
Dartmouth College

SEX AND DEATH IN THE RATIONAL WORLD OF DEFENSE INTELLECTUALS

CAROL COHN

"I can't believe *that*," said Alice.

"Can't you?" the Queen said in a pitying tone. "Try again: draw a long breath, and shut your eyes."

Alice laughed. "There's no use trying," she said. "One *can't* believe impossible things."

"I daresay you haven't had much practice," said the Queen. "When I was your age, I always did it for half-an-hour a day. Why, sometimes I've believed as many as six impossible things before breakfast." [LEWIS CARROLL, *Through the Looking Glass*]

My close encounter with nuclear strategic analysis started in the summer of 1984. I was one of forty-eight college teachers (one of ten women) attending a summer workshop on nuclear weapons, nuclear strategic doctrine, and arms control, taught by distinguished "defense intellectuals." Defense intellectuals are men (and indeed, they are virtually all men) "who use the concept of deterrence to explain why it is safe to have weapons of a kind and number it is not safe to use."[1] They are civilians who move in and out of

[1] Thomas Powers, "How Nuclear War Could Start," *New York Review of Books* (January 17, 1985), 33.

This essay originally appeared in *Signs*, vol. 12, no. 4, Summer 1987.

government, working sometimes as administrative officials or consultants, sometimes at universities and think tanks. They formulate what they call "rational" systems for dealing with the problems created by nuclear weapons: how to manage the arms race; how to deter the use of nuclear weapons; how to fight a nuclear war if deterrence fails. It is their calculations that are used to explain the necessity of having nuclear destructive capability at what George Kennan has called "levels of such grotesque dimensions as to defy rational understanding."[2] At the same time, it is their reasoning that is used to explain why it is not safe to live without nuclear weapons.[3] In short, they create the theory that informs and legitimates American nuclear strategic practice.

For two weeks, I listened to men engage in dispassionate discussion of nuclear war. I found myself aghast, but morbidly fascinated—not by nuclear weaponry, or by images of nuclear destruction, but by the extraordinary abstraction and removal from what I knew as reality that characterized the professional discourse. I became obsessed by the question, How can they think this way? At the end of the summer program, when I was offered the opportunity to stay on at the university's center on defense technology and arms control (hereafter known as "the Center"), I jumped at the chance to find out how they could think "this" way.

I spent the next year of my life immersed in the world of defense intellectuals. As a participant observer, I attended lectures, listened to arguments, conversed with defense analysts, and interviewed graduate students at the beginning, middle, and end of their training. I learned their specialized language, and I tried to understand what they thought and how they thought. I sifted through their logic for its internal inconsistencies and its unspoken assumptions. But as I learned their language, as I became more and more engaged with their information and their arguments, I found that my own thinking was changing. Soon, I could no longer cling to the comfort of studying an external and objectified "them." I had to confront a new question: How can *I* think this way? How can any of us?

Throughout my time in the world of strategic analysis, it was hard not to notice the ubiquitous weight of gender, both in social relations and in the language itself; it is an almost entirely male world (with the exception of the secretaries), and the language contains many rather arresting metaphors.

[2] George Kennan, "A Modest Proposal," *New York Review of Books* (July 16, 1981), 14.

[3] It is unusual for defense intellectuals to write for the public, rather than for their colleagues, but a recent, interesting exception has been made by a group of defense analysts from Harvard. Their two books provide a clear expression of the stance that living with nuclear weapons is not so much a problem to be solved but a condition to be managed rationally. Albert Carnesale and the Harvard Nuclear Study Group, *Living with Nuclear Weapons* (Cambridge, Mass.: Harvard University Press, 1984); and Graham T. Allison, Albert Carnesale, and Joseph Nye, Jr., eds., *Hawks, Doves, and Owls: An Agenda for Avoiding Nuclear War* (New York: W. W. Norton & Co., 1985).

There is, of course, an important and growing body of feminist theory about gender and language.[4] In addition, there is a rich and increasingly vast body of theoretical work exploring the gendered aspects of war and militarism, which examines such issues as men's and women's different relations to militarism and pacifism, and the ways in which gender ideology is used in the service of militarization. Some of the feminist work on gender and war is also part of an emerging, powerful feminist critique of ideas of rationality as they have developed in Western culture.[5] While I am indebted to all of these bodies of work, my own project is most closely linked to the development of feminist critiques of dominant Western concepts of reason. My goal is to discuss the nature of nuclear stragetic thinking; in

[4] For useful introductions to feminist work on gender and language, see Barrie Thorne, Cheris Kramarae, and Nancy Henley, eds., *Language, Gender and Society* (Rowley, Mass.: Newbury Publishing House, 1983); and Elizabeth Abel, ed., *Writing and Sexual Difference* (Chicago: University of Chicago Press, 1982).

[5] For feminist critiques of dominant Western conceptions of rationality, see Nancy Hartsock, *Money, Sex, and Power* (New York: Longman, 1983); Sandra Harding and Merrill Hintikka, eds., *Discovering Reality: Feminist Perspectives on Epistemology, Metaphysics, Methodology and the Philosophy of Science* (Dordrecht: D. Reidel Publishing Co., 1983); Evelyn Fox Keller, *Reflections on Gender and Science* (New Haven, Conn.: Yale University Press, 1985); Jean Bethke Elshtain, *Public Man, Private Woman: Woman in Social and Political Thought* (Princeton, N.J.: Princeton University Press, 1981); Genevieve Lloyd, *The Man of Reason: "Male" and "Female" in Western Philosophy* (Minneapolis: University of Minnesota Press, 1984), which contains a particularly useful bibliographic essay; Sara Ruddick, "Remarks on the Sexual Politics of Reason," in *Women and Moral Theory*, ed. Eva Kittay and Diana Meyers (Totowa, N.J.: Rowman & Allanheld, in press). Some of the growing feminist work on gender and war is explicitly connected to critiques of rationality. See Virginia Woolf, *Three Guineas* (New York: Harcourt, Brace, Jovanovich, 1966); Nancy C. M. Hartsock, "The Feminist Standpoint: Developing the Grounds for a Specifically Feminist Historical Materialism," in Harding and Hintikka, eds., 283–310, and "The Barracks Community in Western Political Thought: Prologomena to a Feminist Critique of War and Politics," in *Women and Men's Wars*, ed. Judith Hicks Stiehm (Oxford: Pergamon Press, 1983); Jean Bethke Elshtain, "Reflections on War and Political Discourse: Realism, Just War and Feminism in a Nuclear Age," *Political Theory* 13, no. 1 (February 1985): 39–57; Sara Ruddick, "Preservative Love and Military Destruction: Some Reflections on Mothering and Peace," in *Mothering: Essays in Feminist Theory*, ed. Joyce Trebilcot (Totowa, N.J.: Rowman & Allanheld, 1984), 231–62; Genevieve Lloyd, "Selfhood, War, and Masculinity," in *Feminist Challenges*, ed. E. Gross and C. Pateman (Boston: Northeastern University Press, 1986). There is a vast and valuable literature on gender and war that indirectly informs my work. See, e.g., Cynthia Enloe, *Does Khaki Become You? The Militarization of Women's Lives* (Boston: South End Press, 1984); Stiehm, ed.; Jean Bethke Elshtain, "On Beautiful Souls, Just Warriors, and Feminist Consciousness," in Stiehm, ed., 341–48; Sara Ruddick, "Pacifying the Forces: Drafting Women in the Interests of Peace," *Signs: Journal of Women in Culture and Society* 8, no. 3 (Spring 1983): 471–89, and "Drafting Women: Pieces of a Puzzle," in *Conscripts and Volunteers: Military Requirements, Social Values, and the All-Volunteer Force*, ed. Robert K. Fullinwider (Totowa, N.J.: Rowman & Allanheld, 1983); Amy Swerdlow, "Women's Strike for Peace versus HUAC," *Feminist Studies* 8, no. 3 (Fall 1982): 493–520; Mary C. Segers, "The Catholic Bishops' Pastoral Letter on War and Peace: A Feminist Perspective," *Feminist Studies* 11, no. 3 (Fall 1985): 619–47.

particular, my emphasis is on the role of its specialized language, a language that I call "technostrategic."[6] I have come to believe that this language both reflects and shapes the nature of the American nuclear strategic project, that it plays a central role in allowing defense intellectuals to think and act as they do, and that feminists who are concerned about nuclear weaponry and nuclear war must give careful attention to the language we choose to use—whom it allows us to communicate with and what it allows us to think as well as say.

State I: Listening

Clean bombs and clean language

Entering the world of defense intellectuals was a bizarre experience—bizarre because it is a world where men spend their days calmly and matter-of-factly discussing nuclear weapons, nuclear strategy, and nuclear war. The discussions are carefully and intricately reasoned, occurring seemingly without any sense of horror, urgency, or moral outrage—in fact, there seems to be no graphic reality behind the words, as they speak of "first strikes," "counterforce exchanges," and "limited nuclear war," or as they debate the comparative values of a "minimum deterrent posture" versus a "nuclear war–fighting capability."

Yet what is striking about the men themselves is not, as the content of their conversations might suggest, their cold-bloodedness. Rather, it is that they are a group of men unusually endowed with charm, humor, intelligence, concern, and decency. Reader, I liked them. At least, I liked many of them. The attempt to understand how such men could contribute to an endeavor that I see as so fundamentally destructive became a continuing obsession for me, a lens through which I came to examine all of my experiences in their world.

In this early stage, I was gripped by the extraordinary language used to discuss nuclear war. What hit me first was the elaborate use of abstraction and euphemism, of words so bland that they never forced the speaker or enabled the listener to touch the realities of nuclear holocaust that lay behind the words.

[6] I have coined the term "technostrategic" to represent the intertwined, inextricable nature of technological and nuclear strategic thinking. The first reason is that strategic thinking seems to change in direct response to technological changes, rather than political thinking, or some independent paradigms that might be isolated as "strategic." (On this point, see Lord Solly Zuckerman, *Nuclear Illusions and Reality* [New York: Viking Press, 1982]). Even more important, strategic theory not only depends on and changes in response to technological objects, it is also based on a kind of thinking, a way of looking at problems—formal, mathematical modeling, systems analysis, game theory, linear programming—that are part of technology itself. So I use the term "technostrategic" to indicate the degree to which nuclear strategic language and thinking are imbued with, indeed constructed out of, modes of thinking that are associated with technology.

Anyone who has seen pictures of Hiroshima burn victims or tried to imagine the pain of hundreds of glass shards blasted into flesh may find it perverse beyond imagination to hear a class of nuclear devices matter-of-factly referred to as "clean bombs." "Clean bombs" are nuclear devices that are largely fusion rather than fission and that therefore release a higher proportion of their energy as prompt radiation, but produce less radioactive fallout than fission bombs of the same yield.[7]

"Clean bombs" may provide the perfect metaphor for the language of defense analysts and arms controllers. This language has enormous destructive power, but without emotional fallout, without the emotional fallout that would result if it were clear one was talking about plans for mass murder, mangled bodies, and unspeakable human suffering. Defense analysts talk about "countervalue attacks" rather than about incinerating cities. Human death, in nuclear parlance, is most often referred to as "collateral damage"; for, as one defense analyst said wryly, "The Air Force doesn't target people, it targets shoe factories."[8]

Some phrases carry this cleaning-up to the point of inverting meaning. The MX missile will carry ten warheads, each with the explosure power of 300–475 kilotons of TNT: *one* missile the bearer of destruction approximately 250–400 times that of the Hiroshima bombing.[9] Ronald Reagan has

[7] Fusion weapons' proportionally smaller yield of radioactive fallout led Atomic Energy Commission Chairman Lewis Strauss to announce in 1956 that hydrogen bomb tests were important "not only from a military point of view but from a humanitarian aspect." Although the bombs being tested were 1,000 times more powerful than those that devastated Hiroshima and Nagasaki, the proportional reduction of fallout apparently qualified them as not only clean but also humanitarian. Lewis Strauss is quoted in Ralph Lapp, "The 'Humanitarian' H-Bomb," *Bulletin of Atomic Scientists* 12, no. 7 (September 1956): 263.

[8] I must point out that we cannot know whether to take this particular example literally: America's list of nuclear targets is, of course, classified. The defense analyst quoted, however, is a man who has had access to that list for at least two decades. He is also a man whose thinking and speaking is careful and precise, so I think it is reasonable to assume that his statement is not a distortion, that "shoe factories," even if not themselves literally targeted, accurately represent a category of target. Shoe factories would be one among many "military targets" other than weapons systems themselves; they would be military targets because an army needs boots. The likelihood of a nuclear war lasting long enough for foot soldiers to wear out their boots might seem to stretch the limits of credibility, but that is an insufficient reason to assume that they are not nuclear targets. Nuclear targeting and nuclear strategic planning in general frequently suffer from "conventionalization"—the tendency of planners to think in the old, familiar terms of "conventional" warfare rather than fully assimilating the ways in which nuclear weaponry has changed warfare. In avoiding talking about murder, the defense community has long been ahead of the State Department. It was not until 1984 that the State Department announced it will no longer use the word "killing," much less "murder," in official reports on the status of human rights in allied countries. The new term is "unlawful or arbitrary deprivation of life" (*New York Times*, February 15, 1984, as cited in *Quarterly Review of Doublespeak* 11, no. 1 [October 1984]: 3).

[9] "Kiloton" (or kt) is a measure of explosive power, measured by the number of thousands of tons of TNT required to release an equivalent amount of energy. The atomic bomb dropped on Hiroshima is estimated to have been approximately 12 kt. An MX missile is designed to

dubbed the MX missile "the Peacekeeper." While this renaming was the object of considerable scorn in the community of defense analysts, these very same analysts refer to the MX as a "damage limitation weapon."[10]

These phrases, only a few of the hundreds that could be discussed, exemplify the astounding chasm between image and reality that characterizes technostrategic language. They also hint at the terrifying way in which the existence of nuclear devices has distorted our perceptions and redefined the world. "Clean bombs" tells us that radioactivity is the only "dirty" part of killing people.

To take this one step further, such phrases can even seem healthful/curative/corrective. So that we not only have "clean bombs" but also "surgically clean strikes" ("counterforce" attacks that can purportedly "take out"—i.e., accurately destroy—an opponent's weapons or command centers without causing significant injury to anything else). The image of excision of the offending weapon is unspeakably ludicrous when the surgical tool is not a delicately controlled scalpel but a nuclear warhead. And somehow it seems to be forgotten that even scalpels spill blood.[11]

White men in ties discussing missile size

Feminists have often suggested that an important aspect of the arms race is phallic worship, that "missile envy" is a significant motivating force in the nuclear build-up.[12] I have always found this an uncomfortably reductionist explanation and hoped that my research at the Center would yield a more complex analysis. But still, I was curious about the extent to which I might find a sexual subtext in the defense professionals' discourse. I was not prepared for what I found.

---

carry up to ten Mk 21 reentry vehicles, each with a W-87 warhead. The yield of W-87 warheads is 300 kt, but they are "upgradable" to 475 kt.

[10] Since the MX would theoretically be able to "take out" Soviet land-based ICBMs in a "disarming first strike," the Soviets would have few ICBMs left for a retaliatory attack, and thus damage to the United States theoretically would be limited. However, to consider the damage that could be inflicted on the United States by the remaining ICBMs, not to mention Soviet bombers and submarine-based missiles as "limited" is to act as though words have no meaning.

[11] Conservative government assessments of the number of deaths resulting from a "surgically clean" counterforce attack vary widely. The Office of Technology Assessment projects 2 million to 20 million immediate deaths. (See James Fallows, *National Defense* [New York: Random House, 1981], 159.) A 1975 Defense Department study estimated 18.3 million fatalities, while the U.S. Arms Control and Disarmament Agency, using different assumptions, arrived at a figure of 50 million (cited by Desmond Ball, "Can Nuclear War Be Controlled?" Adelphi Paper no. 169 [London: International Institute for Strategic Studies, 1981]).

[12] The phrase is Helen Caldicott's in *Missile Envy: The Arms Race and Nuclear War* (Toronto: Bantam Books, 1986).

I think I had naively imagined myself as a feminist spy in the house of death—that I would need to sneak around and eavesdrop on what men said in unguarded moments, using all my subtlety and cunning to unearth whatever sexual imagery might be underneath how they thought and spoke. I had naively believed that these men, at least in public, would appear to be aware of feminist critiques. If they had not changed their language, I thought that at least at some point in a long talk about "penetration aids," someone would suddenly look up, slightly embarrassed to be caught in such blatant confirmation of feminist analyses of What's Going On Here.[13]

Of course, I was wrong. There was no evidence that any feminist critiques had ever reached the ears, much less the minds, of these men. American military dependence on nuclear weapons was explained as "irresistible, because you get more bang for the buck." Another lecturer solemnly and scientifically announced "to disarm is to get rid of all your stuff." (This may, in turn, explain why they see serious talk of nuclear disarmament as perfectly resistable, not to mention foolish. If disarmament is emasculation, how could any real man even consider it?) A professor's explanation of why the MX missile is to be placed in the silos of the newest Minuteman missiles, instead of replacing the older, less accurate ones, was "because they're in the nicest hole—you're not going to take the nicest missile you have and put it in a crummy hole." Other lectures were filled with discussion of vertical erector launchers, thrust-to-weight ratios, soft lay downs, deep penetration, and the comparative advantages of protracted versus spasm attacks—or what one military adviser to the National Security Council has called "releasing 70 to 80 percent of our megatonnage in one orgasmic whump."[14] There was serious concern about the need to harden our missiles and the need to "face it, the Russians are a little harder than we are." Disbelieving glances would occasionally pass between me and my one ally in the summer program, another woman, but no one else seemed to notice.

If the imagery is transparent, its significance may be less so. The temptation is to draw some conclusions about the defense intellectuals themselves—about what they are *really* talking about, or their motivations; but the temptation is worth resisting. Individual motivations cannot necessarily be read directly from imagery; the imagery itself does not originate in these particular individuals but in a broader cultural context.

Sexual imagery has, of course, been a part of the world of warfare since

[13] For the uninitiated, "penetration aids" refers to devices that help bombers or missiles get past the "enemy's" defensive systems; e.g., stealth technology, chaff, or decoys. Within the defense intellectual community, they are also familiarly known as "penaids."

[14] General William Odom, "C³I and Telecommunications at the Policy Level," Incidental Paper, Seminar on C³I: Command, Control, Communications and Intelligence (Cambridge, Mass.: Harvard University, Center for Information Policy Research, Spring 1980), 5.

long before nuclear weapons were even a gleam in a physicist's eye. The history of the atomic bomb project itself is rife with overt images of competitive male sexuality, as is the discourse of the early nuclear physicists, strategists, and SAC commanders.[15] Both the military itself and the arms manufacturers are constantly exploiting the phallic imagery and promise of sexual domination that their weapons so conveniently suggest. A quick glance at the publications that constitute some of the research sources for defense intellectuals makes the depth and pervasiveness of the imagery evident.

Air Force Magazine's advertisements for new weapons, for example, rival *Playboy* as a catalog of men's sexual anxieties and fantasies. Consider the following, from the June 1985 issue: emblazoned in bold letters across the top of a two-page advertisement for the AV-8B Harrier II—"Speak Softly and Carry a Big Stick." The copy below boasts "an exceptional thrust to weight ratio" and "vectored thrust capability that makes the . . . unique rapid response possible." Then, just in case we've failed to get the message, the last line reminds us, "Just the sort of 'Big Stick' Teddy Roosevelt had in mind way back in 1901."[16]

An ad for the BKEP (BLU-106/B) reads:

> The Only Way to Solve Some Problems is to Dig Deep.
> THE BOMB, KINETIC ENERGY
> PENETRATOR
> "Will provide the tactical air commander with efficient power to deny or significantly delay enemy airfield operations."
> "Designed to maximize runway cratering by optimizing penetration dynamics and utilizing the most efficient warhead yet designed."[17]

(In case the symbolism of "cratering" seems far-fetched, I must point out that I am not the first to see it. The French use the Mururoa Atoll in the South Pacific for their nuclear tests and assign a woman's name to each of the craters they gouge out of the earth.)

Another, truly extraordinary, source of phallic imagery is to be found in descriptions of nuclear blasts themselves. Here, for example, is one by journalist William Laurence, who was brought to Nagasaki by the Air Force to witness the bombing. "Then, just when it appeared as though the thing had settled down in to a state of permanence, there came shooting out of the top a giant mushroom that increased the size of the pillar to a total of 45,000 feet. The mushroom top was even more alive than the pillar, seething and boiling in a white fury of creamy foam, sizzling upward and

[15] This point has been amply documented by Brian Easlea, *Fathering the Unthinkable: Masculinity, Scientists and the Nuclear Arms Race* (London: Pluto Press, 1983).

[16] *Air Force Magazine* 68, no. 6 (June 1985): 77–78.

[17] Ibid.

then descending earthward, a thousand geysers rolled into one. It kept struggling in an elemental fury, like a creature in the act of breaking the bonds that held it down."[18]

Given the degree to which it suffuses their world, that defense intellectuals themselves use a lot of sexual imagery does not seem especially surprising. Nor does it, by itself, constitute grounds for imputing motivation. For me, the interesting issue is not so much the imagery's psychodynamic origins, as how it functions. How does it serve to make it possible for strategic planners and other defense intellectuals to do their macabre work? How does it function in their construction of a work world that feels tenable? Several stories illustrate the complexity.

During the summer program, a group of us visited the New London Navy base where nuclear submarines are homeported and the General Dynamics Electric Boat boatyards where a new Trident submarine was being constructed. At one point during the trip we took a tour of a nuclear powered submarine. When we reached the part of the sub where the missiles are housed, the officer accompanying us turned with a grin and asked if we wanted to stick our hands through a hole to "pat the missile." *Pat the missile?*

The image reappeared the next week, when a lecturer scornfully declared that the only real reason for deploying cruise and Pershing II missiles in Western Europe was "so that our allies can pat them." Some months later, another group of us went to be briefed at NORAD (the North American Aerospace Defense Command). On the way back, our plane went to refuel at Offut Air Force Base, the Strategic Air Command headquarters near Omaha, Nebraska. When word leaked out that our landing would be delayed because the new B-1 bomber was in the area, the plane became charged with a tangible excitement that built as we flew in our holding pattern, people craning their necks to try to catch a glimpse of the B-1 in the skies, and climaxed as we touched down on the runway and hurtled past it. Later, when I returned to the Center I encountered a man who, unable to go on the trip, said to me enviously, "I hear you got to pat a B-1."

What is all this "patting"? What are men doing when they "pat" these high-tech phalluses? Patting is an assertion of intimacy, sexual possession, affectionate domination. The thrill and pleasure of "patting the missile" is the proximity of all that phallic power, the possibility of vicariously appropriating it as one's own.

But if the predilection for patting phallic objects indicates something of the homoerotic excitement suggested by the language, it also has another side. For patting is not only an act of sexual intimacy. It is also what one does to babies, small children, the pet dog. One pats that which is small,

[18] William L. Laurence, *Dawn over Zero: The Study of the Atomic Bomb* (London: Museum Press, 1974), 198–99.

cute, and harmless—not terrifyingly destructive. Pat it, and its lethality disappears.

Much of the sexual imagery I heard was rife with the sort of ambiguity suggested by "patting the missiles." The imagery can be construed as a deadly serious display of the connections between masculine sexuality and the arms race. At the same time, it can also be heard as a way of minimizing the seriousness of militarist endeavors, of denying their deadly consequences. A former Pentagon target analyst, in telling me why he thought plans for "limited nuclear war" were ridiculous, said, "Look, you gotta understand that it's a pissing contest—you gotta expect them to use everything they've got." What does this image say? Most obviously, that this is all about competition for manhood, and thus there is tremendous danger. But at the same time, the image diminishes the contest and its outcomes, by representing it as an act of boyish mischief.

Fathers, sons, and virgins

"Virginity" also made frequent, arresting, appearances in nuclear discourse. In the summer program, one professor spoke of India's explosion of a nuclear bomb as "losing her virginity"; the question of how the United States should react was posed as whether or not we should "throw her away." It is a complicated use of metaphor. Initiation into the nuclear world involves being deflowered, losing one's innocence, knowing sin, all wrapped up into one. Although the manly United States is no virgin, and proud of it, the double standard raises its head in the question of whether or not a woman is still worth anything to a man once she has lost her virginity.

New Zealand's refusal to allow nuclear-armed or nuclear-powered warships into its ports prompted similar reflections on virginity. A good example is provided by Retired U.S. Air Force General Ross Milton's angry column in *Air Force Magazine*, entitled, "Nuclear Virginity." His tone is that of a man whose advances have been spurned. He is contemptuous of the woman's protestation that she wants to remain pure, innocent of nuclear weapons; her moral reluctance is a quaint and ridiculous throwback. But beyond contempt, he also feels outraged—after all, this is a woman we have *paid* for, who *still* will not come across. He suggests that we withdraw our goods and services—and then we will see just how long she tries to hold onto her virtue.[19] The patriarchal bargain could not be laid out more clearly.

Another striking metaphor of patriarchal power came early in the summer program, when one of the faculty was giving a lecture on deter-

[19] U.S.A.F. Retired General T. R. Milton, "Nuclear Virginity," *Air Force Magazine* 68, no. 5 (May 1985): 44.

rence. To give us a concrete example from outside the world of military strategy, he described having a seventeen-year-old son of whose TV-watching habits he disapproves. He deals with the situation by threatening to break his son's arm if he turns on the TV again. "That's deterrence!" he said triumphantly.

What is so striking about this analogy is that at first it seems so inappropriate. After all, we have been taught to believe that nuclear deterrence is a relation between two countries of more or less equal strength, in which one is only able to deter the other from doing it great harm by threatening to do the same in return. But in this case, the partners are unequal, and the stronger one is using his superior force not to protect himself or others from grave injury but to coerce.

But if the analogy seems to be a flawed expression of deterrence as we have been taught to view it, it is nonetheless extremely revealing about U.S. nuclear deterrence as an operational, rather than rhetorical or declaratory policy. What it suggests is the speciousness of the defensive rhetoric that surrounds deterrence—of the idea that we face an implacable enemy and that we stockpile nuclear weapons only in an attempt to defend ourselves. Instead, what we see is the drive to superior power as a means to exercise one's will and a readiness to threaten the disproportionate use of force in order to achieve one's own ends. There is no question here of recognizing competing but legitimate needs, no desire to negotiate, discuss, or compromise, and most important, no necessity for that recognition or desire, since the father carries the bigger stick.[20]

The United States frequently appeared in discussions about international politics as "father," sometimes coercive, sometimes benevolent, but always knowing best. The single time that any mention was made of countries other than the United States, our NATO allies, or the USSR was in a lecture on nuclear proliferation. The point was made that younger countries simply could not be trusted to know what was good for them, nor were they yet fully responsible, so nuclear weapons in their hands would be much more dangerous than in ours. The metaphor used was that of parents needing to set limits for their children.

Domestic bliss

Sanitized abstraction and sexual and patriarchal imagery, even if disturbing, seemed to fit easily into the masculinist world of nuclear war planning. What did not fit, what surprised and puzzled me most when I first heard it, was the set of metaphors that evoked images that can only be called domestic.

[20] I am grateful to Margaret Cerullo, a participant in the first summer program, for reporting the use of this analogy to me and sharing her thoughts about this and other events in the program. The interpretation I give here draws strongly on hers.

Nuclear missiles are based in "silos." On a Trident submarine, which carries twenty-four multiple warhead nuclear missiles, crew members call the part of the submarine where the missiles are lined up in their silos ready for launching "the Christmas tree farm." What could be more bucolic—farms, silos, Christmas trees?

In the ever-friendly, even romantic world of nuclear weaponry, enemies "exchange" warheads; one missile "takes out" another; weapons systems can "marry up"; "coupling" is sometimes used to refer to the wiring between mechanisms of warning and response, or to the psychopolitical links between strategic (intercontinental) and theater (European-based) weapons. The patterns in which a MIRVed missile's nuclear warheads land is known as a "footprint."[21] These nuclear explosives are not dropped; a "bus" "delivers" them. In addition, nuclear bombs are not referred to as bombs or even warheads; they are referred to as "reentry vehicles," a term far more bland and benign, which is then shortened to "RVs," a term not only totally abstract and removed from the reality of a bomb but also resonant with the image of the recreational vehicles of the ideal family vacation.

These domestic images must be more than simply one more form of distancing, one more way to remove oneself from the grisly reality behind the words; ordinary abstraction is adequate to that task. Something else, something very peculiar, is going on here. Calling the pattern in which bombs fall a "footprint" almost seems a willful distorting process, a playful, perverse refusal of accountability—because to be accountable to reality is to be unable to do this work.

These words may also serve to domesticate, to *tame* the wild and uncontrollable forces of nuclear destruction. The metaphors minimize; they are a way to make phenomena that are beyond what the mind can encompass smaller and safer, and thus they are a way of gaining mastery over the unmasterable. The fire-breathing dragon under the bed, the one who threatens to incinerate your family, your town, your planet, becomes a pet you can pat.

Using language evocative of everyday experiences also may simply serve to make the nuclear strategic community more comfortable with what they are doing. "PAL" (permissive action links) is the carefully constructed, friendly acronym for the electronic system designed to prevent the unauthorized firing of nuclear warheads. "BAMBI" was the acronym developed for an early version of an antiballistic missile system (for Ballistic Missile Boost Intercept). The president's Annual Nuclear Weapons Stockpile Memorandum, which outlines both short- and long-range plans for production of new nuclear weapons, is benignly referred to

[21] MIRV stands for "multiple independently targetable re-entry vehicles." A MIRVed missile not only carries more than one warhead; its warheads can be aimed at different targets.

as "the shopping list." The National Command Authorities choose from a "menu of options" when deciding among different targeting plans. The "cookie cutter" is a phrase used to describe a particular model of nuclear attack. Apparently it is also used at the Department of Defense to refer to the neutron bomb.[22]

The imagery that domesticates, that humanizes insentient weapons, may also serve, paradoxically, to make it all right to ignore sentient human bodies, human lives.[23] Perhaps it is possible to spend one's time thinking about scenarios for the use of destructive technology and to have human bodies remain invisible in that technological world precisely because that world itself now *includes* the domestic, the human, the warm, and playful—the Christmas trees, the RVs, the affectionate pats. It is a world that is in some sense complete unto itself; it even includes death and loss. But it is weapons, not humans, that get "killed." "Fratricide" occurs when one of your warheads "kills" another of your own warheads. There is much discussion of "vulnerability" and "survivability," but it is about the vulnerability and survival of weapons systems, not people.

Male birth and creation

There is one set of domestic images that demands separate attention—images that suggest men's desire to appropriate from women the power of giving life and that conflate creation and destruction. The bomb project is rife with images of male birth.[24] In December 1942, Ernest Lawrence's

[22] Henry T. Nash, "The Bureaucratization of Homicide," *Bulletin of Atomic Scientists* (April 1980), reprinted in E. P. Thompson and Dan Smith, eds., *Protest and Survive* (New York: Monthly Review Press, 1981), 159. The neutron bomb is notable for the active political contention that has occurred over its use and naming. It is a small warhead that produces six times the prompt radiation but slightly less blast and heat than typical fission warheads of the same yield. Pentagon planners see neutron bombs as useful in killing Soviet tank crews while theoretically leaving the buildings near the tanks intact. Of course, the civilians in the nearby buildings, however, would be killed by the same "enhanced radiation" as the tank crews. It is this design for protecting property while killing civilians along with soldiers that has led people in the antinuclear movement to call the neutron bomb "the ultimate capitalist weapon." However, in official parlance the neutron bomb is not called a weapon at all; it is an "enhanced radiation device." It is worth noting, however, that the designer of the neutron bomb did not conceive of it as an anti-tank personnel weapon to be used against the Russians. Instead, he thought it would be useful in an area where the enemy *did not have* nuclear weapons to use. (Samuel T. Cohen, in an interview on National Public Radio, as reported in Fred Kaplan, "The Neutron Bomb: What It Is, the Way It Works," *Bulletin of Atomic Scientists* [October 1981], 6.)

[23] For a discussion of the functions of imagery that reverses sentient and insentient matter, that "exchange[s] . . . idioms between weapons and bodies," see Elaine Scarry, *The Body in Pain: The Making and Unmaking of the World* (New York: Oxford University Press, 1985), 60–157, esp. 67.

[24] For further discussion of men's desire to appropriate from women the power of giving life and death, and its implications for men's war-making activities, see Dorothy Dinnerstein,

telegram to the physicists at Chicago read, "Congratulations to the new parents. Can hardly wait to see the new arrival."[25] At Los Alamos, the atom bomb was referred to as "Oppenheimer's baby." One of the physicists working at Los Alamos, Richard Feynman, writes that when he was temporarily on leave after his wife's death, he received a telegram saying, "The baby is expected on such and such a day."[26] At Lawrence Livermore, the hydrogen bomb was referred to as "Teller's baby," although those who wanted to disparage Edward Teller's contribution claimed he was not the bomb's father but its mother. They claimed that Stanislaw Ulam was the real father; he had the all important idea and inseminated Teller with it. Teller only "carried it" after that.[27]

Forty years later, this idea of male birth and its accompanying belittling of maternity—the denial of women's role in the process of creation and the reduction of "motherhood" to the provision of nurturance (apparently Teller did not need to provide an egg, only a womb)—seems thoroughly incorporated into the nuclear mentality, as I learned on a subsequent visit to U.S. Space Command in Colorado Springs. One of the briefings I attended included discussion of a new satellite system, the not yet "on line" MILSTAR system.[28] The officer doing the briefing gave an excited recitation of its technical capabilities and then an explanation of the new Unified Space Command's role in the system. Self-effacingly he said, "We'll do the motherhood role—telemetry, tracking, and control—the maintenance."

The Mermaid and the Minotaur (New York: Harper & Row, 1977). For further analysis of male birth imagery in the atomic bomb project, see Evelyn Fox Keller, "From Secrets of Life to Secrets of Death" (paper delivered at the Kansas Seminar, Yale University, New Haven, Conn., November 1986); and Easlea (n. 15 above), 81–116.

[25] Lawrence is quoted by Herbert Childs in *An American Genius: The Life of Ernest Orlando Lawrence* (New York: E. P. Dutton, 1968), 340.

[26] Feynman writes about the telegram in Richard P. Feynman, "Los Alamos from Below," in *Reminiscences of Los Alamos, 1943–1945*, ed. Lawrence Badash, Joseph O. Hirshfelder, and Herbert P. Broida (Dordrecht: D. Reidel Publishing Co., 1980), 130.

[27] Hans Bethe is quoted as saying that "Ulam was the father of the hydrogen bomb and Edward was the mother, because he carried the baby for quite a while" (J. Bernstein, *Hans Bethe: Prophet of Energy* [New York: Basic Books, 1980], 95).

[28] The MILSTAR system is a communications satellite system that is jam resistant, as well as having an "EMP-hardened capability." (This means that the electromagnetic pulse set off by a nuclear explosion would theoretically not destroy the satellites' electronic systems.) There are, of course, many things to say about the sanity and morality of the idea of the MILSTAR system and of spending the millions of dollars necessary to EMP-harden it. The most obvious point is that this is a system designed to enable the United States to fight a "protracted" nuclear war—the EMP-hardening is to allow it to act as a conduit for command and control of successive nuclear shots, long after the initial exchange. The practicality of the idea would also appear to merit some discussion—who and what is going to be communicating to and from after the initial exchange? And why bother to harden it against EMP when all an opponent has to do to prevent the system from functioning is to blow it up, a feat certain to become technologically feasible in a short time? But, needless to say, exploration of these questions was not part of the briefing.

In light of the imagery of male birth, the extraordinary names given to the bombs that reduced Hiroshima and Nagasaki to ash and rubble—"Little Boy" and "Fat Man"—at last become intelligible. These ultimate destroyers were the progeny of the atomic scientists—and emphatically not just any progeny but male progeny. In early tests, before they were certain that the bombs would work, the scientists expressed their concern by saying that they hoped the baby was a boy, not a girl—that is, not a dud.[29] General Grove's triumphant cable to Secretary of War Henry Stimson at the Potsdam conference, informing him that the first atomic bomb test was successful read, after decoding: "Doctor has just returned most enthusiastic and confident that the little boy is as husky as his big brother. The light in his eyes discernible from here to Highhold and I could have heard his screams from here to my farm."[30] Stimson, in turn, informed Churchill by writing him a note that read, "Babies satisfactorily born."[31] In 1952, Teller's exultant telegram to Los Alamos announcing the successful test of the hydrogen bomb, "Mike," at Eniwetok Atoll in the Marshall Islands, read, "It's a boy."[32] The nuclear scientists gave birth to male progeny with the ultimate power of violent domination over female Nature. The defense intellectuals' project is the creation of abstract formulations to control the forces the scientists created—and to participate thereby in their world-creating/destroying power.

The entire history of the bomb project, in fact, seems permeated with imagery that confounds man's overwhelming technological power to destroy nature with the power to create—imagery that inverts men's destruction and asserts in its place the power to create new life and a new world. It converts men's destruction into their rebirth.

William L. Laurence witnessed the Trinity test of the first atomic bomb and wrote: "The big boom came about a hundred seconds after the great flash—the first cry of a new-born world. . . . They clapped their hands as they leaped from the ground—earthbound man symbolising the birth of a new force."[33] Watching "Fat Man" being assembled the day before it was dropped on Nagasaki, he described seeing the bomb as "being fashioned into a living thing."[34] Decades later, General Bruce K. Holloway, the commander in chief of the Strategic Air Command from 1968 to 1972,

[29] The concern about having a boy, not a girl, is written about by Robert Jungk, *Brighter Than a Thousand Suns*, trans. James Cleugh (New York: Harcourt, Brace & Co., 1956), 197.

[30] Richard E. Hewlett and Oscar E. Anderson, *The New World, 1939/46: A History of the United States Atomic Energy Commission*, 2 vols. (University Park: Pennsylvania State University Press, 1962), 1:386.

[31] Winston Churchill, *The Second World War*, vol. 6., *Triumph and Tragedy* (London: Cassell, 1954), 551.

[32] Quoted by Easlea, 130.

[33] Laurence (n. 18 above), 10.

[34] Ibid., 188.

described a nuclear war as involving "a big bang, like the start of the universe."[35]

God and the nuclear priesthood

The possibility that the language reveals an attempt to appropriate ultimate creative power is evident in another striking aspect of the language of nuclear weaponry and doctrine—the religious imagery. In a subculture of hard-nosed realism and hyper-rationality, in a world that claims as a sign of its superiority its vigilant purging of all nonrational elements, and in which people carefully excise from their discourse every possible trace of soft sentimentality, as though purging dangerous nonsterile elements from a lab, the last thing one might expect to find is religious imagery—imagery of the forces that science has been defined in *opposition to*. For surely, given that science's identity was forged by its separation from, by its struggle for freedom from, the constraints of religion, the only thing as unscientific as the female, the subjective, the emotional, would be the religious. And yet, religious imagery permeates the nuclear past and present. The first atomic bomb test was called Trinity—the unity of the Father, the Son, and the Holy Spirit, the male forces of Creation. The imagery is echoed in the language of the physicists who worked on the bomb and witnessed the test: "It was as though we stood at the first day of creation." Robert Oppenheimer thought of Krishna's words to Arjuna in the *Bhagavad Gita:* "I am become Death, the Shatterer of Worlds."[36]

Perhaps most astonishing of all is the fact that the creators of strategic doctrine actually refer to members of their community as "the nuclear priesthood." It is hard to decide what is most extraordinary about this: the easy arrogance of their claim to the virtues and supernatural power of the priesthood; the tacit admission (*never* spoken directly) that rather than being unflinching, hard-nosed, objective, empirically minded scientific describers of reality, they are really the creators of dogma; or the extraordinary implicit statement about who, or rather what, has become god. If this new priesthood attains its status through an inspired knowledge of nuclear weapons, it gives a whole new meaning to the phrase "a mighty fortress is our God."

[35] From a 1985 interview in which Holloway was explaining the logic of a "decapitating" strike against the Soviet leadership and command and control systems—and thus how nuclear war would be different from World War II, which was a "war of attrition," in which transportation, supply depots, and other targets were hit, rather than being a "big bang" (Daniel Ford, "The Button," *New Yorker Magazine* 61, no. 7 [April 8, 1985], 49).

[36] Jungk, 201.

Stage 2: Learning to speak the language

Although I was startled by the combination of dry abstraction and counter-intuitive imagery that characterizes the language of defense intellectuals, my attention and energy were quickly focused on decoding and learning to speak it. The first task was training the tongue in the articulation of acronyms.

Several years of reading the literature of nuclear weaponry and strategy had not prepared me for the degree to which acronyms littered all conversations, nor for the way in which they are used. Formerly, I had thought of them mainly as utilitarian. They allow you to write or speak faster. They act as a form of abstraction, removing you from the reality behind the words. They restrict communication to the initiated, leaving all others both uncomprehending and voiceless in the debate.

But, being at the Center, hearing the defense analysts use the acronyms, and then watching as I and others in the group started to fling acronyms around in our conversation revealed some additional, unexpected dimensions.

First, in speaking and hearing, a lot of these terms can be very sexy. A small supersonic rocket "designed to penetrate any Soviet air defense" is called a SRAM (for short-range attack missile). Submarine-launched cruise missiles are not referred to as SLCMs, but "slick'ems." Ground-launched cruise missiles are "glick'ems." Air-launched cruise missiles are not sexy but magical—"alchems" (ALCMs) replete with the illusion of turning base metals into gold.

TACAMO, the acronym used to refer to the planes designed to provide communications links to submarines, stands for "take charge and move out." The image seems closely related to the nicknames given to the new guidance systems for "smart weapons"—"shoot and scoot" or "fire and forget."

Other acronyms work in other ways. The plane in which the president supposedly will be flying around above a nuclear holocaust, receiving intelligence and issuing commands for the next bombing, is referred to as "kneecap" (for NEACP—National Emergency Airborne Command Post). The edge of derision suggested in referring to it as "kneecap" mirrors the edge of derision implied when it is talked about at all, since few believe that the president really would have the time to get into it, or that the communications systems would be working if he were in it, and some might go so far as to question the usefulness of his being able to direct an extended nuclear war from his kneecap even if it were feasible. (I never heard the morality of this idea addressed.) But it seems to me that speaking about it with that edge of derision is *exactly* what allows it to be spoken about and seriously discussed at all. It is the very ability to make fun of a concept that makes it possible to work with it rather than reject it outright.

In other words, what I learned at the program is that talking about nuclear weapons is fun. I am serious. The words are fun to say; they are racy, sexy, snappy. You can throw them around in rapid-fire succession. They are quick, clean, light; they trip off the tongue. You can reel off dozens of them in seconds, forgetting about how one might just interfere with the next, not to mention with the lives beneath them.

I am not describing a phenomenon experienced only by the perverse, although the phenomenon itself may be perverse indeed. Nearly everyone I observed clearly took pleasure in using the words. It mattered little whether we were lecturers or students, hawks or doves, men or women—we all learned it, and we all spoke it. Some of us may have spoken with a self-consciously ironic edge, but the pleasure was there nonetheless.

Part of the appeal was the thrill of being able to manipulate an arcane language, the power of entering the secret kingdom, being someone in the know. It is a glow that is a significant part of learning about nuclear weaponry. Few know, and those who do are powerful. You can rub elbows with them, perhaps even be one yourself.

That feeling, of course, does not come solely from the language. The whole set-up of the summer program itself, for example, communicated the allures of power and the benefits of white male privileges. We were provided with luxurious accommodations, complete with young black women who came in to clean up after us each day; generous funding paid not only our transportation and food but also a large honorarium for attending; we met in lavishly appointed classrooms and lounges. Access to excellent athletic facilities was guaranteed by a "Temporary Privilege Card," which seemed to me to sum up the essence of the experience. Perhaps most important of all were the endless allusions by our lecturers to "what I told John [Kennedy]" and "and then Henry [Kissinger] said," or the lunches where we could sit next to a prominent political figure and listen to Washington gossip.

A more subtle, but perhaps more important, element of learning the language is that, when you speak it, you feel in control. The experience of mastering the words infuses your relation to the material. You can get so good at manipulating the words that it almost feels as though the whole thing is under control. Learning the language gives a sense of what I would call cognitive mastery; the feeling of mastery of technology that is finally *not* controllable but is instead powerful beyond human comprehension, powerful in a way that stretches and even thrills the imagination.

The more conversations I participated in using this language, the less frightened I was of nuclear war. How can learning to speak a language have such a powerful effect? One answer, I believe, is that the *process* of learning the language is itself a part of what removes you from the reality of nuclear war.

I entered a world where people spoke what amounted to a foreign language, a language I had to learn if we were to communicate with one another. So I became engaged in the challenge of it—of decoding the acronyms and figuring out which were the proper verbs to use. My focus was on the task of solving the puzzles, developing language competency—not on the weapons and wars behind the words. Although my interest was in thinking about nuclear war and its prevention, my energy was elsewhere.

By the time I was through, I had learned far more than a set of abstract words that refers to grisly subjects, for even when the subjects of a standard English and nukespeak description seem to be the same, they are, in fact, about utterly different phenomena. Consider the following descriptions, in each of which the subject is the aftermath of a nuclear attack:

> Everything was black, had vanished into the black dust, was destroyed. Only the flames that were beginning to lick their way up had any color. From the dust that was like a fog, figures began to loom up, black, hairless, faceless. They screamed with voices that were no longer human. Their screams drowned out the groans rising everywhere from the rubble, groans that seemed to rise from the very earth itself.[37]

> [You have to have ways to maintain communications in a] nuclear environment, a situation bound to include EMP blackout, brute force damage to systems, a heavy jamming environment, and so on.[38]

There are no ways to describe the phenomena represented in the first with the language of the second. Learning to speak the language of defense analysts is not a conscious, cold-blooded decision to ignore the effects of nuclear weapons on real live human beings, to ignore the sensory, the emotional experience, the human impact. It is simply learning a new language, but by the time you are through, the content of what you can talk about is monumentally different, as is the perspective from which you speak.

In the example above, the differences in the two descriptions of a "nuclear environment" stem partly from a difference in the vividness of the words themselves—the words of the first intensely immediate and evoca-

[37] Hisako Matsubara, *Cranes at Dusk* (Garden City, N.Y.: Dial Press, 1985). The author was a child in Kyoto at the time the atomic bomb was dropped. Her description is based on the memories of survivors.

[38] General Robert Rosenberg (formerly on the National Security Council staff during the Carter Administration), "The Influence of Policymaking on C³I," Incidental Paper, Seminar on C³I (Cambridge, Mass.: Harvard University, Center for Information Policy Research, Spring 1980), 59.

tive, the words of the second abstract and distancing. The passages also differ in their content; the first describes the effects of a nuclear blast on human beings, the second describes the impact of a nuclear blast on technical systems designed to assure the "command and control" of nuclear weapons. Both of these differences may stem from the difference of perspective: the speaker in the first is a victim of nuclear weapons, the speaker in the second is a user. The speaker in the first is using words to try to name and contain the horror of human suffering all around her; the speaker in the second is using words to ensure the possibility of launching the next nuclear attack. Technostrategic language can be used only to articulate the perspective of the users of nuclear weapons, not that of the victims.[39]

Thus, speaking the expert language not only offers distance, a feeling of control, and an alternative focus for one's energies; it also offers escape—escape from thinking of oneself as a victim of nuclear war. I do not mean this on the level of individual consciousness; it is not that defense analysts somehow convince themselves that they would not be among the victims of nuclear war, should it occur. But I do mean it in terms of the structural position the speakers of the language occupy and the perspective they get from that position. *Structurally*, speaking technostrategic language removes them from the position of victim and puts them in the position of the planner, the user, the actor. From that position, there is neither need nor way to see oneself as a victim; no matter what one deeply knows or believes about the likelihood of nuclear war, and no matter what sort of terror or despair the knowledge of nuclear war's reality might inspire, the speakers of technostrategic language are positionally allowed, even forced, to escape that awareness, to escape viewing nuclear war from the position of the victim, by virtue of their linguistic stance as users, rather than victims, of nuclear weaponry.

Finally, then, I suspect that much of the reduced anxiety about nuclear

[39] Two other writers who have remarked on this division of languages between the "victims" and the professionals (variously named) are Freeman Dyson and Glenn D. Hook. Dyson, in *Weapons and Hope* (New York: Harper & Row, 1984), notes that there are two languages in the current discussion of nuclear weapons, which he calls the language of "the victims"and the language of "the warriors." He sees the resulting problem as being the difficulty the two groups have in communicating with each other and, thus, in appreciating each other's valid concerns. His project, then, is the search for a common language, and a good portion of the rest of the book is directed toward that end. Hook, in "Making Nuclear Weapons Easier to Live With: The Political Role of Language in Nuclearization," *Journal of Peace Research* 22, no. 1 (1985): 67–77, follows Camus in naming the two groups "the victims" and "the executioners." He is more explicit than Dyson about naming these as perspectives, as coming from positions of greater or lesser power, and points out that those with the most power are able to dominate and define the terms in which we speak about nuclear issues, so that no matter who we are, we find ourselves speaking as though we were the users, rather than the victims of nuclear weapons. Although my analysis of perspectives and the ways in which language inscribes relations of power is similar to his, I differ from Hook in finding in this fact one of the sources of the experts' relative lack of fear of nuclear war.

war commonly experienced by both new speakers of the language and long-time experts comes from characteristics of the language itself: the distance afforded by its abstraction; the sense of control afforded by mastering it; and the fact that its content and concerns are that of the users rather than the victims of nuclear weapons. In learning the language, one goes from being the passive, powerless victim to the competent, wily, powerful purveyor of nuclear threats and nuclear explosive power. The enormous destructive effects of nuclear weapons systems become extensions of the self, rather than threats to it.

Stage 3: Dialogue

It did not take very long to learn the language of nuclear war and much of the specialized information it contained. My focus quickly changed from mastering technical information and doctrinal arcana to attempting to understand more about how the dogma was rationalized. Instead of trying, for example, to find out why submarines are so hard to detect or why, prior to the Trident II, submarine-based ballistic missiles were not considered counterforce weapons, I now wanted to know why we really "need" a strategic triad, given submarines' "invulnerability."[40] I also wanted to know why it is considered reasonable to base U.S. military planning on the Soviet Union's military capabilities rather than seriously attempting to gauge what their intentions might be. This standard practice is one I found particularly troubling. Military analysts say that since we cannot know for certain what Soviet intentions are, we must plan our military forces and strategies as if we knew that the Soviets planned to use all of their weapons. While this might appear to have the benefit of prudence, it leads to a major problem. When we ask only what the Soviets *can* do, we quickly come to assume that that is what they *intend* to do. We base our planning on "worst-case scenarios" and then come to believe that we live in a world where vast resources must be committed to "prevent" them from happening.

Since underlying rationales are rarely discussed in the everyday business of defense planning, I had to start asking more questions. At first,

[40] The "strategic triad" refers to the three different modes of basing nuclear warheads: at land, on intercontinental ballistic missiles; at sea, on missiles in submarines; and "in the air," on the Strategic Air Command's bombers. Given that nuclear weapons based on submarines are "invulnerable" (i.e., not subject to attack), since there is not now nor likely to be in the future any reliable way to find and target submarines, many commentators (mostly from outside the community of defense intellectuals) have suggested that the Navy's leg of the triad is all we need to ensure a capacity to retaliate against a nuclear attack. This suggestion that submarine-based missiles are an adequate deterrent becomes especially appealing when it is remembered that the other basing modes—ICBMs and bombers—act as targets that would draw thousands of nuclear attacks to the American mainland in time of war.

although I was tempted to use my newly acquired proficiency in technostrategic jargon, I vowed to speak English. I had long believed that one of the most important functions of an expert language is exclusion—the denial of a voice to those outside the professional community.[41] I wanted to see whether a well-informed person could speak English and still carry on a knowledgeable conversation.

What I found was that no matter how well-informed or complex my questions were, if I spoke English rather than expert jargon, the men responded to me as though I were ignorant, simpleminded, or both. It did not appear to occur to anyone that I might actually be choosing not to speak their language.

A strong distaste for being patronized and dismissed made my experiment in English short-lived. I adapted my everyday speech to the vocabulary of strategic analysis. I spoke of "escalation dominance," "preemptive strikes," and, one of my favorites, "subholocaust engagements." Using the right phrases opened my way into long, elaborate discussions that taught me a lot about technostrategic reasoning and how to manipulate it.

I found, however, that the better I got at engaging in this discourse, the more impossible it became for me to express my own ideas, my own values. I could adopt the language and gain a wealth of new concepts and reasoning strategies—but at the same time as the language gave me access to things I had been unable to speak about before, it radically excluded others. I could not use the language to express my concerns because it was physically impossible. This language does not allow certain questions to be asked or certain values to be expressed.

To pick a bald example: the word "peace" is not a part of this discourse. As close as one can come is "strategic stability," a term that refers to a balance of numbers and types of weapons systems—not the political, social, economic, and psychological conditions implied by the word "peace." Not only is there no word signifying peace in this discourse, but the word "peace" itself cannot be used. To speak it is immediately to brand oneself as a soft-headed activist instead of an expert, a professional to be taken seriously.

If I was unable to speak my concerns in this language, more disturbing still was that I found it hard even to keep them in my own head. I had begun my research expecting abstract and sanitized discussions of nuclear war and had readied myself to replace my words for theirs, to be ever vigilant against slipping into the never-never land of abstraction. But no matter how prepared I was, no matter how firm my commitment to staying aware of the reality behind the words, over and over I found that I could not stay

[41] For an interesting recent discussion of the role of language in the creation of professional power, see JoAnne Brown, "Professional Language: Words That Succeed," *Radical History Review*, no. 34 (1986), 33–51.

connected, could not keep human lives as my reference point. I found I could go for days speaking about nuclear weapons without once thinking about the people who would be incinerated by them.

It is tempting to attribute this problem to qualities of the language, the words themselves—the abstractness, the euphemisms, the sanitized, friendly, sexy acronyms. Then all we would need to do is change the words, make them more vivid; get the military planners to say "mass murder" instead of "collateral damage" and their thinking would change.

The problem, however, is not only that defense intellectuals use abstract terminology that removes them from the realities of which they speak. There *is* no reality of which they speak. Or, rather, the "reality" of which they speak is itself a world of abstractions. Deterrence theory, and much of strategic doctrine altogether, was invented largely by mathematicians, economists, and a few political scientists. It was invented to hold together abstractly, its validity judged by its internal logic. Questions of the correspondence to observable reality were not the issue. These abstract systems were developed as a way to make it possible to "think about the unthinkable"—not as a way to describe or codify relations on the ground.[42]

So the greatest problem with the idea of "limited nuclear war," for example, is not that it is grotesque to refer to the death and suffering caused by *any* use of nuclear weapons as "limited" or that "limited nuclear war" is an abstraction that is disconnected from human reality but, rather, that "limited nuclear war" is itself an abstract conceptual system, designed, embodied, achieved by computer modeling. It is an abstract world in which hypothetical, calm, rational actors have sufficient information to know exactly what size nuclear weapon the opponent has used against which targets, and in which they have adequate command and control to make sure that their response is precisely equilibrated to the attack. In this scenario, no field commander would use the tactical "mini-nukes" at his disposal in the height of a losing battle; no EMP-generated electronic failures, or direct attacks on command and control centers, or human errors would destroy communications networks. Our rational actors would be free of emotional response to being attacked, free of political pressures from the populace, free from madness or despair or any of the myriad other factors that regularly affect human actions and decision making. They would act solely on the basis of a perfectly informed mathematical calculus of megatonnage.

So to refer to "limited nuclear war" is already to enter into a system that is de facto abstract and removed from reality. To use more descriptive

[42] For fascinating, detailed accounts of the development of strategic doctrine, see Fred Kaplan, *The Wizards of Armageddon* (New York: Simon & Schuster, 1983); and Gregg F. Herken, *The Counsels of War* (New York: Alfred A. Knopf, 1985).

language would not, by itself, change that. In fact, I am tempted to say that the abstractness of the entire conceptual system makes descriptive language nearly beside the point. In a discussion of "limited nuclear war," for example, it might make some difference if in place of saying "In a counterforce attack against hard targets collateral damage could be limited," a strategic analyst had to use words that were less abstract—if he had to say, for instance, "If we launch the missiles we have aimed at their missile silos, the explosions would cause the immediate mass murder of 10 million women, men, and children, as well as the extended illness, suffering, and eventual death of many millions more." It is true that the second sentence does not roll off the tongue or slide across one's consciousness quite as easily. But it is also true, I believe, that the ability to speak about "limited nuclear war" stems as much, if not more, from the fact that the term "limited nuclear war" refers to an abstract conceptual system rather than to events that might take place in the real world. As such, there is no need to think about the concrete human realities behind the model; what counts is the internal logic of the system.[43]

This realization that the abstraction was not just in the words but also characterized the entire conceptual system itself helped me make sense of my difficulty in staying connected to human lives. But there was still a piece missing. How is it possible, for example, to make sense of the following paragraph? It is taken from a discussion of a scenario ("regime A") in which the United States and the USSR have revised their offensive weaponry, banned MIRVs, and gone to a regime of single warhead (Midgetman) missiles, with no "defensive shield" (or what is familiarly known as "Star Wars" or SDI):

> The strategic stability of regime A is based on the fact that both sides are deprived of any incentive ever to strike first. Since it takes roughly two warheads to destroy one enemy silo, an attacker must expend two of his missiles to destroy one of the enemy's. A first strike disarms the attacker. The aggressor ends up worse off than the aggressed.[44]

"The aggressor ends up worse off than the aggressed"? The homeland of "the aggressed" has just been devastated by the explosions of, say, a thousand nuclear bombs, each likely to be ten to one hundred times more

[43] Steven Kull's interviews with nuclear strategists can be read to show that on some level, some of the time, some of these men are aware that there is a serious disjunction between their models and the real world. Their justification for continuing to use these models is that "other people" (unnamed, and on asking, unnameable) believe in them and that they therefore have an important reality ("Nuclear Nonsense," *Foreign Policy*, no. 58 [Spring 1985], 28–52).

[44] Charles Krauthammer, "Will Star Wars Kill Arms Control?" *New Republic*, no. 3,653 (January 21, 1985), 12–16.

powerful than the bomb dropped on Hiroshima, and the aggressor, whose homeland is still untouched, "ends up worse off"? How is it possible to think this? Even abstract language and abstract thinking do not seem to be a sufficient explanation.

I was only able to "make sense of it" when I finally asked myself the question that feminists have been asking about theories in every discipline: What is the reference point? Who (or what) is the *subject* here?

In other disciplines, we have frequently found that the reference point for theories about "universal human phenomena" has actually been white men. In technostrategic discourse, the reference point is not white men, it is not human beings at all; it is the weapons themselves. The aggressor thus ends up worse off than the aggressed because he has fewer weapons left; human factors are irrelevant to the calculus of gain and loss.

In "regime A" and throughout strategic discourse, the concept of "incentive" is similarly distorted by the fact that weapons are the subjects of strategic paradigms. Incentive to strike first is present or absent according to a mathematical calculus of numbers of "surviving" weapons. That is, incentive to start a nuclear war is discussed not in terms of what possible military or political ends it might serve but, instead, in terms of numbers of weapons, with the goal being to make sure that you are the guy who still has the most left at the end. Hence, it is frequently stated that MIRVed missiles create strategic instability because they "give you the incentive to strike first." Calculating that two warheads must be targeted on each enemy missile, one MIRVed missile with ten warheads would, in theory, be able to destroy five enemy missiles in their silos; you destroy more of theirs than you have expended of your own. You win the numbers game. In addition, if you do not strike first, it would theoretically take relatively few of their MIRVed missiles to destroy a larger number of your own—so you must, as they say in the business, "use 'em or lose 'em." Many strategic analysts fear that in a period of escalating political tensions, when it begins to look as though war may be inevitable, this combination makes "the incentive to strike first" well nigh irresistible.

Incentive to launch a nuclear war arises from a particular configuration of weapons and their hypothetical mathematical interaction. Incentive can only be so narrowly defined because the referents of technostrategic paradigms are weapons—not human lives, not even states and state power.

The fact that the subjects of strategic paradigms are weapons has several important implications. First, and perhaps most critically, there simply is no way to talk about human death or human societies when you are using a language designed to talk about weapons. Human death simply *is* "collateral damage"—collateral to the real subject, which is the weapons themselves.

Second, if human lives are not the reference point, then it is not only impossible to talk about humans in this language, it also becomes in some sense illegitimate to ask the paradigm to reflect human concerns. Hence, questions that break through the numbing language of strategic analysis and raise issues in human terms can be dismissed easily. No one will claim that the questions are unimportant, but they are inexpert, unprofessional, irrelevant to the business at hand to ask. The discourse among the experts remains hermetically sealed.

The problem, then, is not only that the language is narrow but also that it is seen by its speakers as complete or whole unto itself—as representing a body of truths that exist independently of any other truth or knowledge. The isolation of this technical knowledge from social or psychological or moral thought, or feelings, is all seen as legitimate and necessary. The outcome is that defense intellectuals can talk about the weapons that are supposed to protect particular political entities, particular peoples and their way of life, without actually asking if weapons *can* do it, or if they are the best *way* to do it, or whether they may even damage the entities you are supposedly protecting. It is not that the men I spoke with would say that these are invalid questions. They would, however, simply say that they are separate questions, questions that are outside what they do, outside their realm of expertise. So their deliberations go on quite independently, as though with a life of their own, disconnected from the functions and values they are supposedly to serve.

Finally, the third problem is that this discourse has become virtually the only legitimate form of response to the question of how to achieve security. If the language of weaponry was one competing voice in the discussion, or one that was integrated with others, the fact that the referents of strategic paradigms are only weapons would be of little note. But when we realize that the only language and expertise offered to those interested in pursuing peace refers to nothing but weapons, its limits become staggering, and its entrapping qualities—the way in which, once you adopt it, it becomes so hard to stay connected to human concerns—become more comprehensible.

Stage 4: The terror

As a newcomer to the world of defense analysts, I was continually startled by likeable and admirable men, by their gallows humor, by the bloodcurdling casualness with which they regularly blew up the world while standing and chatting over the coffee pot. I also *heard* the language they spoke—heard the acronyms and euphemisms, and abstractions, heard the imagery, heard the pleasure with which they used it.

Within a few weeks, what had once been remarkable became unnoticeable. As I learned to speak, my perspective changed. I no longer stood outside the impermeable wall of technostrategic language and, once inside, I could no longer see it. Speaking the language, I could no longer really hear it. And once inside its protective walls, I began to find it difficult to get out. The impermeability worked both ways.

I had not only learned to speak a language: I had started to think in it. Its questions became my questions, its concepts shaped my responses to new ideas. Its definitions of the parameters of reality became mine. Like the White Queen, I began to believe six impossible things before breakfast. Not because I consciously believed, for instance, that a "surgically clean counterforce strike" was really possible, but instead because some elaborate piece of doctrinal reasoning I used was already predicated on the possibility of those strikes, as well as on a host of other impossible things.[45]

My grasp on what *I* knew as reality seemed to slip. I might get very excited, for example, about a new strategic justification for a "no first use" policy and spend time discussing the ways in which its implications for our force structure in Western Europe were superior to the older version.[46] And after a day or two I would suddenly step back, aghast that I was so involved with the military justifications for not using nuclear weapons—as though the moral ones were not enough. What I was actually talking about—the mass incineration caused by a nuclear attack—was no longer in my head.

Or I might hear some proposals that seemed to me infinitely superior to the usual arms control fare. First I would work out how and why these proposals were better and then work out all the ways to counter the arguments against them. But then, it might dawn on me that even though these two proposals sounded so different, they still shared a host of assumptions that I was not willing to make (e.g., about the inevitable, eternal conflict of interests between the United States and the USSR, or the desirability of having some form of nuclear deterrent, or the goal of "managing," rather than ending, the nuclear arms race). After struggling to this point of seeing what united both positions, I would first feel as though I had really accomplished something. And then all of a sudden, I would realize that these new insights were things I actually knew *before I ever entered* this community. Apparently, I had since forgotten them, at least functionally, if not absolutely.

I began to feel that I had fallen down the rabbit hole—and it was a struggle to climb back out.

[45] For an excellent discussion of the myriad uncertainties that make it ludicrous to assume the targeting accuracies posited in the notion of "surgically clean counterforce strikes," see Fallows (n. 11 above), chap. 6.

[46] "No first use" refers to the commitment not to be the first side to introduce nuclear weapons into a "conventional" war. The Soviet Union has a "no first use" policy, but the United States does not. In fact, it is NATO doctrine to use nuclear weapons in a conventional war in Western Europe, as a way of overcoming the Warsaw Pact's supposed superiority in conventional weaponry and troop strength.

Conclusions

Suffice it to say that the issues about language do not disappear after you have mastered technostrategic discourse. The seductions remain great. You can find all sorts of ways to seemingly beat the boys at their own game; you can show how even within their own definitions of rationality, most of what is happening in the development and deployment of nuclear forces is wildly irrational. You can also impress your friends and colleagues with sickly humorous stories about the way things really happen on the inside. There is tremendous pleasure in it, especially for those of us who have been closed out, who have been told that it is really all beyond us and we should just leave it to the benevolently paternal men in charge.

But as the pleasures deepen, so do the dangers. The activity of trying to out-reason defense intellectuals in their own games gets you thinking inside their rules, tacitly accepting all the unspoken assumptions of their paradigms. You become subject to the tyranny of concepts. The language shapes your categories of thought (e.g., here it becomes "good nukes" or "bad nukes," not, nukes or no nukes) and defines the boundaries of imagination (as you try to imagine a "minimally destabilizing basing mode" rather than a way to prevent the weapon from being deployed at all).

Yet, the issues of language have now become somewhat less vivid and central to me. Some of the questions raised by the experiences described here remain important, but others have faded and been superseded by new questions. These, while still not precisely the questions of an "insider," are questions I could not have had without being inside, without having access to the knowledge and perspective the inside position affords. Many of my questions now are more practical—which individuals and institutions are actually responsible for the endless "modernization" and proliferation of nuclear weaponry? What role does technostrategic rationality actually play in their thinking? What would a reasonable, genuinely defensive "defense" policy look like? Others are more philosophical. What is the nature of the rationality and "realism" claimed by defense intellectuals for their mode of thinking? What are the many different grounds on which their claims to rationality can be shown to be spurious?

My own move away from a focus on the language is quite typical. Other recent entrants into this world have commented to me that, while it is the cold-blooded, abstract discussions that are most striking at first, within a short time "you get past it—you stop hearing it, it stops bothering you, it becomes normal—and you come to see that the language, itself, is not the problem."

However, I think it would be a mistake to dismiss these early impressions. They can help us learn something about the militarization of the mind, and they have, I believe, important implications for feminist scholars and activists who seek to create a more just and peaceful world.

Mechanisms of the mind's militarization are revealed through both listening to the language and learning to speak it. *Listening*, it becomes clear that participation in the world of nuclear strategic analysis does not necessarily require confrontation with the central fact about military activity—that the purpose of all weaponry and all strategy is to injure human bodies.[47] In fact, as Elaine Scarry points out, participation in military thinking does not require confrontation with, and actually demands the elision of, this reality.[48]

Listening to the discourse of nuclear experts reveals a series of culturally grounded and culturally acceptable mechanisms that serve this purpose and that make it possible to "think about the unthinkable," to work in institutions that foster the proliferation of nuclear weapons, to plan mass incinerations of millions of human beings for a living. Language that is abstract, sanitized, full of euphemisms; language that is sexy and fun to use; paradigms whose referent is weapons; imagery that domesticates and deflates the forces of mass destruction; imagery that reverses sentient and nonsentient matter, that conflates birth and death, destruction and creation—all of these are part of what makes it possible to be radically removed from the reality of what one is talking about and from the realities one is creating through the discourse.[49]

Learning to speak the language reveals something about how thinking can become more abstract, more focused on parts disembedded from their context, more attentive to the survival of weapons than the survival of human beings. That is, it reveals something about the process of militarization—and the way in which that process may be undergone by man or woman, hawk or dove.

Most often, the act of learning technostrategic language is conceived of as an additive process: you add a new set of vocabulary words; you add the reflex ability to decode and use endless numbers of acronyms; you add some new information that the specialized language contains; you add the conceptual tools that will allow you to "think strategically." This additive view appears to be held by defense intellectuals themselves; as one said to

[47] For an eloquent and graphic exploration of this point, see Scarry (n. 23 above), 73.

[48] Scarry catalogs a variety of mechanisms that serve this purpose (ibid., 60–157). The point is further developed by Sara Ruddick, "The Rationality of Care," in *Thinking about Women, War, and the Military*, ed. Jean Bethke Elshtain and Sheila Tobias (Totowa, N.J.: Rowman & Allanheld, in press).

[49] My discussion of the specific ways in which this discourse creates new realities is in the next part of this project, entitled, "The Emperor's New Armor." I, like many other social scientists, have been influenced by poststructuralist literary theory's discussion of deconstructing texts, point of view, and narrative authority within texts, and I take the language and social practice of the defense intellectuals as a text to be read in this way. For a classic introduction to this literature, see Josue Harari, ed., *Textual Strategies: Perspectives in Post-structuralist Criticism* (Ithaca, N.Y.: Cornell University Press, 1979); and Jacques Derrida, *Of Grammatology* (Baltimore: Johns Hopkins University Press, 1976).

me, "Much of the debate is in technical terms—learn it, and decide whether it's relevant later." This view also appears to be held by many who think of themselves as antinuclear, be they scholars and professionals attempting to change the field from within, or public interest lobbyists and educational organizations, or some feminist antimilitarists.[50] Some believe that our nuclear policies are so riddled with irrationality that there is a lot of room for well-reasoned, well-informed arguments to make a difference; others, even if they do not believe that the technical information is very important, see it as necessary to master the language simply because it is too difficult to attain public legitimacy without it. In either case, the idea is that you add the expert language and information and proceed from there.

However, I have been arguing throughout this paper that learning the language is a transformative, rather than an additive, process. When you choose to learn it you enter a new mode of thinking—a mode of thinking not only about nuclear weapons but also, de facto, about military and political power and about the relationship between human ends and technological means.

Thus, those of us who find U.S. nuclear policy desperately misguided appear to face a serious quandary. If we refuse to learn the language, we are virtually guaranteed that our voices will remain outside the "politically relevant" spectrum of opinion. Yet, if we do learn and speak it, we not only severely limit what we can say but we also invite the transformation, the militarization, of our own thinking.

I have no solutions to this dilemma, but I would like to offer a few thoughts in an effort to reformulate its terms. First, it is important to recognize an assumption implicit in adopting the strategy of learning the language. When we assume that learning and speaking the language will give us a voice recognized as legitimate and will give us greater political influence, *we are assuming that the language itself actually articulates the criteria and reasoning strategies upon which nuclear weapons development and deployment decisions are made.* I believe that this is largely an illusion. Instead, I want to suggest that technostrategic discourse functions more as a gloss, as an ideological curtain behind which the actual reasons for these decisions hide. That rather than informing and shaping decisions, it far more often functions as a legitimation for political outcomes that have occurred for utterly different reasons. If this is true, it raises some serious questions about the extent of the political returns we might get from using technostrategic discourse, and whether they can ever balance out the potential problems and inherent costs.

[50] Perhaps the most prominent proponent of this strategy is Sheila Tobias. See, e.g., "Demystifying Defense: Closing the Knowledge Gap," *Social Policy* 13, no. 3 (1983): 29–32; and Sheila Tobias, Peter Goudinoff, Stefan Leader, and Shelah Leader, *What Kinds of Guns Are They Buying for Your Butter?* (New York: William Morrow & Co., 1982).

I do not, however, want to suggest that none of us should learn the language. I do not believe that this language is well suited to achieving the goals desired by antimilitarists, yet at the same time, I, for one, have found the experience of learning the language useful and worthwhile (even if at times traumatic). The question for those of us who do choose to learn it, I think, is what use are we going to make of that knowledge?

One of the most intriguing options opened by learning the language is that it suggests a basis upon which to challenge the legitimacy of the defense intellectuals' dominance of the discourse on nuclear issues. When defense intellectuals are criticized for the cold-blooded inhumanity of the scenarios they plan, their response is to claim the high ground of rationality; they are the only ones whose response to the existence of nuclear weapons is objective and realistic. They portray those who are radically opposed to the nuclear status quo as irrational, unrealistic, too emotional. "Idealistic activists" is the pejorative they set against their own hard-nosed professionalism.

Much of their claim to legitimacy, then, is a claim to objectivity born of technical expertise and to the disciplined purging of the emotional valences that might threaten their objectivity. But if the surface of their discourse—its abstraction and technical jargon—appears at first to support these claims, a look just below the surface does not. There we find currents of homoerotic excitement, heterosexual domination, the drive toward competency and mastery, the pleasures of membership in an elite and privileged group, the ultimate importance and meaning of membership in the priesthood, and the thrilling power of becoming Death, shatterer of worlds. How is it possible to hold this up as a paragon of cool-headed objectivity?

I do not wish here to discuss or judge the holding of "objectivity" as an epistemological goal. I would simply point out that, as defense intellectuals rest their claims to legitimacy on the untainted rationality of their discourse, their project fails according to its own criteria. Deconstructing strategic discourse's claims to rationality is, then, in and of itself, an important way to challenge its hegemony as the sole legitimate language for public debate about nuclear policy.

I believe that feminists, and others who seek a more just and peaceful world, have a dual task before us—a deconstructive project and a reconstructive project that are intimately linked.[51] Our deconstructive task requires close attention to, and the dismantling of, technostrategic discourse. The dominant voice of militarized masculinity and decontextualized rationality speaks so loudly in our culture, it will remain difficult for any other voices to be heard until that voice loses some of its power to

[51] Harding and Hintikka, eds. (n. 5 above), ix–xix, esp. x.

define what we hear and how we name the world—until that voice is delegitimated.

Our reconstructive task is a task of creating compelling alternative visions of possible futures, a task of recognizing and developing alternative conceptions of rationality, a task of creating rich and imaginative alternative voices—diverse voices whose conversations with each other will invent those futures.

Center for Psychological Studies in the Nuclear Age
Harvard University Medical School

THE DAUGHTER'S SEDUCTION: SEXUAL VIOLENCE AND LITERARY HISTORY

CHRISTINE FROULA

> A still, small voice has warned me again to postpone the description of hysteria. [FREUD to Fliess, January 1, 1896][1]

> I felt sorry for mama. Trying to believe his story kilt her. [ALICE WALKER'S Celie][2]

In her speech before the London/National Society for Women's Service on January 21, 1931, Virginia Woolf figured the woman novelist as a fisherwoman who lets the hook of her imagination down into the depths "of the world that lies submerged in our unconscious being." Feeling a violent jerk, she pulls the line up short, and the "imagination comes to the top in a state of fury":

I thank Paul Wallich, Elizabeth Abel, Margaret Ferguson, Margaret Homans, Patricia Joplin, Claire Kahane, Adrienne Munich, Julie Rivkin, and Patricia Spacks for helpful readings and comments.

[1] Sigmund Freud, *The Origins of Psychoanalysis: Letters to Wilhelm Fliess, Drafts and Notes: 1887–1902*, ed. Marie Bonaparte, Anna Freud, and Ernst Kris, trans. Eric Mosbacher and James Strachey (New York: Basic Books, 1954), 141; hereafter cited in the text as *Origins*.

[2] Alice Walker, *The Color Purple* (New York: Harcourt Brace Jovanovich, 1982), 15; hereafter cited in the text as *Color*.

This essay originally appeared in *Signs*, vol. 11, no. 4, Summer 1986.

> Good heavens she cries—how dare you interfere with me. . . . And I—that is the reason—have to reply, "My dear you were going altogether too far. Men would be shocked." Calm yourself. . . . In fifty years I shall be able to use all this very queer knowledge that you are ready to bring me. But not now. You see I go on, trying to calm her, I cannot make use of what you tell me—about women's bodies for instance—their passions—and so on, because the conventions are still very strong. If I were to overcome the conventions I should need the courage of a hero, and I am not a hero. . . .
>
> Very well says the imagination, dressing herself up again in her petticoat and skirts. . . . We will wait another fifty years. But it seems to me a pity.[3]

Woman's freedom to tell her stories—and indeed, as this fable shows, to know them fully herself—would come, Woolf went on to predict, once she is no longer the dependent daughter, wife, and servant. Given that condition, Woolf envisioned "a step upon the stair": "You will hear somebody coming. You will open the door. And then—this at least is my guess—there will take place between you and some one else the most interesting, exciting, and important conversation that has ever been heard" (*Pargiters*, xliv).

But that was to be in "fifty years." In 1931, Woolf still felt a silence even within all the writing by women that she knew—even, indeed, within her own. Woolf's fable of silences that go unheard within women's writing points to a violence that is all the more powerful for being nearly invisible, and it interprets women's silence in literary history as an effect of repression, not of absence. In this essay, I will explore the literary history implied by Woolf's fisherwoman image, reading it backward, through Homer and Freud, to elucidate the "conventions" that bound her imagination; and forward, to contemporary works by women that fulfill Woolf's "guess" that women would soon break a very significant silence. Drawing upon feminist analyses of Freud's discovery and rejection of the seduction theory of hysteria, I will argue that the relations of literary daughters and fathers resemble in some important ways the model developed by Judith Herman and Lisa Hirschman to describe the family situations of incest victims: a dominating, authoritarian father; an absent, ill, or complicitous mother; and a daughter who, prohibited by her father from speaking about the abuse, is unable to sort out her contradictory

[3] Virginia Woolf, *The Pargiters: The Novel-Essay Portion of "The Years,"* ed. Mitchell A. Leaska (New York: Harcourt Brace Jovanovich, 1978), xxxviii–xxxix. See also Woolf's *A Room of One's Own* (New York: Harcourt, Brace & World, 1929), 5–6, and "Professions for Women" (written in 1932) in *The Death of the Moth and Other Essays* (New York: Harcourt Brace Jovanovich, 1942), 240–41.

feelings of love for her father and terror of him, of desire to end the abuse and fear that if she speaks she will destroy the family structure that is her only security.[4] By aligning a paradigmatic father-daughter dialogue in Homer's *Iliad* with Freud's dialogue with the hysterics, we can grasp the outline of what I shall call the hysterical cultural script: the cultural text that dictates to males and females alike the necessity of silencing woman's speech when it threatens the father's power. This silencing insures that the cultural daughter remains a daughter, her power suppressed and muted; while the father, his power protected, makes culture and history in his own image. Yet, as the hysterics' speech cured their symptoms, so women, telling stories formerly repressed, have begun to realize the prediction of Woolf's fisherwoman. Maya Angelou's *I Know Why the Caged Bird Sings* (1969) and Alice Walker's *The Color Purple* (1982) exemplify the breaking of women's forbidden stories into literary history—an event that reverberates far beyond their heroes' individual histories to reshape our sense of our cultural past and its possible future directions.

Cultural fathers and daughters: Some interesting conversations

What is the fisherwoman's story, the one that got away? The answer I wish to pursue begins with the earliest conversation between man and woman in our literary tradition, that between Helen and Priam in the *Iliad*, book 3. Although readers tend to remember the Helen of the *Iliad* as silent—beauty of body her only speech—the text reveals not Helen's silence but her silen*cing*. As they stand upon the city wall gazing down at the battlefield, the Trojan king and patriarch Priam asks Helen to point out to him the Greek heroes whose famous names he knows. Her answer exceeds Priam's request:

> "Revere you as I do,
> I dread you, too, dear father. Painful death
> would have been sweeter for me, on that day
> I joined your son, and left my bridal chamber,
> my brothers, my grown child, my childhood friends!
> But no death came, though I have pined and wept.

[4] See Judith Lewis Herman with Lisa Hirschman, *Father-Daughter Incest* (Cambridge, Mass.: Harvard University Press, 1981), esp. chaps. 1, 4–7. For a history of twentieth-century sociological scholarship on incest, see pp. 9–21. My reading of women's literary history augments Harold Bloom's model of male literary history as oedipal family romance. On the same question, see Sandra M. Gilbert's "Notes toward a Literary Daughteronomy," *Critical Inquiry* 11, no. 3 (1985): 355–84.

> Your question, now: yes, I can answer it:
> that man is Agamemnon, son of Atreus,
> lord of the plains of Argos, ever both
> a good king and a formidable soldier—
> brother to the husband of a wanton . . .
> or was that life a dream?"[5]

Helen first invokes her own fear of and reverence for Priam. But this daughterly homage to her cultural father only frames her expression of her longing for her former life and companions. Helen, however, is powerless to escape the male war economy that requires her presence to give meaning to its conflicts, and so she translates her desire for her old life into a death wish that expresses at once culturally induced masochism and the intensity of her resistance to her own entanglement in the warriors' plot.

Priam appears to reply only to the words that answer his query:

> The old man gazed and mused and softly cried:
> "O fortunate son of Atreus! Child of destiny,
> O happy soul! How many sons of Akhaia
> serve under you! In the old days once I went
> into the vineyard country of Phrygia
> and saw the Phrygian host on nimble ponies,
>
> . . . .
>
> And they allotted me as their ally
> my place among them when the Amazons
> came down, those women who were fighting men;
> but that host never equaled this,
> the army of the keen-eyed men of Akhaia."
>
> [*Iliad*, 74]

Priam seems not to notice Helen's misery as he turns to imaginary competition with the admired and envied Agamemnon. What links his speech to Helen's, however, is the extraordinary fact that the occasion he invokes as his most memorable experience of troops arrayed for battle is a battle against the Amazons. That Amazons come to his mind suggests that, on some level, he *has* heard Helen's desires. Priam's speech recapitulates his conflict with Helen, and hers with Greek culture, as an archetypal conflict between male and female powers. Significantly, Priam does not say which of these forces triumphed. But in leaving the action suspended, he connects past with present, the Amazons' challenge with this moment's conflict between his desires and Helen's, who, merely in having desires that

[5] *The Iliad* of Homer, trans. Robert Fitzgerald (New York: Doubleday & Co., 1974), 73; hereafter cited in the text as *Iliad*.

would interfere with her role as battle prize, becomes for Priam the Amazon.

What does it mean that Helen should become the Amazon in Priam's imagination? Page duBois and William Blake Tyrrell analyze the Amazon myth as a representation of female power that has escaped the bounds within which Greek culture, specifically the marriage structure, strives to contain it.[6] The Amazon myth, Tyrrell writes, is about daughters, warriors, and marriage. It projects male fear that women will challenge their subordinate status in marriage and with it the rule of the father. In Varro's account of the mythology of Athens's origins, the female citizens of Athens were, under Cecrops, dispossessed of their social and political authority after they banded together to vote for Athena as their city's presiding deity and brought down Poseidon's jealous wrath: "'They could no longer cast a vote, no new-born child would take the mother's name,' . . . [and] they are no longer called Athenians but daughters of Athenians."[7] From the Greek woman's lifelong role of daughter, her deprivation of political, economic, and social power, the Amazon myth emerges as "the specter of daughters who refuse their destiny and fail to make the accepted transition through marriage to wife and motherhood" (*Amazons*, 65). Such unruly daughters threatened to be "rivals of men," "opposed or antithetical to the male as father" (*Amazons*, 83). Becoming a rival in the male imagination, the daughter also becomes a warrior—as Helen does to Priam, as Clytemnestra does to Apollo when, in the *Eumenides*, he laments that Agamemnon was not cut down by an Amazon instead of by her, as Dido does to Aeneas in his premonitory conflation of her with Penthesilea in *Aeneid* 1. These allusions suggest that the Amazon figure, a figment of the male imagination, expresses male desire to contain the threat of a female uprising within the arena of the battlefield; that is, to transform the invisible threat of female revolt into a clear and present danger that males might then band together to combat in the regulated violence of war. In linking Helen with the Amazons, Priam dramatizes the threat that female desire poses to the male war culture predicated on its subjugation. Their conversation replicates the larger design of Homer's epic, which, being "his" story, not hers, turns the tale of a woman's abduction and silencing into the story of a ten-year war between two male cultures. Priam's battle with the Amazons remains suspended in his speech because that battle has

[6] Page duBois, *Centaurs and Amazons: Women and the Pre-History of the Great Chain of Being* (Ann Arbor: University of Michigan Press, 1982); and William Blake Tyrrell, *Amazons: A Study in Athenian Mythmaking* (Baltimore: Johns Hopkins University Press, 1984); cited in the text as *Amazons*. DuBois writes that marriage, "in Lévi-Strauss' sense, the exchange of women between men of the same kind, was culture for the Greeks" (41).

[7] Tyrrell, p. 29, citing Simon Pembroke, "Women in Charge: The Function of Alternatives in Early Greek Tradition and the Ancient Idea of Matriarchy," *Journal of the Warburg and Courtauld Institutes* 30 (1967): 26–27.

not ended. But in this conversation, it is Priam, the cultural father, who triumphs, while Helen's story, by his refusal to hear it, becomes the repressed but discernible shadow of Priam's own.

Helen's exchange with Priam is one skirmish in her culture's war against the Amazons, and a subsequent conversation between Helen and Aphrodite depicts another battle in the form of a cultural daughter's seduction. Here, Helen opposes Aphrodite's demand that she join Paris in bed while the battle rages outside: "'O immortal madness, / why do you have this craving to seduce me? / . . . Go take your place beside Alexandros! / . . . Be / unhappy for him, shield him, till at last / he marries you—or, as he will, enslaves you. / I shall not join him there!'" (*Iliad*, 81–82). Helen passionately and eloquently resists her cultural fate, but Homer's Olympian magic conquers her. Aphrodite silences Helen and enforces her role as object, not agent, of desire by threatening her: "Better not be so difficult. / . . . I can make hatred for you grow / amid both Trojans and Danaäns, / and if I do, you'll come to a bad end" (*Iliad*, 82).[8] The male-authored goddess, embodying the sublimated social authority of Greek culture, forces Helen to relinquish control over her sexuality to the "higher" power of male culture and, like a complicitous mother, presses her to conform to its rule. Helen easily resists being "seduced," angrily thrusting back upon Aphrodite the role of compliant wife/slave that the goddess recommends to her. But this scene makes no distinction between seduction and rape—between being "led astray" and being sexually violated—for Helen can resist sexual complicity only on pain of being cast out altogether from the social world, which is constructed upon marriage. She can be a faithful wife or a "wanton," a "nightmare," a "whore"; she can be a dutiful daughter or an unruly one. But she cannot act out her own desire as Menelaus and Paris, Agamemnon and Akhilleus, Khryses and Hektor, can theirs. Indeed, if wanton in Troy and wife in the bridal chamber are the only choices her culture allows her, she cannot choose even from these. Whereas Paris can propose to settle the dispute by single combat with Menelaus, or the Trojan elders, seeing Helen on the wall, can murmur "let her go [back to Greece] in the ships / and take her scourge from us" (*Iliad*, 73), there is never a question of Helen's deciding the conflict by choosing between the two men.[9]

[8] Compare Shakespeare's use of magic to quell unruly female desire in *A Midsummer Night's Dream*, in which Amazon power—embodied in Hippolyta, whom Theseus wooed by his sword and won while doing her injuries—also symbolizes disruptions to marriage caused by female solidarity and independent female desire. Shakespeare resolves the conflict between Oberon and Titania over the changeling her votaress left her in favor of patriarchal rule by the violence of a figure: the *magic* flower upon which Oberon's power depends.

[9] Ann L. T. Bergren analyzes Helen's ambiguous status in Greek culture as object of exchange and agent of her own desire. Gorgias, defending Helen, poses three readings of her flight with Paris—abduction by force, persuasion by speech, and capture by love—all of which

Although not literally silenced by Aphrodite's metaphysical violence, Helen, surrendering her sexuality, is simultaneously subdued to her culture's dominant text of male desire. "Brother dear," she tells Hektor,

> dear to a whore, a nightmare of a woman!
> That day my mother gave me to the world
> I wish a hurricane blast had torn me away
> to wild mountains, or into tumbling sea
> to be washed under by a breaking wave,
> before these evil days could come! . . .
>
> [*Iliad*, 152]

Helen's will to escape the warriors' marriage plot here turns against the only object her culture permits: herself. She names herself from its lexicon for wayward daughters and passionately imagines death as her only possible freedom. Using the names her culture provides her, weighted with its judgments, Helen loses power even to name herself, her speech confined between the narrow bounds of patriarchal culture and death. That she imagines her death as an entering into the wild turbulence of nature allegorizes the radical opposition of male culture to female nature which the Greek marriage plot enforces: Helen, the Greeks' most exalted image of woman, is also a powerfully expressive subject who must, because of her power, be violently driven back into nature.[10]

Death failing, Helen fulfills her prescribed role by participating in her culture's metaphysical violence against herself: "You [Hektor] are the one afflicted most / by harlotry in me and by his madness, / our portion, all of misery, given by Zeus / that we might live in song for men to come" (*Iliad*, 153). She sacrifices herself upon the altar of patriarchal art, a willing victim

---

represent her as compelled "not otherwise than if she had been raped" ("Language and the Female in Early Greek Thought," *Arethusa* 16 [1983]: 69–95, esp. 83). But such a defense also denies Helen the agency of her own desire, circumscribing it within the male ethical scheme attendant upon the marriage structure. Priam's exoneration of Helen—"You are not to blame, / I hold the gods to blame" (*Iliad*, 73)—similarly exemplifies the attempt to circumscribe female desire within the male ethical scheme attendant upon the marriage structure, which maintains its eminence in pronouncing her "guilty" or "innocent."

[10] Sherry B. Ortner, "Is Female to Nature as Male Is to Culture?" in *Women, Culture, and Society*, ed. Michelle Zimbalist Rosaldo and Louise Lamphere (Stanford, Calif.: Stanford University Press, 1974), 67–87, argues that childbearing and attendant social responsibilities and psychic structures cause women to be seen as closer to nature than men. Further, as the *Iliad* suggests, the founding texts of Western culture manifest an active antagonism to female desire, social power, and language—in a word, to female culture making. If, as de Beauvoir, Dinnerstein, and others have argued, it is *woman as nature* that male culture seeks to bring under control, the effect of men's and women's equal involvement in "projects of creativity and transcendence" (Ortner, 87) would be not only to dissolve the male culture/female nature dichotomy but to transform the "nature" of culture.

who not only suffers but justifies her culture's violence. (Men too suffer the violence of the Greek marriage plot—Helen's "we" includes Hektor—but whereas Hektor resists Andromakhe's pleas and follows his desire for honor into battle, Helen's and Andromakhe's desires are entirely ineffectual.) If the poem, like the war, seems to glorify Helen, in fact she and all the female characters serve primarily to structure the dynamics of male desire in a culture that makes women the pawns of men's bonds *with each other* and the scapegoats for their broken allegiances. The poem's opening scene portrays woman's role in Greek culture as the silent object of male desire, not the speaker of her own. While Agamemnon and Akhilleus rage eloquently over their battle prizes Khryseis and Briseis, the women themselves do not speak at all. They are as interchangeable as their names make them sound, mere circulating tokens of male power and pride—as Akhilleus's apology to Agamemnon upon rejoining the battle confirms: "Agamemnon, was it better for us / in any way, when we were sore at heart, / to waste ourselves in strife over a girl? / If only Artemis had shot her down / among the ships on the day I made her mine, / after I took Lyrnessos!" (*Iliad*, 459).

The *Iliad* suggests that women's silence in culture is neither a natural nor an accidental phenomenon but a cultural achievement, indeed, a constitutive accomplishment of male culture. In Helen's conversations, Homer writes the silencing of woman into epic history as deliberate, strategic, and necessary—a crucial aspect of the complex struggle that is the epic enterprise. In Helen, the *Iliad* represents the subjugation of female desire to male rule by means of a continuum of violence, from physical abduction to the metaphysical violence that Greek culture exerts against woman's words and wishes. To a greater extent than we have yet realized, Homer's epic is about marriage, daughters, and warriors. It is about the Amazon.

The *Iliad* is an ancient text, and we have moved very far from the world that produced it—a fact often invoked to distance readers from the violence against women in which the poem participates. But if we set Helen's conversations next to a powerful analogue of our century, Sigmund Freud's dialogues with hysterics and with the phenomenon of hysteria, the paradigmatic force of her "abduction" into the cultural father's script becomes apparent. As the *Iliad* tells the story of a woman's abduction as a male war story, so Freud turned the hysterics' stories of sexual abuse into a tale to soothe a father's ear. And just as Priam's repressed fears seep into his speech in his allusion to the Amazons, so Freud's repression of the daughter's story generates symptomatic moments that "chatter through the fingertips" of his psychoanalytic theory.[11]

[11] See Sigmund Freud, *Dora: An Analysis of a Case of Hysteria*, ed. Philip Rieff (New York: Collier, 1963), 96: "He that has eyes to see and ears to hear may convince himself that no

Freud's conversations with hysterical patients began in the 1880s. At first, Freud, unlike Priam, was able to hear his patients' stories, and he found that in every case, analysis elicited an account of sexual abuse suffered in childhood at the hands of a member of the patient's own family—almost always the father, as he belatedly reported.[12] On this evidence, Freud developed his "seduction theory"—the theory that hysterical symptoms have their origin in sexual abuse suffered in childhood, which is repressed and eventually assimilated to later sexual experience. Freud first formulated the seduction theory in a letter to his colleague and confidant Wilhelm Fliess in October 1895, and he presented it to the Vienna psychiatric establishment on April 21, 1896, in a paper titled "The Aetiology of Hysteria." The paper, Freud wrote to Fliess, "met with an icy reception,"[13] summed up in Krafft-Ebing's dismissal of it as "a scientific fairytale" (*Origins*, 167n.). For a time Freud pursued the research by which he hoped to prove the seduction theory, writing to Fliess in December 1896: "My psychology of hysteria will be preceded by the proud words: "*Introite et hic dii sunt* [Enter, for here too are gods]" (*Origins*, 172). His pride in his discovery was shortlived, however, for within a year, he would write again to confide "the great secret which has been slowly dawning on me in recent months. I no longer believe in my *neurotica*" (*Origins*, 215). From this point, Freud went on to found psychoanalytic theory upon the oedipal complex.

Historians of psychoanalysis consider Freud's turn from the seduction theory to the oedipal complex crucial to the development of psychoanalysis. Anna Freud wrote that "keeping up the seduction theory would mean to abandon the Oedipus complex, and with it the whole importance of phantasy life. . . . In fact, I think there would have been no psychoanalysis afterwards."[14] But a more critical reading of Freud's abandonment of his seduction theory has emerged from feminist scholarship over the last decade. Several critics have argued—Luce Irigaray from feminist theory, Alice Miller as well as Herman and Hirschman from clinical evidence, Marie Balmary from a psychoanalytic reading of the "text" of Freud's life

---

mortal can keep a secret. If his lips are silent, he chatters with his finger-tips; betrayal oozes out of him at every pore."

[12] See Sigmund Freud, *New Introductory Lectures on Psychoanalysis*, in *Standard Edition of the Complete Psychological Works*, trans. and ed. James Strachey, 24 vols. (London: Hogarth Press, 1953–74), 22:120n. (editor's note).

[13] Max Schur, *Freud: Living and Dying* (New York: International Universities Press, 1972), 104.

[14] Anna Freud, cited in Jeffrey Moussaieff Masson, *The Assault on Truth: Freud's Suppression of the Seduction Theory* (New York: Farrar, Straus & Giroux, 1984), 113. This view has prevailed among psychoanalysts, but since Freud was already discovering the unconscious, infantile sexuality, and symbolic process in treating hysterics, it does not appear to be well-founded.

and work, Florence Rush and Jeffrey Moussaieff Masson from historical evidence, among others—that Freud turned away from the seduction theory not because it lacked explanatory power but because he was unable to come to terms with what he was the first to discover: the crucial role played in neurosis by the abuse of paternal power.[15]

For purposes of the present argument, the issue is best put in terms of credit or authority: the hysterics, Breuer's and his own, confronted Freud with the problem of whose story to believe, the father's or the daughter's. From the first, Freud identified with the hysterics strongly enough that he could hear what they told him. Yet, although he could trace the etiology of hysteria to sexual abuse suffered in childhood, Freud could not bring himself to draw the conclusion that his evidence presented to him: that the abuser was most often the father. The cases of Anna O., Lucy R., Katharina, Elizabeth von R., and Rosalia H. described in *Studies on Hysteria* all connect symptoms more or less closely with fathers or, in Lucy's case, with a father substitute. In two cases, however, Freud represented the father as an uncle, a misrepresentation that he corrected only in 1924; and his reluctance to implicate the father appears strikingly in a supplemental narrative of an unnamed patient whose physician-father accompanied her during her hypnotic sessions with Freud. When Freud challenged her to acknowledge that "something else had happened which she had not mentioned," she "gave way to the extent of letting fall a single significant phrase; but she had hardly said a word before she stopped, and her old father, who was sitting behind her, began to sob bitterly." Freud concludes: "Naturally I pressed my investigation no further; but I never saw the patient again."[16] Here Freud's sympathies divide: had the father not intruded, Freud undoubtedly would have heard her out as he had Katharina; but, made aware of the father's anguish, he "naturally" cooperated with it even to the extent of repressing from his text the "single significant phrase" that may have held the key to her neurosis.

In larger terms, too, Freud's work on hysteria posed the dilemma of whether to elicit and credit the daughter's story, with which rested, as other cases had shown, his hope of curing her limping walk; or to honor the father's sob, which corroborated even as it silenced the girl's significant word. The list of reasons Freud gave Fliess for abandoning the seduction

[15] See Luce Irigaray, *Speculum de l'autre femme* (Paris: Editions de Minuit, 1974); Alice Miller, *Thou Shalt Not Be Aware: Society's Betrayal of the Child*, trans. Hildegarde Hannum and Hunter Hannum (1981; New York: Farrar, Straus & Giroux, 1984); Herman with Hirschman (n. 4 above), chaps. 1, 4; Marie Balmary, *Psychoanalyzing Psychoanalysis: Freud and the Hidden Fault of the Father*, trans. Ned Lukacher (Baltimore: Johns Hopkins University Press, 1982; originally published in France in 1979), chaps. 5–7; Florence Rush, *The Best Kept Secret: Sexual Abuse of Children* (Englewood Cliffs, N.J.: Prentice-Hall, Inc., 1980), chap. 7; and Masson (n. 14 above).

[16] Sigmund Freud and Marcel Breuer, *Studies on Hysteria*, in *Standard Edition*, 2:100–101n.

theory is, as Balmary points out, not very compelling; indeed, it contradicts the evidence of *Studies on Hysteria*. Freud complains that he cannot terminate the analyses, even though several cases (notably Anna O./Bertha Pappenheim, who was Breuer's patient) are there described as terminating in a lasting cure. He complains of not being able to distinguish between truth and "emotionally charged fiction" in his patients, even though he had linked the vanishing of symptoms with the recovery of traumatic experience through memory—whether narrated with apparent fidelity to literal fact, as in Katharina's case, or in dream imagery, as by Anna O., whom Breuer wrote that he always found "entirely truthful and trustworthy" (*Studies on Hysteria*, 43). And Freud claims to have been frustrated in his attempt to recover the buried trauma, despite his success in some instances. Only one item on the list is upheld by the earlier cases: "the astonishing thing that in every case *my own not excluded*, blame was laid on perverse acts by the father, and realization of the unexpected frequency of hysteria, in every case of which the same thing applied, though it was hardly credible that perverted acts against children were so general."[17]

The problem was precisely that sexual abuse of children by fathers appeared "so general." In the years between conceiving and abandoning the seduction theory, Freud was engaged in his own self-analysis, in which he discovered, through dreams, his own incestuous wishes toward his daughter Mathilde and, through symptoms exhibited by his siblings, the possibility that his father Jakob had abused his children. Jakob himself died on October 23, 1896, initiating in Freud a complex process of mourning that ultimately strengthened his idealization of his father. Freud's dream of Irma's injection, which concerned a patient who shared his daughter Mathilde's name, superimposed a destructive father-daughter relationship upon one between physician and patient. Nor could the father's fault be contained within the bounds of the hysterics' individual histories. Recent research, for example Herman's, has traced many continuities between the problem of father-daughter incest and the dominance of male/paternal authority in society as a whole; Freud too faced implications that would have changed the focus of his work from individual therapy to social criticism. The "icy reception" with which the professional community of fin de siècle Vienna greeted his 1896 lecture, which did not explicitly implicate fathers in hysteria, was indication enough that Freud, if he credited the daughters, would risk sharing their fate of being silenced and ignored. The stakes for Freud were very high, for the fathers who paid him his (at that time meager) living also represented, as had Jakob, the privileged place that Freud, as a male, could himself hope to attain in the culture. Acceding, upon Jakob's death, to the place of the father, he acceded also to

[17] Freud, *Origins*, 215–16. Balmary supplies the italicized phrase, omitted in *Origins*, from the 1975 German edition of the Freud/Fliess correspondence.

the father's text, which gave him small choice but to judge the daughters' stories "hardly credible."

Yet Freud could not easily call in the credit that he had already invested in the daughters' stories. As Jane Gallop notes, he continued to speak of "actual seduction" long after he had supposedly repudiated it, with the difference that he now deflected guilt from the father to, variously, the nurse, the mother, and, by way of the oedipal complex, the child herself.[18] Balmary argues persuasively that Freud's own hysterical symptoms grew more pronounced as he undertook to deny what he was the first to discover, that "the secret of hysteria is the father's hidden fault"; and that the texts documenting his turn to the oedipal complex betray that turn as a symptomatic effort to conceal the father's fault.[19] Seduced by the father's sob story, Freud took upon himself the burden his patients bore of concealing the father's fault in mute symptomology. Hysterics, Freud wrote, suffer from reminiscence.[20] As Priam in his reply to Helen does not forget her words, so Freud in his later writings does not forget the daughter's story but rewrites it as the story of "femininity," attributing to mothers, nurses, and a female "Nature" the damage to female subjectivity and desire wrought by specific historical events.[21] Yet when Freud concludes in "Femininity" that woman has an inferior sense of justice and suggests that the "one technique" she has contributed to culture, the invention of plaiting and weaving, is designed to conceal the shame of her genital lack, it is he who, like Priam, is weaving a cultural text whose obscured but still legible design is to protect the *father* (conceived broadly as general and cultural, that is, as male authority) from suspicion of an insufficiently developed sense of justice. Like Priam, Freud makes subtle war on woman's desire and on the credibility of her language in order to avert its perceived threat to the father's cultural preeminence. If, in doing so, he

[18] Jane Gallop, *The Daughter's Seduction: Feminism and Psychoanalysis* (Ithaca, N.Y.: Cornell University Press, 1982), 144–45. While I have found Gallop's treatment of father/daughter seduction provocative and enlightening, both my approach and the sociological and literary texts I consider place more emphasis than she does on the damaging effects of seduction on the daughter, who is by virtue of age, family role, and gender far weaker than the father.

[19] Balmary powerfully reinterprets the oedipal myth, recovering aspects suppressed in Sophocles' and Freud's accounts that reveal Oedipus's crimes to be an unconscious repetition of his father's, as well as biographical materials, also suppressed, that uncover the sudden, unexplained disappearance of Jakob's second wife Rebecca and the likelihood that Freud was conceived before Jakob married Freud's mother Amalie, his third wife.

[20] Marcel Breuer and Sigmund Freud, "The Mechanism of Hysterical Phenomena," in *Standard Edition*, 2:7.

[21] Feminist critiques of "Female Sexuality," "Femininity," and the Dora case engage the issue of femininity in Freud's treatment of hysteria; see esp. Catherine Clément and Hélène Cixous, *La jeune née* (Paris: UGE, 1975), and the essays collected in *In Dora's Case: Freud—Hysteria—Feminism*, ed. Charles Bernheimer and Claire Kahane (New York: Columbia University Press, 1985).

produces a theory that Krafft-Ebing could have approved, he also composes a genuine "scientific fairytale."

It appears, then, that Freud undertook not to believe the hysterics not because the weight of scientific evidence was on the father's side but because so much was at stake in maintaining the father's credit: the "innocence" not only of particular fathers—Freud's, Freud himself, the hysterics'—but also of the cultural structure that credits male authority at the expense of female authority, reproducing a social and political hierarchy of metaphorical fathers and daughters. The history of the seduction theory shows Freud's genius, but it also shows his seduction by the hysterical cultural script that protects the father's credit, and Freud's consequent inability, not unlike Helen's, the hysterics', or Woolf's fisherwoman's, to bring the story of sexual abuse and silencing to light. When Helen sublimely paints herself and Hektor as willing victims upon the altar of an art that serves the divine plan of Zeus, "father of gods and men," she speaks this cultural script; as Priam does in reminiscing about Amazons; as the hysterics with their bodily reminiscences and Freud with his theory of femininity did; and as Woolf's fisherwoman does, with her imagination gagged and petticoated in deference to the "conventions."

Women's literary history has important continuities with the actual and imaginative histories told by Homer, Freud, and Herman. Woman's cultural seduction is not merely analogous to the physical abuses that Freud's patients claimed to have suffered but *continuous* with them. Herman shows that the abusive or seductive father does serious harm to the daughter's mind as well as to her body, damaging her sense of her own identity and depriving her voice of authority and strength. For the literary daughter—the woman reader/writer as daughter of her culture—the metaphysical violence against women inscribed in the literary tradition, although more subtle and no less difficult to acknowledge and understand, has serious consequences. Metaphysically, the woman reader of a literary tradition that inscribes violence against women is an abused daughter. Like physical abuse, literary violence against women works to privilege the cultural father's voice and story over those of women, the cultural daughters, and indeed to silence women's voices. If Freud had difficulty telling the difference between his patients' histories and their fantasies, the power of such cultural fantasies as Homer's and Freud's to shape their audiences' sense of the world is self-evident.

But the Freud of 1892 understood the power of language to cure. Woolf, we remember, predicted a moment when women would break through the constraints of the cultural text. If the literary family history resembles the histories Freud elicited from his patients, we could expect the cultural daughter's telling of her story to work not only a "cure" of her silence in culture but, eventually, a more radical cure of the hysterical cultural text that entangles both women and men. To explore these possibilities, I will turn to a daughter's text that breaks even as it represents the daughter's hysterical silence, in doing so, crossing images of literal and literary sexual abuse: Maya Angelou's autobiographical *I Know Why the Caged Bird Sings*.

The daughter's story and the father's law

Early in her memoir, Angelou presents a brief but rich *biographia literaria* in the form of a childhood romance: "During these years in Stamps, I met and fell in love with William Shakespeare. He was my first white love. Although I enjoyed and respected Kipling, Poe, Butler, Thackeray and Henley, I saved my young and loyal passion for Paul Lawrence Dunbar, Langston Hughes, James Weldon Johnson and W.E.B. DuBois' 'Litany at Atlanta.' But it was Shakespeare who said, 'When in disgrace with fortune and men's eyes.' It was a state with which I felt myself most familiar. I pacified myself about his whiteness by saying that after all he had been dead so long that it couldn't matter to anyone any more."[22] Maya and her brother Bailey reluctantly abandon their plan to memorize a scene from Shakespeare—"we realized that Momma would question us about the author and that we'd have to tell her that Shakespeare was white, and it wouldn't matter to her whether he was dead or not" (*I Know Why*, 11)—and choose Johnson's "The Creation" instead. This passage, depicting the trials attending those interracial affairs of the mind that Maya must keep hidden from her vigilant grandmother, raises the question of what it means for a female reader and fledgling writer to carry on a love affair with Shakespeare or with male authors in general. While the text overtly confronts and disarms the issue of race, the seduction issue is only glancingly acknowledged. But this literary father-daughter romance resonates quietly alongside Angelou's more disturbing account of the quasi-incestuous rape of the eight-year-old Maya by her mother's lover, Mr. Freeman—particularly by virtue of the line she finds so sympathetic in Shakespeare, "When in disgrace with fortune and men's eyes."

Mr. Freeman's abuse of Maya occurs in two episodes. In the first, her mother rescues her from a nightmare by taking her into her own bed, and Maya then wakes to find her mother gone to work and Mr. Freeman grasping her tightly. The child feels, first, bewilderment and terror: "His right hand was moving so fast and his heart was beating so hard that I was afraid that he would die." When Mr. Freeman subsides, however, so does Maya's fright: "Finally he was quiet, and then came the nice part. He held me so softly that I wished he wouldn't ever let me go. . . . This was

[22] Maya Angelou, *I Know Why the Caged Bird Sings* (New York: Bantam Books, 1971), 11; hereafter cited in the text as *I Know Why*.

probably my real father and we had found each other at last" (*I Know Why*, 61). After the abuse comes the silencing: Mr. Freeman enlists the child's complicity by an act of metaphysical violence, informing her that he will kill her beloved brother Bailey if she tells anyone what "they" have done. For the child, this prohibition prevents not so much telling as asking, for, confused as she is by her conflicting feelings, she has no idea what has happened. One day, however, Mr. Freeman stops her as she is setting out for the library, and it is then that he commits the actual rape on the terrified child, "a breaking and entering when even the senses are torn apart" (*I Know Why*, 65). Again threatened with violence if she tells, Maya retreats to her bed in a silent delirium, but the story emerges when her mother discovers her stained drawers, and Mr. Freeman is duly arrested and brought to trial.

At the trial, the defense lawyer as usual attempts to blame the victim for her own rape. When she cannot remember what Mr. Freeman was wearing, "he snickered as though I had raped Mr. Freeman" (*I Know Why*, 70). His next question, as to whether Mr. Freeman had ever touched her prior to that Saturday, reduces her to confusion because her memory of her own pleasure in being held by him seems to her to implicate her in his crime: "I couldn't say yes and tell them how he had loved me once for a few minutes and how he had held me close. . . . My uncles would kill me and Grandmother Baxter would stop speaking. . . . And all those people in the court would stone me as they had stoned the harlot in the Bible. And mother, who thought I was such a good girl, would be so disappointed" (*I Know Why*, 70–71). An adult can see that the daughter's need for a father's affection does not cancel his culpability for sexually abusing her. But the child cannot resolve the conflict between her desire to tell the truth, which means acknowledging the pleasure she felt when Mr. Freeman gently held her, and her awareness of the social condemnation that would greet this revelation. She knows the cultural script and its hermeneutic traditions, which hold all female pleasure guilty, all too well, and so she betrays her actual experience with a lie: "Everyone in the court knew that the answer had to be No. Everyone except Mr. Freeman and me. . . . I said No" (*I Know Why*, 71). But she chokes on the lie and has to be taken down from the stand. Mr. Freeman is sentenced to a year and a day, but somehow manages to be released that very afternoon; and not long thereafter, he is killed by her Baxter uncles. Hearing of Mr. Freeman's death, Maya is overwhelmed with terror and remorse: "A man was dead because I lied" (*I Know Why*, 72). Taking his death as proof that her words have power to kill, she descends into a silence that lasts for a year. Like Helen's sacrificial speech, Maya's silence speaks the hysterical cultural script: it expresses guilt and anguish at her own aggression against the father and voluntarily sacrifices the cure of truthful words.

Maya's self-silencing recalls the link between sexual violation and silence in the archetypal rape myth of Philomela. Ovid's retelling of the Greek myth entwines rape with incest as Tereus, watching Philomela cajole her father into allowing her to visit her sister Procne, puts himself in her father's place: "He would like to be / Her father at that moment, and if he were / He would be as wicked a father as he is a husband."[23] After the rape, in Ovid's story as in Angelou's, the victim's power of speech becomes a threat to the rapist and another victim of his violence: "Tereus did not kill her. He seized her tongue / With pincers, though it cried against the outrage, / Babbled and made a sound like *Father*, / Till the sword cut it off."[24] The tongue's ambiguous cry connects rape/incest with the sanctioned ownership of daughters by fathers in the marriage structure and interprets Procne's symmetrical violation of killing her son Itys: she becomes a bad mother to her son as Tereus has been a bad father to the daughter entrusted to him. In the suspension wrought by metamorphosis, Tereus becomes a war bird and Procne and Philomela become nightingales whose unintelligible song resembles the hysterics' speech. In silencing herself, Maya—who knows why the caged bird sings—plays all the parts in this cultural drama. She suffers as victim, speaks the father's death, and cuts out her own tongue for fear of its crying "Father."

Maya breaks her silence when a woman befriends her by taking her home and reading aloud to her, then sending her off with a book of poems, one of which she is to recite on her next visit. We are not told which poem it was, but later we find that the pinnacle of her literary achievement at age twelve was to have learned by heart the whole of Shakespeare's *Rape of Lucrece*—nearly two thousand lines. Maya, it appears, emerges from her literal silence into a literary one. Fitting her voice to Shakespeare's words, she writes safe limits around the exclamations of her wounded tongue and in this way is able to reenter the cultural text that her words had formerly disrupted. But if Shakespeare's poem redeems Maya from her hysterical silence, it is also a lover that she embraces at her peril. In Angelou's text, Shakespeare's Lucrece represents that violation of the spirit which

[23] Ovid, *Metamorphoses*, trans. Rolfe Humphries (Bloomington: Indiana University Press, 1955), 144–45. See Patricia Joplin, "The Voice of the Shuttle Is Ours," *Stanford Literature Review* 1 (1984): 25–53 for an excellent study of the complex inscription of cultural violence against women in the Philomela myth.

[24] A parody of castration, this scene, like Priam's thoughts of Amazons, projects the war between the father's desire, represented by the penis/sword, and the daughter's, represented by a phallus-like tongue with power to tell her story. The ambiguity of father figures in Ovid's retelling points to the fact that the father's ownership of his daughter gives him privileged sexual access to her, whether or not he avails himself of it. Herman (n. 4 above), 98 notes that incest victims frequently report that men find their histories arousing, as though they too envy the place of the bad father; see also Susan Brownmiller, who concludes that the cultural taboo against acknowledging the high incidence of father rape arises from the "patriarchal philosophy of sexual private property," of which children are an extension (*Against Our Wills: Men, Women, and Rape* [New York: Simon & Schuster, 1975], 311).

Shakespeare's and all stories of sleeping beauties commit upon the female reader. Maya's feat of memory signals a double seduction: by the white culture that her grandmother wished her black child not to love and by the male culture which imposes upon the rape victim, epitomized in Lucrece, the double silence of a beauty that serves male fantasy and a death that serves male honor.[25] The black child's identification with an exquisite rape fantasy of white male culture violates her reality. Wouldn't everyone be surprised, she muses, "when one day I woke out of my black ugly dream, and my real hair, which was long and blond, would take the place of the kinky mass that Momma wouldn't let me straighten? My light-blue eyes were going to hypnotize them. . . . Because I was really white and because a cruel fairy stepmother, who was understandably jealous of my beauty, had turned me into a too-big Negro girl, with nappy black hair, broad feet, and a space between her teeth that would hold a number two pencil" (*I Know Why*, 2). Maya's fantasy bespeaks her cultural seduction, but Angelou's powerful memoir, recovering the history that frames it, rescues the child's voice from this seduction by telling the prohibited story.

Re-creating the universe

If Angelou presents one woman's emergence from the hysterical cultural text, Alice Walker's *The Color Purple* deepens and elaborates its themes to work a more powerful cure. Published in 1982 (right on schedule with respect to Woolf's prediction), Walker's novel not only portrays a cure of one daughter's hysterical silence but rewrites from the ground up the cultural text that sanctions her violation and dictates her silence. Whereas the memoir form holds Angelou's story within the limits of history, Walker stages her cure in the imaginary spaces of fiction. Yet Walker conceived *The Color Purple* as a historical novel, and her transformation of the daughter's story into a fiction that lays claim to historical truth challenges the foundation of the "conventions," social and cultural, that enforce women's silence.[26] Walker retells the founding story of Western culture from a woman's point of view, and in an important sense, her historical

[25] Maya's identification with Lucrece conceals by revealing, exemplifying Freud's view of the hysterical symptom as "a compromise between two opposite affective and instinctual impulses," one trying to bring to light and the other trying to repress ("Hysterical Phantasies and Their Relation to Bisexuality," in *Standard Edition*, 9:164). Freud posits a conflict between homosexual and heterosexual desire as the symptom's cause, but, as Maya's case shows, the conflictual nature of the symptom is better explained by the social danger in which the victim finds herself. See Coppélia Kahn, "The Rape in Shakespeare's *Lucrece*," *Shakespeare Studies* 9 (1976): 45–72, for the earliest treatment of rape in the poem.

[26] Alice Walker, "Writing *The Color Purple*," in *In Search of Our Mothers' Gardens: Womanist Prose* (New York: Harcourt Brace Jovanovich, 1983), 356.

novel—already celebrated as a landmark in the traditions of Black women's, Black, and women's writing—also stands in the tradition inaugurated by Homer and Genesis. Her hero Celie is a woman reborn to desire and language; and Walker, while not one with Celie as Angelou is with Maya, is a woman writer whom Woolf might well have considered a hero.

The Color Purple tells the story of a fourteen-year-old daughter's rape by her "Pa." It begins in its own prohibition: its first words, inscribed like an epigraph over Celie's letters, are her "Pa"'s warning, "*You better not never tell nobody but God. It'd kill your mammy*" (*Color*, 11). Thus is Celie robbed, in the name of her mother, of her story and her voice. Later, her pa further discredits her when he hands Celie over to Mr. ______ (ironically reduced to generic cultural father), a widower in need of a wife-housekeeper-caretaker of his children, with the warning: "She tell lies" (*Color*, 18). Isolated, ignorant, and confused, Celie follows her pa's prohibition literally, obediently silencing her speech but writing stumblingly of her bewilderment in letters to God: "Dear God, I am fourteen years old. ~~I am~~ I have always been a good girl. Maybe you can give me a sign letting me know what is happening to me" (*Color*, 11).[27] Celie's rape leaves her with guilt that blocks her words. But through her letter writing she is able at once to follow the letter of the father's law and to tell her story, first to that imaginary listener, the God of her father's command, and later, to the friend who saves her from silence, Shug Avery.

These ends are all the more powerful in that they emerge from Celie's seemingly hopeless beginnings. With the first of Celie's two pregnancies by her pa, he forces her to leave school: "He never care that I love it" (*Color*, 19). Celie keeps studying under her younger sister Nettie's tutelage, but the world recedes from her grasp. "Look like nothing she say can git in my brain and stay," Celie writes God. "She try to tell me something bout the ground not being flat. I just say, Yeah, like I know it. I never tell her how flat it look to me" (*Color*, 20). While this passage conveys the pathos of Celie's isolation, it also reveals what will eventually prove the source of her strength, for Celie's eventual emergence from silence, ignorance, and misery depends upon her fidelity to the way things look to her. One important instance is her feeling for her mother, who is too weak and ill to intervene in the incest and who dies soon after Celie's second child is born. "Maybe cause my mama cuss me you think I kept mad at her," Celie tells God. "But I ain't. I felt sorry for mama. Trying to believe his story kilt her" (*Color*, 15).

As Celie never loses her identification with her mother, so she is saved from her isolation by three other women who become her companions and examples and whose voices foil Celie's submissive silence. Sofia, who

[27] Compare the incest victim in Herman's study (n. 4 above) who "wrote private letters to God," 99.

marries Mr. ______'s son Harpo, is at first a problem for Celie, who tells God: "I like Sofia, but she don't act like me at all. If she talking when Harpo and Mr. ______ come in the room, she keep right on. If they ast her where something at, she say she don't know. Keep talking" (*Color*, 42). When Harpo consults her about how to make Sofia mind, Celie advises: "Beat her" (*Color*, 43)—propounding the cultural script of violent male rule in marriage, the only one she knows. But when Sofia angrily confronts Celie, a friendship forms, and Celie begins to abandon her numb allegiance to the father's law. Shug Avery, a brilliant blues singer and Mr. ______'s long-time lover, enters Celie's life when Mr. ______ brings her home ill for Celie to nurse. Like Sofia, Shug talks: "she say whatever come to mind, forgit about polite" (*Color*, 73). Mary Agnes, Harpo's girl friend after Sofia's departure, begins, like Celie, as a relatively weak and silent woman. Yet when she is elected to go ask help from the white warden for Sofia in prison, she returns from her mission battered and bruised, and only after some urging—"Yeah, say Shug, if you can't tell us, who you gon tell, God?" (*Color*, 95)—is she able to tell the others that the warden has raped her. Telling the story, she becomes her own authority, symbolized in her self-naming: when Harpo says, "I love you, Squeak," she replies, "My name Mary Agnes" (*Color*, 95).

Mary Agnes's example is important for Celie, who, until now, has buried her story in her letters. One night soon afterward, when their husbands are away, Shug comes into bed with Celie for warmth and company, and Celie tells her everything: "I cry and cry and cry. Seem like it all come back to me, laying there in Shug arms. . . . Nobody ever love me, I say. She say, I love you, Miss Celie. And then she haul off and kiss me on the mouth. *Um*, she say, like she surprise. . . . Then I feels something real soft and wet on my breast, feel like one of my little lost babies mouth. Way after while, I act like a little lost baby too" (*Color*, 108–9). To know all alone, Balmary writes, is to know as if one did not know. To know with another is conscious knowledge, social knowledge, *con-science*.[28] Celie's telling of her story is an act of knowing-with that breaks the father's law, his prohibition of conscience. Knowing her story with Shug begins to heal Celie's long-hidden wounds of body and voice.

The radical conscience of Walker's novel goes beyond restoring Celie's voice to break down the patriarchal marriage plot that sanctions violence against women. This dismantling begins with another wound when Shug and Celie find the letters from Nettie that Mr. ______ has spitefully hidden since the sisters' separation. From them, Celie learns her lost history: that their father had been lynched when they were babies for having a store that did too well; that their mother, then a wealthy widow, had lost her reason and married a stranger, the man Celie knew as her "Pa";

[28] Balmary (n. 15 above), 159 ff.; see also Herman with Hirschman (n. 4 above), 178 ff.

that he had given Celie's two children to Samuel and Corrine, the missionaries to whom Nettie had also fled; and that, Corrine having died, Samuel, Nettie, and Celie's children are returning to the United States from their African mission. Celie's first response when she finds the intercepted letters is a murderous fury toward fathers both physical and metaphysical. Shug has to disarm her of the razor she is about to use to kill Mr. ______, and the scales fall from her eyes with respect to the God to whom she has been writing: "Dear God, . . . My daddy lynch. My mama crazy. All my little half-brothers and sisters no kin to me. My children not my sister and brother. Pa not pa. You must be sleep" (*Color*, 163).

With Shug's help, Celie is able to translate her murderous rage into powerful speech and to meet Mr. ______ on the battlefield of language. Patriarchal family rule and patriarchal metaphysics break down simultaneously as Shug and Celie leave Mr. ______'s house for Shug's Memphis estate. Celie's self-assertion is met with scorn by Mr. ______: "Shug got talent, he say. She can sing. She got spunk, he say. She can talk to anybody. Shug got looks, he say. She can stand up and be notice. But what you got? You ugly. You skinny. You shape funny. You too scared to open your mouth to people" (*Color*, 186). But Celie's voice gains strength as she comes into possession of her history, and for the first time, she finds words to resist Mr. ______:

> I curse you, I say.
>
> What that mean? he say.
>
> I say, Until you do right by me, everything you touch will crumble.
>
> He laugh. Who you think you is? he say. . . .
>
> A dust devil flew up on the porch between us, fill my mouth with dirt. The dirt say, Anything you do to me, already done to you.
>
> Then I feel Shug shake me. Celie, she say. And I come to myself.
>
> I'm pore, I'm black, I may be ugly and can't cook, a voice say to everything listening. But I'm here.
>
> Amen, say Shug. Amen, amen. [*Color*, 187]

Celie's curse, which Walker enhances with epic machinery, is powerful. But unlike the razor which Shug takes out of her hand, it does not return Mr. ______'s violence in kind. Instead, the decline of the father's law in Walker's novel creates temporary separate spheres for women and men in which gender hierarchy breaks down in the absence of the "other," enabling women and men eventually to share the world again. Celie's authority is consolidated as she comes into economic independence. Earlier, Shug had distracted Celie from her murderous rage toward Mr. ______ by suggesting that the two of them sew her a pair of pants.

"What I need pants for?" Celie objects. "I ain't no man" (*Color*, 136). In Memphis, while trying to think what she wants to do for a living, Celie sits "making pants after pants" (*Color*, 190) and soon finds her vocation, founding "Folkpants, Unlimited." In this comic reversal, the garment that Celie at first associates strictly with men becomes the means, symbolic and material, of her economic independence and her self-possession.

The magical ease with which Celie emerges from poverty and silence classes Walker's "historical novel" with epic and romance rather than with realist or socialist realist fiction. Walker's Shug has a power that is historically rare indeed, and Celie's and Nettie's inheritance of their father's house, in particular, indulges in narrative magic that well exceeds the requirements of the plot. But Celie's utopian history allegorizes not only women's need to be economically independent of men but the daughter's need to inherit the symbolic estate of culture and language that has always belonged to the father, a "place" in culture and language from which she, like Archimedes, can move her world. When Celie comes into the power of language, work, and love, her curse temporarily comes true. As the daughter learns to speak, Mr. ______ falls into a hysterical depression. Mr. ______'s crisis signals the death of the cultural father whom he had earlier embodied: "Harpo ast his daddy why he beat me. Mr. ______ say, Cause she my wife. Plus, she stubborn. All women good for—he don't finish. He just tuck his chin over the paper like he do. Remind me of Pa" (*Color*, 30). As cultural father, Mr. ______'s law was unspoken, his ways immutable, and his words so close to the patriarchal script that he didn't have to finish his sentences. By the end of the novel, however, Mr. ______ has abandoned that role to become Albert and to "enter into the Creation" (*Color*, 181). By the novel's last scenes, Albert's life is scarcely differentiable from Celie's, and he tells her, "Celie, I'm satisfied this the first time I ever lived on Earth as a natural man" (*Color*, 230).

An important effect of Albert's transition from patriarch to natural man is the abandonment of that strictly literal stake in paternity that the marriage structure serves. As a "natural man," Albert, like everyone else, spends a lot of time concocting devious recipes to hide the taste of yams from Henrietta—who, Celie explains, has to eat yams to control her chronic blood disease but "Just our luck she hate yams and she not too polite to let us know" (*Color*, 222). Henrietta, Sofia's youngest child, whose "little face always look like stormy weather" (*Color*, 196), is a crucial figure in the novel. Though Harpo tries to claim her as his sixth child, she is nobody's baby; only Sofia (if anyone) knows who her father is. Nonetheless, Harpo, Albert, and everyone else feel a special affection for "ole evil Henrietta" (*Color*, 247), and, as they knock themselves out making yam peanut butter and yam tuna casserole, it becomes apparent that, in Walker's recreated universe, the care of children by men and women without respect to proprietary biological parenthood is an important means of undoing the exploitative hierarchy of gender roles.[29] If Celie's discovery that "Pa not pa" liberates her from the law of the father that makes women and children its spiritual and sexual subjects, Albert, in learning to "wonder" and to "ast" (*Color*, 247) and to care for Henrietta, escapes the confines of the patriarchal role. As the functions of father and mother merge, the formerly rigid boundaries of the family become fluid: Celie, Shug, and Albert feel "right" sitting on the porch together; love partners change with desire; and, most important, children circulate among many parents: Samuel, Corrine, and Nettie raise Celie's; Celie raises Mr. ______'s and Annie Julia's; Sofia, Odessa, and Mary Agnes exchange theirs; and the whole community, including the white Eleanor Jane, becomes involved with yams and Henrietta. Whereas, in the patriarchal societies analyzed by Lévi-Strauss, the exchange of women forges bonds between men that support male culture, in Walker's creation story children are the miracle and mystery that bond all her characters to the world, each other, and the future.

Undoing the gender hierarchy necessitates a rewriting of the Creation myth and a dismantling of the hierarchical concepts of God and authority that underwrite them in Western tradition. The God to whom Celie writes her early letters loses credibility once she learns, through Nettie's letters, that nothing is as the law of the father proclaimed it. When Shug hears her venting her wrath, she is shocked: "Miss Celie, You better hush. God might hear you." "Let 'im hear me, I say. If he ever listened to poor colored women the world would be a different place, I can tell you." Shug deconstructs Celie's theology: "You have to git man off your eyeball, before you can see anything a 'tall," she explains. "He on your box of grits, in your head, and all over the radio. He try to make you think he everywhere. Soon as you think he everywhere, you think he God. But he ain't"; "God ain't a he or a she, but a It. . . . It ain't something you can look at apart from everything else, including yourself. I believe God is everything . . . that is or ever was or ever will be. And when you can feel that, and be happy to feel that, you've found It" (*Color*, 175–79). In Walker's cosmos, the monotheistic Western myth of origins gives way to one of multiple, indeed infinite, beginnings that the new myth of Celie's fall and self-redemption celebrates. Hers is not a Creation finished in the first seven days of the world but one in which all creators are celebrated, if at times reluctantly. When Sofia, with what Harpo calls her "amazon sisters," insists on bearing her mother's casket, Harpo asks,

> Why you like this, huh? Why you always think you have to do things your own way? I ast your mama bout it one time, while you was in jail.

[29] See Dorothy Dinnerstein, *The Mermaid and the Minotaur: Sexual Arrangements and Human Malaise* (New York: Harper & Row, 1976); and Nancy Chodorow, *The Reproduction of Mothering* (Berkeley: University of California Press, 1978).

> What she say? ast Sofia.
> She say you think your way as good as anybody else's. Plus, it yours. [*Color*, 196]

Walker echoes this moment in her epigraph, which translates Harpo's "here come the amazons" (*Color*, 198) into: "Show me how to do like you. Show me how to do it" (*Color*, i). She fills her historical novel with creators, authorities, beginnings, "others." Like all authors of epic, she collapses transcendence and history; but her history differs from that of earlier epics. Originating in a violation of the patriarchal law, it undoes the patriarchal cultural order and builds upon new ground. "Womanlike," Walker writes, "my 'history' starts not with the taking of lands, or the births, battles, and deaths of Great Men, but with one woman asking another for her underwear."[30] The violation of "conventions" that this exchange of underwear stages breaks through the patriarchal sexual and spiritual economy, writing into history a story long suppressed and revising history by doing so. Celie's last letter—addressed to "Dear God. Dear stars, dear trees, dear sky, dear peoples. Dear Everything. Dear God"—records a conversation about history:

> Why us always have family reunion on July 4th, say Henrietta, mouth poke out, full of complaint. It so hot.
> White people busy celebrating they independence from England July 4th, say Harpo, so most black folks don't have to work. Us can spend the day celebrating each other.
> Ah, Harpo, say Mary Agnes, sipping some lemonade. I didn't know you knowed history. [*Color*, 249–50]

Harpo's decentering history is a microcosm of Walker's, which ends with a beginning: "I feel a little peculiar round the children," Celie writes. "And I see they think [us] real old and don't know much what going on. But I don't think us feel old at all. . . . Matter of fact, I think this the youngest us ever felt" (*Color*, 251). As Celie's beginning could have been a silent end, so her ending continues the proliferating beginnings that the novel captures in its epistolary form, its characters' histories, and the daily revelations that Shug names "God."

Walker's telling of the daughter's long-repressed story marks an important beginning for literary history. In her hands, the forbidden story recreates the world by reclaiming female subjectivity. "What I love best bout Shug," Celie tells Albert, "is what she been through. When you look in Shug's eyes, you know she been where she been, seen what she seen, did what she did. And now she know. . . . And if you don't git out the way,

[30] Walker, "Writing *The Color Purple*," 356. Compare the title of Jacob's essay, "'Does History Consist of the Biographies of Great Men?'" in Virginia Woolf's *Jacob's Room* (1922; New York: Harcourt Brace Jovanovich, 1978), 39.

she'll tell you about it" (*Color*, 236). Walker's woman as hero, whose history is her identity and who recreates the universe by telling her story to the world, is not new in real life. But she is only now making her presence felt in the literary tradition, opening a powerfully transformative dialogue between herself and the world, between her story and his, and between ourselves and our cultural past. As she does so, we can look forward to that "most interesting, exciting, and important conversation" that Woolf predicted would begin once woman recovered her voice.

Department of English
Yale University

RACISM AND FEMINIST AESTHETICS: THE PROVOCATION OF ANNE DUDEN'S *OPENING OF THE MOUTH*

LESLIE A. ADELSON

The contemporary West German discussion of what it means to write a text appropriate to women's experience began with the 1975 publication of a slim volume entitled *Shedding*, in which Verena Stefan explores the various power structures inherent in the relationship between a young physical therapist and her lover, a male Marxist activist.[1] Specifically, it was Stefan's critical focus on the limitations of sexist language and male-oriented sexuality that attracted the attention of West German feminists. What has generally gone unnoticed, however, is that this historically

[1] Verena Stefan, *Häutungen* (Munich: Frauenoffensive, 1975). The English translation of this was published as *Shedding*, trans. Johanna Moore and Beth Weckmueller (New York: Daughter's Publishing Co., 1978). Ricarda Schmidt cites the sale, by 1980 alone, of 200,000 copies of Stefan's book (*Westdeutsche Frauenliteratur in den 70er Jahren* [Frankfurt am Main: Rita G. Fischer, 1982], 120). Jeanette Clausen provides an early English-language essay on *Shedding* in "Our Language, Our Selves: Verena Stefan's Critique of Patriarchal Language," in *Beyond the Eternal Feminine: Critical Essays on Women and German Literature*, ed. Susan L. Cocalis and Kay Goodman (Stuttgart: Hans-Dieter Heinz, 1982), 381–400. Silvia Bovenschen's essay on female aesthetics prompted much theoretical debate on women's writing. See Bovenschen, "Über die Frage: Gibt es eine weibliche Ästhetik?" *Ästhetik und Kommunikation* 25 (September 1976): 60–75, or "Is There a Feminine Aesthetic?" trans. Beth Weckmueller, *New German Critique* (Winter 1977), 111–37. The English translation is also reprinted in *Feminist Aesthetics*, ed. Gisela Ecker (Boston: Beacon Press, 1985), 23–50.

This essay originally appeared in *Signs*, vol. 13, no. 2, Winter 1988.

important text also perpetuates racist stereotypes regarding the sexual sensibilities of blacks. The protagonist is sorely disappointed to learn that her black male lover is no less sexist than her white boyfriend, a disappointment that stems from two assumptions: that one oppressed group is automatically more sensitized to the sufferings of any other oppressed group and that black people in general are *by nature* more "in their bodies" than whites.[2] The common denominator here is a blindness to the historical specificity of various manifestations and imbrications of sexism and racism in very different social contexts. The protagonist does not wonder, for example, why white American women as a whole did not all denounce the institutionalized enslavement of black men and women. Since the author never subjects the protagonist's experiences or her interpretations of them to any form of critical distancing, what has passed as a watershed feminist critique in West Germany explicitly asserts that sexism goes deeper than racism or economic oppression—an assertion that does not account for the very real possibility that specific manifestations of feminism may be implicated in systems of oppression not determined by gender alone.

The fact that racist stereotypes exist in a book that was of such initial importance to the contemporary West German discussion of feminist aesthetics may be an unfortunate coincidence. The textual significance accorded yet another racist premise in a more recent, far more complex text by another German woman writer suggests, however, that it behooves us as feminist critics to examine the potentially racist abuses and implications of some aspects of feminist aesthetics. By analyzing the varying functions of blackness in Anne Duden's *Opening of the Mouth* as they relate to the notion of negativity in feminist theories of women's culture, we can explore how it is that a racist image becomes the pivot on which a text that aspires to feminist aesthetics comes to turn.[3] What bearing do the textual complexities of *Opening of the Mouth* have on the more general questions we do and do not ask regarding the relationship between racism and feminist aesthetics?[4]

[2] Stefan, *Shedding*, esp. 28.

[3] Anne Duden, *Übergang* (Berlin: Rotbuch, 1982). Further references to this work, cited in parentheses in the text by page number, will be to the English translation, *Opening of the Mouth*, trans. Della Couling (London and Sydney: Pluto Press, 1985). The story from which the German text takes its title bears in English a title different from the book title: "Transition."

[4] I should emphasize at the outset that my comments will not provide a comprehensive picture of racist elements in contemporary German women's writing or in West German society. Rather, I will explore the issue of racism, which is, of course, not primarily textual, by examining its structural function in the text. I wish to draw critical attention to the much too muffled issue of racism against persons of color in the German tradition of women's writing, obviously a complex tradition, for which neither Stefan's book nor Duden's work alone can stand as exemplary. What I hope other scholars will help provide is a more systematic

Duden's tendentially positive appropriation of blackness on behalf of a female subjectivity evidences, on the one hand, a close affinity to generally held premises about *écriture féminine*. On the other hand, however, the racist core-image of this text underscores the issue of positionality vis-à-vis the dominant order for author, character, and reader alike. Ignoring the racism of the text's central image allows for a reading that is all too compatible with a "universal" understanding of what it means to write a text we might be tempted to call woman-centered. The racism in Duden's aesthetic, once it is named, forces us to acknowledge that the experience of femaleness is historically, socially, and racially specific. The political recognition of differences among women in the same or different cultures and societies thus suggests a far more rigorously differentiated understanding of feminist aesthetics than is often practiced.[5]

Duden's creative debut on the literary scene met with high praise from both establishment literary critics and feminists.[6] Only in rare instances, however, did the reviewers ever mention that the central episode, in which the protagonist, her brother, and two friends suffer an apparently unprovoked attack by a group of GIs in a West Berlin discotheque, involves a group of *black* GIs.[7] The attackers are never named, their faces never

---

investigation of the different ways in which writing by German women has or has not appropriated the racism of the culture at large. I hope, further, that my elaborations on the problems and challenges of *Opening of the Mouth* will also provoke fruitful discussion among feminist theorists who do not necessarily concern themselves with German feminism or German literature per se. For a critical survey of the image of blackness in German culture generally from the eighteenth century to the mid-twentieth century, see Sander L. Gilman, *On Blackness without Blacks: Essays on the Image of the Black in Germany* (Boston: G. K. Hall & Co., 1982). One important article that does examine the issue of race in a piece by Ingeborg Bachmann is Sara Lennox's "Geschlecht, Rasse und Geschichte in 'Der Fall Franza,'" trans. Frank Mecklenburg, in *Ingeborg Bachmann*, ed. Sigrid Weigel (Munich: Text & Kritik, 1984), 156–79.

[5] A German text may lend itself particularly well to this provocation, given that West German discussions of feminist theory have until very recently been more influenced by dialectical materialism than by the Anglo-French terms of poststructuralist feminist discourse. Sigrid Weigel's work (which will be cited in the discussion to follow) is particularly notable for its intelligent attempts to integrate these two strains of critical analysis. Inasmuch as a useful discussion of the particularities of German feminist theory would lead us well beyond the confines of this paper, I can only refer interested readers to the collection of diverse essays gathered together by Gisela Ecker and published, in English, as *Feminist Aesthetics* (n. 1 above). For those readers fluent in German, I would recommend, as an update, Margret Brügmann's essay, "Weiblichkeit im Spiel der Sprache: Über das Verhältnis von Psychoanalyse und 'écriture féminine,'" in *Frauen Literatur Geschichte: Schreibende Frauen vom Mittelalter bis zur Gegenwart*, ed. Hiltrud Gnüg and Renate Möhrmann (Stuttgart: Metzler, 1985), 395–415.

[6] The same can be said of Anne Duden's second book, *Das Judasschaf* (Berlin: Rotbuch, 1985), which has not yet been translated into English.

[7] This tendency to colorblindness was echoed at the May 1986 annual meeting of "Frauen in der Literaturwissenschaft" (Women in literary studies) at the University of Hamburg (West

described, their motivations never analyzed, nor are their numbers ever properly counted. They are characterized only by ruthless, unexplained violence, which takes the form of "a moveable but impenetrable wall" (57). This highly questionable equation of a group of faceless blacks with what functions implicitly in the text as indiscriminate evil is rendered all the more problematic by the consequences of this attack for the female narrator. The brick that smashes through the windshield as she tries to drive herself and her companions to safety literally destroys the lower half of her face, necessitating a long hospital stay and the painful reconstruction of the part of her that violence has decimated. What we have here, one might contend, is the affirmation of the racist stereotype that black men pose an inherent danger to white people and to white women in particular.

Yet, if Duden does affirm this prejudice, she fails to reproduce it in its pure form. The sexual connotations of this particular stereotype would lead one to expect a sexual assault on Duden's protagonist. It is, however, not her vaginal opening but her mouth that is violated. She is, quite literally, *ent-mündigt* (the unconventionally hyphenated version of the German term implies that she has been deprived of her mouth as well as of her right to speak for herself).[8] The focus of the cultural critique articulated by the text is thus not woman's sex in the narrow sense of the term but her gender (the experience of which is of course based on her sex). The threat of indistinguishable darkness, perceived as a threat to life itself (60) and embodied by the black GIs, is thus linked and likened to the protagonist's inability to speak.

Before closely examining how blackness relates to speechlessness in *Opening of the Mouth*, it will be useful to recall some of the more common premises found in feminist theory regarding the problem women encounter in finding a voice of their own. What follows does not by any means pretend to be a complete account of feminist theories of language, which are both varied and complex; rather, it sketches some of the steps leading from the understanding of language as oppression to the manifestation of the female body as a voice that cannot be silenced, even by language. This progression is crucial to the textual analysis at hand since it is around the function of the body in Duden's text that, first, a feminist notion of negativity as opposition to the dominant order crystallizes, and, second,

Germany), where I presented a shorter version of this article. One of the some 400 participants asked if we could not just as easily consider the race of the GIs irrelevant to our reading of the text. My impression was that Duden had become a kind of cult favorite for a large percentage of the German women attending the conference. They seemed noticeably unsettled and quite surprised by my critical reading of her text.

[8] Duden actually uses the word in the chapter entitled "Heart and Mouth." The English translation of *Opening of the Mouth* lacks the double entendre: "I was without my right of say—it had been taken away" (43).

the issue of what I call positionality asserts itself, thereby throwing into question that very assumption of feminist negativity as opposition. In this instance it is the racist core-image of the text that insists that we acknowledge the weight of positionality. For the purposes of this paper, negativity as opposition, manifestations of a feminist "bodyspeak," racist imagery, and positionality must all be thought *together*, or else none of the above will be properly understood in context.

Feminist critics of Western patriarchal literature see language as a phallocentric system that controls and dominates women as "other." Many women writers and theorists speak to, and beyond, these barriers by giving voice to women's bodies. Stefan's *Shedding* was an early, admittedly problematic, attempt at this. In "The Sex Which Is Not One," Luce Irigaray's famous arguments against "fixed, immobilized" meanings and identities are based on the implications of female organs for female sexuality and subjectivity.[9] Hélène Cixous notes, "Women must write through their bodies," a conviction also expressed by writers such as Adrienne Rich and Christa Reinig.[10] However, as Elaine Showalter points out in her review of the biological perspective of feminist criticism, "there can be no expression of the body which is unmediated by linguistic, social, and literary structures."[11] Woman's body can nonetheless be said to assume particular significance in the context of feminist writing, since the cultural notion of femaleness (*Weiblichkeit*) is inscribed on it. As Sigrid Weigel argues, "Woman . . . *embodies* femaleness, that is to say, her body is defined and pinpointed as the locus of femaleness in the male order."[12] This would clearly indicate something of a double bind for the woman trying to

[9] Luce Irigaray, "The Sex Which Is Not One," trans. Claudia Reeder, in *New French Feminisms: An Anthology*, ed. Elaine Marks and Isabelle de Courtivron (Amherst: University of Massachusetts Press, 1980), 99–106.

[10] Hélène Cixous, "Laugh of the Medusa," trans. Keith Cohen and Paula Cohen, in Marks and de Courtivron, eds., 256; see also Hélène Cixous, "Schreiben, Feminität, Veränderung," trans. Monika Bellan, *Alternative* 19, nos. 108/109 (June/August 1976): 145. The original French text of the latter can be found in Cixous's *La jeune née* (Paris: Union Générale d'Editions, 1975), 115 ff. For an English translation see the "Sorties" chapter of Hélène Cixous and Catherine Clement, *The Newly Born Woman*, trans. Betsy Wing (Minneapolis: University of Minnesota Press, 1986), 94. See Adrienne Rich, *Of Woman Born: Motherhood as Experience and Institution* (New York: W. W. Norton & Co., 1977), 62; and Christa Reinig, "Das weibliche Ich," *Alternative* 19, nos. 108/109 (June/August 1976): 120. American readers unfamiliar with Reinig may wish to read Angelika Bammer's article, "Testing the Limits: Christa Reinig's Radical Vision," in *Women in German Yearbook 2: Feminist Studies and German Culture*, ed. Marianne Burkhard and Edith Waldstein (Lanham/New York/London: University Press of America, 1986), 107–27.

[11] Elaine Showalter, "Feminist Criticism in the Wilderness," in *Writing and Sexual Difference*, ed. Elizabeth Abel (Chicago: University of Chicago Press, 1982), 19.

[12] Sigrid Weigel, "Frau und 'Weiblichkeit': Theoretische Überlegungen zur feministischen Literaturkritik," in *Feministische Literaturwissenschaft*, ed. Inge Stephan and Sigrid Weigel (Berlin: Argument, 1984), 109.

write through her body. On the one hand, feminist theory cites that body as resistant or in opposition to the dominant system of order and signification. On the other hand, and at the same time, that body is a cultural construct through and on which that system is inscribed. Analyzing images of women in the tradition of bourgeois literature, Weigel has concluded that "the actual battlefield is the female body."[13] The same might be said, I would argue, albeit for different reasons, of the female body in feminist texts.

In the unconventionally materialist social theory of Oskar Negt and Alexander Kluge, the body is seen concretely as that through which all human experience is filtered, processed, and pursued; it is at once an organ for both personal and social orientation. Never privy to a fixed, permanent identity, they contend, it can sometimes be the battleground for conflicting social antagonisms in the same person.[14] This allowance for multiple, conflicting subjectivities within the same body comes very close to some instances of feminist theory that owe more to poststructuralism than to dialectical materialism.[15] Negt and Kluge do not, however, address the specific cultural value assigned to the female body as the embodiment of femaleness. Feminist writing may well provide the meeting ground between theories that assume the primacy of material relations and those that assume the primacy of discourse and signification. The female body is a material organ of woman's own (self-determined) orientation *as well as* the locus of her cultural signification. What this means concretely for the feminist author is that the female body must be charted as both friendly and enemy territory.

This of course renders *opposition* to dominant structures of language and signification problematic. The Lacanian designation of woman as lack or absence, the negative to the phallocentric positive, must be distinguished from the negative perceived as opposition (resistance) to the dominant order. It is the former to which Cixous refers when she asserts, "We have no womanly reason to pledge allegiance to the negative."[16] Kristeva means oppositional subversion when she claims that "a feminist practice can only be negative."[17] Weigel assesses this type of negativity as

[13] Sigrid Weigel, "Die geopferte Heldin und das Opfer als Heldin," in Inge Stephan and Sigrid Weigel, *Die verborgene Frau: Sechs Beiträge zu einer feministischen Literaturwissenschaft* (Berlin: Argument, 1983), 142.

[14] Oskar Negt and Alexander Kluge, *Geschichte und Eigensinn* (Frankfurt am Main: Zweitausendeins, 1981), 782.

[15] See, e.g., Irigaray (n. 9 above).

[16] Cixous, "Laugh of the Medusa," 255.

[17] Julia Kristeva, "Woman Can Never Be Defined," trans. Marilyn A. August, in Marks and de Courtivron, eds. (n. 9 above), 137; see also Julia Kristeva, "Produktivität der Frau: Interview von Eliane Boucquey," trans. Lily Leder, *Alternative* 19, nos. 108/109 (June/August 1976): 168. The latter is translated from the French: *Les cahiers du Grif* (Brussels: Transédition, 1975), 22 ff.

opposition to the "claim of universality" from which women's experience and self-articulation have traditionally been excluded and warns repeatedly against the dangers of filling in the real gaps of women's experience with the projected presence of utopian images.[18]

This danger of positively occupying a negative movement (movement in the sense of passage or, if one will, *Übergang* or "transition") has its unfortunate counterpart in the tendency to celebrate oppositional negativity for women in a way that confuses the negative with absence or silence, which is, after all, the space that patriarchy has accorded women all along. It is, for example, extremely problematic when Susan Guber extrapolates from Isak Dinesen's short story "The Blank Page" to imply that resistance in general, for women, articulates itself on a blank page and, further, that women writers should "contribute to the blank pages of our future history."[19] The distinction we make between women and "woman" as a cultural construct in traditional male discourse[20] must also be kept in mind when we grapple with femaleness in women's literature. Weigel cautions against what she perceives as Cixous's and Irigaray's tendency to mystify and hence dehistoricize femaleness and urges us to differentiate more carefully between real women, images of women, and utopia.[21] We are further cautioned not to define femaleness in literature as writing characterized predominantly by discontinuity and rupture. Weigel thus takes up Cixous's notion of the impossibility of defining "a feminine practice of writing" but warns us against making this resistance to definition into yet another metaphor for femaleness.[22]

The negative or oppositional value of feminist writing is both circumscribed and complicated by the positionality of the woman author with regard to the dominant order. Inge Stephan and Sigrid Weigel refer to her position as one of "simultaneous exclusion and participation."[23] Assessing

[18] Sigrid Weigel, "Overcoming Absence: Contemporary German Women's Literature (Part Two)," *New German Critique* 32 (Spring/Summer 1984): 9, 11, "Frau und 'Weiblichkeit'" (n. 12 above), 107, "Double Focus: On the History of Women's Writing," trans. Harriet Anderson, in Ecker, ed. (n. 1 above), 59, 74, and "'Das Weibliche als Metapher des Metonymischen': Kritische Überlegungen zur Konstitution des Weiblichen als Verfahren oder Schreibweise," in *Kontroversen, alte und neue: Akten des VII. Internationalen Germanisten-Kongresses Göttingen 1985*, vol. 6, *Fraeunsprache—Frauenliteratur?* ed. Albrecht Schöne (Tübingen: Niemeyer, 1986).

[19] Susan Gubar, "'The Blank Page' and the Issues of Female Creativity," in *Abel*, ed. (n. 11 above), 93.

[20] See Biddy Martin, "Weiblichkeit als kulturelle Konstruktion," *Das Argument* 25, no. 138 (March/April 1983): 212, and "Feminism, Criticism, and Foucault," *New German Critique* 27 (Fall 1982): 3–30.

[21] Weigel, "Double Focus," 77, 78, and "Frau und 'Weiblichkeit.'"

[22] Weigel, "'Das Weibliche als Metapher des Metonymischen'"; Cixous, "Laugh of the Medusa" (n. 10 above), 253.

[23] Inge Stephan and Sigrid Weigel, "Vorwort," in Stephan and Weigel (n. 13 above), 5. See also Martin, "Weiblichkeit als kulturelle Konstruktion," 213–14.

the relevance of Foucault's work for feminist theory, Biddy Martin similarly stresses the need to "deconstruct monolithic concepts of *the* oppressor and *the* oppressed."[24] Not surprisingly, both Weigel and Martin argue for a "doubled strategy" based on their understanding of women's "double existence."[25] This cuts deeper than Cixous's call for women writing their selves "to break up, to destroy; and to foresee the unforeseeable, to project"[26] because it speaks for the historical contextualization of writing strategies for women. Feminist writing strategies are necessarily bound to the extraliterary struggle for social and cultural self-determination, a struggle that requires some working notion of historical agency for women.[27] Accepting negativity as a mere metaphor for simplistic opposition to dominant structures of signification and subject-hood would deny women this agency, relegating them to their own form of nonspeech and confining them to a "safe" corner from which they can oppose but not change the dominant order. When Weigel speaks of feminist utopia as "imaginable and testable only in a fragmentary fashion," it is not in allegiance to the negative as lack but in awareness of women's double existence both inside and outside language and ideology.[28] Any utopian undertaking must take this double existence into account.[29]

How then does this understanding of a "concrete utopia" (to borrow a phrase from the German philosopher Ernst Bloch) relate to images of blackness in *Opening*?[30] On one level, blackness is used to represent the female protagonist's exclusion from the patriarchal order of signification, an exclusion that Duden intermittently inverts into *positive* images of blackness: this yields negativity as opposition. On another level, however, we must realize that women are both included and excluded from dominant orders *in different ways* depending on factors such as race, class, age,

[24] Martin, "Weiblichkeit als kulturelle Konstruktion," 210, and "Feminism, Criticism, and Foucault."

[25] Martin, "Weiblichkeit als kulturelle Konstruktion," 212, and "Feminism, Criticism, and Foucault," 13; Weigel, "Double Focus," passim.

[26] Cixous, "Laugh of the Medusa," 245.

[27] Toril Moi's recently published book on *Sexual/Textual Politics* (London/New York: Methuen, Inc., 1985) was intended to address this need for a feminist notion of historical agency if the subject (as phallocentric) is to be deconstructed. Weigel's essay, "Double Focus," may also be read in this context.

[28] Weigel, "Frau und 'Weiblichkeit'" (n. 12 above), 107. Martin is of the same mind. See "Weiblichkeit als kulturelle Konstruktion," 213–14.

[29] Sigrid Weigel's review of *Opening* in fact claims the following: "Anne Duden's book deals with what precedes a utopia in now-time, a utopia which is not projected onto a matriarchal prehistory or an unattainable future: the book deals with a radical opening to the world" ("Ohne Schutzhaut," *Courage* 8, no. 6 [June 1983]: 47).

[30] Ernst Bloch's phrase, taken from his treatise on *Das Prinzip Hoffnung* (The principle of hope), which was written between 1938 and 1947 but not published until 1959 (Frankfurt am Main: Suhrkamp), implies that utopia is more oriented to real possibilities for an unalienated present than to an eternally distant future.

religion, sexual preference, and national context. This demands that we acknowledge how the factor of positionality effectively challenges any simplistic or universalized assumption of negativity as opposition for women. Duden's protagonist is not Everywoman. She is a white, German, non-Jewish woman who, having been a young girl during World War II, feels herself victimized by her culture and yet realizes that she belongs to "the species of those responsible" (64), that is, responsible for the genocide of the Jews. How much of her experience is German, how much of it female, how much of it white? It is to Duden's great credit that she does not allow us to isolate surgically one from the other, for it is only historically, in the context of these other factors, that gender can be experienced. While certain images of blackness may adequately depict some aspects of the protagonist's existence as a woman in West German society, the specifically racist image of the black GIs reflects back only the whiteness of her own skin and experience.[31] As a white German woman she is caught in the crossfire of racial tensions in a culture whose present sensibilities with regard to race are determined by responses to the Nazi past, the presence of black American soldiers stationed in West Germany and West Berlin, and the continued employment of the so-called guest workers from countries such as Turkey, Yugoslavia, Italy, and Greece. The conditions under which Duden's protagonist experiences "simultaneous exclusion and participation" vis-à-vis the dominant order cannot be considered identical to those experienced by an Afro-German woman reading this text or by the sister of a black GI reading it. Neither can I, as a white, American, Jewish woman find the terms of my own existence mimetically reflected in the experience of Duden's female protagonist or in the images of blackness that she has appropriated. It is only in particular shards of the mirror she holds out to me that I am able to recognize myself at all. The shock of simultaneous recognition in and alienation from this feminist text is what makes the images of blackness in *Opening* and the issue of positionality they suggest both deeply unsettling and potentially productive.

The chapter that lends its title to Duden's book in the German edition is situated in the middle of a series of shorter texts, all of which challenge the traditional distinction between inner and outer space by rendering that barrier so ambiguous as to be meaningless. This spatial ambiguity is echoed in a more general dissolution of boundaries. In one text it rains up as well as down, in another everything fuses into "a gigantic unit," and in a third the narrator cannot distinguish between noise and silence (38, 48, 98). It is

[31] I wish to stress that my analysis addresses the aesthetic function of blackness in the text *as Duden has chosen to structure it*. Interestingly enough, class affiliations make up one social specification that recedes from the text. One may *surmise* that the black GIs and female protagonist do not belong to the same economic class, but the text provides no real corroboration for this, an omission that further foregrounds the question of race.

significant that Duden asserts the primacy of space over temporality. There are enough intertextual allusions for us to assume that the different figures and narrative voices in this series of texts refer to "the same person," but, if so, we are compelled to see her as a composite of multiple subjectivities. As Duden herself writes in one text: "I and I, we hear each other" (44). "Heart and Mouth," a story that precedes "Transition," might well refer to the psychological and physical aftermath of the attack that does not occur until three stories later. Duden's refusal to adhere to linear time or to single, clearly delineated identities allows her images of spatial ambiguity to speak more forcefully than they otherwise might. Duden makes us listen to the silence of women's experience by making us feel the fullness of the empty space traditionally accorded us.[32]

The ambiguity between inner and outer space in "Transition" is developed primarily through the "bodyspeak" of the female protagonist and through her ambivalent attitudes toward darkness and light. "The Country Cottage," the first story in the series, relates the experience of a woman housesitting in the countryside. Initially the blinding white light outside the house, the seemingly endless darkness inside, and the discomfort she experiences making the transition from one to the other (13–14) cause her to lose all sense of orientation. "I couldn't focus my gaze on anything any more" (14). Gradually there is an approximation of the light conditions inside and outside the house (23) until one night, when the woman becomes obsessed with her fear of an intruder who might be lurking in the darkness outside the lit house, waiting to do her harm. "The darkness immediately opened up—especially behind me—like a bottomless sack which, billowing and lurching, was lying in wait to throw itself over my head and thus throw me right out of control and fell me once and for all" (27). She is finally able to lock herself into the bedroom, hoping to sleep in spite of her fears. "Instead the impenetrable darkness towered omnipotently around me and over me" (27). Not any human attacker but darkness itself emerges as the real invader here. While darkness is seen as life-threatening in "The Country Cottage," it is perceived as desirable in "The Art of Drowning." "During the day I mainly keep myself busy by waiting for it to get dark again. In the dark the invisible behaves more casually and naturally" (124). In the context of women's relegation to absence, darkness is considered the home of that which has been rendered invisible, that is, women's experience and subjectivity. The following passage reads almost like a direct contribution to the feminist commentary on the patriarchal

[32] On woman's relation to space and time, see Claudia Herrmann, "Women in Space and Time," trans. Marilyn R. Schuster, in Marks and de Courtivron, eds. (n. 9 above), 168–73; and Julia Kristeva, "Women's Time," trans. Alice Jardine and Harry Blake, in *Feminist Theory: A Critique of Ideology*, ed. Nannerl O. Keohane (Chicago: University of Chicago Press, 1982), 31–53.

order: "Compared with the prevailing peace, the light and the order, however, the darkness is too weak and too short. It has long been no effective alternative. But perhaps the day will come when it will no longer be light" (124).

The ambivalence toward darkness finds its most critical articulation in "Transition," the same text in which the death threat associated with loss of contours or dissolution of boundaries is most trenchantly conveyed. The text actually begins not with the injury to the woman but with an attack on her brother, who is beaten at night by a group of black GIs. The same group, "a dark, man-high wall" (59), waits outside the discotheque to attack the car in which its victims try to flee. The sister's subsequent injury brings her to the hospital, where she sees her anesthetist as a "black face" (66) against the neon hospital light. "He belongs to them. They want to kill me" (66). Here blackness is clearly reserved for perceived threats to her life, although the customary distinction between helper and attacker is negated by their shared blackness. Elsewhere, however, she perceives the darkness of night as her ally (68). In a reversal of what is generally considered normal, she claims: "The emergency lighting extinguished any orientation" (73).

By the same token, the injured woman's reaction to the partial destruction of her face is not what we might expect. We as readers are spared few of the unpleasant details either of her injury or of the reconstruction of her mouth. Going to feel her lips after being hit, she feels instead "torn and burst pulp and loose teeth hanging in it" (60). The nurse at the hospital gives her a basin to catch the "stream of blood, slime and saliva," and, were she to lie down, she would be suffocated by all these fluids that would flow back into her (61). Tellingly, the narrative voice shifts from the third to the first person at the point of the operation. While the account of the attack is narrated in the third person, the first person asserts itself when the doctor begins to reconstruct the formless mess she has where her face should be. This is, however, not the same first person that would have spoken had it been given a voice prior to the attack. "With a bloodless, precise cut the doctor separated me from what was" (62). "What was" was society's imposition and the woman's assumption of an identity inappropriate to her own subjectivity. One is tempted to call this a reversal of the familiar Freudian dictate: *Wo Ich war, soll Es werden.* (Where ego was, id shall be.) But the narrative voice speaks as *Ich* (I), not as *Es* (id). She does not relinquish her claims to an *Ich* altogether but problematizes her choices by welcoming the destruction of her mouth.[33] "The hole, the trap was to be stopped up,

[33] Recall Martin's comments on Foucault's relevance for feminists: "Foucault's work does not negate the possibility of concrete political struggle and resistance. It does insist that we understand and take account of the ways in which we are implicated in power relations and the fact that we are never outside of power. He does not advocate *a* position; however, he is

scarcely had it been ripped open. Yet in fact I could consider it fortunate that now, finally, my anatomy too had cracked, that my body could begin to catch up on what had until then been reserved only for my brainhead: following the limitless chaos of the world along all its secret pathways and everywhere where it made itself noticeable, to let it break into me then, and rage in me. Basically, I was relieved" (63). The terror we would normally associate with such an attack is experienced instead when medicine attempts to repair the damage. "The terror would abate to the degree in which what was broken could not be mended and intactness could not be restored" (63), an image that binds her old face, the attackers, and the medical personnel in a collusion of constriction. That which is soft and formless resists the penetration of the phallic "muzzle protector"; she considers herself "impaled" (75–76). Each stage of the "recovery" brings with it a growing sense of confinement. Her mouth is literally wired shut for weeks: "A feeling of inescapable narrowness, as though I were shut into myself and the key had been taken away" (84). She does not want to accept this: "That constantly something would be forced together in me that wasn't supposed to be. An exasperated, frantic speechlessness wanted to scream itself hoarse" (84). Duden's text speaks the speechlessness that refuses its own negation but struggles to find words to speak. For this reason the female protagonist suffers her injury as both pain and opportunity.[34] Her I.V. is both "gallows" and "umbilical cord" (67). The positive value of her effacement lies in the negativity not of nonidentity but of anti-identity in the dominant scheme of things. The narrative voice rejects identification; the I she does claim lies outside the *image* that others seek to recognize as her (see 69). Her physical disfigurement thus represents an approximation between the inner space of her subjectivity and the outer space of its representation.

This is how darkness portrayed as threat emerges as a source of potential liberation. The standard association of darkness with absence (of light) and silence is inverted when the woman fills that darkness with her own presence and her struggle for self-articulation. At least, this is one possible reading of "Transition." The black holes of history that mine the German protagonist's childhood experience of World War II and later postwar Germany are similarly illuminated by her physical responses to her most recent *Ent-mündigung*. She is constantly battling bouts of nausea. The vomit and blood in her stomach are the fluids inside her that resist the confinement delineated by the contours of the body. As Kristeva says of nausea and vomit, "'I' am in the process of becoming an other at the

obviously aware of the possibilities for new pleasures and new forms of resistance created in every confrontation" ("Feminism, Criticism, and Foucault" [n. 20 above], 12).

[34] See Weigel's review of *Opening*, "Ohne Schutzhaut," 46.

expense of my own death."[35] And yet, the protagonist can hardly be said to enjoy her vomit. Her mouth wired shut, she feels it rise and fall inside her as she struggles to keep it down and dreams a scream that can neither be released nor returned (85). This ambivalence toward her vomit has to do with the parallels between the functions of her mouth and her recollections of history.

The flashbacks scattered throughout "Transition" are adult recollections of childhood impressions in which the war and its aftermath figure predominantly. "Outside was the war, that no one wasted words on, that no one described as such" (70). Silence negates the war as it does female subjectivity. Not surprisingly then, the narrative voice notes a kinship with a historical presence denied: "I the war" (70). The mouth becomes an organ of orientation for the young girl, for whom seeing is swallowing. "I swallowed whole battles away, mountains of corpses of the conquered. . . . I put away what they had put up with. I only did it, I couldn't have said anything about it, as language itself was what was being eaten and swallowed. And I was like a tablet which is uninterruptedly being written on, but not a single letter remains and can be gleaned: the body the unwritten page. Proof for the disappearance of wars" (71). This female body is left as a blank page on the surface only.[36] Inside it is filled with the unarticulated trauma of war, silenced by social convention. Her individual speechlessness is thus indicted along with a collective speechlessness peculiar to the German national experience. As Negt and Kluge have noted, no bodily organ alone has the capacity to yield orientation. Orientation, they contend, stems from the production of a public sphere that links what is public with what is intimate.[37] Duden writes: "The vacuum mouth became the most important organ." But because there is no public sphere to acknowledge what that female mouth has swallowed, the mouth has only one choice: "to take in and swallow down inwardly. The opposite didn't work" (65). The woman's inner space becomes the site where unarticulated, unappropriated history, both individual and collective, is deposited and left to fester. "I grew up, as though nothing had happened. Only somewhere, unlocatable and unfathomable, something was getting worse and worse" (71). "It slowly became manifest that all those individually overpowered and aborted moments of my life had secretly remained in my body" (80–81). The "vacuum mouth" has become a "mouth of ruins" (83). Rather than building up from the rubble, this *Trümmerfrau* ("woman of ruins") has been condemned to swallow it. (*Trümmerfrauen* were German women who literally

[35] Julia Kristeva, *Powers of Horror: An Essay on Abjection*, trans. Leon S. Roudiez (New York: Columbia University Press, 1982), 3.

[36] Contrast this with Gubar's analysis of "'The Blank Page' and the Issues of Female Creativity" (n. 19. above).

[37] Negt and Kluge, *Geschichte und Eigensinn* (n. 14 above), 1005.

cleaned up much of the rubble after the war.) The nausea with which she is plagued is thus also historical: she gags on her own unarticulated experience of the Third Reich and World War II. What has been swallowed revolts inside her.[38]

In this historical sense, too, the attack on her person causes that which has been repressed into controllable form to resume movement. Her housing or casing has been crushed (82), much as the snail shells in her path are crushed by the woman in "The Country Cottage" (17). The woman in "Transition" knows that in all statistical probability medicine will restore her appearance to "normal," but she also knows that what this most recent attack has set into motion cannot and should not be stopped. "What had just happened simply could not be handled yet, neither by memory nor by suppression. . . . What had happened had already almost totally become something invisible, was shapeless and unpredictable. What to do with it?" (81–82).[39] The text flatly refuses to provide answers to this question. The woman feels no relief whatsoever once her wires are removed. "I could open my mouth again but that was just what I was trying to avoid, because it was as though I had to stem stones apart" (91). During the final removal of the tracks that had been laid in her mouth during surgery, she experiences her head as a kind of inverted "construction site," where beams creak and ceilings cave in (91–92). Once again the distinction between construction and destruction is dissolved. The female subject experiences herself as the *object* both of the attackers' destruction and the doctor's reconstruction. The initial destruction allows for the integration between inner and outer space that would be the prerequisite for her self-construction. The medical reconstruction, on the other hand, imposes order from without. No wonder that the woman leaves the doctor's office with a "hollow thank you" (*Übergang*, 101; the official English translation reads "muttered a thank you very much," *Opening*, 92). Note, however, that it is not the attack that the protagonist welcomes but the movement precipitated by it.[40]

Yet Duden carefully eschews the glorification of movement for its own sake. Once the pain and physical discomfort subside, the reconstructed woman is left with the emotional residue of the attack. The ending, anything but optimistic, reverts to the image of blackness as a source of death and silence. The protagonist returns from shopping in the "wintry

[38] Cixous argues against the homogenized understanding of woman as historical subject that would deny that she occupies multiple sites simultaneously (see "Laugh of the Medusa" [n. 10 above], 252–53, and "Schreiben, Feminität, Veränderung" [n. 10 above], 138; or Cixous and Clement, *The Newly Born Woman* [n. 10 above], 88).

[39] This question has its counterpart in the final "But where to?" of "The Country Cottage" (39), where the woman has succumbed to the erasure of boundaries between inner and outer space.

[40] This distinction is important if we are to avoid the sexist assumption that women "like" the violence to which they are often subjected.

darkness," passes the second, "inner courtyard," and enters the "pitchdark entrance to the lift" (93). Darkness reigns as we realize that this woman identifies with the darkness that fills the inner courtyard. The dark spaces that she has had to traverse are in fact her own, but, given the dissolution of boundaries between inner and outer space, we must realize that this inner space is not private but social. "I have laboriously made my way through it, where in fact nothing should move; several times I had the impression the whole world, like this inner courtyard, was empty of people, sold into slavery" (94).

How then does this qualify as "concrete utopia"? The answer lies in the assertion of an "I" that resists external definitions but stops short of celebrating discontinuity for discontinuity's sake. The dark courtyard is described as "a terrain of ruins that has not yet been cleared. The choking sadness so often, the states of pain, the numbness, the sheer boredom of taking one step after another, and the constantly recurring uneasiness, the hunt, the grip on the throat, tighter and tighter. . . . I don't want to have to go through rooms or to buildings like that any more" (93). This "I" anticipates a brighter present without projecting misleadingly positive images onto the present, the future, or the past. As Weigel writes of Inga Buhmann's *Ich habe mir eine Geschichte geschrieben* (I wrote myself a story, 1977): "The detours would be wrong ways only if they were not grasped as *transit*, if the woman contented herself in her development with conquering male spaces."[41] Duden clearly does not conquer the spaces she has us traverse. The transition invoked by the title is one of constant movement and exploration. Its destination cannot be ascribed to any one place since the woman herself is both in and outside the dominant order. The protagonist in Duden's text is thus a working subject, and therein lies the "concrete utopia."

If the analysis ends here, we are left with the impression that the racism in the image of a group of faceless blacks characterized as unmitigated evil is itself mitigated when feminist aesthetics appropriates this image of blackness for its own.[42] Evil becomes good, absence assumes presence, and silence speaks. This is of course an oversimplification of the binary oppositions, which do not, as such, play a role in "Transition." Nonetheless, it can be argued that an attack by a group of black GIs allows the female protagonist to assert her subjectivity somewhere between the positive-negative pull of the dominant order and that which it negates. Blackness, one might

[41] Sigrid Weigel, "Der schielende Blick: Thesen zur Geschichte weiblicher Praxis," in Stephan and Weigel (n. 13 above), 117. The German original, from which "Double Focus" is translated, is cited (in my translation) for this particular passage, as it is omitted from Anderson's translation.

[42] Cixous's admonishment to "hurry: the continent is not impenetrably dark" ("Laugh of the Medusa," 255) is similarly problematic.

conclude, cannot be all bad or badness all black. Indeed a dream-like recollection of harassment by a group of young, *blond* youths is fused with an image of blacks in a way that momentarily binds black and white together in a conspiracy of evil (77, 79). Yet, this poses no effective challenge to the fundamentally racist image of the black attackers. They do have other qualities besides being black and evil; they are also Americans, soldiers, and males. And yet, none of these latter qualities is stressed or reinforced throughout the text as only blackness is. Prompted in part by Barbara Smith's contention that "much feminist scholarship has been written as if black women did not exist," Adrienne Rich writes in a lengthy essay: "I no longer believe that 'colorblindness'—if it even exists—is the opposite of racism; I think it is, in this world, a form of naivete and moral stupidity."[43] I have asked myself to what extent *Opening* is tainted with the "white solipsism" (Rich) indicted by Smith and Rich. In other words, does the fact that Duden's text claims blackness *on behalf* of female subjectivity excuse it from the charge of racism?

Whereas images of blackness and darkness are scattered throughout *Opening*, the GIs are the only human figures onto whom blackness is permanently projected. This has striking consequences when we consider that dark spaces are after all not the same as dark men or women.[44] I have already discussed the relationship between the darkness inside the protagonist and the darkness outside her. What does it mean for the dissolution of the boundaries between inner and outer space for this darkness to be projected, as a fixed characteristic, onto a group of human beings? By citing black GIs as aggressors, Duden fuses blackness, otherwise treated positively in the text in its association with the oppressed, with the qualities of the oppressor (male, "impenetrable wall"). While blackness in its other forms can be treated both as the repository of hope and the instrument of its destruction, the particular linkage in the black GIs yields black human beings who function in the text *only* as evil. Duden in fact has the attackers represent what men traditionally fear in women: darkness, loss of self, threat to life. Yet, the GIs do pose a real threat to the woman. She is attacked, one might argue, by the male projection of woman projected back onto another group of men. The woman is caught here between the dominant (white) order and the blackness that comes back to haunt it.

[43] Adrienne Rich, "Disloyal to Civilization: Feminism, Racism, Gynephobia (1978)," in her *On Lies, Secrets, and Silence: Selected Prose, 1966–1978* (New York: W. W. Norton & Co., 1979), 300. Barbara Smith's essay, to which Rich refers, is "Toward a Black Feminist Criticism," *Conditions* 2 (1977): 25–44.

[44] Consider, e.g., the analyses of dark spaces in Sandra M. Gilbert and Susan Gubar's "The Parables of the Dark Cave," in their *The Madwoman in the Attic: The Woman Writer and the Nineteenth-Century Imagination*, 2d ed. (New Haven, Conn., and London: Yale University Press, 1980), 93–104

"Caught" is a good word for her situation because the two identifying characteristics that the narrative voice cannot flow into and out of are her gender and her race. This constitutes a textual thorn in the theory of oppositional negativity for women. If the story is not about the narrator's relationship to blacks as persons, and it is not, then why use them as a symbol? The particular role of black persons in the text forces the issue of positionality in a way that the other, metaphorical images of blackness in and of themselves do not. The story would surely read differently if the narrator herself were black. A writer like Toni Morrison can use images of "nightshade" and "blackberry" to refer to black experience in a way that is blocked to Duden as a white woman writer.[45] Any appropriation of blackness on her part is necessarily predicated on the experience that white skin brings in a predominantly white society, even if the white woman consciously rejects the dominant order.[46]

Although the race of the female persona is never named, it is clear from the context that she is a white woman in a culture that identifies itself as white. Foreign and appropriated by the text as a symbol of unabashed evil, the black GIs can pose a serious threat to her because they embody what has been severed, silenced, effaced, and repressed. This holds for her personal history as a woman as well as for the missing collective coming to terms with the (Nazi) past (*Vergangenheitsbewältigung*), in which her life as a German is bound. And yet this symbol of the "evil" blacks can function only on the basis of her "privilege." In spite of all the black holes of her history, the narrator is white and can speak only from that perspective. Not all cows are black or even gray in the night in which Duden erases the boundaries between inner and outer space.[47] For her own dark spaces (absences) the narrator lets stand a dark presence (the GIs), but, by giving this presence a human form, she reinforces the racist premise of her privileged position—one from which, however, she clearly derives no satisfaction and certainly no identity. While she speaks from the disrupted vantage point of an oppressed gender, the inversions that *Opening* enacts in the relationship between oppressor and oppressed rely on a symbolism that qualifies the narrator as privileged. She is, to be sure, *injured* by the blacks who attack her and her companions, but she is *oppressed* by her entrapment in the privileged position that allows the symbol to function at all.

[45] See the passage from Toni Morrison's *Sula* cited in Susan S. Lanser, *The Narrative Act: Point of View in Prose Fiction* (Princeton, N.J.: Princeton University Press, 1981), 234–35.

[46] The "double existence" cited by Weigel and Martin for women in general is doubly true in the context of white women's role in the oppression of other races. See Rich, "Disloyal to Civilization."

[47] The pastoral allusion is to G. W. F. Hegel's *The Phenomenology of Mind*, rev. 2d ed., trans. J. B. Baillie (New York: Humanities Press, 1971), 79.

This particular manifestation of positionality is, furthermore, culturally specific to the West German context. The female protagonist, who realizes that she belongs to "the species of those responsible" for the genocide of the Jews (64), has too much historical consciousness to equate her own victimization as a woman with the victimization of the Jews by the Nazis. This non-Jewish German woman is precluded from appropriating Jewishness as a symbol or as a vehicle with which to express her own, culturally and socially determined victimization. Blackness, on the other hand, would *seem* to provide a more neutral medium with which both to articulate and to challenge this victimization. Such appropriation is, however, *textually* prohibited by the racist image of the black GIs, which essentially undermines the feminist, racially "neutral" expectations evoked by the text. While the piece provides a historical context for its discussion of Jews, there is no comparable context provided explicitly by the text for its treatment of blacks or blackness. Nevertheless, even though the central attack is depicted by the narrator as unprovoked, it seems logical to assume that racial tension must be at least a contributing factor. And yet, this assumption is a misleadingly simplistic one if we too glibly conclude that the blacks attack the Germans *because* they are white or that the racist image of the GIs is *merely* a function of the protagonist's white skin per se. We need to know what it means to be black- or white-skinned in any given context. What is missing here is an articulation of the historical context in which the manifestation of racial conflict acquires historically and socially particular meaning. The GIs' own racial awareness has surely been shaped primarily by experiences in the United States, and yet these figures function in the story outside that context. It is their skin color, not the context of their lives, that links the incident to both the textual imagery of blackness and to the life history of the white German protagonist. Although feminist readers may be eager to emphasize the femaleness of the woman's injuries, the latter have just as much to do with the protagonist being a German who grew up during the Third Reich as with her being a woman. While we may reasonably assume that extratextual racial tension between Afro-Americans and Germans continues to bear traces of the ideology of the "master race," it would be patently ridiculous to contend that the soldiers in the story enact or in any way speak for the vengeance of the Jews. The cross-cultural *specificity* of racial conflict in this particular context is very clearly *not* woven into the texture of the story, which is why the exact relationship between this German woman, Jews, and black GIs remains so disturbingly murky. And yet the unequivocally racist imagery with which the attack at the discotheque is depicted signals that the apparent racial neutrality of the textual appropriation of blackness is bogus. In other words, the racist image of the GIs points a finger at a sociohistorical context that the text itself does not elaborate. In that sense, the real "dark presence" of the text is not the group of GIs, nor is it even the collective history of the Germans who were somehow part of the Third Reich. We have seen how the movement of the protagonist's vomit traces the progression from suppression and repression into consciousness and articulation. The presence that *remains* in the darkness in this text are the social and historical forces that are brought to bear on a confrontation between a white, non-Jewish, German woman and a group of black, male soldiers from the United States.

As to whether *Opening* explodes a racist premise or reproduces it, I can only answer, yes, it does both. It is perhaps one of those images that women writers must traverse in all its ugly familiarity in order to destroy.[48] Its racist implications challenge the simple appropriation of images of blackness by feminist aesthetics on behalf of a female subjectivity in whose name this text might otherwise be hailed. *Opening* poses an ineluctable confrontation with women's positionality vis-à-vis the dominant order in specific historical contexts. The racist premise that yields this confrontation is cause not for celebration but for self-reflection. It demands, at the very least, that we examine more rigorously the concrete and hence theoretical implications of any alleged universality of *écriture féminine*.

Department of German
Ohio State University

[48] I am alluding here to Weigel's critique of Cixous and Irigaray, in which she calls for women writers "to traverse" the regressive images we have internalized ("Frau und 'Weiblichkeit'" [n. 12 above], 112, and "Double Focus" [n. 18 above], 79–80, or "Der schielende Blick" [n. 41 above], 112–16). Weigel makes brief references to some of the many similarities between *Opening* and "Der Fall Franza" by Ingeborg Bachmann in her review of the former ("Ohne Schutzhaut" [n. 29 above], 47). One significant difference, however, is that Franza is ill, whereas the woman in Duden's text is injured in an attack. Franza internalizes the attacks on her person in a way that Duden's protagonist does not. By smashing her head against the wall, Franza fails to make the most crucial distinction between her self and the image that inadequately represents her. In other words, Franza destroys herself *along with* the image.

ON MATERNAL SPLITTING: A PROPOS OF MARY GORDON'S *MEN AND ANGELS*

SUSAN RUBIN SULEIMAN

When I first began to think about writing this essay, I envisaged it as a sequel to my earlier essay on "Writing and Motherhood."[1] There my chief concern had been with the inner conflicts of the writing mother and, more generally, of any creative woman who feels herself torn between two seemingly irreconcilable allegiances: on the one hand, her commitment to and love for her child, whom she perceives as totally dependent on her and needing her in order to survive and flourish; on the other hand, her commitment to her own creative self and to *its* particular offspring—her work, her writing. Although this conflict, I argued, can be seen as produced in large part by the mother's internalization of the dominant cultural discourses about motherhood and the mother-child bond (including the discourse of psychoanalysis, which has tended to see women's creativity and motherhood as an "either/or" relation), my emphasis in that essay was less on the social and cultural determinants of the mother's inner conflict than on a description of the experience of that conflict—a phenomenology, if you will—as it is manifested in the writings, both discursive and fictional, of women who are moth-

I am grateful to the "other mothers" in the Cambridge mothers' group—Mieke Bal, Teresa Bernardez, Carol Gilligan, Marianne Hirsch, Evelyn Keller, Amy Lang, Ruth Perry, and Gail Reimer—for our ongoing discussions, in 1985 and 1986, of the issues treated in this essay.

[1] Susan Rubin Suleiman, "Writing and Motherhood," in *The (M)other Tongue: Essays in Feminist Psychoanalytic Interpretation*, ed. C. Kahane, S. Garner, and M. Sprengnether (Ithaca, N.Y.: Cornell University Press, 1985), 352–77.

This essay originally appeared in *Signs*, vol. 14, no. 1, Autumn 1988.

ers. I felt that this emphasis on the mother's subjectivity was especially important, given the silence to which mothers in our culture have traditionally been reduced.

In planning this new essay—and from the very beginning it was linked in my mind to Mary Gordon's *Men and Angels*, a novel that intrigued me even before I had read it—I thought I would continue my exploration of the mother's subjectivity by focusing not on the triangle of mother, work, and child, but on that of mother, mother-surrogate, and child. In the first case what seemed to be involved was a struggle between the mother's creative needs and the child's needs, the issue being that of work. The second case (so I told myself) could be seen as a logical and chronological sequel to the former. Here the mother would no longer experience herself as pitted against her child over her work or against her work over her child. Rather, she would see herself as somehow threatened by the intrusion of a third person, an "other mother" or maternal figure who might displace her in her child's affections while she was away pursuing her nonmaternal activities.

I knew from my own experience and from discussions with other feminist friends engaged in self-absorptive creative careers that this anxiety does in fact exist, whatever its basis in reality. And two popular books, Nancy Friday's *Jealousy* and Phyllis Chesler's *Mothers on Trial*, reinforced this conviction.[2] Friday shows, at great length, that jealousy, or the fear of the loss of love by the intrusion of a third party, is a well-nigh universal feeling. Chesler, in turn, documents with terrifying (and terrified) relentlessness a number of recent cases in which mothers have been legally deprived of their children by fathers who are often aided and abetted by what she calls "mother-competitors," women bent on replacing the child's biological mother both in the father's bed and in the child's affections. Even if such cases are statistically rarer than Chesler suggests, they still indicate that in contemporary America the mother's anxiety is not always a matter of fantasy but may be founded on a perception of real danger.

Nevertheless, my beginning intention was to explore the question of the "other mother" not as a political issue but as a powerful maternal fantasy, especially as it is manifested in fiction by writing mothers. When it came time to actually work out this essay and do the necessary reading and writing, however, an interesting discovery emerged. I began to see that the fantasies and conflicts I had thought of as different and separate (my two "triangles") were in

[2] Nancy Friday, *Jealousy* (New York: Wm. Morrow, 1985); Phyllis Chesler, *Mothers on Trial: The Battle for Children and Custody* (New York: McGraw-Hill, 1986).

fact closely related. I also realized, more forcefully than ever before, that personal fantasy, fictional representation, and social and cultural reality are so interconnected where motherhood is concerned that it is impossible to talk about one without the others. The notion of maternal splitting links maternal fantasies about the "other mother" with fantasies about the child and work and provides one perspective on the important question of the relations between maternal fantasy and the realities of mothering in our culture today.

Splitting the mother: Some psychoanalytic views

As the fairy tales about wicked stepmothers and fairy godmothers tell us, the impulse to split the maternal figure into "good" and "bad" personae is very old indeed. Bruno Bettelheim has remarked, "Far from being a device used only by fairy tales, such a splitting up of one person into two to keep the good image uncontaminated occurs to many children as a solution to a relationship too difficult to manage or comprehend. . . . The fantasy of the wicked stepmother not only preserves the good mother intact, it also prevents having to feel guilty about one's angry thoughts or wishes about her."[3] Bettelheim is restating here what has long been recognized as a psychoanalytic truism: the child's feelings toward the mother are ambivalent, a conflicting mixture of tenderness, gratitude, and destructive rage. According to Melanie Klein, these feelings are already present in the very young infant, who experiences the mother's breast alternately as gratifying and pleasure giving and (when it is delayed or withheld) as hateful and frustrating. "The baby reacts to unpleasant stimuli, and to the frustration of [her] pleasure, with feelings of hatred and aggression. These feelings of hatred are directed towards the same objects as are the pleasurable ones, namely, the breasts of the mother."[4] Later on, the child sees the mother as a whole person, but the coexistence of opposing feelings persists: "Feelings both of a destructive and of a loving nature are experienced towards one and the same person and this gives rise to deep and disturbing conflicts in the child's mind."[5] In Klein's theory, if all goes well, these conflicts will produce guilt in the child for her or his destructive fantasies, which in turn will lead to a desire for reparation. Or, Bettelheim suggests, these conflicts may produce

[3] B. Bettelheim, *The Uses of Enchantment: The Meaning and Importance of Fairy Tales* (New York: Vintage, 1987), 67, 69.

[4] M. Klein, "Weaning," in *Love, Guilt, and Reparation and Other Works, 1921–1945* (New York: Delta, 1977), 290.

[5] Ibid., 293.

fantasies such as that of the wicked stepmother, which deflect the child's destructive feelings away from the good mother. Or yet again, as Margaret Mahler has observed in the behavior of toddlers, ambivalence toward the mother may produce a splitting of the real object world around the child into "good" and "bad"; one of the child's caretakers then becomes the "bad" mother, "protecting the good mother image from [the child's] destructive anger."[6] Splitting thus functions as a defense mechanism, enabling the child to preserve the image of a protective and nurturant mother—an image that *must* be preserved (so the theory goes), given the child's sense of total dependence on her. Ultimately, according to Mahler, if the child is to develop a stable and harmonious sense of self, splitting must give way to the "unifying of 'good' and 'bad' objects into one whole representation."[7] This unifying might correspond to Klein's notion of repairing the mother's body or to Bettelheim's idea that, once a child grows older and more secure, no longer quite so dependent on her mother, she "can rework the double picture into one."[8]

If in these versions of splitting what is at stake is maternal nurturance, there exists another version, first analyzed by Freud, in which splitting refers specifically to the erotic realm: what is at stake in this instance is maternal asexuality. In his essay "The Most Prevalent Form of Degradation in Erotic Life," Freud diagnosed the "mother/whore" syndrome so common in men as the result of a disassociation of sensual and tender feelings, aiming to maintain the mother's asexual "purity" by deflecting all sensual feelings onto an other, degraded object. Recently, Jim Swan has analyzed Freud's own discovery of the Oedipus complex as resulting from a similar splitting: the splitting between Freud's Catholic Nannie, who initiated him into sex (he called her his "first seductress and shamer"), and his mother, who remained the "pure object of desire."[9] It is perhaps explicable in historical terms, as a Victorian phenomenon, that the kind of splitting in which Freud himself was most interested and personally implicated was the splitting of the mother in the erotic realm. Object-relations theorists, on the other hand, seem less concerned with the child's view of the mother as asexual or

[6] M. Mahler, Fred Pine, and Anni Bergman, *The Psychological Birth of the Human Infant* (New York: Basic, 1975), 99.

[7] Ibid., 110.

[8] Bettelheim, 68.

[9] Freud's 1912 essay can be found in Sigmund Freud, *Sexuality and the Psychology of Love* (New York: Collier, 1963), 58–69. J. Swan, "*Mater* and Nannie: Freud's Two Mothers and the Discovery of the Oedipus Complex," *American Imago* 31 (1974): 50 and passim.

sexual than with the child's view of the mother as benevolent or destructive.[10]

Whether of the strictly Freudian or the object-relations variety, however, all of the theories I have mentioned assume that the "unique love-object," as well as the single most powerful and important figure in the life of the infant and small child—and consequently, according to these theories, in the life of the adult the child will become—is her or his mother.[11] They also assume, by and large, that this is the natural and necessary way things should be. This is not the place to survey the various critiques and modifications that have been proposed with regard to this psychoanalytic model, whether one considers it as a model of child development (positing that the individual personality is fully formed in the first few years of life) or as a model of mothering (positing that the mother-child dyad is the determining one). Such critiques have come both from male psychoanalysts like Erik Erikson, who proposes a less infant-centered as well as a more socially oriented model of child development, and from feminist theorists like Nancy Chodorow and Dorothy Dinnerstein, who propose a less biologically based model of mothering. However, the dominant analytic and cultural discourse about mothers and their children—what Ann Kaplan has called the "Master Mother Discourse"—continues to emphasize the mother's crucial, determining role in the development and continuing welfare of the child.[12] This discourse fosters what Chodorow and Susan Contratto have called the "myth of maternal omnipotence"—the belief that whatever happens to the child on the way to becoming an adult is ultimately attributable to its "good" or "bad" mother.[13]

[10] Interestingly, the question of the mother's sexuality is once again foregrounded in Sue Miller's best-selling novel, *The Good Mother* (New York: Harper & Row, 1986)—in which, perhaps most significantly, the mother's sexuality becomes a determining factor in a legal conflict over what is beneficial or destructive to the child. The cultural-ideological implications of this novel and of its extraordinary popular success are yet to be fully explored.

[11] The phrase "unique love-object" occurs in Mahler, Pine, and Bergman, 110.

[12] Erik H. Erikson, *Childhood and Society,* 2d ed. (New York: Norton, 1963); Nancy Chodorow, *The Reproduction of Mothering: Psychoanalysis and the Sociology of Gender* (Berkeley: University of California Press, 1978); Dorothy Dinnerstein, *The Mermaid and the Minotaur: Sexual Arrangements and the Human Malaise* (New York: Harper & Row, 1976); E. Ann Kaplan, "Mothering, Feminism and Representation: The Maternal in Melodrama and the Woman's Film, 1910–1940," in *Home Is Where the Heart Is,* ed. Christine Gledhill (London: British Film Institute, 1987), 113–37.

[13] N. Chodorow and S. Contratto, "The Fantasy of the Perfect Mother," in *Rethinking the Family,* ed. Barrie Thorne with Marilyn Yalom (New York: Longman, 1982), 71.

Chodorow and Contratto make an impassioned plea for an alternative to our "cultural ideology" of "blame and idealization of mothers," which has been internalized by so many women.[14] They mount an impressive critique of some of the more influential feminist writings by mothers about their experience of motherhood, on the grounds that even feminists have not succeeded in freeing themselves from the myth of maternal omnipotence.[15] Although the feminist mothers "blame patriarchy" instead of "blaming Mom," they do not question the dominant assumption that Mom is all-important. Chodorow and Contratto claim that this assumption is itself based on fantasies whose source is in infancy about the omnipotent mother, but that such fantasies exist precisely because children in our culture are being "mothered exclusively by one woman." It seems that we are trapped in a vicious circle. The way out of the circle, Contratto and Chodorow suggest, is for feminists to be very wary and self-critical about their own assumptions concerning motherhood and child development. They should seek models of development that "recognize collaboration and compromise as well as conflict" and that "look at times other than infancy in the developmental life span and relationships over time to people other than the mother to get a more accurate picture of what growing up is about."[16]

Intellectually, I find myself very attracted to this conclusion, as well as to the analysis that precedes it. The idea that even feminists writing about motherhood are expressing infantile fantasies about the omnipotent mother, for example, could explain the phenomenon of *maternal* splitting, in which it is not the child who through fantasy splits the mother into "good" and "bad," but the mother herself who does so. Consider the guilt fantasy about work versus child, for example: "With every word I write, with every act of genuine creation, I hurt my child."[17] This fear on the part of the mother that each moment of creative self-absorption is destructive to her child is widespread and powerful, and has found some powerful expressions in fiction. Now, if Chodorow and Contratto are right, this fantasy "repeats" both the infant's own fantasy and the cultural ideology of maternal omnipotence. If the mother did not somehow imagine herself as omnipotent in relation to her child, she would

[14] Ibid., 65.

[15] Among the works that Chodorow and Contratto critique are Adrienne Rich, *Of Woman Born: Motherhood as Experience and Institution* (New York: Norton, 1976); Jane Lazarre, *The Mother Knot* (New York: McGraw-Hill, 1976); *Feminist Studies*, vol. 4, no. 2 (Summer 1978), a special issue entitled "Toward a Feminist Theory of Motherhood."

[16] Chodorow and Contratto, 71.

[17] Suleiman (n. 1 above), 374.

not need to feel so guilty and murderous every time she turned away from the child to pursue other self-absorptive goals.[18]

Sara Ruddick has suggested to me that the term "maternal omnipotence" does not accurately name what is involved both in the cultural ideology and in the maternal fantasy I have been describing. Ruddick proposes, instead, the term "maternal responsibility," which suggests not so much a feeling of power (mothers often feel powerless, even in relation to their infants) as the feeling that what happens to the child is ultimately attributable to the mother—hence the cultural "blame Mom" syndrome, but also the mother's own potential sense of guilt or self-blame. I find Ruddick's argument convincing, but I would propose the term "absolute responsibility" or "ultimate responsibility" to suggest the hyperbolic nature of what is involved. One could then say, refining Chodorow and Contratto's terminology, that what the young child perceives as maternal omnipotence, the mother perceives as absolute or ultimate maternal responsibility. The two perceptions are symmetrical and both are fantasies, for in reality the mother is neither all-powerful in relation to the child nor absolutely (exclusively) responsible for the child's fate.

Questions of terminology aside, I agree with Chodorow and Contratto's suggestion that a more reality-oriented attitude—an attitude reinforced or made possible by new theories of mothering and child development, a new cultural discourse—would be healthy for mothers. At the same time, when I think of my own experience as a woman with a commitment to intellectual creativity and to motherhood, as well as that of other women whom I have read or with whom I have spoken about this subject, I become painfully aware of the difficulties, both personal and social, that the realization of such a "program for mothers" entails. Can we choose or discard at will our most deep-seated fantasies and self-representations? Do we dare, in a time of increasing social conservatism and

[18] Carol Gilligan has noted that women with an absorbing career generally feel strong conflict "between achievement and care," even if they are not mothers. In her study of women pursuing advanced degrees, she found that "these highly successful and achieving women do not mention their academic and professional distinction in the context of describing themselves, and the conflict they encounter between achievement and care leaves them either divided in judgment or feeling betrayed" (Gilligan, *In a Different Voice: Psychological Theory and Women's Development* [Cambridge, Mass.: Harvard University Press, 1982], 159). If, as Gilligan suggests, the phenomenon of splitting is experienced by women in general, it is all the more strong when the "care" involved is that of a mother for her child. In both cases, however, cultural ideology plays at least as important a role as the feminine specificity one might wish to attribute to women or to mothers.

disintegrating family life, to give up our sense of an absolutely privileged relationship with our children?

I am not going to try and answer these questions directly—at least not yet. Rather, I want to reinscribe them in my reading of *Men and Angels,* a novel that I think poses them in an extremely compelling and disturbing way.

Maternal splitting: *Men and Angels*

About a month before the publication of *Men and Angels,* Mary Gordon published some excerpts from her diary in the *New York Times Book Review.* The diary entries covered the period from December 1983 to the fall of 1984. During this time, Mary Gordon gave birth to her second child, a boy, and also finished her novel and delivered it to the publisher. In the first entry, Gordon is in a New York apartment waiting for the birth of her son, who is late in coming; she has with her her unfinished manuscript and her other child, a three-year-old girl, who is sick. Sitting at her sick daughter's bedside, she thinks of the fact that she has not even looked at the manuscript: "I have not even looked at it, partly because any action is physically difficult for me; I could excuse myself this way. But the truth is, it is impossible for me to believe that anything I write could have a fraction of the importance of the child growing inside me, or of the child who lies now, her head on my belly, with the sweet yet offhand stoicism of a sick child."[19]

When I read that, my first reaction was, "Here we go again—not mothership and authorhood, but writing versus motherhood! The same old conflict, resolved here by a somewhat sentimental renunciation of the writing self. Will we writing mothers never get beyond this split, always having to choose the work or the child, always convinced that choosing one means sacrificing the other?" The rest of the diary entries show, however, that in reality Mary Gordon was able to choose both. After a few months of total immersion in/with her baby, she went back to writing and finished her novel. And when the novel was reviewed by Margaret Drabble (another famous writing mother) on the front page of the *New York Times Book Review,* a short boxed interview by Herbert Mitgang with Mary Gordon on an inside page showed a reassuringly unconflicted and practical author talking about her life. "I probably have it a lot easier than most writers with children. When the baby

[19] Mary Gordon, "On Mothership and Authorhood," *New York Times Book Review* (February 10, 1985), 1.

sitter takes over after breakfast, I leave the house, get into my car and drive for 15 minutes to a little cabin on the Hudson River. There I light the fire and gain the physical separation that I need to work. Between 9:30 and 1:30, I turn into a writer." "In *Men and Angels*," noted Mitgang, "Miss Gordon's heroine is happily married and has two children and a baby sitter. So does Miss Gordon, whose husband teaches English at the University of New York at New Paltz, where they live."[20]

In Margaret Drabble's review of *Men and Angels*, however, I read the following: "The bloody denouement is both predictable and plausible. Presented with a stark choice . . . , Anne, in effect, saves her children and sacrifices Laura."[21] Anne is the writing mother, Laura is the live-in babysitter; Anne writes, and Laura is sacrificed. It occurred to me then that "Miss Gordon's heroine" may lead a more complicated life, and be related to Miss Gordon in more complicated ways, than Mr. Mitgang realized.

A few weeks later, I went to hear Mary Gordon talk about the book and read excerpts from it at the Boston Public Library. "Who has written seriously about the inner world of mothers?" she asked, uncannily echoing a question by Julia Kristeva that I had used as an epigraph for "Writing and Motherhood": "Que savons-nous du discours que (se) fait une mère?" (What do we know about the [inner] discourse of a mother?)

In the first passage from *Men and Angels* that Mary Gordon read, Anne Foster, the heroine, has just finished her day's work up in her study. She has recently accepted an important assignment: to curate and write the catalog essay for the first major retrospective exhibition of an American expatriate painter, Caroline Watson, who lived and worked in Paris and died there in 1939. (Caroline Watson is an invented figure.) Anne has been poring over Caroline's letters and feels that she is beginning to know this woman "in the bone." Now, however, it's time for her to go and join her children, in the familiar kitchen downstairs. Walking down the stairs, "hearing her heels on the wooden floor as if they were somebody else's," Anne feels the difference within herself: "In the room with Caroline she was weightless. Sometimes it frightened her, the speed of her blood, the giddy sense of being somewhere else, in some high territory, inaccessible. With the children, there was never any flying off, flying up. A mother was encumbered and held down. Anne felt that

[20] "A Cabin of One's Own," *New York Times Book Review* (March 31, 1985), 30.

[21] Margaret Drabble, "The Limits of Mother Love," *New York Times Book Review* (March 31, 1985), 30.

she was fortunate in that she loved the weighing down."[22] When she reaches the kitchen, the children are not there. They are out in the woods with Laura, the au pair girl Anne has hired to make her writing possible while her husband is away on a year's sabbatical in France. Anne feels disappointed, then happy when the children appear. But Laura is with them, diffident, watching her—an intrusive presence. Anne, intuitively understanding how starved Laura is for affection ("She was a girl who had not, it was clear, been held enough, been treasured"), tries to convince herself that her discomfort is only momentary: "She was sure that when she got more used to living with a stranger, her unpleasant feelings would just disappear. She brought the cups to the sink, ashamed of herself for wishing Laura were not there" (48).

The second passage read by Mary Gordon occurs in the novel's time a few weeks later. Once again, Anne is reading Caroline's letters, and this time the text of one letter is quoted in full; it is from Caroline in Paris to her son Stephen and his wife Jane, who are in Cambridge, Massachusetts. It is a warm, witty, loving letter, but all the warmth is addressed to Jane, not to Stephen. Caroline did not love Stephen; she had barely ever lived with him, had left him in the care of others in the States while she chose to work in Paris, the only place where she could paint. Stephen died young, miserable. Jane is still alive, an old and vigorous woman, childless, flourishing, with a distinguished academic career behind her.

> Whenever Anne thought of Caroline's treatment of Stephen she came upon a barrier between them that was as profound as one of language. . . . She couldn't imagine Peter or Sarah [her children] marrying anyone she would prefer to them, as Caroline has preferred Jane to Stephen. You have done wrong, she always wanted to tell Caroline. Caroline, the ghost who had taken over her life, hovering, accepting worship. . . . And even as she wanted to tell Caroline, "You have done wrong," an anger rose up in her as if the accusation had come from someone else. No one would have pored through a male artist's letters to his children as she had through Caroline's to Stephen. It was that Caroline was a woman and had a child and had created art; because the three could be connected in some grammar, it was as though the pressure to do so were one of logic. Then she wanted to defend Caroline from the accusation she herself had laid against her. What did it matter,

[22] Mary Gordon, *Men and Angels* (New York: Random, 1985), 45. Further page references will be given in parentheses in the text.

> she wanted to say to the shivering ghost whom she had left unsheltered. You were a great painter. You did what you had to do. Yet even as she shielded the ghost, she could not still the accusation: "You should not have let your child die young." For as a mother, she felt it was the most important thing in the world. You did not hurt your children. You kept your children safe. [68–69]

Hearing these two passages read by the author, I realized that *Men and Angels* was a book I had to read and write about. It is an extraordinarily powerful book, and a veritable gold mine for anyone interested in the phenomenon of maternal splitting. This is a rather crude way of putting it, for I don't mean that Mary Gordon gives us a guided tour or a handy little catalog of maternal fantasies relating to children, creativity, and "other" mothers. I mean, rather, that for those who share my current preoccupations, this novel will reveal a marvelously rich and complex terrain, offering multiple paths for exploration. I want to explore here the direction of maternal splitting, to see how this notion makes possible both a detailed (albeit necessarily partial) reading of this novel[23] and a renewed consideration of the conflicts and dilemmas that real-life mothers face.

As the passages above suggest, the three principal characters in the novel variously mirror and read each other; more exactly, Anne is the central figure "doubled" on two sides by Caroline and Laura. Like Caroline, whose life and work she pores over, Anne is a creative woman and a mother. However, unlike Caroline, Anne has a passionate commitment to motherhood: whereas Caroline was a "bad" mother to her son, "allowing" him to die young (shades of the maternal omnipotence fantasy), Anne is a totally "good" mother to her children and has their safety uppermost in her mind. Caroline, on the other hand, was a good "other" mother to Jane, whose feelings toward her own biological mother were no warmer than (as she puts it) feelings toward "a rather distant cousin" (167). Caroline is therefore split into a murderous and a nurturing mother, depending on whether one looks at Stephen or Jane. But she can

[23] I call my reading of *Men and Angels* both detailed and partial because, although it explores at some length the phenomenon of maternal splitting and uses it to make sense of the novel as a whole, that is all it does. In other words, it makes *one* sense of a work that obviously invites many other readings and constructions of sense. Such a partial reading is inevitable, given my theoretical frame; in any case, no reading of a novel can claim completeness (although some may be more complete than others).

also be seen as the "bad" version or double of Anne—a mother who chooses to sacrifice her own child to her work.

Structurally, Laura occupies the most interesting position, for she functions as a negative double both for Anne *and* for Anne's children: as the "bad" "other mother," she allows Peter and Sarah to walk on the thin ice of a pond while she herself sits engrossed in a book (as it happens, the Bible—it's the only book she reads); it is Anne herself who, rushing down to the pond, saves the children and then turns in a fury on Laura: "As strong as her love for her children, for her husband, stronger than the things that made the center of her life was her desire to inflict damage on the smiling face of this girl who might have let her children die" (203). We can read Anne's destructive rage here as directed against the bad, murderous mother, who sits reading while the children are in danger; but as the text emphasizes in various ways, this bad mother is a mirror image—what I call a negative double, and what in psychoanalytic terms might be called a split-off projection—of Anne herself. This is made most clear at the moment when, after Laura's suicide, Anne painfully drags the young woman's body to her own bed and proceeds to dress the body in her own bathrobe. It is also significant that the narrative itself is divided into alternating sections with now Anne, now Laura, as the center of consciousness. The narration thus mirrors in its language and point of view the psychological doubling between Anne and Laura.

If Laura is the negative double who must be destroyed in order to preserve the "good" Anne, the good mother, she is also the negative double of Anne's children. Caroline, we recall, had one unloved child (her biological son) who died young, and another, chosen child (Jane) whom she loved. In Anne's case, the position of the unloved child is occupied by Laura, and it is this child who, like Caroline's son Stephen, is sacrificed by Anne to her work: "Each time now that [Anne] thought of her work on Caroline, she would have to wonder if Laura had been its sacrifice. Her death would touch even that. Had she not met me, she would not have died, Anne thought, listening to the priest. Had I not ignored her distress trying to finish my work" (233). Paradoxically, then, in destroying Laura, Anne destroys the bad mother, but she also destroys a child, thus reintroducing the bad mother into herself.[24]

Although the complicated mirrorings among Anne, Caroline, and Laura dominate the novel, there are at least two other mothers who

[24] The novel emphasizes at various points the adoring love that Laura feels for Anne. Having been rejected by her own mother, Laura is seeking a substitute. Anne knows this but is unable to respond.

figure secondarily but significantly in the story. Anne's mother has two daughters—she has been a good, loving mother to Anne's sister, but a rejecting mother to Anne herself. In relation to Anne, the good mother slot may be considered occupied by her father, and possibly also by the older woman, Jane (who enters her life quite late, however, through her work on Caroline). Laura's mother also has two daughters, of whom Laura is the unloved one. By their similar position in relation to their biological mothers, Anne and Laura again turn out to be structural twins—with the crucial difference that whereas Anne finds one or perhaps two good "other" mothers, Laura does not. Laura's pathological attachment to Anne is precisely an attempt to find in her a loving mother with whom she can identify. This attempt fails, however, because Anne cannot love Laura—Laura, like Stephen, is not lovable.[25] When, in the end, Anne vents her fury on Laura, the young woman commits suicide—like a child who has suddenly discovered, to her horror, that she does not possess any "good" mother, only a murderously punitive one (and that consequently she cannot herself be "good"?).

The web of connections between the characters in the novel suggests several observations. First, the structural similarity between Caroline and Anne is evident, but so is Anne's greater complexity (and more complicated splitting), which rightly confers on her the title of protagonist, if not necessarily of heroine. Caroline is divided internally into a good and a bad mother, with her work as a crucial element in both cases (it "kills" Stephen, but it creates an emotional and intellectual bond between her and Jane). Anne, too, is divided internally, though her work functions only in a negative way: it destroys Laura (as Anne herself thinks in a passage I quoted earlier), but it also, indirectly, harms Anne's own children. After Laura's death, nothing can ever be the same for them—they would "grow up knowing life was terrible and they were never safe" (237).

[25] This may seem a highly problematic statement. Is there such a thing as an "essentially unlovable" child? Or are people like Laura and Stephen, who appear so unlovable, already the "products"—and victims—of a lack of maternal love? The very asking of this question entangles one in the fantasy of ultimate maternal responsibility: if the child turns out unlovable because of the mother's care-lessness, then the mother is the ultimately responsible agent of the child's destiny. If this view appears unduly harsh, what shall we say about the alternative explanation that some people are "born unlovable"? Could the fantasy of ultimate maternal responsibility be one way to deflect the perhaps more horrifying notion (horrifying to a mother and to a child) that some human beings are unlovable by nature? At this point, the religious and theological dimensions of Gordon's novel, introduced by the character of Laura, take on a new resonance: is grace given or withheld at birth, or is it acquired (or lost) through the course of one's life—and if the latter, who is the agent responsible for that process?

In addition to this internal split, Anne is split in a quasi-pathological way: the "bad" mother in her is externalized in a separate figure (Laura), on whom she vents her murderous rage. One wonders whether this rage is only that of the good mother, whether it is not also, in some sense, the rage of a small child at *her* bad mother. Anne, Margaret Mahler might say, has never successfully integrated her own childish images of the good and bad mother. Or we could say that, if she experiences a kind of maternal schizophrenia, that is because she occupies, at one and the same time, both the position of the small child and of the mother. This would be a confirmation of Chodorow and Contratto's thesis that the maternal fantasy of omnipotence is a repetition of an infantile fantasy, only I would qualify that thesis by saying that the infantile fantasy (of maternal omnipotence) reinforces the maternal fantasy (of ultimate responsibility) without being its only source. The other source is in the mother herself as mother—perhaps because she has internalized the cultural discourse about mothering, but also perhaps because the very fact of being a mother places her in a position symmetrical to the child. The psychoanalyst Alice Balint suggested in an essay published almost fifty years ago that "maternal love is the almost perfect counterpart to the love for the mother"—both of them being archaic, instinctual, and absolute.[26] If there is even a slight bit of truth in this, then it may be too simple to declare that mothers should give up their "infantile" fantasies and become more "realistic." For the mother may always reply, "Yes, I know, but still." "Yes, I know I'm not the only one ultimately responsible for my child's life," says the mother, "I know it's only a fantasy, and a terrifying one at that—but I still want to pretend it's true." Some fantasies are simply too satisfying to give up.

The second observation my reading suggests is a truism, but significant: in order to survive, a child needs at least one good mother, whether it is the biological mother or an "other" one. Stephen and Laura, who find no nurturing mother, die.

Finally, in this novel no child (except perhaps Anne?) has more than one "good" mother. And that raises once again the question of maternal fantasy and its relation to social reality.

Beyond fantasy? American motherhood in the 1980s

If I read *Men and Angels* as a multiple fantasy of maternal splitting, whose ultimate source or "author" is not so much the individual

[26] A. Balint, "Love for the Mother and Mother Love," in *Primary Love and Psycho-Analytic Technique*, by Michael Balint (New York: Liveright, 1965), 101.

Mary Gordon but a kind of collective contemporary American Mother, then I must finally ask: Why is it that mothers—even enlightened, creative, feminist mothers—in the United States today find it so difficult to acknowledge, in their deepest fantasies about their children, the possibility that they are not the only ones on whom the child's welfare, the child's whole life and self, depend? In reality, most mothers will readily admit that the father, the grandparents, teachers, friends, aunts, uncles, and other adult figures can and often do play a significant mothering role. Many feminist mothers are ardent exponents of Dinnerstein's and Chodorow's thesis that fathers in particular must share that role. And yet when we really dig down, when we really try to understand how we feel about our children, even the most enlightened among us will often discover in ourselves the stubborn belief that mother is the one who really counts. Why?

Whatever psychological explanations one can offer (regression, identification with the child, internalization of the "Master mother discourse," and so on), I think that there is a specifically contemporary sociopolitical explanation as well. Erik Erikson has noted that in order to benefit both mother and child, "biological motherhood needs at least three links with social experience: the mother's past experience of being mothered; a conception of motherhood shared with trustworthy contemporary surroundings; and an all-enveloping world-image tying past, present and future into a convincing pattern of providence."[27] The third condition, which has religious overtones, is probably not specific to mothering: in order to do anything worthwhile, one has to have a certain sense of continuity and faith in the future. The first condition, we all more or less fulfill—which is not to belittle its importance, for we know that a mother's past history is crucial to her mothering. But it seems to me that as a *social* problem, the first condition merges with the second; and it is precisely Erikson's second condition that has become most problematic in American society today.

In order to relinquish her fantasy of ultimate responsibility, a mother needs a "conception of motherhood shared with trustworthy contemporary surroundings"; but we live in a society where divorce is rampant, where the old presumptions no longer hold (witness the conundrum of surrogate motherhood, as well as those posed by various reproductive technologies), where women feel increasingly threatened as mothers, financially, emotionally, and legally. Even if Phyllis Chesler's *Mothers on Trial* exaggerates in viewing all fathers as potential sadists and mother haters, and all mothers as

[27] E. Erikson, "Human Strength and the Cycle of Generations," in *Insight and Responsibility* (New York: Norton, 1964), 116.

potential victims, the fact that this view exists at all has both symbolic and social significance. (It is a similar perception of mothers as victims and its attendant fear that may account for the extraordinary popular success of Sue Miller's novel, *The Good Mother*).[28] Lenore Weitzman has shown that in divorce negotiations fathers often blackmail their wives into accepting disadvantageous financial terms by threatening to sue for custody of the children and that in any case mothers end up much more impoverished than fathers after divorce.[29] However, if that is the case, if mothers really cannot feel secure in their attempt to pursue full and integrated personal lives and remain mothers, if they feel or fear that society through its legal system is ready to punish them by depriving them of their children any time they stray from the traditional, constraining path of "true mother-and-wife," then it makes a certain practical and logical sense for them to hold on to one thing they can affirm with certainty: that they have a natural, biological bond, and right, as mothers, to their children.

I read Chesler's book as a terrified reaction to what she perceives as a terrifying reality. To reaffirm, as she does, the biological bonding between mother and child and to claim that the mother is the child's "natural" guardian may be an ideologically and psychologically regressive move, but if so, it is also a self-protective move, as regression often is.[30] Until and unless American women can feel that society offers them a trustworthy surrounding in which to pursue both their desire for self-creation and their desire to mother, they will be unwilling to share their child with "other mothers" and will cling to the fantasy of ultimate responsibility. For it will appear to them as their only hope.

The popularity of Chesler's book underscores the connections between the fantasy of maternal splitting that I have analyzed in *Men and Angels* and women's real-life situations. Although it is theoretically hazardous to draw neat parallels between fiction and life, in practice we often do read fiction as an illumination of, and commentary on, real-life predicaments. That being the case, I would suggest that changes in the representation of maternal conflicts and

[28] Miller (n. 10 above).

[29] Lenore J. Weitzman, *The Divorce Revolution: The Unexpected Social and Economic Consequences for Women and Children in America* (New York: Free Press, 1985) chaps. 9, 10.

[30] This is even clearer in Chesler's more recent book, based on her involvement on the behalf of Mary Beth Whitehead in the "Baby M" case (*Sacred Bond: The Legacy of Baby M* [New York: Times Books, 1988]). Here, too, although Chesler's claims may be sweeping, the cases she documents are sobering. See also Daniel Golden's "What Makes Mommy Run?" *Boston Globe Magazine* (April 24, 1988).

fantasies in fiction by American women writers will have to be accompanied (perhaps even preceded) by efforts to create a trustworthy surrounding for women in American social life. As a first step, such efforts might be directed at the creation of a system of excellent, universally available day care that would allow biological mothers to rely on "other mothers" instead of feeling threatened by them and would encourage all of us to think of motherhood and self-creation as complementary rather than as mutually exclusive categories in women's lives. In concert with other social policy reforms, this action would contribute to and reflect the broader thinking that is necessary about the family, the social roles of women and men (both those who are parents and those who are not), and how these will be linked to the needs, values, and ultimate goals of American society at the turn of a new century.

Department of Romance Languages and Literatures
Harvard University

TOWARD A DEFINITION OF THE LESBIAN LITERARY IMAGINATION

MARILYN R. FARWELL

In a review of Adrienne Rich's *Diving into the Wreck,* Margaret Atwood claims that "it is not enough to state the truth; it must be imaged, imagined."[1] Contemporary women writers have waged a war of images in order to define an autonomous female imagination, and in the process they have questioned traditional literary images and offered radical reevaluations of the creative act. Women writers have chosen images and metaphors that have ranged from demon and sickness—images that evince the conflict and turmoil surrounding the woman's effort to create—to mother and androgyne—images designed to affirm and empower the creative woman. Some writers, such as Adrienne Rich and Monique Wittig, have recently proposed lesbian as the latest metaphor for female creativity.[2] Although no little controversy surrounds a female creativity vested in lesbian sexuality, feminist theorists from different and sometimes opposing philosophical traditions have suggested and developed this metaphor as a positive, utopian image of woman's creativity.

I wish to thank the University of Oregon's Center for the Study of Women in Society for its generous support. The opinions expressed in this paper are those of the author and not necessarily those of the center. I wish also to thank the referees for *Signs* for their helpful comments and critiques.

[1] Margaret Atwood, "Review of *Diving into the Wreck,*" in *Reading Adrienne Rich: Review and Revisions, 1951–81,* ed. Jane Roberta Cooper (Ann Arbor: University of Michigan Press, 1984), 238–41, esp. 241.

[2] Adrienne Rich, "It Is the Lesbian in Us . . . ," in her *On Lies, Secrets, and Silence: Selected Prose, 1966–1978* (New York: Norton, 1979), 199–202, esp. 201; and Monique Wittig, *The Lesbian Body,* trans. David Le Vay (New York: Avon, 1975).

This essay originally appeared in *Signs,* vol. 14, no. 1, Autumn 1988.

Traditionally and fundamentally, Western metaphors for creativity present images—lover, androgyne, or mother—that exclude lesbian sexuality by privileging heterosexuality in assuming an analogy between creative production and reproduction. "Lesbian" is one of the few words in our language, if not the only one, that privileges female sexuality. For a cultural tradition that identifies sexual energy with creativity, then, lesbian as a metaphor is crucial to the redefinition of female autonomy and creativity, and although contemporary definitions of lesbian at times seem at odds, feminist theorists have begun to evolve a complex, problematic, and yet flexible image that both deconstructs the heterosexual pattern for creativity and creates a space for redefining the relationship of the woman writer to other women writers, to readers, and to the text.

Although contemporary feminist writers are not the first to connect lesbian with creativity—for example, Virginia Woolf, in a letter to Ethel Smyth, writes, "Women alone stir my imagination"—current feminist theory forges parameters and introduces problems not central to the earlier uses of the idea.[3] In the most well-known metaphoric use of lesbian, Rich claims that the woman who is self-defined, the lesbian, differs from the female who is constructed by the patriarchy, the "dutiful daughter." She ascribes creativity to this reified lesbian only: "It is the lesbian in us who is creative, for the dutiful daughter of the fathers in us is only a hack."[4] The controversy that ensued over Rich's definition and over other generalized, less sexually dependent definitions from writers such as Lillian Faderman, Blanche Wiesen Cook, and Bertha Harris involved many of the major issues of contemporary feminism.[5] Lesbian as metaphor, it was argued, ignored specificity, subsuming racial and historical differences among women or, in our contemporary philosophical vocabulary, lesbian writ large essentialized and ahistoricized lesbian and female existence. On this basis, some theorists criticized Rich's later proposal of the phrase, "lesbian continuum," which she described as the "primary intensity between and among women" existing at various stages in women's lives and at various times

[3] Virginia Woolf, *The Letters of Virginia Woolf*, vol. 4, *1929–31*, ed. Nigel Nicolson and Joanne Trautman (New York: Harcourt Brace Jovanovich, 1978), 203.

[4] Rich, "It Is the Lesbian in Us . . . ," 201.

[5] Lillian Faderman, *Surpassing the Love of Men: Romantic Friendship and Love between Women from the Renaissance to the Present* (New York: Morrow, 1981); Blanche Wiesen Cook, "Support Networks and Political Activism: Lillian Wald, Crystal Eastman, Emma Goldman," *Chrysalis: A Magazine of Women's Culture* 3 (Spring 1977): 43–60; and Bertha Harris, "Lesbians and Literature" (paper presented at the Modern Language Association Convention, New York City, 1976), cited in Barbara Smith, "Toward a Black Feminist Criticism," *Women's Studies International Quarterly* 2, no. 2 (1979): 183–94, esp. 188.

throughout history.[6] A number of literary critics also objected to a generalized metaphoric definition: Bonnie Zimmerman, for instance, called it reductionist; Gloria Bowles argued that the term was too general; and Catharine R. Stimpson derided it as "a fancily labelled metaphor."[7] In the early debate, straight women feared that naming female creativity lesbian meant that only lesbians could be creative. In one telling example, a prominent woman poet, upon hearing a paper on Rich's definition of lesbian, objected to the connection between lesbian and creativity because she "liked men." Alicia Ostriker simply termed it the "Lesbian Imperative."[8] But lesbians also objected out of the fear that any metaphoric definition of the word would negate the uniqueness of lesbian existence in which women relate to women sexually and form communities around this choice. Not acknowledging sexuality as the core of the definition of lesbian was, for some lesbians, missing the point. One lesbian, in response to Rich's definition of the "lesbian in us," said that if the word lesbian was going to be used in such a general way, she wanted another term for women who physically love other women.[9] As if to seal the coffin of a dangerous idea, Elaine Showalter recently claimed the end of an era: "By the 1980s, the lesbian aesthetic had differentiated itself from the female aesthetic . . . and the figure of the mother replaced that of the Amazon for theorists of the female aesthetic."[10]

Despite these objections, the development and exploration of this idea have continued in the pages of contemporary feminist theory, fiction, poetry, and criticism, with writers like Judy Grahn, Monique Wittig, and Alice Walker expanding and deepening the metaphoric meaning, agreeing and disagreeing over the definition of lesbian, and, in the attempt to refine the metaphor, addressing

[6] Adrienne Rich, "Compulsory Heterosexuality and Lesbian Existence," *Signs: Journal of Women in Culture and Society* 5, no. 4 (Summer 1980): 631–60, esp. 648. For the controversy, see Ann Ferguson, Jacqueline N. Zita, and Kathryn Pyne Addelson, "On 'Compulsory Heterosexuality and Lesbian Existence': Defining the Issues," *Signs* 7, no. 1 (Autumn 1981): 158–99.

[7] Bonnie Zimmerman, "What Has Never Been: An Overview of Lesbian Feminist Criticism," in *Making a Difference: Feminist Literary Criticism,* ed. Gayle Greene and Coppélia Kahn (London and New York: Methuen, 1985), 177–210, esp. 184; Gloria Bowles, "Adrienne Rich as Feminist Theorist," in Cooper, ed., 319–28, esp. 322; and Catharine R. Stimpson, "Adrienne Rich and Lesbian/Feminist Poetry," *Parnassus* 12, no. 2/13, no. 1 (Spring/Summer/Fall/Winter 1985): 249–68, esp. 255.

[8] Alicia Ostriker, *Writing Like a Woman* (Ann Arbor: University of Michigan Press, 1983), 121.

[9] Summarized in Rich, "It Is the Lesbian in Us . . . ," 202.

[10] Elaine Showalter, "Introduction: The Feminist Critical Revolution," in *The New Feminist Criticism: Essays on Women, Literature, and Theory,* ed. Elaine Showalter (New York: Random House, 1985), 3–17, esp. 7.

some of the main objections to the term.[11] In fact, Bonnie Zimmerman, in her comprehensive essay on lesbian criticism, claims that definition is now the primary concern of lesbian feminist criticism.[12] The parameters of this debate can be found in differences among feminist theorists, particularly in the debates between those who wish to name a new feminist reality and those who insist on the centrality of deconstructing the old patriarchal reality. Those feminists influenced by French theories of language argue that only opposition is possible within a language determined by a structure in which male is the subject and the center, female is the other and the marginal. Thus, Rachel Blau DuPlessis, citing and echoing Margaret Homans's earlier objection to Adrienne Rich's essentializing, claims that Rich's use of lesbian is effective only when "oppositional."[13] American Black feminist critic, Barbara Smith, also sees the use of lesbian as oppositional when she calls Toni Morrison's novel *Sula* lesbian, not because of any lesbian characters but because of a political perspective critical of heterosexual institutions.[14] Monique Wittig has most fully developed the definition of the lesbian as "not-woman," economically, politically, or ideologically.[15] On the other side stand those writers—primarily American radical feminists—who affirm the need for women to rename ourselves, to define what is essential to being female. In this context the metaphoric lesbian becomes what Rich calls the creative element in all women or what Judy Grahn declares is "by extension, every woman."[16] Adrienne Rich most fully represents this philosophical position in her prose writings of the late 1970s when she ascribed to words like androgyne, mother, and, finally, lesbian the power to rename and therefore reclaim female experience.

[11] See Judy Grahn, *The Highest Apple: Sappho and the Lesbian Poetic Tradition* (San Francisco: Spinsters Ink, 1985); Monique Wittig, *The Lesbian Body* (n. 2 above); and Alice Walker, *The Color Purple* (New York and London: Harcourt Brace Jovanovich, 1982). See also the significant discussions by Mary J. Carruthers, "The Re-Vision of the Muse: Adrienne Rich, Audre Lorde, Judy Grahn, Olga Broumas," *Hudson Review* 36 (Summer 1983): 293–327; and Susan Gubar, "Sapphistries," *Signs* 10, no. 1 (Autumn 1984): 43–62.

[12] Zimmerman, 183.

[13] Rachel Blau DuPlessis, *Writing beyond the Ending: Narrative Strategies of Twentieth-Century Women Writers* (Bloomington: Indiana University Press, 1985), 135, 139. See also Margaret Homans, *Women Writers and Poetic Identity: Dorothy Wordsworth, Emily Brontë, and Emily Dickinson* (Princeton, N.J.: Princeton University Press, 1980).

[14] Smith (n. 5 above), 189.

[15] Monique Wittig, "One Is Not Born a Woman," in *Feminist Frameworks: Alternative Theoretical Accounts of Relations between Women and Men*, ed. Alison M. Jaggar and Paula S. Rothenberg (New York: McGraw-Hill, 1984), 148–52, esp. 150.

[16] Grahn, 40.

Both theories of lesbian as metaphor accept as vital the notion that lesbian is a word sufficient and necessary to describe the autonomous and creative woman. Thus both approaches can be placed in the long history of Western metaphors that connect sexual energy to imaginative creativity. In this context the problems and possibilities for the metaphoric meaning of lesbian can best be described in a phrase that Adrienne Rich uses to denote truth: "increasing complexity."[17]

The Western tradition offers two important sexual, and distinctly heterosexual, images of creativity—lover and androgyne—which women writers at various times have attempted to appropriate, usually unsuccessfully, for their own use. In these two metaphors, male sexuality is privileged as the source of reproduction; the female functions as the other to male subjectivity and as the margin to the male center. She is only a means to an end, for in this union of opposites woman becomes the means to man's ecstatic transcendence of the material and contingent world, a transcendence that is rooted in the male orgasm and metaphorically replicated in his poetic inspiration. Male sexuality, then, is central to the creative process because it is the only sexuality acknowledged in the heterosexual paradigm. In the Western images of androgyne and lover, then, the metaphoric union of male and female qualities—of soul and body, intellect and emotion, idea and matter—requires the absorption by the male of the female and the qualities that she represents.

Men have long assumed that their sex alone could create. Aristotle set the stage for centuries of biological and eventually symbolic theory which credits the male alone with the powers of reproduction by arguing that the semen contains the principle of motion, the potentiality as well as the actuality of the soul. The female contribution is relegated to inert matter.[18] This identification of maleness with the powers of creativity mirrors the theology that has dominated Western culture: a male god who creates the world through his own powers. Male poets and theorists have claimed even this for themselves. For Renaissance theorist J. C. Scaliger, the poet "transforms himself almost into a second deity," an idea also taken up by the better-known Renaissance critic, Sir Philip Sidney.[19] For the central Romantic theorist, S. T. Coleridge, imagination became the "repetition in the finite mind of the eternal act

[17] Adrienne Rich, "Women and Honor: Some Notes on Lying," in *On Lies, Secrets, and Silence* (n. 2 above), 185–94, esp. 187.

[18] Aristotle, "De Generatione Animalium," in *The Works of Aristotle Translated into English*, ed. J. A. Smith and W. D. Ross (Oxford: Clarendon Press, 1912), 5:729a.

[19] Julius Caesar Scaliger, "Poetics," in *Critical Theory since Plato*, ed. Hazard Adams (New York: Harcourt Brace Jovanovich, 1971), 137–43, esp. 139; Sir Philip Sidney, "An Apology for Poetry," in Adams, ed., 155–77, esp. 157.

of creation in the infinite *I am*."[20] Creativity, reproduction, and god are collapsed into a single expression of man's identity.

Virginia Woolf was not the first to suggest that androgyny as a balance of gender opposites, a kind of psychological intercourse, best describes the fertile imagination. With a nod to Coleridge, Woolf sketches the powers that form the "fully fertilised" soul: "If one is a man, still the woman part of the brain must have effect; and a woman also must have intercourse with the man in her."[21] Woolf's use of the word "intercourse" in reference to woman's internal relation with her "male" side suggests an ambivalence about androgyny indicative of contemporary feminist debates.[22] In the historical paradigm, one that influenced much philosophical and theological thinking from Plato to Carl Jung, androgyny is a combination of male and female qualities that devalues the female. The female most often represents those qualities that need to be controlled—emotion, darkness, desire, intuition—and the result is a paradigm that focuses on male control of the dangerous side of human nature. Gerrard Winstanley, a seventeenth-century radical, defines the value system inherent in this juxtaposition of male and female principles when he describes the original fall from androgynous perfection as a time when "man" was "led by the powers of the curse in flesh, which is the *Feminine* part; not by the power of the righteous Spirit which is Christ, the *Masculine* power."[23] Carl Jung's notion of androgynous behavior is the male who, in touch with his anima, opens up to his creative side, or a female who, in touch with her animus, becomes an opinionated woman.[24] Andro-

[20] Samuel Taylor Coleridge, *Biographia Literaria*, ed. J. C. Metcalf (New York: Macmillan, 1926), 189–90. The best discussion of the identification of the male with literary authority can be found in Sandra Gilbert and Susan Gubar, *The Madwoman in the Attic: The Woman Writer and the Nineteenth-Century Literary Imagination* (New Haven, Conn.: Yale University Press, 1979).

[21] Virginia Woolf, *A Room of One's Own* (1929; reprint, New York: Harcourt, Brace & World, 1957), 102.

[22] "Special Issue: The Androgyny Papers," *Women's Studies* 2, no. 2 (1974); Adrienne Rich, "Diving into the Wreck," in her *Diving into the Wreck: Poems 1971–72* (New York: Norton, 1973), 56, and *Of Woman Born: Motherhood as Experience and Institution* (New York: Norton, 1976), 83; Mary Daly, *Beyond God the Father: Toward a Philosophy of Women's Liberation* (Boston: Beacon, 1973), and *Gyn/Ecology: The Metaethics of Radical Feminism* (Boston: Beacon, 1978), 387–88. Contemporary feminist criticism has, in some instances, turned to a new and more favorable view of androgyny. For example, for a discussion of androgyny as multiplicity in Virginia Woolf's *Orlando*, see DuPlessis (n. 13 above), 63.

[23] Gerrard Winstanley, "The New Law of Righteousness," in *The Works of Gerrard Winstanley*, ed. George H. Sabine (Ithaca, N.Y.: Cornell University Press, 1941), 149–244, esp. 157.

[24] Carl Jung, *Two Essays on Analytical Psychology*, trans. R. F. C. Hull (New York: Meridian, 1956), 218.

gyny brings creativity to men, but its benefits for women are less clear. Sally B. Allen and Joanna Hubbs have noted that the androgynous union of male and female in a seventeenth-century alchemical theory was "achieved by denying the independent status of the feminine and by containing and arrogating her creative powers."[25] By using a sexual metaphor that implies transcendence of dualism and the concomitant transcendence of the female, androgyny describes an imagination located in male subjectivity and sexuality, an imagination that is as a result free from gender and presumably from other contingencies—history, class, and race. This metaphor positions the imagination as an essence that is bound by nothing in material existence. It claims for the Western man the exclusive centrality of his consciousness. This realization led writers like Adrienne Rich to reject androgyny as a model for female wholeness, for as Rich concludes, "The very structure of the word replicates the sexual dichotomy and the priority of *andros* (male) over *gyne* (female)."[26]

The notion of male centrality also pervades the metaphor of the poet as lover. This image, like that of the androgyne, has historically been associated with the poet's muse. In Mary K. DeShazer's analysis of the concept of the muse in Western literature, she identifies three types of muses: the sexual, the spiritual, and the natural, each linking the poet to a primary force. In each case, DeShazer maintains, "the active male engenders his poetry upon the body of a passive female muse."[27] In the courtly and Petrarchan love poems of the Middle Ages and Renaissance that founded this tradition, the poet/lover is almost always identified as male. He is active and creative; he is the one who speaks. The female, the beloved, is acted upon, her usual response to the ardent declarations of her lover being "no." This answer is not an expression of her own sexual choice, but, rather, it is an expression of woman's symbolic function vis-à-vis men: to help the poet transcend the lower world of change and physicality by reminding him that the real object of his sexual passion is his own creativity. Frederick Goldin, in an aptly titled book on courtly love, *The Mirror of Narcissus*, describes the lady of these poets as "the localization of the ideal," the mirror by which the poet learns to know and love heavenly perfection.[28] Feminist

[25] Sally B. Allen and Joanna Hubbs, "Outrunning Atalanta: Feminine Destiny in Alchemical Transmutation," in *Signs* 6, no. 2 (Winter 1980): 210–29, esp. 215.

[26] Rich, *Of Woman Born*, 77n.

[27] Mary K. DeShazer, *Inspiring Women: Reimagining the Muse* (New York: Pergamon, 1986), 8–10.

[28] Frederick Goldin, *The Mirror of Narcissus* (Ithaca, N.Y.: Cornell University Press, 1967), 14.

critics see the image of woman as mirror for male imagination as more self-serving than does Goldin.[29] The woman remains a means by which the male completes his quest, not a lover with her own sexual/spiritual needs. In many of these poems the pains of the lover are articulated in great detail, but little is said about the lady. In Petrarchan poetry the lover is a ship tossed at sea, a hart wounded by an arrow, an actor on a stage; the lady is at best described in idealistic physical detail and at worst as the cause of all of the poet's pain. In a standard example, the sixteenth-century poet Thomas Wyatt describes the lover's turmoil: "I find no peace, and all my war is done. / I fear and hope, I burn, and freeze like ice." The poem continues in this vein for thirteen of its fourteen lines, leaving the last line for the beloved: "And my delight is causer of this strife."[30]

The connection of sexuality with imaginative creativity is paramount to this tradition. The muse of these poems, partly because she refuses physical sex, inspires the poet to write. It is here that the heterosexual paradigm is most obvious, for in communing on a symbolic sexual level with the absent, objectified "other," the poet must absorb the obviously female creative function of reproduction. In order to complete the metaphor, he not only expends his seed on an object, but he also bears the fruit: in other words he has a self-sufficient power to create. This tradition can still be found in modern writers, most obviously in Robert Graves's *The White Goddess*.[31] The contemporary male poet can invoke the muse—whether a real woman or a mythical figure—and thereby claim a creativity based on a notion of heterosexual coupling as a catalyst for *his* offspring. However, when a writer like May Sarton attempts to adopt the poet-as-lover imagery to describe a woman's creativity, as she did in *Mrs. Stevens Hears the Mermaids Singing*, she is forced into the same center/margin linguistic rules—the male as creator, the female as inspirer. Sarton's key statement on the woman writer is thus disappointing: "The crucial question seems to me to be this: what is the *source* of creativity in the woman who wants to be an

[29] Feminist critic Luce Irigaray uses the image of the mirror to argue that woman exists in the male symbolic economy to reflect back to man *his* identity, what she calls "*the same re-marking itself*" (*Speculum of the Other Woman*, trans. Gillian C. Gill [Ithaca, N.Y.: Cornell University Press, 1985], 21). Virginia Woolf notes a similar function for women, the "looking-glasses possessing the magic and delicious power of reflecting the figure of man at twice its natural size" (*A Room of One's Own*, 35).

[30] Thomas Wyatt, "Description of the Contrarious Passions in a Lover," in *The Renaissance in England*, ed. Hyder E. Rollins and Herschel Baker (Boston: Heath, 1954), 198.

[31] Robert Graves, *The White Goddess: A Historical Grammar of Poetic Myth* (1948; reprint, New York: Farrar, Straus, & Giroux, 1973), 24.

artist? After all, admit it, a woman is meant to create children not works of art—that's what she has been engined to do, so to speak. A man with a talent does what is expected of him, makes his way. . . . It's the natural order of things that he construct objects outside himself and his family. The woman who does so is aberrant."[32] In this symbolic world, woman, who does not have a sexuality beyond reproduction and therefore does not have creative energy except in relation to man, cannot name her creativity with impunity.

Another common patriarchal metaphor for imaginative creativity is mother, a seemingly ironic metaphor in light of the above images that claim male sexuality as central to creativity. Yet mother is related to the above metaphors because in androgyne and lover the male who creates by himself, in effect, becomes a mother by absorbing the female power to create. In this confusion and appropriation of all gender roles, the androgyne and lover become pregnant and deliver their creative product through the impregnating inspiration of the female other. Mother, then, is related to these two heterosexual metaphors, for although it lacks the connection between ecstatic love and inspiration, it does follow the heterosexual model that associates reproduction with imaginative production. At the same time, it is essential for understanding the development of lesbian as a metaphor. Men have often found motherhood and pregnancy viable transcriptions of imaginative creativity, and women have found these images more congenial, on the surface, than other sexual images for creation. Tillie Olsen, commenting on Balzac's appropriation of pregnancy and motherhood as a description of his creative activity, agrees at first that "in intelligent passionate motherhood there are similarities, and in more than the toil and patience," for, she continues, motherhood, as does art, demands one's "total capacities."[33] Nonetheless, the fact is that this image, like lover and androgyne, has more often excluded rather than included women; for the very power to bear children has been an argument against women's ability to create books, as if physical labor precludes mental muscle. The male fascination with this metaphor is merely an extension of the absorption of the female that takes place in the images of androgyne and lover.

Women writers have exhibited a strong and ambivalent relationship to the image of the mother as one who both creates—births—and nurtures an imaginative product. Olsen ultimately finds the image absurd because, having experienced motherhood, she

[32] May Sarton, *Mrs. Stevens Hears the Mermaids Singing* (New York: Norton, 1965), 190.

[33] Tillie Olsen, *Silences* (1978; reprint, New York: Dell, 1979), 18.

does not romanticize it; in fact, in the end, she sees motherhood as the antithesis of imagination.[34] Monique Wittig, as we shall see, refuses any idealization of mother because it is motherhood that domesticated the energies of the "lesbian peoples."[35] Others have found the image more compatible: Domna Stanton claims that French feminists Hélène Cixous, Luce Irigaray, and Julia Kristeva currently use the image of the mother to encapsulate the ideal female.[36] Two important American radical feminists, however, have used as a stepping-stone to their theories of lesbian the image of mother. Early in her feminist theorizing, Adrienne Rich suggests that a connecting rather than a separating of physical and imaginative creativity could "tell us, among many other things, more about the physical capacity for gestation and nourishment of infants and how it relates to psychological gestation and nurture as an intellectual and creative force."[37] Audre Lorde also forges a maternal definition of creativity when she answers Adrienne Rich's interview question, "Who is the poet?" Lorde replies, "The Black mother who is the poet exists in every one of us."[38] The argument that valorizes and essentializes this natural female function was prominent in American radical feminist thought of the 1970s because the image seemed to claim for women their own power in birth, to declare its connection to the power of nature to reproduce itself, and to insist on taking back women's fecundity.

This image has become less palatable for many radical feminists because, within the context of the present symbolic system, to claim the female power to give birth is to acquiesce to assumptions that have traditionally colonized women: all women must become mothers inseminated by men to bear sons. An idealization of the mother, the reification of physical birth and gestation, was quickly dropped by most American radical feminists, as they began to develop a different idea of the mother as a stepping-stone to the less co-opted image of lesbian. In their definition of lesbian, mother is divested of male control and defined not primarily by the act of giving birth but by her relationship to the daughter. The lesbian is the woman

[34] Ibid., 18–19.

[35] Monique Wittig and Sande Zeig, *Lesbian Peoples: Material for a Dictionary*, trans. Monique Wittig and Sande Zeig (New York: Avon, 1979).

[36] Domna C. Stanton, "Difference on Trial: A Critique of the Maternal Metaphor in Cixous, Irigaray, and Kristeva," in *The Poetics of Gender*, ed. Nancy K. Miller (New York: Columbia University Press, 1986), 157–82.

[37] Adrienne Rich, "The Anti-Feminist Woman," in *On Lies, Secrets, and Silence* (n. 2 above), 69–84, esp. 77.

[38] Audre Lorde, "An Interview: Audre Lorde and Adrienne Rich," in *Sister Outsider: Essays and Speeches by Audre Lorde* (Trumansburg, N.Y.: Crossing Press, 1984), 81–109, esp. 100.

who returns to the girl's original love for a woman, her mother, the fulfillment of which Freud denied the girl—although not the boy—but which the lesbian affirms as possible.

Lesbian as a metaphor for female creativity is unlike heterosexual images because it refuses the transcendence and reproduction model that informs the heterosexual connection between sexuality and creativity. At the same time it remains within the tradition that highlights sexuality as the core of creativity, but because it privileges a female sexuality that does not need or want male energy, it radically revises the symbolic order. For a woman to claim a sexuality and therefore a subjectivity of her own, outside of male influence or control, defies the symbology of the Western tradition. As a metaphor for creativity, lesbian also refuses many of the elements essential to the connection between heterosexuality and creativity: dualism, transcendence, ecstasy, reproduction, and a product. Instead it emphasizes the autonomy of the creative self, the community of readers and writers, and the diffuse physicality of the creative act and of the text itself. The shift in emphasis is crucial.

As a metaphor, lesbian, like the other metaphors, trades on both similarities and differences between tenor and vehicle. As a metaphor, lesbian must be held separate from actual women who form relationships and communities outside of and in resistance to the patriarchy; at the same time, it depends on abstractions from these experiences, sometimes on idealizations of these experiences. In abstracting from the literal experience, the metaphor gains a wider range of meaning but loses specificity and, of course, loses some connection with its source—lesbians. A woman who is a lesbian, then, may not necessarily be a metaphoric lesbian, as Mary Daly says when she dissociates female homosexuals who give "their allegiance to men and male myths" from women who have "rejected false loyalties to men on all levels."[39] From this perspective Adrienne Rich claims that "even before I wholly knew I was a lesbian, it was the lesbian in me who pursued that elusive configuration. . . . It is the lesbian in us who drives us to feel imaginatively, render in language, grasp, the full connection between woman and woman."[40] What is called lesbian does not depend on women loving women genitally but, rather, on the presence and attention of women to other women that is analogous to the act of loving sexually another like oneself. In fact, words like presence, attention, and sight are used most often to describe this metaphoric lesbian. While this

[39] Daly, *Gyn/Ecology* (n. 22 above), 26n.

[40] Rich, "It Is the Lesbian in Us . . . ," (n. 2 above), 200–201.

process of abstraction has indeed been the source of much critical debate, my argument is that the word does not lose its power merely because it abstracts from lesbian experience. Instead, it functions on the symbolic level analogously to the human being who defines herself sexually as a lesbian: it stands as a disruption of the Western tradition that portrays the female and her imagination as marginal.

In her writings of the late 1970s, Rich describes the lesbian as that core of self-knowledge, power, and creativity that is potentially in all women. For many reasons, critics have shied away from a full description of Rich's development of this idea,[41] and Rich herself now disagrees with this early radical feminist formula for female identity because it does not encompass the "simultaneity of oppressions" women encounter.[42] Yet her exploration of the topic in the late 1970s remains central to any discussion of it. For Rich, the lesbian is she who, in defiance of male linguistic and social hegemony, separates herself from male constructions—Rich's "dutiful daughter"—and discovers in herself the truly unfettered woman. Lesbian, she states, "was nothing so simple and dismissible as the fact that two women might go to bed together. It was a sense of desiring oneself; above all, of choosing oneself."[43] For the poet, this choice of self opens the window on a revised notion of creativity. In her insightful essay on the metaphoric lesbian, Mary J. Carruthers groups Rich with other poets—Audre Lorde, Judy Grahn, and Olga Broumas—who remythologize lesbian as a way of "seeing the poet in the woman, not as alien or monstrous, but as an aspect of her womanhood."[44]

But Rich's distinction between physical sex and self-affirmation does not eliminate sexuality from the metaphor. Sexuality becomes self-knowledge and power because it is redefined as a diffuse and omnipresent energy, not as orgasmic sexuality associated with transcendence. Audre Lorde defines the erotic in this largest possible sense: "When I speak of the erotic, then, I speak of it as an assertion of the lifeforce of women; of that creative energy empowered, the knowledge and use of which we are now reclaiming in our language, our history, our dancing, our loving, our work, our lives."[45] Rich

[41] Some recent books minimize Rich's lesbian stance, such as Paula Bennett, *My Life a Loaded Gun: Female Creativity and Feminist Poetics* (Boston: Beacon, 1986); or Deborah Pope, *A Separate Vision: Isolation in Contemporary Women's Poetry* (Baton Rouge: Louisiana State University Press, 1984).

[42] Adrienne Rich, foreword in her *Blood, Bread, and Poetry: Selected Prose 1979–1985* (New York and London: Norton, 1986), vii–xiv, esp. xii.

[43] Rich, "It Is the Lesbian in Us . . . ," 200.

[44] Carruthers (n. 11 above), 296.

[45] Audre Lorde, "Uses of the Erotic: The Erotic as Power," in *Sister Outsider*, 53–59, esp. 55.

alludes to this statement in her discussion of the "lesbian continuum" when she defines the lesbian as not only she who says "no" to the patriarchy but also she who discovers the "erotic in female terms," the erotic as a diffuse and omnipresent energy "unconfined to any single part of the body or solely to the body itself."[46] The nature of this energy is often described in terms of women's attention to one another, their presence to one another, their sight of one another in a world where women's attention and presence are compelled, sometimes by force, to focus on men. In this awareness of self and the attention to another like the self, eroticism flourishes, as feminist philosopher Marilyn Frye notes: "When one's attention is on something, one is present in a particular way to that thing. This presence is, among other things, an element of erotic presence."[47] It is this omnipresent energy, this attention to another rather than an orgiastic experience of transcendence that explains the metaphoric sexuality of the female creative act.

Rich also describes the "*primary presence of women to ourselves and each other*" as the "crucible of a new language."[48] The attention to ourselves demands a new language because, as Luce Irigaray says in "When Our Lips Speak Together," "If we keep on speaking the same language together, we're going to reproduce the same history. . . . If we keep on speaking sameness, if we speak to each other as men have been doing for centuries, as we have been taught to speak, we'll miss each other, fail ourselves."[49] Rich, too, sees the necessity for a new language, a common language, which can accommodate women who speak to one another, a language where women are the authors/speakers, readers/auditors, and subjects. In this act of attention, women become both the lover and the beloved, subject and object, and the resulting fecundity does not focus on a product owned by the author but on a network of relationships among author, reader, text, and even literary foremothers.

Yet the autonomous self who chooses her lesbian potential is paradoxically defined through relationship. No contradiction exists between an autonomous self and a self in relationship, no contradiction between creativity as an autonomous and as a communal

[46] Rich, "Compulsory Heterosexuality and Lesbian Existence" (n. 6 above), 650.

[47] Marilyn Frye, "To See and Be Seen: The Politics of Reality," in her *The Politics of Reality: Essays in Feminist Theory* (Trumansburg, N.Y.: Crossing Press, 1983), 152–74, esp. 172.

[48] Adrienne Rich, "Power and Danger: Works of a Common Woman," in *On Lies, Secrets, and Silence* (n. 2 above), 247–58, esp. 250.

[49] Luce Irigaray, "When Our Lips Speak Together," in her *This Sex which Is Not One*, trans. Catherine Porter with Carolyn Burke (Ithaca, N.Y.: Cornell University Press, 1985), 205–13, esp. 205.

act. Not dependent on a sexuality of transcendence, which demands the "other" for its ascent, this metaphor focuses on the communication within a community of subjects. The imagination described by such a metaphor is not universal or disembodied, not isolated, or egotistical but, rather, part of a community and of the contingent world.

The paradigmatic relationship of this community is the mother-daughter relationship, the return of the woman to her original love. Mother as an image of female creativity is subsumed by the larger image of the lesbian, the one whose creativity springs from her primary attention to women. Rich has made much of the story of Demeter and Persephone, of the mother finding the daughter and of the Earth's fertile growth that follows.[50] This shared subjectivity comes from what Rich calls the original homesickness: "*This is what she was to me, and this / is how I can love myself— / as only a woman can love me. / Homesick for myself, for her.*"[51] Through this notion of community, Rich destroys the dualism that underscores heterosexual images of creativity, although it may be argued that the refusal of dualism is superficial because Rich still allows for female uniqueness in traditional terms. Unlike Wittig, who calls for an end to gender, Rich remains inside the historically accepted definitions of male and female. Her radical potential appears in her attempt—a successful one, I believe—to wrest the female from male control and position the woman at the center of her discourse.

One of Adrienne Rich's most unusual essays, "Women and Honor: Some Notes on Lying," illustrates many of these points with audacity and vision. This key text rarely mentions the word lesbian but does explore the meaning of women's relationships with one another and invites translation to the metaphoric realm. Here, where her prose strategy, usually highly rhetorical, is poetic, Rich measures the erotic charge between women by their trust of one another. In the patriarchal world, woman's honor is acknowledged only by her sexual loyalty to men; in a brave new world of relationships among women, a new code of honor based on truth and trust can begin to unfold. Trust is the primary way of being attentive to one another, and, on this trust, truth is based. Trust, she implies, is another way of making love, a way of allowing the full freedom of imagination and of sexuality. Because truth itself is based on trust and not on mere facts, it is created between two people as they

[50] Adrienne Rich, "Caryatid: Two Columns," in *On Lies, Secrets, and Silence* (n. 2 above), 107–19, esp. 115.

[51] Adrienne Rich, "Transcendental Etude," in her *The Dream of a Common Language: Poems 1974–1977* (New York: Norton, 1978), 76.

open to one another. This point leads Rich to a curious epistemological place, one in which the universe is created on the trust two people share, including the universe created when the beloved declares "It is seventy degrees outside and the sun is shining."[52] Both trust and truth become the foundation of the female creative imagination: "The unconscious wants truth, as the body does. The complexity and fecundity of dreams come from the complexity and fecundity of the unconscious struggling to fulfill that desire. The complexity and fecundity of poetry come from the same struggle."[53] Because women have been alienated from their bodies and their own sexuality, they have also been alienated from their own creativity. A bond with another woman puts each in touch with her own body and her imagination because that bond opens each to the unconscious. Untimately, the connection is with the void, the power understood by the matriarchal religions that allowed "Out of death, rebirth; out of nothing, something."[54] Thus the erotic energy of two women becomes the source of creative energy because it puts each in touch with the profound creativity of universe. It is a creativity not described in terms of ecstasy or inspiration but in terms of a human bond.

Monique Wittig, philosophically quite separate from Adrienne Rich, has also evolved a definition of lesbian in which the word assumes a broader meaning than two women making love. In the space Wittig calls lesbian, any female can reject the socially defined category of woman. Significantly, lesbian can also be a metaphor for the woman writer, as Hélène Vivienne Wenzel has noted of the narrator in Wittig's last work of fiction: "The lover *j/e* in *Le corps lesbien* is also the writer whose violent lovemaking both as subject and as object with *tu* is a metaphor for the craft of the writer."[55] In this space of subjectivity that the lesbian occupies, textuality and sexuality are closely intertwined.

As a socialist feminist, Wittig does not accept theories of innate differences between woman and man or of a unique female sexuality and creativity. The lesbian is one who is beyond all gender, who is not woman, essentially the one who occupies a space from which the marginal can claim subjectivity. In her critique of contemporary French feminists' psychoanalytic theories of women and writing, Ann Rosalind Jones notes Wittig's suspicions "both of the oppositional thinking that defines woman in terms of man and of

[52] Rich, "Women and Honor" (n. 17 above), 192.

[53] Ibid., 188.

[54] Ibid., 191.

[55] Hélène Vivienne Wenzel, "The Text as Body/Politics: Appreciations of Monique Wittig's Writings in Context," *Feminist Studies* 7, no. 2 (Summer 1981): 264–87, esp. 284.

the mythical-idealist strain in certain formulations of *féminité*."[56] The source of oppression is gender itself, what Wittig calls artificial categories of man and woman that "conceal the fact that social differences always belong to an economic, political, ideological order."[57] Lesbian is the only word she knows that obliterates gender, the only concept in which women are not dependent on men economically, politically, socially, or emotionally. Although theoretically at odds, both Wittig and Rich differentiate the lesbian from the woman who is constructed by patriarchal codes. What lesbian as a metaphor becomes for Rich is a capacious room walled from patriarchal constraints but unlimited inside; for Wittig the space is larger, what she has called, echoing Pascal, the circle "whose center is everywhere and whose circumference is nowhere."[58]

From this place, Wittig notes, the marginal subject refuses dualism and gains an "axis of categorization from which to universalize."[59] Rich eschews a claim to the universal with its attendant implications of noncorporeality; Wittig, however, insists on the necessity of a universal point of view without losing the corporeal, for without a point from which to universalize, she explains, one exists as a contingent being, an ontological impossibility. Men are given such absolute existence because, in effect, they are already genderless; only women must exist under the sword of gender. She is marked; he is unmarked. This dualistic structure is "based on the primacy of difference" and the "thought of domination."[60] Like Rich, Wittig refuses this dualism, although Wittig eliminates it entirely and Rich dismisses one side of it, the male. Thus, in her radical fiction, *The Lesbian Body,* Wittig startles us with her goal to "lesbianize the symbols, lesbianize the gods and goddesses, lesbianize men and women."[61] Ulysses, for example, becomes Ulyssea, Achilles and Patrocles become Achillea and Patroclea. In her groundbreaking essay on this work, Namascar Shaktini rightly notes that Wittig's method of displacement is to put the subject "outside of the presence/absence and center/margin dichotomies."[62] Wittig allows the reader no recognizable point of view, nor does she give

[56] Ann Rosalind Jones, "Writing the Body: Toward an Understanding of l'Écriture féminine," in Showalter, ed. (n. 10 above), 361–77, esp. 370.

[57] Monique Wittig, "The Category of Sex," in *Feminist Issues* 2 (Fall 1982): 63–68, esp. 64.

[58] Monique Wittig, "The Point of View: Universal or Particular," *Feminist Issues* 3 (Fall 1983): 63–69, esp. 65.

[59] Ibid.

[60] Wittig, "The Category of Sex," 65.

[61] Monique Wittig, "The Mark of Gender," in *Feminist Issues* 5 (Fall 1985): 3–12, esp. 11.

[62] Namascar Shaktini, "Displacing the Phallic Subject: Wittig's Lesbian Writing," *Signs* 8, no. 1 (Autumn 1982): 29–44, esp. 39.

any specific identity to the lovers. They are interchangeable. Wittig accomplishes most of this shift through her use of pronouns, which she considers the center of subjectivity in language: the "elles" in *Les Guérillères* and the "j/e" of *The Lesbian Body.* These pronouns give to the marginal and other a centrality and universality, just as she argues that Djuna Barnes and Proust succeed because they posit a homosexual subject as a point from which to universalize.[63]

But this insistence on a claim to the universal does not avoid the necessity for the concrete, the physical, the particular, or the sexual. Wittig assumes both the materiality of the body and of the text. While she insists that a text, to be successful, must be universal, or it will lose "its polysemy" and become "univocal," she also claims that the marginal text must also assume a particular point of view.[64] The materiality of the body/text allows Wittig to include sexuality in her definition of lesbian as metaphor, but this sexuality is not powerful because of the woman's innate sexual uniqueness. Rather, the power of lesbian sexuality is determined by its position outside of any category; it is, as Elaine Marks states, "undomesticated."[65] The centrality of sexuality can best be seen in some of Wittig's fiction, especially in *The Lesbian Body,* a series of poems that focuses on lesbian lovers whose eroticism is neither transcendent nor within the traditional images of Western eroticism. It is a violent, disruptive, tender, grotesque sexuality, and, like the sexuality described by Adrienne Rich, it is also diffuse and omnipresent.

Outside of any categories, Wittig's lovers release creative as well as sexual energy. The text, too, is a sensual body that the lover caresses and violently puts together. As Marks states: "The power of the word and the pleasures of the female body are intimately related. Love-making is the primary source of inspiration. It opens and defines a world whose existence had been suspected but never so explicitly stated."[66] The imagination posited by this new eroticism leads the speaker to burst the bonds of recognizable sexual imagery and forge a textuality/sexuality of her own, with its own reality and language. To be outside the dichotomies, undomesticated and uncategorized, means, then, to create new images, new languages, and a new "axis of categorization."

Wittig could not be expected to rhapsodize about a tender relationship of subjects based on the archetypal mother-daughter bond.

[63] Wittig, "The Point of View," 64.

[64] Ibid., 65–68.

[65] Elaine Marks, "Lesbian Intertextuality," in *Homosexualities and French Literature: Cultural Contexts/Critical Texts,* ed. Elaine Marks and George Stambolian (Ithaca, N.Y.: Cornell University Press, 1979), 353–77, esp. 372.

[66] Ibid., 374–75.

In fact, for Wittig, the mother is everything that *is* the socially constructed woman; she is the domesticated woman. In her futurist dictionary (written with Sande Zeig), Wittig opposes the amazon to the mother, the betrayer of free women: "Then came a time when some daughters, and some mothers did not like wandering anymore in the terrestrial garden. They began to stay in the cities and most often they watched their abdomens grow. This activity brought them, it is said, great satisfaction. Things went so far in this direction that they refused to have any other interests. . . . The first generation of static mothers who refused to leave their cities, began. From then on, they called the others 'eternal, immature daughters, amazons.' "[67] As in *Les Guérillères,* this lesbian community is not constituted by similar but by uncategorized females, females who are not defined by any ontological term, least of all by mother. The community is, then, a collection of these undomesticated women, not an ontological entity.

The imaginative process that is circumscribed by lesbian is for Rich and Wittig a shattering of old images and language, a space in which the woman writer can both oppose patriarchal categories and begin to define a new concept of reality. By removing the male from the audience, text, and authorial stance, Rich, like Wittig, moves the woman writer from the margins to the center of her own language. Rich does not ask or care for Wittig's universality but relies on the text's ability to communicate to and draw from the "lesbian continuum," a continuum that must include the tradition of women writers as well as contemporary readers. In her latest book of poetry, for example, Rich asks for this admittedly Romantic aesthetic relationship: "I wasn't looking for a muse / only a reader by whom I could not be mistaken."[68] Her emphasis is on the poet-reader connection, the lesbian community that forges its own identity outside the patriarchy and therefore discovers its own truth. Rich is willing to let her text be univocal in Wittig's sense. Wittig is more concerned with the position of the subject in the linguistic order, with pronouns in particular, and with the linguistic space in which the lesbian can claim universality. But for both, the word lesbian provides a key term for the woman writer to position herself anew in an alien language.

I am not arguing that these two approaches to the metaphoric lesbian are essentially the same or that they can be resolved in some Hegelian synthesis. I am arguing that lesbian as metaphor is

[67] Wittig and Zeig (n. 35 above), 108–9.

[68] Adrienne Rich, "Contradictions: Tracking Poems, no. 20," in her *Your Native Land, Your Life: Poems* (New York: Norton, 1986), 102.

one of the most vital concepts in feminist critical theory today and deserves more and not less attention. I am also arguing that, while these two definitions of lesbian depend on different and, at times, radically opposed philosophies of language, they also have important elements in common, elements that deconstruct Western sexual metaphors for creativity and point to the possibility of female autonomy. This approach, I hope, will also address some of the important objections to lesbian as a metaphor for female creativity. To argue, for instance, that this metaphor eschews sexuality is to limit sexuality primarily to genital sexuality; sexuality, I would argue, is the core of the metaphor. Yet to state that it abstracts and generalizes is, of course, true because any metaphor must; but even as a metaphor, lesbian is a constant linguistic and conceptual challenge to the patriarchy. Unlike, for instance, the image of mother, which not only fixes women in a patriarchal category but also can and has been appropriated by men, lesbian as an image is too threatening to be blithely absorbed by the male artist.

As a metaphor for creativity, "lesbian" expands our concept of the author's and the reader's relationships to the text. They both become a relation of exchanged honesty and trust; and the writing of the text becomes an act that affirms self in community with others. As a broader literary symbol of women's lives, the metaphor can revise our reading of many texts, making, for instance, the lesbians in novels such as *The Color Purple* and *The Women of Brewster Place* symbols of as well as catalysts for the existence of autonomous women's communities.[69] Thus, while the recent theoretical history of this image offers problems and controversy, the creative strengths of lesbian as metaphor can significantly enrich and complicate our culture's symbolic representation of women.

Department of English
University of Oregon

[69] Walker (n. 11 above); and Gloria Naylor, *The Women of Brewster Place* (New York: Penguin, 1983).

HISTORY, CRITICAL THEORY, AND WOMEN'S SOCIAL PRACTICES: "WOMEN'S TIME" AND *HOUSEKEEPING*

THOMAS FOSTER

The value of the deconstructive critique to feminist theory and the form it should take within a political reading practice continue to be debated by feminist critics.[1] However, the relevance of Julia Kristeva's essay "Women's Time" to this debate has not been generally acknowledged.[2] "Women's Time" offers a historical model of recent developments in the women's movement, a model that presents feminist expropriation of deconstruction as a possibility

I would like to thank Jane Marcus for her readings of this paper, her support, and her encouragement, as well as the other participants in her seminars at the University of Texas on women's writing and feminist criticism.

[1] See Elizabeth A. Meese, *Crossing the Double-Cross: The Practice of Feminist Criticism* (Chapel Hill: University of North Carolina Press, 1986), esp. chaps. 5 and 8; Celeste M. Schenck, "Feminism and Deconstruction: Re-constructing the Elegy," *Tulsa Studies in Women's Literature* 5, no. 1 (Spring 1986): 13–27; and Gayatri Chakravorty Spivak, "Displacement and the Discourse of Woman," in *Displacement: Derrida and After*, ed. Mark Krupnick (Bloomington: Indiana University Press, 1983), 169–95.

[2] Julia Kristeva, "Women's Time," trans. Alice Jardine and Harry Blake, in *Feminist Theory: A Critique of Ideology*, ed. Nannerl O. Keohane, Michelle Z. Rosaldo, and Barbara C. Gelpi (Chicago: University of Chicago Press, 1982). Subsequent citations of this article will appear in parentheses in the text as *WT*. The main exception is Toril Moi, *Sexual/Textual Politics: Feminist Literary Theory* (London: Methuen, 1985), 12–13, who offers a schematic outline of Kristeva's model and uses it to argue for the need to deconstruct male/female gender roles.

This essay originally appeared in *Signs*, vol. 14, no. 1, Autumn 1988.

generated by (at least) Western women's historical situation. Kristeva suggests that there is a material basis for feminist use of deconstructive strategies, but her model of the forms feminist self-consciousness can take also implies that those forms stand in specific relation to historical materialism, including its use of dialectics in critical analysis. Feminist practices as Kristeva presents them function as an immanent critique of both materialist and deconstructive theories, while implying the need to retain as well as modify their analytic categories and procedures. Kristeva's essay presents itself as a commentary on the European women's movement, particularly in France and Italy, but the questions it raises find enough correspondence in the work of socialist feminists and critics engaged in politicizing deconstruction to interest Anglo-American readers.[3] As a literary representation of the lives of several generations of women, Marilynne Robinson's novel *Housekeeping* shows how an analysis like Kristeva's might organize a narrative of women's resistance to the historical limitations imposed on them.

Living (in) history

"Women's Time" (1979) begins with two examples of collectivities that cut across the linear history of the nation-state and unsettle the national identity founded on that shared history. Harking back to the student revolts of May 1968, women and young people are the examples Kristeva gives of groups causing this "loss of identity" through their participation in what she calls "monumental time" (*WT*, 32). In an early essay, Kristeva defines monumental history as "a plurality of productions that cannot be reduced to one another," in contrast to the unitary narrative posited by "the concept of *linear*

[3] Socialist feminist work discussed below will include Joan Kelly, *Women, History, and Theory: The Essays of Joan Kelly* (Chicago: University of Chicago Press, 1984); Elizabeth Fox-Genovese, "Placing Women's History in History," *New Left Review* 133 (May–June 1982): 5–29; Michéle Barrett, *Women's Oppression Today: Problems in Marxist Feminist Analysis* (London: Verso, 1980); and (more briefly) Sheila Rowbotham, Lynne Segal, and Hilary Wainwright, *Beyond the Fragments: Feminism and the Making of Socialism* (Boston: Alyson Publications, 1981). Michael Ryan, *Marxism and Deconstruction: A Critical Articulation* (Baltimore: Johns Hopkins University Press, 1982), chap. 9, treats socialist feminism in relation to dialectics and deconstruction. Gayatri Spivak's work is concerned with the same issues, and Meese sets out "to provoke critical theory, especially American manifestations of deconstruction, to be more radically political" (x).

historicity."[4] In "Women's Time," this heterogeneity results from the "diagonal" relation established between European, North and South American, Indian, or Chinese women who retain their own particularity but also share a "structural place in reproduction and its representations" (*WT*, 33). Kristeva's historical model distinguishes three "generations" in the women's movement according to whether women seek to synchronize their time with the progress of linear history, affirm a cyclic or monumental time with archaic connotations, or establish a prefigurative practice that both exists in the "Now" and belongs to a different future.[5]

The first two moments in this model correspond to the "oscillation between power and denial" Kristeva described in an interview, five years before writing "Women's Time."[6] In the emergence of a third moment, Kristeva finds an alternative to those two extremes. Associated with suffrage movements and the impact of existential ideas on feminism, the first generation seeks "to gain a place in linear time as the time of project and history" (*WT*, 36). This "insertion into history" is structured by a "logic of identification" with the values of "a rationality dominant in the nation-state," values which are also masculine; this generation rejects traditional feminine or maternal traits when they come into conflict

[4] Julia Kristeva, "Semiotics: A Critical Science and/or a Critique of Science," trans. Sean Hand, in *The Kristeva Reader*, ed. Toril Moi (New York: Columbia University Press, 1986), 85. Kristeva takes this term from Philippe Sollers's distinction between linear and monumental histories in his "Programme," *Tel Quel* 31 (Autumn 1967): 3–7. See Jacques Derrida, *Positions*, trans. Alan Bass (Chicago: University of Chicago Press, 1981), for an indication of what this concept came to mean in French theoretical discourse. In an interview from this collection, Guy Scarpetta asks Derrida if it is not possible to retain a notion of "history conceived no longer as a linear scheme, but as a stratified, differential, contradictory" group of social practices (56).

[5] Ernst Bloch's essay, "Nonsynchronism and the Obligation to Its Dialectics," *New German Critique* 11 (Spring 1977), offers a way of reading Kristeva's notion of women's time. Bloch begins: "Not all people exist in the same Now. They do so only externally, by virtue of the fact that they may all be seen today. But that does not mean that they are living at the same time with others. . . . One has one's times according to where one stands corporeally" (22). Writing originally in response to the rise of fascism in the 1930s, Bloch points to the prefiguratively nonsynchronic position of young people, a position Kristeva also claims for women: "For the most part, *Youth* turns away from the day that it has. It is a day that the young do not have today. But their dreams are nourished just as materially by an empty condition of being-young, which is not of the present" (23).

[6] Julia Kristeva, "Oscillation between Power and Denial," in *New French Feminisms*, ed. Elaine Marks and Isabelle de Courtivron (New York: Schocken, 1981), 165–67.

with the goal of entering history (*WT*, 37). As the phallic rhetoric of insertion and entry indicates, for Kristeva this stage is marked by a desire for mastery, which seizes power without transforming or adequately questioning it.[7] Despite this criticism, she recognizes the political benefits of such activism, whose effects in her view exceed those of the industrial revolution (*WT*, 37). What this generation's efforts fail to exceed is the hegemonic culture's capacity to absorb and thrive on contradiction and challenge.

The second generation constitutes itself in reaction to the initial project of "modernization" and the attempt to synchronize women's time with a history that has excluded women. This reaction is characterized by a reaffirmation of "the specificity of female psychology and its symbolic realizations" (*WT*, 37). Women reject the linear time of historiography in favor of a cyclic and monumental temporality traditionally associated with female subjectivity and with ritual, marginalized religious practices, and mysticism. More importantly, women at this point reject a unitary image of self-identity, unmarked by internal contradictions such as differences between women: "By demanding recognition of an irreducible identity, without equal in the other sex and as such exploded, plural, fluid, in a certain way nonidentical, this feminism situates itself outside the linear time of identities which communicate through projection and revindication" (*WT*, 37–38).

In this passage, Kristeva's use of "identity" to name nonidentity or difference emphasizes that the second, separatist generation is constituting and reclaiming "nonidentity" as a subject position from which to speak and act, an oppositional potential the third generation in her model will realize. But the same designation of difference as identity points to Kristeva's criticism of this second moment for a tendency to imagine itself as transcending differences of class, race, or sexuality and the tensions they create and instead thinking of itself as "harmonious, without prohibitions, free and fulfilling" (*WT*, 45). Such a "countersociety" recapitulates the sacrificial foundation of the social and symbolic contracts based on transactions between separate and equal individuals—that is, "the expulsion of an excluded element, a scapegoat charged with the evil of which the community duly constituted can then purge itself" (*WT*, 45). In *Revolution in Poetic Language*, Kristeva describes the insight that sacrifice provides into the institution and functioning of the symbolic order of language and other semiotic systems: "Sacrifice shows how representing . . . violence is enough to stop it and to concatenate an order. Conversely it indicates that all order is based on

[7] Ibid., 166; Kristeva, "Women's Time," 44–48.

representation: what is violent is the irruption of the symbol, killing substance to make it signify."[8] The idea is not to eradicate this violence, which is seen as the basis of language acquisition, but to transform it by intervening to prevent violence and the power it represents from being organized along the lines of social hierarchies. Kristeva's third generation raises the possibility of "an ethics which, conscious of the fact that its order is sacrificial, reserves part of the burden for each of its adherents, therefore declaring them guilty while immediately affording them the possibility for *jouissance,* for various productions, for a life made up of both challenges and differences" (*WT*, 53). The current mode of social organization instead divides the social order into victims and executioners (*WT*, 52).

The third generation in Kristeva's model combines the responses of the first two: "insertion into history and the radical *refusal* of the subjective limitations imposed by this history's time on an experiment carried out in the name of the irreducible difference" (*WT*, 38). The separatist moment is not abandoned, but neither do women refuse to engage with the dominant culture; rather they enter society and history to introduce into it the possibility of radical change and the fact of heterogenous social elements, the "irreducible difference." For Kristeva as for Luce Irigaray, "It is in order to bring their difference to light that women are demanding their rights."[9] In "Women's Time" and other essays like "Stabat Mater,"[10] Kristeva treats mothering as a social practice with transformative cultural force when it comes into conflict with the dominant culture. I want to extend her analysis to the sexual division of labor, the exploitation of women's productive and reproductive work by an economic system that privileges exchange-value and the production of surplus-value over use-value, and the ideology of the home as a separate sphere, a private domestic space.

Kristeva's definition of a third generation of feminists who combine an entry into history with an affirmation of difference implies the possibility of radicalizing what Temma Kaplan calls "female consciousness," the socially legitimated assumptions about qualities and activities required of women within specific cultures, as-

[8] Julia Kristeva, *Revolution in Poetic Language,* trans. Margaret Waller (New York: Columbia University Press, 1984), 75.

[9] Luce Irigaray, *This Sex Which Is Not One,* trans. Catherine Porter (Ithaca, N.Y.: Cornell University Press, 1985), 166.

[10] Kristeva, "Women's Time," 48–49; Julia Kristeva, "Stabat Mater," trans. Arthur Goldhammer, in *The Female Body in Western Culture: Contemporary Perspectives,* ed. Susan Rubin Suleiman (Cambridge: Harvard University Press, 1986), 99–118.

sumptions women themselves internalize.[11] This third generation affirms the value and specificity of the consciousness produced by exclusion from an official history that uses women as a specular image to confirm masculine self-identity. But they reject the material and symbolic limitations, especially enclosure within a domestic space as well as the teleology of motherhood, that produced that consciousness.

Kristeva ends "Women's Time" with the statement that her historical model does not describe a progression with a clear beginning and end; each generation is "less a chronology than a signifying space, a both corporeal and desiring mental space" (*WT*, 51). Mary Jacobus's distinction between liberal and radical feminist attitudes toward language corresponds to the signifying spaces of Kristeva's first two generations. For Jacobus, liberal feminists tend to treat dominant discourses as if they were neutral forms, to be filled with the content of female experience, while radical feminists insist on a separatist position, demanding a whole new language.[12] Margaret Homans aligns this distinction with Elaine Marks's definition of the different conceptions of women's situation within patriarchy used by Anglo-American and French feminists; the first group tends to treat women's oppression while the French focus on women's repression and difference. Kristeva's location of a third possibility suggests the emergence of productive conjunctions between the opposing positions these American critics have outlined.[13] Adrienne

[11] Temma Kaplan, "Female Consciousness and Collective Action: The Case of Barcelona, 1910–1918," in Keohane, Rosaldo, and Gelpi, eds. (n. 2 above), 55–76, esp. 55–57, 75–76. See Sondra Hale, "The Wing of the Patriarch: Sudanese Women and Revolutionary Parties," *Merip: Middle East Report* 16 (January–February 1986), 28–30, for an application of Kaplan's ideas to one group of non-Western women. Rather than revalorizing domestic space, Hale proposes that Sudanese women could draw upon other, culturally specific women-only spaces in order to avoid a cooptation that ignores women's issues. Hale also relates these spaces to what Sheila Rowbotham in *Beyond the Fragments* (n. 3 above) calls "prefigurative forms," which I will discuss in the last section of the present essay. Susan Willis makes an argument about domestic space similar to mine in her book on Afro-American women's writing. See Willis, *Specifying: Black Women Writing the American Experience* (Madison: University of Wisconsin Press, 1987), 159–60.

[12] Mary Jacobus, "The Difference of View," in *Women Writers and Writing about Women*, ed. Mary Jacobus (Totowa, N.J.: Barnes & Noble, 1979), 10–21, esp. 14.

[13] Margaret Homans, " 'Her Very Own Howl': The Ambiguities of Representation in Recent Women's Fiction," *Signs: Journal of Women in Culture and Society* 9, no. 2 (Winter 1983): 186–205, esp. 186–87; Elaine Marks, "Women and Literature in France," *Signs* 3, no. 4 (Summer 1978): 832–42, esp. 835–36. Homans's essay defines one such conjunction when she argues that contemporary women's fiction displaces the French feminist concern with women's exclusion from the symbolic order of language onto the thematic level, thus continuing to use and to revise given discursive forms (205).

Rich's lesbian continuum represents one response to the need for retaining a perspective exceeding the hegemony's capacity to appropriate feminist activities, in order to "*change the social relations of the sexes.*"[14] A comparable statement is Luce Irigaray's description of "non-integration" as both a necessity and a desire for women.[15]

Luce Irigaray's work exemplifies the emergence in France of Kristeva's third generation. When Irigaray tells an interviewer that for women it is not a question of "installing" themselves within a masculine definition of woman as negativity, "nor of reversing the economy of sameness by turning the feminine into *the standard for 'sexual difference,'* " but instead it is "a matter of trying to practice that difference," she defines a combination of entry into history and maintenance of difference.[16] Her comments on Freud's need to arrange differences into hierarchies pose the alternative that Kristeva locates in the third moment of her historical model:

> Let us imagine that man (Freud in the event) had discovered that the rarest thing—. . . the most faithful to factual materiality and the most historically curative—would be to articulate directly, *without catacombs* . . . these two syntaxes. Irreducible in their strangeness and eccentricity one to the other. . . . Had the man Freud preferred the play, or even the clash of those two economies rather than their disposition in hierarchical stages by means of one barrier (or two), one censorship (or two), then perhaps he would not finally have cracked his head against all that remains irreducibly "obscure" to him in his speculations.[17]

For readers of Kristeva, this passage recalls her description of the preverbal negativity of the semiotic which always appears as a disruption within the symbolic order. Such disruptions call attention both to the contradictions on which that order is founded and to the subject's capacity to exceed and to transgress the preexisting social and linguistic structures in which we are inscribed.[18]

This thematics of heterogeneity and doubleness finds a parallel in recent socialist feminist theory that asserts the need to treat gender and class systems as neither separate nor reducible one to

[14] Adrienne Rich, "Compulsory Heterosexuality and Lesbian Existence," in *Blood, Bread, and Poetry: Selected Prose 1979–1985* (New York: Norton, 1986), 63.

[15] Irigaray, *This Sex* (n. 9 above), 135.

[16] Ibid., 159.

[17] Luce Irigaray, *Speculum of the Other Woman*, trans. Gillian C. Gill (Ithaca, N.Y.: Cornell University Press, 1985), 139.

[18] Kristeva, *Revolution* (n. 8 above), 68.

the other. In "The Doubled Vision of Feminist Theory," Joan Kelly argues that the political goals of feminism "are neither to participate as equals in man's world, nor to restore to woman's realm and values their dignity and worth. Conceptions such as these are superseded in the present will to extirpate gender and sex hierarchy altogether, and with them all forms of domination."[19] Elizabeth Fox-Genovese extends this analysis while stressing the importance of retaining the separatist moment that restores "to woman's realm and values their dignity and worth." In "Placing Women's History in History," Fox-Genovese implies that feminism confronts a masculine logic of identity: "the expansion of capitalism and modern representative government has attempted to bind men of different classes, races, and ethnic groups together through the double promise of individualism in the public sphere and male dominance in the home."[20] In what can be read as a variant of (or gloss on) Kristeva's critique of the second generation, Fox-Genovese believes that the rejection of "all official history as irrelevant to female experience" only "perpetuates the most pernicious myths" of that history, particularly its "insistence upon the universal claims of female biology."[21] For her, the "confrontation between women's history . . . and mainstream history offers a special opportunity to rethink the basic premises that inform historical interpretation."[22] The form that challenge takes is "not to substitute the chronicle of the female subject for that of the male, but rather to restore conflict, ambiguity, and tragedy to the centre of historical process," elements excluded from "the perspective of the authoritative male subject—the single, triumphant consciousness."[23]

Both Kelly and Fox-Genovese are implicitly modifying the traditional Marxist analysis of capitalist class relations as the totalizing final instance to which all forms of oppression can be reduced. The privilege accorded to a unified working class as the vehicle of significant change, the motor of history, results from this reduction. Georg Lukacs refers to this status of the proletariat in Marxist theory when he calls it "the identical subject-object of the historical process."[24] The proletariat is unified as a class precisely through its function as the dialectic negation of an exploitation organized along class lines. In "Women's Time," Kristeva comments on the problem

[19] Kelly (n. 3 above), 59–60.

[20] Fox-Genovese (n. 3 above), 7.

[21] Ibid., 14.

[22] Ibid.

[23] Ibid., 29.

[24] Georg Lukacs, *History and Class Consciousness: Studies in Marxist Dialectics*, trans. Rodney Livingstone (Cambridge: MIT Press, 1971), 199.

with regarding the proletariat as "the last oppressed class," to quote Lukacs again.[25] Because of an ideology that emphasizes productive labor in the marketplace, in most socialist countries (specifically Eastern Europe) feminist issues like birth control and more generally the role of domestic labor in the reproduction of capitalist social relations have appeared "nonessential or even nonexistent" (*WT*, 38–39).

But Michéle Barrett stresses that, while forms of oppression involving ideologies of separate gender roles preceded the transition to capitalism and so would not automatically be eradicated by a socialist revolution, the sexual division of labor has been appropriated by and become functional for capitalism, to the extent that only radical changes in the existing relations of production would have a significant impact on the exploitation of women's work.[26] In Barrett's account, women have a dual relationship to the class structure. The heterogeneity may result from *indirect* dependence on the wage of a husband or father or, in the case of many working women, combine direct involvement in wage-labor with the obligation to perform domestic work traditionally defined as unpaid.[27] For Kelly, socialist feminism's "doubled vision" works against attempts either "to reduce sex oppression to class interests or to see the relation of the sexes as always and ever the same, regardless of race, class, or society."[28] From this point of view, feminism complicates the notion that a dialectical resolution can securely place diversity under the sign of unity to transcend contradiction and conflict.

Dialectic (and) deconstruction

Kristeva's historical model participates in this critique of dialectics. Its three-step design deliberately invites comparison to the movement of the dialectic, which is a version of the linear time of the first generation in her model. The contradiction inherent in an initial social formation determines and generates its own negation. Women's attempts to enter history by accepting the masculine values on which it is based (including separation from the domestic space) lead to or are accompanied by the return to female specificity, which Kristeva elsewhere calls the "valorization of a silent under-

[25] Ibid., 224.
[26] Barrett (n. 3 above), 226.
[27] Ibid., 134–38.
[28] Kelly (n. 3 above), 61.

water body."[29] The third step, then, would be the synthesis or *Aufhebung*, the negation of the second generation's negation of the first, which should produce an affirmation of unity out of seeming contradiction. But Kristeva asserts that the "insertion into history" is accompanied by an irruption of "irreducible difference" (*WT*, 38); her third moment is one of heterogenous mixture, not final unity. This departure from traditional dialectics focuses on the category of contradiction as a permanent feature of historical process, not merely a strategic moment within it.

However, Kristeva's model follows a deconstructive trajectory as much as a dialectic one. The second generation in her model is responding to the counter-productive results of declaring equality without, in Derrida's terms, first overturning the structure of privilege that marginalizes women:

> We must traverse a phase of *overturning*. To do justice to this necessity is to recognize that . . . we are not dealing with the peaceful coexistence of a *vis-à-vis*, but rather with a violent hierarchy. One of the two terms governs the other . . . or has the upper hand. To deconstruct the opposition, first of all, is to overturn the hierarchy at a given moment. To overlook this phase of overturning is to forget the conflictual and subordinating structure of opposition. Therefore one might proceed too quickly to a *neutralization* that *in practice* would leave the previous field untouched, leaving one no hold on the previous opposition, thereby preventing any means of *intervening* in the field effectively. We know what always have been the practical (particularly political) effects of immediately jumping beyond oppositions.[30]

The separatist moment in Kristeva's model performs this inversion, giving priority to a privatized feminine subjectivity and field of action over a male-dominated history, but without necessarily challenging the opposition between public and private. The next step is the displacement of the power structure and the dominant term's claim to a privileged identity, by marking an interval, an irreducible and necessary alterity, that exists within both terms of the opposition and stands as a return of the repressed within self-identity. Recalling the title of Fox-Genovese's article, this interval locates the excluded

[29] Kristeva, "Oscillation" (n. 6 above), 166.

[30] Derrida, *Positions* (n. 4 above), 41. These negative political effects are what Moi seems to chance or to attribute to Kristeva when she describes Kristeva's model simply as a deconstruction of gender roles; see n. 2 above.

and subordinated term of the opposition within the self-identity of the term governing the opposition.[31] Women claim historical agency as women, refusing to identify with the supposedly universal values that have supported masculine privilege. But women also reject a unitary notion of "Woman," thus marking a difference operating within the social construction of both genders. Kristeva describes the logic of identity as a circular projection and revindication, a repetition of sameness. Her third generation's rejection of that logic corresponds to Derrida's moment of displacement. This rejection occurs both on a subjective and a collective level, and its goal is "to avoid the centralization of power, . . . to detach women from it, and . . . to proceed through their critical, differential, and autonomous interventions, to render decision-making institutions more flexible" (*WT*, 45).

Kristeva's third generation retains the separatist moment of inversion, putting it into practice against the mystifications of official culture, with the aim of transforming social structures, including those that define the subject. The moment of inversion is "not a question of a chronological phase"; rather the analyst interminably operates "both an overturning deconstruction and a positively displacing, transgressive, deconstruction."[32] This remark underscores the repetitive and cyclic character of deconstruction, in contrast to the dialectic model; the temporality of the deconstructive operation embraces the monumental time of Kristeva's second generation.

The combination of two kinds of temporality, linear dialectic and cyclic deconstruction, within Kristeva's historical model itself repeats the combination of linear, historical time and nonsynchronous women's time achieved by the third generation her model discusses. By implication, deconstruction *and* dialectic are modified. In *Revolution in Poetic Language,* Kristeva criticizes Derrida for carrying both his desire to "think short" of the institution of hierarchies and his rejection of linear teleology to the point of ignoring or minimizing the possibility of deconstructive social practices: "The grammatological deluge of meaning gives up on the subject and must remain ignorant not only of his [sic] functioning as social practice but also of his chances for experiencing jouissance or being put to death. . . . Demonstrating disinterestedness toward (symbolic and/or social) structure, grammatology remains silent when faced with its destruction or renewal."[33] In Kristeva's model, the deconstructive moment of inversion is assimilated to the necessity

[31] Derrida, *Positions,* 42.
[32] Ibid., 66.
[33] Kristeva, *Revolution* (n. 8 above), 142.

of defining a counterhegemonic subject position whose full potential for resistance is realized in the third moment of the operation.

Kristeva's third generation offers a solution to the problem for Marxist theory posed by Stanley Aronowitz: "It remains for us to find the bearers of a non-identical dialectic."[34] Aronowitz's idea of the "crisis in historical materialism" draws on his reading of Theodor Adorno's "negative dialectics" and Ernst Bloch's "polyphonous dialectics," both of which try to redefine a dialectic that avoids final unity, as Kristeva's historical model does in tracing the development of feminist practice.[35] "Women's Time" also responds to Derrida's suggestion that feminism remains caught in the second moment of the deconstructive operation and only inverts traditional hierarchies without subverting the concept of hierarchy itself: "Feminism is nothing but the operation of a woman who aspires to be like a man. And in order to resemble the masculine dogmatic philosopher this woman lays claim—just as much claim as he—to truth, science, and objectivity in all their castrated delusions of virility."[36] Kristeva's historical model reveals this statement for the misreading of feminist possibilities that it is.[37]

The deconstructive strategy Kristeva sees as informing the development of the women's movement involves questioning material and symbolic boundaries between inside and outside, between the public space of political action and productive labor and the private, domestic space to which women's values and activities have historically been confined. The third generation of feminists in her model rejects the limitations placed on those values, both their spatial enclosure and the ideology that situates women's lives within a horizon of motherhood. The women's movement has begun to expose the contradictions inherent in representing home as a private space, when for women that space has functioned as the

[34] Stanley Aronowitz, *The Crisis in Historical Materialism: Class, Politics, and Culture in Marxist Theory* (New York: Praeger, 1982), 31.

[35] Ibid., 24–34, 116–17, 121; Bloch (n. 5 above), 38; see Ryan (n. 3 above), 73–81, on Adorno.

[36] Jacques Derrida, *Spurs/Eperons*, trans. Barbara Harlow (Chicago: University of Chicago Press, 1979), 65.

[37] Alice Jardine, *Gynesis: Configurations of Woman and Modernity* (Ithaca, N.Y.: Cornell University Press, 1985), 194–95, points out how Derrida seems to endorse Nietszche's perspective on feminism in this passage, treating it merely as a moment of inversion which fails to challenge the hierarchies of man/woman or truth/untruth. Kristeva's model asks whether the moment of inversion is necessary to give purpose to "skepticism" and "dissimilation" (Jardine, 194) as social practice and to link it to a material subject position, thus giving substance to her critique of grammatology for remaining silent about the subject.

site of social responsibilities.[38] Marilynne Robinson's novel *Housekeeping* provides us with a literary representation of the (nonidentical) dialectic development Kristeva's model follows and of an alternative, prefigurative practice that comes into contradiction with dominant social forms precisely through the performance of deconstructive strategies.

Burning down the house

As Elizabeth Meese has pointed out, Marilynne Robinson's first novel performs a separatist inversion by offering a narrative of small-town American life in which men appear only marginally, as intruders.[39] The narrative follows two sisters, Ruth (the narrator) and Lucille, as they are cared for by a succession of relatives after their mother's suicide. After their grandmother's death, two of her sisters come to live with the children until they can arrange for the girls' aunt, Sylvie, to stay with them. Before her arrival in Fingerbone, Sylvie was living as a transient, riding the rails and sleeping in bus stops and on park benches. By the end of the novel, the community decides Sylvie is unfit to be entrusted with the care of children. She then returns to the life of a drifter and takes Ruth with her, after setting fire to the grandmother's house. Meese calls this final defiance of the confinement of "women's work" to a private sphere a "gesture to the permanence of family relationships, one that stands in strict contrast to Kerouac's male fantasy of life on the road."[40] The novel ends with the two women never knowing for certain whether the house was actually destroyed or whether Ruth's sister Lucille might be living there, since Lucille had rejected Sylvie's alternative economy of the home by running away to live with her Home Economics teacher. Through the choices the two sisters make,

[38] Jean Bethke Elshtain, *Public Man, Private Woman: Women in Social and Political Thought* (Princeton, N.J.: Princeton University Press, 1981), 12, describes a logic of the supplement in the separation of the Greek *polis* from the household: "First the relations and activities occurring within and serving as the raison d'être of the *polis* were defined as existing outside the realms of nature and necessity. Second, the free space of the *polis*, though apart from necessity, existed in a *necessary* relation to those activities lodged within the private realm, held by the Greeks to be the sphere of unfreedom."

[39] Marilynne Robinson, *Housekeeping* (New York: Farrar, Straus, & Giroux, 1980), subsequent citations of this novel will appear in parentheses in the text as *H;* Meese (n. 1 above), 57.

[40] Meese, 64.

Ruth accepting Sylvie's way of life and Lucille accepting a conventional gender role, the narrative asks the reader to choose one or the other of these two perspectives and thus to undertake the political act of either endorsing or rejecting Ruth and Sylvie's rebellion.[41] But the novel contextualizes the alternative Sylvie represents in other ways, as well.

Early in the novel, the grandmother's relation to society is defined in terms of her exclusion from access to the public domain. She looks forward to her death, Ruth tells us, because it will result in the execution of her will: "Since my grandmother had a little income and owned her house outright, she always took some satisfaction in thinking ahead to the time when her simple private destiny would intersect with the great public processes of law and finance—that is, to the time of her death" (*H*, 27). Significantly, the only men to appear in the narrative are public figures, a school principal and a sheriff who arrives to legislate Ruth and Sylvie's family arrangements. The specification of death as the point when this woman would gain the power to exert her will within the public realm is important for an understanding of the novel's ending, where this standard narrative of women's powerlessness is revised even as it presents Ruth and Sylvie's decision to become drifters as a kind of death. The ending foregrounds and dramatizes the contradictions women live when they refuse to abide within their "proper place," but it also implies the possibility of putting these contradictions into practice as a form of historical agency with potentially radical results. The grandmother's death prefigures the way of life Ruth and Sylvie choose by leaving the house. At the time of her death "all the habits and patterns and properties that had settled around her, the monthly checks from the bank, the house she had lived in since she came to it as a bride, the weedy orchard that surrounded the yard on three sides where smaller and wormier apples and apricots and plums had fallen every year of her widowhood, all these things would suddenly become liquid, capable of assuming new forms" (*H*, 27). The significance of linking the separation of public and private spheres to ownership will become apparent in Sylvie's attitude toward private property, especially when she "steals" a boat. Sylvie's economy of the home will be marked by a fluidity in the structures effecting that separation, a fluidity the grandmother could imagine occurring only after her death. Sylvie will reject the logic of exclusion that circumscribes the grandmother's life and will bring Ruth to reject it also.

[41] Ibid., 61.

Still, Ruth demonstrates her sensitivity to the values of a traditional female consciousness by trying to think back through her grandmother and imagine how this woman felt while hanging up clothes to dry and while working in her garden, which Ruth presents as a "resurrection of the ordinary" (*H*, 18). But the grandmother's moment of self-consciousness about the value of her way of life is accompanied by a recognition of the limitations imposed on her by the domestic enclosure that forms the material basis of that way of life. This recognition appears as a feeling of loneliness, in response to which "old women she had known, first her grandmother and then her mother, rocked on their porches in the evenings and sang sad songs, and did not wish to be spoken to" (*H*, 18). Ruth expresses the same dissatisfied awareness of limits in describing how the grandmother combined her private life and personal habits with her social function of caring for the girls: "Say that my grandmother sang in her throat while she sat on her bed and we laced up her big black shoes. Such details are merely accidental. Who could know but us?" (*H*, 116). Ruth's question indicates an awareness that the openness and productive complexity the grandmother's attitude displays is confined to the domestic sphere and excluded from the standard life stories in which "such details" would be "merely accidental" to the real plot. As long as the home continues to define a rigid boundary between public and private spaces, the potential alternative to that public/private dichotomy will remain a private experience rather than a social movement or practice.

In contrast to the grandmother, the girls' mother, Helen, had internalized a masculine concept of individuality as detachment rather than the engagement prominent in the grandmother's behavior. Ruth refers to her mother's "gentle indifference" toward her children and the abstraction which often made them think there was someone else in the room with her that they could not see. Ruth's comment about being left on the grandmother's porch before Helen drove her car into the lake at Fingerbone is, "At last we had slid from her lap like one of those magazines full of responsible opinion about discipline and balanced meals" (*H*, 109–10). Besides having had to jettison the traditional role of mother to the extent that it interfered with her need to make a living, Helen's status as a working mother and the actual division of her time between the marketplace and the home had become part of her way of life even within the home. Unlike the grandmother, Helen excluded the children from her private thoughts and feelings and made them feel excluded, just as she denied them access to information about their absent father in maintaining that it was her business and hers alone (*H*, 52). She treated domestic work as the kind of regimen that might be contained in one of those "magazines full of responsible opinion" and subordinated her private life to her public activities, as if nothing private could make "any significant demands on her attention" (*H*, 109). This division is presented as the major factor in her decision to commit suicide.

The girls' mother corresponds to the first generation in Kristeva's model, an entry into history made on masculine terms, an appropriation of the detached position of the male subject. The return to the grandmother, then, performs a narrative function equivalent to the rejection of official history that characterizes the second moment in Kristeva's model. Sylvie's appearance marks the beginning of the third generation, the combination of these two attitudes. Soon after Sylvie's arrival, the lake by Fingerbone rises, and the grandmother's house is flooded. When they come down to check on the ground floor, Ruth describes how "Sylvie took me by the hands and pulled me after her through six grand waltz steps. The house flowed around us" (*H*, 64). The remark prefigures both the change Sylvie will introduce into the traditional domestic economy and the relationship she establishes with Ruth.

Meese refers to Sylvie's housekeeping as a "tending to and nurturing of the exterior world, an opening up of the outside to the inside."[42] Her housekeeping is the other side of her vagrancy, which treats the exterior world and public spaces like parks as if they were a domestic space where one would be perfectly justified in satisfying a need, say, to sleep. Ruth remembers Sylvie walking around the house with a scarf around her hair and a broom in her hand, but at the same time the house began to accumulate leaves in the corners, along with scraps of paper bearing phrases like "Powers Meet" and "I think of you" (*H*, 84–85). The change occurs as a function of Sylvie's belief that air is the best cleaning agent, since she would open doors and windows and not think to close them. Ruth tells us "it was for the sake of air that on one early splendid day she wrestled my grandmother's plum-colored davenport into the front yard, where it remained until it weathered pink" (*H*, 85–86). In Sylvie's hands, the house becomes "attuned to the orchard and the particularities of weather, even in the first days of Sylvie's housekeeping," with the leaves in the corners "lifted up by something that came before the wind" (*H*, 85).

Another of Sylvie's habits underscores her rejection of the home as a mechanism of exclusion. She prefers to leave the lights off when evening arrives and to eat dinner in the dark. Ruth says that Sylvie "seemed to dislike the disequilibrium of counterpoising a

[42] Ibid., 59.

roomful of light against a worldful of darkness. Sylvie in a house was more or less like a mermaid in a ship's cabin. She preferred it sunk in the very element it was meant to exclude. We had crickets in the pantry, squirrels in the eaves, sparrows in the attic. Lucille and I stepped through the door from sheer night to sheer night" (*H*, 99). Sylvie works against the binary logic of "counterpoising" an inside and an outside. One night, while eating dinner in the moonlight, Lucille suddenly turns on the lights in the kitchen. The passage suggests that Sylvie's housekeeping and the attitude toward women's social situation to which it corresponds can only be criticized from within the dualistic structures of thought and social existence to which Sylvie's way of life stands as an alternative. Turning on the light restores the separation of interior and exterior that Lucille wishes to uphold: "The window went black and the cluttered kitchen leaped, so it seemed, into being, as remote from what had gone before as this world was from the primal darkness. We saw that we ate from plates that came in detergent boxes, and we drank from jelly glasses. . . . Lucille had startled us all, flooding the room so suddenly with light, exposing heaps of pots and dishes, the two cupboard doors which had come unhinged and were propped against the boxes of china" (*H*, 100–101). The episode ends with a comic detail that looks ahead to what Ruth and Sylvie will eventually feel forced to do to the house, since another thing they can see is a curtain "which had been half consumed by fire once when a birthday cake had been set too close to it. Sylvie had beaten out the flames with a back issue of *Good Housekeeping*, but she had never replaced the curtain" (*H*, 101).

Being inside a lighted room establishes a barrier between those inside and the exterior, making it difficult to see outside; but the lights make it easier for those outside to see in. In this way, Robinson's novel encodes women's confinement and the masculine privilege of moving freely between the public sphere and the family space. At the same time, that privilege sets substantive male existence outside the home, so that the traditional position of men within the domestic space resembles the picture Ruth conjures up of her grandfather "just outside [the women's] conversation, like a difficult memory, or a ghost" (*H*, 96). That description also conveys a sense of the woman-identified quality of Ruth's imagination and narrative. This ghost is the only figure in the text offered to male readers to situate themselves in opposition to the sheriff, the law, with respect to the events and characters of the narrative. To take the position of that ghost, a reader like me must acknowledge that feminist discourses both speak critically to me and demand a reply that heeds the various boundaries by which women define themselves. As male critic, *I* must make this ghost speak. This essay is, I hope, marked by a sense of the political urgency and the risks such an undertaking carries.

The narrative does place women within such lighted and enclosed spaces. Soon after Sylvie's arrival, Ruth and Lucille run alongside a train "to stay abreast of the window of a young woman with a small head and a small hat and a brightly painted face" (*H*, 54). She looks "at the window," caught up in the closure of her own reflected and painted image, "clearly absorbed by what she saw, which was not but merely seemed to be Lucille and me scrambling to stay beside her, too breathless to shout" (*H*, 54). This passage is introduced by Ruth's comment that "memories are by their nature fragmented, isolated, and arbitrary as glimpses one has at night through lighted windows" (*H*, 53). Later, Ruth describes the result of being inside as a mystification of difference:

> When one looks from inside at a lighted window, or looks from above at the lake, one sees the image of oneself in a lighted room, the image of oneself among trees and sky—the deception is obvious, but flattering all the same. When one looks from the darkness into the light, however, one sees all the difference between here and there, this and that. Perhaps all unsheltered people are angry in their hearts, and would like to break the roof, spine, and ribs, and smash the windows and flood the floor and spindle the curtains and bloat the couch. [*H*, 157–58][43]

These remarks indicate an awareness of the privileges many American women do possess, but they also suggest those privileges function socially to contain an anger at gender-based oppression which once released, would cut across class lines. The same awareness of how women are encouraged to reproduce their own oppression (like an image in a mirror, a fixed identity) informs Sylvie's story of a woman who, out of loneliness, got married and "had four children in five years," although "none of it helped at all" (*H*, 66).

Ruth also displays an awareness of the difficulty of getting beyond habits of thought that will allow "no permanent displacement," which encourage women to remain "indifferent," unaware of difference, and which make the separation of public and private seem as self-evident and unchanging as the surface appearances of objects: "It would be terrible to stand outside in the dark and watch a woman in a lighted room studying her face in a window, and to

[43] Meese also discusses these passages, 66–67.

throw a stone at her, shattering the glass, and then to watch the window knit itself up again and the bright bits of lip and throat and hair piece themselves seamlessly again into that unknown, indifferent woman" (*H*, 162–63). At the end of the novel, Ruth and Sylvie literally choose a life of "permanent displacement," in becoming transients together, which is how the narrative represents what Gayatri Spivak calls the attempt "to operate from displacement as such."[44] The extremity of this decision indicates that their practice is not only prefigurative, in Sheila Rowbotham's terms, but *u-topian;* in the eyes of the community Sylvie's housekeeping and attitude toward child rearing have no place and will be allowed none.[45] The novel suggests that it is only through such oppositional practices that the conditions for change might be created. When those practices become the basis for a new story, the anger in the heart of "unsheltered" women can begin to come into play in a social field. Their anger would be a function of their continuing relation to domestic values and the limitations placed on them; but the "difference between here and there, this and that" would be the difference between freedom and constraint, not public impoverishment and a desired, conventional comfort.

Sylvie's opening up the house is the correlative of her transient habits of living out in the public world. At one point, Lucille and Ruth find Sylvie sleeping on a bench "in the fallow little park that memorialized war dead," with "her ankles and her arms crossed and a newspaper tented over her face" (*H*, 105). Unlike Lucille, Ruth is willing to put up with this behavior because she feels that if Sylvie "could remain transient here, she would not have to leave," as their mother left (*H*, 103). Lucille, on the other hand, "hated everything that had to do with transience," and her hatred is directed at transience in both time and space: "Lucille saw in everything its potential for invidious change" (*H*, 103, 93). The same crossing of the categories of time and space occurs in the comment, "Memories are by their nature fragmented, isolated, and arbitrary as glimpses one has at night through lighted windows" (*H*, 53), and the significance of the displacement of that opposition for women is implied by Kristeva in "Women's Time": "When evoking the name and destiny of women, one thinks more of the *space* generating and forming the human species than of *time*, becoming, or

[44] Spivak, "Displacement" (n. 1 above), 186.

[45] Rowbotham, Segal, and Wainwright (n. 3 above), 147 ff. Rowbotham's contribution to this book describes feminist organizational forms as a prefigurative model of social change and as a model for socialist movements. Ryan (n. 3 above), 202–4, comments on this passage.

history" (*WT*, 33). Sylvie is teaching the girls how to feel at home outside the space traditionally assigned to women, rather than participating in the "reproduction of mothering." She is the mother as sister, as companion in becoming, not the mother as role model. It is precisely for that reason the community decides to take Ruth from Sylvie; the sheriff comes because "we returned to Fingerbone [from a trip to the lake] in a freight car. Sylvie was an unredeemed transient, and she was making a transient of me" (*H*, 177).[46]

Joan Kirkby discusses this novel's rejection of a "patriarchal notion of housekeeping in which ends are emphasized almost to the exclusion of performance."[47] In other words, the standard ideology of women's work is structured by a proleptic troping, a logic of the future perfect, in which the ongoing process of making a home is represented in terms of the end toward which that process is aimed, imaged in the house itself as a static object. A housekeeping that accepts that representation sees "in everything its potential for invidious change" and seeks an eternal repetition of the same, the unaltered house. Sylvie's housekeeping is instead based on a belief in "accumulation" as "the essence of housekeeping" and remains open to process, becoming, and the contingency implied by the leaves and scraps of paper in the corners of the rooms (*H*, 180). The grandmother's house, built for her by her husband, makes this shift easier since it bears within itself the marks of its own production—a stairway that leads up to a blank wall, a sloping hallway with a single step in the middle. The implication is that the house is not just a material but a social construct which does not have to be received simply as self-evident and natural. In effect, the grandmother's house is a text in which it is possible to read traces of the creation of a boundary between public and private fields of endeavor, within which women are confined. That patriarchal text begins to be rewritten when Sylvie allows scraps of paper to filter in, conveying messages like "Powers Meet" and "I think of you"—messages of conflict and relatedness.

In the course of Ruth's narrative, the trope of anticipation is wrested from its function within an oppressive ideology. Ruth tells us that Sylvie "inhabited a millennial present" (*H*, 94). As she practices it, anticipation becomes not reification of the future, but transfiguration of the present, the creation of prefigurative forms that

[46] See Meese, 61–62, for a similar reading and a discussion of transiency as an option for women and as indicating a feminist consciousness.

[47] Joan Kirkby, "Is There Life after Art? The Metaphysics of Marilynne Robinson's *Housekeeping*," *Tulsa Studies in Women's Literature* 5 (Spring 1986): 91–109, esp. 107.

Rowbotham calls for, to "release the imagination of what could be."[48] It is through her anticipation of a radically different future that Sylvie exists in a process of becoming, as a transient; anticipation of the future precludes conceptualizing the present moment as a state of plentitude or full presence. Instead the present contains its own future status as past and so is lived as already historical. Sylvie's "millennial present" is a way of inscribing her existence historically, in its temporal transience and mutability. Her prefigurative practice is demonstrated in her attitudes toward housekeeping, when she proceeds as if standard ideas of the separation of public and private spheres were already transformed and so helps to create the preconditions for such change, if only in the readers of Ruth's narrative. But Sylvie's anticipation of an altered social structure also appears in her attitude toward private property.

Sylvie leads Ruth down to the shore of the lake, where she expects to find a boat that is usually moored there. However, "someone" has tried to hide it, and Sylvie finds that action inexplicable: "I always put it right back where I find it. I don't care if someone else uses it. You know, so long as they don't damage it" (*H*, 145). As they shove off, a man appears, "yelling and dancing his wrath and pitching stones" at them (*H*, 146–47). Sylvie's comment is, "Ignore him. . . . He always acts like that. If he thinks someone's watching him, he just carries on more" (*H*, 147). The narrative here affords us a glimpse of a system in which distribution would be based on need. Moreover, for Sylvie, objects are owned only as long as the person claiming them is actually making use of them as well. One of Sylvie's stories centers on a woman who died while riding a freight train one winter. She was wearing, "besides her rubbers and her hunting jacket, two dresses and seven flannel shirts, not to keep off the cold, Sylvie said, but to show herself a woman of substance" (*H*, 87). In Sylvie's world, the world of the transient, the only way to accumulate property is by physically making use of it, all at once.

Michael Ryan notes how an emphasis on needs "moves beyond the limits of productive struggle [traditional Marxist class struggle] toward an examination of how power, domination, and exploitation operate in social relations and everyday life."[49] Fox-Genovese offers an analysis of the association of women with the labor required to satisfy basic needs—that is, with the production of immediate use-value.[50] The separation of use-value and exchange-value is one of

[48] Rowbotham, Segal, and Wainwright, 147.
[49] Ryan, 201.
[50] Fox-Genovese (n. 3 above), 25–26.

the defining features of the capitalist system, with exchange-value being associated with public transactions and especially the production of surplus-value. Use-value then becomes excluded from public life, at least officially, and confined to the home where labor-power is reproduced, so as not to interfere with the exploitation of labor and pursuit of profit. When Sylvie takes the man's boat, she again demonstrates the kind of strategy Kristeva locates in the third generation of her model; she refuses to reject the traditional association of women with use-value and the fulfillment of needs, and she refuses to limit that attitude to the confines of the home or to accept that fulfillment requires female self-sacrifice.

Sylvie takes a similarly prefigurative attitude with regard to consumer items. Ruth's comment on Sylvie's existence in a "millennial present" is made in the context of an attempt to understand why Sylvie buys blue velveteen ballet slippers at the five-and-dime for the girls to use as school shoes: "Sylvie, on her side, inhabited a millennial present. To her the deteriorations of things were always a fresh surprise, a disappointment not to be dwelt on. However a day's or a week's use might have maimed the velvet bows and plastic belts, the atomizers and gilt dresser sets, the scalloped nylon gloves and angora-trimmed anklets, Sylvie always brought us treasures" (*H*, 94). Sylvie expects these objects to combine utility with her "taste for the fanciful" (*H*, 93), pleasure with need.[51] In the most striking use of a proleptic trope in the novel, that figure is presented specifically as a woman's trope and is used to represent the daughter's conception as the embryo's becoming pregnant with herself, rounding and growing heavy: "Of my conception I know only what you know of yours. It occurred in darkness and I was unconsenting. I (and that slenderest word is too gross for the rare thing I was then) walked forever through reachless oblivion, in the mood of one smelling night-blooming flowers, and suddenly—My ravishers left their traces in me, male and female, and over the months I rounded, grew heavy, until the scandal could no longer be concealed and oblivion expelled me" (*H*, 214–15). This anticipatory identification of daughter and mother in the process of giving birth could be disruptive, a scandal to traditional concepts of separate gender roles, or it could be a reproduction of those roles. The description of birth as rape recalls Kristeva's remarks on the third generation of feminists, who assert that they are forced to submit to a symbolic order

[51] Gayatri Chakravorty Spivak, in "Scattered Speculations on the Question of Value," in Spivak, *In Other Worlds: Essays in Cultural Politics* (New York: Methuen, 1987), 162–63, comments on "affectively necessary labor" in relation to women's work, in opposition to socially necessary labor and the reproduction of labor-power.

dominated by men against their wills ("unconsenting"; *WT*, 43). Ruth's ravishers in the passage above are both male and female, and it is the married women of Fingerbone, Ruth and Sylvie's inquisitive visitors, who are instrumental in alerting the authorities to Sylvie's dangerous habits, perpetuating social and familial relations that oppress women. As Ruth says, these women "were obliged to come by their notions of piety and good breeding, and by a desire, a determination, to keep me, so to speak, safely within doors" (*H*, 183).

Ruth's grandmother identified the fluidity of her house and grounds and the dissolution of boundaries established by ownership of private property with her death (*H*, 27). The same references to separation as the basis for establishing a secure domestic space that simultaneously functions to contain and exclude women are applied to the constitution of the subject. In this case death becomes a trope for the differences within that interrupt the closure and isolation of a self-presence imaged in the novel as absorption in the closed circuit of oneself and one's reflection. After Ruth and Sylvie take the boat and arrive at their destination across the lake, Ruth begins to feel Sylvie has deserted her and thinks, "Let them come unhouse me of this flesh, and pry this house apart. It was no shelter now, it only kept me here alone" (*H*, 159). During an earlier trip to the lake with Lucille, they had to spend the night outside. Rather than fall asleep, Ruth lets "the darkness in the sky become coextensive with the darkness in my skull and bowels and bones" (*H*, 116), echoing the statement that, in Sylvie's house, with the lights off, she and Lucille "stepped through the door from sheer night to sheer night" (*H*, 99). When the girls return to Sylvie the next morning, Ruth falls asleep sitting up and dreams that she is not sleeping but dead (*H*, 118–19).

Death also functions to combine a sense of personal history and becoming with a consciousness defined by place, specifically the home, as Kristeva suggests of the third moment in her model. To anticipate death is to become aware of one's transience and, for a woman, to step outside a conventional feminine identity (as well as the middle-class identity of home and property owner; *H*, 177–79). Intimations of mortality are the negative side of the lesson Sylvie teaches Ruth, but the redeeming side is Sylvie's openness to the possibility of women remaining transient without leaving the home, without denying their connection to alternative, feminine values. The combination of critique and prefiguration of a positively different social order manifests itself at the novel's end as an ambiguity that joins the literal and figurative senses of death, much like the yoking of time and space in the pun on transience.

Ruth refers to Lucille's rejection of Sylvie's unconventional life when she states that "Lucille's loyalties were with the other world" (*H*, 95). Ruth also describes the townspeople's attitude toward transients: "Like the dead, we could consider their histories complete, and we wondered only what had brought them to transiency, to drifting, since their lives as drifters were like pacings and broodings and skirmishings among ghosts who cannot pay their way across the Styx. However long a postscript to however short a life, it was still no part of the story" (*H*, 179).[52] She adds that, in this condition, it becomes difficult "to distinguish mine from thine" (*H*, 179). Ruth's comments about her escape from Fingerbone strongly suggest that she and Sylvie have similarly undergone an experience comparable to death. Like the transients, their state of existence is one which exceeds the closure of dominant stories or histories. When Ruth and Sylvie have to walk across the railroad bridge over the lake after setting fire to the grandmother's house, Ruth remembers that "something happened, something so memorable that when I think back to the crossing of the bridge, one moment bulges like the belly of a lens and all the others are at the peripheries and diminished. Was it only that the wind rose suddenly, so that we had to cower and lean against it like blind women groping their way along a wall? or did we really hear some sound too loud to be heard, some word so true we did not understand it?" (*H*, 215). The townspeople assume they drowned (*H*, 213), but for Ruth, "it was the crossing of the bridge that changed me finally" (*H*, 215). After several years seem to have passed, Ruth imagines that Lucille now lives in the grandmother's house, that "Sylvie and I have stood outside her window a thousand times," have entered the house, "brought in leaves" (as Sylvie let leaves gather in the corners), and left again "before she could run downstairs, leaving behind us a strong smell of lake water" (*H*, 218). Kirkby points to the unsettling refusal here to distinguish whether the pair are metaphorically dead to the social world that refused to tolerate Sylvie's prefigurative practices or whether they have actually died.[53] In the latter case the entire narrative would take the form of a proleptic anticipation of the narrator's death, described in the past tense.[54] The same proleptic construction informs Emily Dickinson's poem "I heard a Fly buzz—

[52] Meese (n. 1 above), 62–63, cites this passage as fitting into the novel's reflexivity about narrative construction, its own and the social "stories" we tell.

[53] Kirkby (n. 47 above), 106.

[54] In seminar discussions of the novel, Jane Marcus and Ingeborg O'Sickey have suggested that the ending displaces Ruth as narrator. The final descriptions of Lucille can be read as indicating that the narrative originates with the sister who stayed behind and who is imagining an alternative way of life.

when I died," a poem Ruth was required to recite in school and which she remembers as one of the few events interrupting the tedium of her time there (*H*, 76–77). This undecidability that holds together two apparently mutually exclusive possibilities underscores what Meese calls the "double gesture," the "negation of certainty and affirmation of possibility"[55] that ends the novel, as Ruth imagines Lucille sitting in a restaurant where no one could know "how she does not watch, does not listen, does not wait, does not hope, and always for me and Sylvie" (*H*, 219).

Prefiguration and practice

Like Kristeva's historical model of the development of feminist responses to marginalization, *Housekeeping* offers some support for the conclusion that women have in practice already begun "to operate from displacement as such."[56] Kristeva and Marilynne Robinson's writings together imply that there is a social subtext to the female thematics of the home, as an enclosure frequently conflated with the female body itself. Sandra Gilbert and Susan Gubar argue that the "paradigmatic female story" centers on "the psychic split between the lady who submits to male dicta and the lunatic who rebels," a paradigm derived from *Jane Eyre*.[57] Kristeva and Robinson, however, construct narratives grounded in social practices and the possibility of social transformation.

Housekeeping and "Women's Time" also offer some insight into a psychodynamic of women's writing that would connect textual production to women's prefigurative social practices. The problem women writers have to negotiate may not always be a sense of "belatedness" or even a gender-based "anxiety of authorship," as in Gilbert and Gubar's appropriation of Harold Bloom's ideas.[58] As Annette Kolodny points out, Bloom's theory of the anxiety of authorship applies only to authors who think of themselves as securely working within a tradition where their texts can be situated.[59] As Emily Dickinson's line, "I lingered with Before—" suggests, women

[55] Meese (n. 1 above), 67.

[56] Spivak, "Displacement" (n. 1 above), 186.

[57] Sandra M. Gilbert and Susan Gubar, *The Madwoman in the Attic: The Woman Writer and the Nineteenth-Century Literary Imagination* (New Haven, Conn.: Yale University Press, 1979), 82.

[58] Ibid., 48–49.

[59] Annette Kolodny, "A Map for Rereading: Gender and the Interpretation of Literary Texts," in *The New Feminist Criticism: Essays on Women, Literature, and Theory*, ed. Elaine Showalter (New York: Pantheon, 1985), 47–48.

trying to produce literary texts may suffer from a sense of earliness, of writing in advance of a tradition that would accord their work the same significance male texts receive.[60] Kolodny implies that women's writing often anticipates its own misreading by men.[61] I would argue that women can use strategies of anticipation by writing *as if* there were already a tradition and a community of readers prepared to receive their work. Such strategies would empower individual women but could also have a collective effect, giving meaning to existing practices by helping to create the conditions for a significant body of women's texts to come into being. This proleptic troping of a possible future condition would be prefigurative—in Rowbotham's sense of the word.

Kristeva's theoretical writing calls for a prefigurative practice like the one Rowbotham describes in *Beyond the Fragments:* "We need to make the creation of prefigurative forms an explicit part of our movement against capitalism. I do not mean that we try to hold an imaginary future in the present, straining against the boundaries of the possible until we collapse in exhaustion and despair. This would be utopian. Instead such forms would seek both to consolidate existing practice and release the imagination of what could be."[62] In "Women's Time" Kristeva uses the term "future perfect," in quotes, with reference to the cyclic temporality that she later associates with the traditional ideas of women's subjectivity recuperated by the separatist moment in her model (*WT*, 32).[63] For Derrida, the logic of the future perfect only objectifies the future as what will have been and so "reduces the future to the form of manifest presence."[64] But for Kristeva, this logic of anticipation can

[60] *The Complete Poems of Emily Dickinson*, ed. Thomas Johnson (Boston: Little, Brown, 1955), 300.

[61] Kolodny, 51–52, 57–58.

[62] Rowbotham, Segal, and Wainwright (n. 3 above), 147.

[63] Kristeva's earliest use of this term takes it from Jacques Lacan; Julia Kristeva, *Séméiotiké: Recherches pur une sémanalyse* (Paris: Editions du Seuil, 1969), 242, n. 32. For Lacan as for Derrida, this kind of anticipation is a reification, underlying the formation of the autonomous ego in the mirror stage; Lacan, *Ecrits: A Selection*, trans. Alan Sheridan (New York: Norton, 1977), 306–7. Louis Althusser makes a similar argument about the negative effects of tropes of anticipation in his discussion of how "expecting" a child already assimilates her or him to a position in a preexisting ideological formation; Althusser, *Lenin and Philosophy and Other Essays*, trans. Ben Brewster (New York: Monthly Review Press, 1971), 176.

[64] Jacques Derrida, *Dissemination*, trans. Barbara Johnson (Chicago: University of Chicago Press, 1981), 7. However, in an earlier text, Derrida uses the term "future perfect" in a more positive way; Jacques Derrida, *Of Grammatology*, trans. Gayatri Chakravorty Spivak (Baltimore: Johns Hopkins University Press, 1976), 5 (Derrida here uses the French phrase for the verb tense of the future perfect, *futur antérieur*, and it is translated literally as "future anterior").

also operate as a form of critical negativity, opening the possibility of transforming present conditions by bringing to light elements or potentialities that have been repressed and excluded. Alice Jardine summarizes Kristeva's future perfect as "a modality that implies neither that we are helpless before some inevitable destiny nor that we can somehow, given enough time and thought, engineer an ultimately perfect future."[65] The idea is not to hold an imaginary, perfect future in the present, as Rowbotham says, but to hold and practice a possible future, whose possibility is precisely what the dominant culture ensconced in that present tries to deny. Kristeva's third generation is nonsynchronous in relation to linear history, but this heterogeneity is no longer the remnant of an overtaken past. It is rather a future like that of the young in Ernst Bloch's analysis: "[Women] turn away from the day that [they have]. It is a day that [women] do not have today," but are in the process of creating.[66]

In her historical and political analysis of male avant-garde writers like Leautréamont, Kristeva argues that their work is "social" because it "speaks to subjects in immediate desire for play, knowledge and constructive activity"; it is addressed to a new collective subjectivity before the fact, since that subjectivity's "realization is impossible in the interior of the present social body."[67] In "Women's Time" and women's writing like Robinson's we find that it *is* possible to proceed from the marginality of an aesthetic avant-garde "to linking the placing in process/on trial of the subject in a text to social subversion, to the struggle for a society where production will not be the imperative rule and where expenditure will be the principle of a constant renovation of ephemeral structures."[68]

Department of English
University of Wisconsin—Madison

[65] Alice Jardine, "Introduction to Julia Kristeva's 'Women's Time,'" *Signs* 7, no. 1 (Autumn 1981): 5–12, esp. 5.

[66] Bloch (n. 5 above), 23.

[67] Julia Kristeva, *La révolution du langage poétique* (Paris: Editions du Seuil, 1974), 419, my translation. The English version contains only the first section of this longer work.

[68] Ibid., 366.

"SHAHBANO"

ZAKIA PATHAK AND RAJESWARI SUNDER RAJAN

In April 1985, the Supreme Court of India, the highest court of the land, passed a judgment in favor of Shahbano in the case of Mohammad Ahmed Khan, appellant, versus Shahbano and others, respondents.[1] The judgment created a furor unequaled, according to one journal, since "the great upheaval of 1857."[2]

The Supreme Court confirmed the judgment of the High Court awarding Shahbano, a divorced Muslim woman, maintenance of Rs 179.20 (approximately $14) per month from her husband, Mohammad Ahmed Khan, and dismissed the husband's appeal against the

This paper was presented at the Third National Conference on Women's Studies in Chandigarh, India, in October 1986, at the invitation of Uma Chakravorty and Sudesh Vaid. Our thanks to them. Our special gratitude to our colleague Rashmi Bhatnagar for her indefatigable enthusiasm and support.

[1] Mohd. Ahmed Khan, Appellant, v. Shah Bano and others, Respondents. The Supreme Court of India, Criminal Appellate Jurisdiction. Criminal Appeal No. 103 of 1981, D/–23.4.1985. A.I.R. 1985 Supreme Court 945 = 1985 Cri.L.J. 875 = M.L.R. (1985) 202.

[2] Shekhar Gupta with Farzand Ahmed and Inderjit Badhwar, "The Muslims, a Community in Turmoil," *India Today* (January 31, 1986), 90–104, esp. 90.

This essay originally appeared in *Signs*, vol. 14, no. 3, Spring 1989.

award of maintenance under section 125 of the 1973 Code of Criminal Procedure.[3]

For Shahbano this victory came after ten years of struggle. A lower court had awarded her only Rs 25 a month (the average daily wage of a laborer in India is Rs 11.50, or roughly a dollar). Shahbano was not the first Muslim woman to apply for (and be granted) maintenance under the 1973 Code of Criminal Procedure.[4] The repercussions of the Supreme Court judgment therefore took many, including the government, by surprise. When some by-elections fell due in December 1985, the sizeable Muslim vote turned against the ruling party (the Congress-I) partly because it supported the judgment. Its candidate at Kishengunj, although a Muslim, was defeated by the opposition's Muslim candidate, Syed Shahabuddin, who would play a major role in the events that followed. When an independent member of Parliament, a Muslim, introduced a bill to save Muslim personal law (with the support of the Muslim Personal Law Board), the ruling party reversed its earlier position and resorted to a whip to ensure the bill's passage. The bill was passed in May 1986 and became the Muslim Women (Protection of Rights in Divorce) Act.

The relationship of state or secular law to personal or religious law has always been a vexed one in India. Although Hinduism is the majority religion, there are sizeable minority populations.[5] Most rulers, including the British, recognizing that interference in religious issues could be explosive in its consequences, respected the traditional laws of religious communities in personal matters relating to family and inheritance rights. As a result, matters relating to the family (such as marriage, divorce, maintenance, succession to property, inheritance, and custody and guardianship of children, as well as adoption), which came to be known as "personal laws" and would vary from one religious community to another, remained uncodified. During the nineteenth century, however, several British acts and legislative measures empowered the courts to recognize

[3] Section 125 is an "order for maintenance of wives, children, and parents." "If any person having sufficient means neglects or refuses to maintain" his wife, children, or parents in need, a magistrate may "upon proof of such neglect, or refusal, order such person to make a monthly allowance for the maintenance . . . at such monthly rate not exceeding five hundred rupees in the whole"; see Ratanlal Ranchhoddas and Dhirajlal Keshavlal Thakore, *The Code of Criminal Procedure* (Nagpur: Wadwa, 1987), 94–112, esp. 110.

[4] The Supreme Court judgment (A.I.R. 1985 SC) quotes two earlier decisions of the Court confirming the applicability of sec. 125 of the code to Muslims: Bai Tahira v. Ali Hussain Fidaalli Chotia, 1979, and Fazlunbi v. V. Khader Vali, 1980 (946).

[5] There are 75 million Muslims, forming 11.35 percent of India's population.

and apply local customs and usages; these often prevailed uniformly over an area, irrespective of religion. In fact, in some instances, they were less liberal than religious laws, as in the case of Muslim women and property inheritance. It was largely due to this conflict that the Shariat Law was passed in 1937. The Shariat law provides that Muslims in India will be governed by Muslim religious laws in matters relating to the family.

In 1949, when the Constitution of Independent India was framed, the founding fathers saw the necessity of continuing to recognize personal law at the same time that, moved by the unifying secular impulse, they also declared as an objective of the state the adoption of a uniform civil code (art. 44). (Other articles of the constitution that relate to religious freedom are art. 14, which guarantees the right to equal protection of laws; art. 15, which forbids discrimination on grounds only of religion, race, caste, sex, place of birth, and so forth; art. 25, which guarantees freedom of religion and conscience; and art. 29, which guarantees to minorities the right to conserve their culture.)

The interests of women in this dual legal structure are particularly vulnerable to exploitation by alliance of religious and secular interests. Personal law concerns women intimately, pronouncing as it does on marriage, divorce, maintenance, adoption, succession, and inheritance. Women's rights activists in India have long been protesting against the gender-discriminatory nature of the personal laws of all religious communities which regulate most spheres of women's activity. Under all personal laws, the male is the head of the family and succession is through the male line—women have no right to inherit an equal share of property, and the father is the natural guardian of minor children.[6] Since 1872, divorced and abandoned women of all faiths have been regularly applying for maintenance under the Criminal Procedure Code (which relates to "maintenance of wives, children and parents").[7]

[6] Some other examples of personal law relating to women, taken from Indira Jaisingh, "Personal Law: A Matter of Politics," *Bombay*, March 7–21, 1986, 56–57. In spite of the Hindu Succession Act, 1956, Hindu daughters cannot be coparceners in a Hindu undivided family. The Travancore Christian Succession Act, 1916, totally disinherits a daughter who has received a dowry and limits her share to Rs 5,000. Under Parsi law, daughters get only half the share of a son in inheritance. Under Muslim law, a Muslim male can marry four wives and can divorce a wife by unilateral pronouncement of the triple *talaq*.

[7] Vasudha Dhagamvar has described the code as one "whose universal applicability has never been challenged"; see "Uniform Civil Code: Don't We Have It Already?" *Mainstream* (July 6, 1985), 15–17, 34, esp. 16.

The religion of the divorced woman seeking maintenance under section 488 of the 1872 code piloted by Sir James Fitzjames (forerunner to sec. 125 of the Code of Criminal Procedure, 1973) was immaterial. Since criminal law procedures are quicker and more effective than civil law procedures, many divorced women of all communities (by appealing under a legal provision intended primarily to prevent vagrancy) bypassed the personal law of their religions.

Muslim fundamentalists have been disturbed by what they perceive as a trend away from honoring religious law. The Shahbano judgment gave them an opportunity to mount an attack on what they perceived as the Hindus' homogenizing influence, an influence that would eventually lead to the assimilation and destruction of Muslim identity. The Muslim Personal Law Board intervened in the Shahbano case on behalf of the husband and, having been unsuccessful in the Supreme Court, carried the battle to Parliament.

Under the provisions of the Muslim Women (Protection of Rights in Divorce) Act, divorced Muslim women would fall outside the purview of section 125 of the Code of Criminal Procedure. According to this newly codified Muslim personal law, the divorced woman's husband is obliged only to return the *mehr* (dower, or marriage settlement) and pay her maintenance during the period of *iddat* (the period of three months following the divorce). If the divorced woman is not able to maintain herself after the *iddat* period, her maintenance will be the responsibility of her children, or parents, or those relatives who would be entitled to inherit her property upon her death; if she has no relatives or if they have no means to pay her maintenance, the magistrate may direct the State *Wakf* Boards (administrators of Muslim trust funds) to pay the maintenance determined by him.

This has not resolved the crisis sparked by the Supreme Court judgment in favor of Shahbano, however. The Muslim community continues to find itself divided into "progressives" (those supporting the judgment) and "fundamentalists" (those opposing it). The act has been challenged in the courts. The government of India, possibly in an attempt to appease feminists and Muslim progressives and to refurbish its secular image, is engaged in drafting a uniform civil code.

The terms "fundamentalist" and "progressive" have been used both descriptively and pejoratively in this debate when referring to the positions of Muslim groups on their personal law. Syed Shahabuddin, the acknowledged spokesman for the Muslim fundamentalist position and president of the Muslim *Majlis-e-Mushawarat*, accepts the term "fundamentalist" as accurately descriptive of his allegiance to the Quran: "Historically, the Quran was revealed to the Prophet 1400 years ago but it is the final message of God to mankind. Not one syllable is subject to change. . . . It is in this sense that the Muslim is by definition a fundamentalist."[8]

Arif Mohammed Khan, Muslim minister in the government of India, who, at its behest, initially defended the Supreme Court judgment and subsequently refused to follow the government when it reversed its position, rejects such fundamentalism: "My faith has always been progressive on matters relating to women. . . . The Prophet's grandson gave his wife 10,000 *dirhams* while divorcing her. It was to clear doubts on this that God revealed verse 11.241 that says: 'And for the divorced women let there be a fair provision.' " He goes on to say: "Gandhi was shown black flags across the country when he spoke against untouchability. Any suggestion of change or reform upsets fundamentalists and that should not deter any progressive person, least of all a right thinking Muslim."[9] Thus the term "progressives" defines those Muslims who endorse reform in the personal law.

Some experts on Islamic law, however, deride those Muslims who demand the uniform civil code: "They want to project their image as progressives and support the demand without knowing what they are talking about."[10] The term "fundamentalist" is also applied to extremist members of the Hindu religious parties who, as part of a sustained anti-Muslim campaign, opposed the Muslim Women Bill.

In what follows, we explore the sense of crisis produced in a society through a women's issue and the possibilities for change that it may provoke. From the narrative of Shahbano we describe the formation of a discontinuous female subjectivity in response to the displacement of the Muslim woman question onto several discourses. These discourses are marked, and unified, by the assumptions of an ideology of protection. We explore the possibilities of resistance within such a discourse. Our notion of a "subaltern consciousness" assumes an operative "will" that functions as resistance; it destabilizes the family's ideology of protection and the law's ideology of evolution. Thus a space is created from which a woman can speak.

[8] Syed Shahabuddin, "The Turmoil in the Muslim Mind," *Onlooker* (March 16–31, 1986), 32–37, esp. 36.

[9] Arif Mohammed Khan in an interview with Shekhar Gupta, *India Today* (January 16–31, 1986), 94.

[10] See, e.g., Tahir Mahmood's comments in an interview with Kuldeep Kumar, *Sunday Observer* (March 9, 1986).

Discursive displacements

To be framed by a certain kind of discourse is to be objectified as the "other," represented without the characteristic features of the "subject," sensibility and/or volition.[11] The Muslim woman, as subject, is either absent or fragmented in the various legal, religious, sexual, and political texts that develop into a discourse supposedly about her. Discourse, in this conceptual sense, works in fact only by significantly excluding certain possibilities (in this case full representation of the subject). It achieves its internal coherence by working within parameters which are ideologically fixed. The different textual strands achieve discursive coherence by these two related procedures, that is, exclusion and limitation within ideologically fixed boundaries. Working within the contours of a conceptually unified field, discourse seeks to produce knowledge. Such knowledge is implicated in the structures of power. At this level, social action itself is textualized into legal, religious, political, and other texts. In any stable society, the texts must exist harmoniously. This harmony is disturbed and a crisis results when a proposition accommodated in one text is displaced onto another.

We do not want to invoke an actual Freudian/psychoanalytic narrative of history. But we do wish to suggest, analogically, that both the decentering and the substitution of the "truth" of a situation, which are characteristics of the "disguise" that the dream wears,[12] are diagnosable in the route traveled by the plea for maintenance initiated by Shahbano.

The narrative of displacement begins when this plea for maintenance moved out of domestic discourse into the realm of law and law courts, when Shahbano, a woman of seventy-three, after over forty years of marriage, was driven out of her house by the triple pronouncement of *talaq* (oral and unilateral divorce) by her husband.

The narrative intersects with religious discourse when the Muslim Personal Law Board intervenes for the husband in the Supreme

[11] It seems to us that much historical as well as religious narrative represses the subject. For a discussion of the repression of female subjectivity in *Paradise Lost*, see Christine Froula, "When Eve Reads Milton: Undoing the Canonical Economy," *Critical Inquiry* 10, no. 2 (December 1983): 321–47.

[12] Richard Wollheim explains the place of displacement in Freud's dream theory: "By 'displacement' . . . Freud meant two distinct but related processes. One is that whereby the dream is differently 'centered' from the dream thoughts, so that it does not reflect the relative importance of these thoughts. The other is that whereby elements in the dream do duty for elements in the dream thoughts, the substitution being in accordance with a chain of association. Displacement is peculiarly connected with the disguise that the dream wears" (*Sigmund Freud* [New York: Viking, 1971], 65).

Court. Daniel Latifi, counsel for Shahbano, located the significance of the case in the elevation of the Muslim Personal Law Board: "Why was the Bill brought forward at all? . . . Some Machiavelli seems to have masterminded this entire operation. . . . The act that preceded the Bill, the recognition of the so-called Muslim Personal Law Board as a College of Cardinals for Indian Muslims is not only against Islam but is also the most flagrant exercise of a power-drunk autocracy since Caligula installed Incitatus, his favourite horse, as Governor of Rome. The Muslim intelligentsia who have opposed this Act will continue the struggle against this illegitimate Papacy."[13]

The discourse now appears in the area of electoral politics. A cover story of the influential magazine, *India Today,* traced the trajectory of the case: "[Shahbano's] search for a small sustenance has led to an unprecedented Islamic resurgence, not seen in the country for decades. . . . More vitally, it threatens to upset the very electoral equation on which the arithmetic of national political fortunes has been based since Independence." The article goes on to detail the reverses suffered by the Congress-I in the by-elections in Uttar Pradesh, Assam, and Gujarat.[14]

After the judgment, the battle is joined in Parliament. Reformists and activists continued the debate into the liberal discourse of secularism and constitutional rights. Kuldip Nayar, a leading journalist who pressed for a secular solution, asked: "Should the country join issue with the community on a point which is a non-issue? Some argue that one thing will lead to another; probably it will if we continue to concentrate our attention and energy on non-issues like maintenance of a divorced woman in Muslim society."[15]

Fundamentalists, both Muslim and Hindu, take up positions. Syed Shahabuddin, M.P., depersonalized Shahbano completely while relocating her predicament within a Muslim identity problematic: "In the current turmoil, the Shahbano case, celebrated as it became, recedes into the background and pales into insignificance. Stripped to its bones, the case was no more than a conflict of opinion among the Muslims on whether what is desirable can be made obligatory, whether a recommendation [in the Quran] to treat the divorcees generously can be made into a legal mandate. Thus it was a very limited issue though the Muslim Indians saw it as the beginning of state interference with the Shariat."[16]

[13] Daniel Latifi, "The Unfriendly Act," *Sunday* (June 8–14, 1986), 32–37, esp. 37.

[14] Gupta, Ahmed, and Badhwar (n. 2 above), 90.

[15] Kuldip Nayar, "Separate Personal Laws Do Not Dilute Secularism," *Telegraph* (March 15, 1986).

[16] Shahabuddin, 34.

Once the disturbances of the peace break out, the discourses can no longer be kept clear of each other.

The displacements nonetheless continue. In an attempt to assert her faith and restore communal harmony, Shahbano is driven to announce her rejection of the Supreme Court's judgment, asserting her Muslim loyalty. (We see in this the attempt to highlight the Muslim identity problematic at the expense of all others.) The counterattempt to anchor the crisis in a limited legal discourse has resulted in a challenge to the Muslim Women Act in the Supreme Court. The drafting of a common civil code is promised by the government.

Where, in all these discursive displacements, is Shahbano the woman?[17] Has the discourse on the Muslim woman, torn away from its existential moorings, sucked her in and swallowed her up? Though, as the pronouncements above show, the several discourses attend to only one or the other dimension of her identity, the dominant consciousness tends to homogenize the subaltern subject for its purposes:[18] here as that which is to be "protected."

The discourse of protection

All the parties to the discourse share the common assumption that they are protecting the Muslim woman; but statements from the discourse reveal the ubiquity of this argument, either as a claim or as a rebuttal:

> This Government will never deviate from the path of protecting the legitimate interests of the minority. [Asoke Sen, law minister]
>
> The Bill intends to safeguard the majority voice of the community. [Syed Shahabuddin, Opposition Muslim member of Parliament]
>
> The Bill protects the husbands who would divorce their wives. [Zoya Hassan, Muslim women's rights activist]

[17] We use here the argument put forward by Gayatri Chakravorty Spivak, "Subaltern Studies: Deconstructing Historiography," in *Subaltern Studies IV: Writings on South Asian History and Society,* ed. Ranajit Guha (Delhi: Oxford University Press, 1985), 330–63. She uses the phrase "discursive displacement" to mean "functional changes in sign systems." Our indebtedness to the work of Gayatri Spivak goes beyond the actual quotations used in this essay.

[18] Subaltern: Of inferior rank: A particular not a universal (OED). Of inferior rank: A particular in relation to a universal of the same quality. Therefore, here, a subject relating to the societal universal norm of a unified, freely choosing subject—tangentially or marginally, or in opposition to, or opaquely.

We have to protect ourselves from such protection. [Justice Chowdhary, Supreme Court judge[19]]

"Protection" can confer upon the protector the right to interfere in areas hitherto out of bounds or the authority to speak for the silent victim; or it can serve as a camouflage for power politics. An alliance is formed between protector and protected against a common opponent from whom danger is perceived and protection offered or sought, and this alliance tends to efface the will to power exercised by the protector. Thus the term conceals the opposition between protector and protected, a hierarchical opposition that assigns higher value to the first term: strong/weak, man/woman, majority/minority, state/individual.

At the propositional level, we understand the discourse of protection as meaning-in-use. By this we mean language in a contextual frame, that is, as having a certain meaning in communication which cannot be accounted for by its grammatical or objective properties.[20] Considered thus, utterances are explicable only in terms of the activities in which they play a role and in the way they negotiate relationships (therefore, to ask whether these propositions are true or false is to miss the force which informs the sentences). Three such propositions from the discourse of protection that show sentential force are:

Hindu men are saving Muslim women from Muslim men.
Islam is in danger.
The perceptions of the minority community must govern the pace of change.

The attack of Hindu fundamentalists (often members of communalist political parties like Shiv Sena, Vishwa Hindu Parishad, Rashtriya Swayam Sevak Sangh) upon the proposed Muslim Women Act, upon Muslim religious law in general, and upon the Muslim community at large on behalf of oppressed Muslim women translates into the proposition "Hindu men are saving Muslim women

[19] Asoke Sen, May 5, 1986; Syed Shahabuddin, May 1986; Zoya Hassan, March 1986; Justice Chowdhary, March 22, 1986; as cited in a publicity pamphlet issued by Mediastorm at the inaugural screening, September 14, 1986, of "In Secular India," a video film on the Muslim Women (Protection of Rights in Divorce) Bill.

[20] This theory of language was propounded by Ludwig Wittgenstein (*Philosophical Investigations*, trans. G.E.M. Anscombe [New York: Macmillan, 1958]); and J. L. Austin (*How to Do Things with Words* [Cambridge, Mass.: Harvard University Press, 1962]), and is fully formulated in the speech-act theory of language.

from Muslim men."[21] It is a bizarre as well as sinister claim. It invokes the stereotypes of the Muslim woman as invariably destitute, and the Muslim male as polygamous, callous, and barbaric. This scenario clears the way for Hindu intervention in the form of a demand for reform or outright removal of the Muslim personal law. The protection of women of a minority community thus emerges as the ploy of a majority community to repress the religious freedom of that minority and ensure its own dominance.

When the interventionary intentions of the protection of Muslim women became clear, the cry "Islam is in danger!" was sounded from within the community. Some Muslim women's organizations also opposed the judgment for the same reason. The government gave primacy to the Muslims' perception that their community identity was threatened.[22]

When the government somersaulted and supported the bill that created the Muslim Women Act, it came under pressure to explain its *volte face,* which was widely seen as panicked capitulation to the fundamentalist lobby in order to ensure the ruling party's political future. Speaking on its behalf in Parliament, Minister K. C. Pant declared that what mattered was not whether the Supreme Court was right or wrong, but how the Muslims perceived it. Law Minister Sen also emphasized this.[23]

By adopting "perception theory," the government was able to present the situation as a conflict of two minority interests, that is, Muslim versus woman. Calling upon all the power of Solomon to adjudicate in the matter, it assumed its traditional benevolent role,

[21] This sentence is analogous to "white men are saving brown women from brown men" in Spivak's essay on *Sati,* "Can the Subaltern Speak? Speculations on Widow Sacrifice," *Wedge* 7/8 (Winter/Spring 1985), 120–30, esp. 121.

[22] Through a strategy of synedochic substitution, the Muslim Personal Law Board has claimed to represent the sentiments of the entire Muslim population. "Progressive" Muslims have felt alienated from their community because their call for Islamic reform has been dismissed either as irrelevant or as opposed to mass opinion. Women of the Muslim community have also been ignored; no referendum on the bill among Muslims was held, though it was repeatedly promised.

[23] In an article in *Statesman* (May 8, 1986), the editor described the law minister as an acknowledged legal luminary who could argue both sides of a case with equal facility. He pointed out that "perception theory" had not been applied to the Sikh minority's demand for a separate state, or to their perception that Sikh temples were sacred places which the army could not enter. Castigating the perception theory as dangerous, the article held: "In a plural society such as ours, the rulers, though not impervious to public opinion, are expected to lead society—to mould it, rather than surrender to its darker mood. If the 'perception theory' were to prevail, no reform would ever be possible. . . . Dowry is considered a necessary evil among the Hindus. Will the Government make it a ground for not reforming society?"

its commitment to the protection of all minorities. The real exigencies of power struggles in party politics were successfully downplayed in this deployment of the ideology of protection. When the government emerged to take up its role, it was as deus ex machina. In response to the accusation implicit in the Supreme Court judgment, as well as in Hindu fundamentalist attacks, that Islam offered inadequate protection to women, influential members of Parliament argued that the provisions for women in Muslim religious laws were liberal and farsighted. The proposed Muslim Women Act was persuasively presented as a means of protecting women's rights: instead of being dependent on the whims of a recalcitrant and hostile ex-husband, the Muslim woman by the provisions of the new act would be able to fall back on the affection and duty of the natal family, and failing that, the *Wakf* Board. In this way her protection would be guaranteed. By passing the bill and foregrounding these arguments in favor of the progressiveness of the provisions for divorced women in Muslim religious law, the government successfully "protected" both Muslims in general and Muslim women in particular.[24]

The government's strategy of reconciling these conflicts is not one that liberal intellectuals have been able to adopt, since the act is clearly regressive. Yet, the sensitivity of the minority community to any form of interference in their personal law makes a primarily feminist position, that is, outright condemnation of the act, equally difficult to adopt. An article in *Manushi,* a leading feminist journal, expressed it this way:

> [A] minority community's reactions have a logic of their own and cannot be lightly dismissed, especially if the minority has been a disadvantaged community. . . .
>
> The most important task is to prevent the Hindu communalists from using what is essentially a women's rights issue for the purpose of stirring up communal hatred against the Muslims and other minorities.[25]

The indulgence toward a minority's insecurity cannot altogether avoid the aspect of liberal "protection." Feminist discourses have

[24] Seema Mustafa, "Behind the Veil," points out how the prime minister, Rajiv Gandhi, himself defended the bill in Parliament "on the grounds that it was secular, that it did not deprive Muslim women of their rights but was superior to even Section 125, Cr.P.C., and that, as Hindus, Parsis and Christians had modified bills why should this be denied to Muslim women" (see *The Telegraph* [March 2, 1986]).

[25] Madhu Kishwar, "Pro Women or Anti Muslim? The Shahbano Controversy," *Manushi,* no. 32 (1986), 4–13, esp. 12–13.

tried to steer clear of choosing between supporting a minority community or condemning them on feminist grounds by emphasizing the shared predicament of all Indian women within the personal laws of all religious communities—thus displacing the religious identity of Muslim women by highlighting their gender identity.

Shahbano's emergence from and retreat into the family suggest that the family is a site and an ideology that needs to be considered in relation to the law and the state. The state is sensitive about issues relating to the family, first, because of their regulation by religious law (as we have already pointed out). For religion, too, is a "protected" sphere in India (the constitutional commitment to secularism does not imply, as in many western countries, a separation of church and state, or a state in which "religion or religious considerations are not only ignored but also purposely excluded from the sphere of State activities"; on the contrary, it has meant "the co-existence of various religions under the benevolent supervision of the State").[26] Second, the demarcation of the spheres of influence of family and state into the private and the public, respectively, enables them to work together in a collaborative hegemony. Since the entitlement of the family to privacy and autonomy is widely recognized and granted, any rights granted to the woman as an individual citizen by the state can only be imperfectly enforced within that state-within-a-state. When women become victimized within the family—and the most significant site of violence against women in India today is the household—the state (read: police) is reluctant to move in to prevent or punish the crime.[27] The conflict between the state and the patriarchal family over the rights of women is caught up in the problematic of "protection." In the Muslim woman's case, her legal right to maintenance from her estranged husband has resulted in an act that has not only taken away that right but driven her back to total dependence upon (the protection of) her natal family. The family has reclaimed the erstwhile "vagrant." Thus the discourse of women's rights becomes implicated in a discourse of protection, shifting imperceptibly from a question of establishing that to which women are entitled to that to which women have (for the moment) the privilege.

Protectionist arguments would then appear to be inherent in any women's issue. They are not altogether easy to avoid, as the predicament of women's groups outlined earlier suggests, nor are they

[26] See K. K. Wadhwa, *Minority Safeguards in India* (Delhi: Thomson, 1975), 85, 96.

[27] In recent times, it has been the task of women's groups to question the sanctified space of the family and to demand that women's cries for help be heard and addressed.

invariably "insincere." We only argue that the will to power contaminates even the most sincere claims of protection. There are multifarious relations of dominance and subordination that circulate within the term "protection," so that its meaning is always deferred.

A protectionist argument succeeds in effacing the protector's will to power, but it also effaces the recalcitrant (nonsubmissive) will of the protected. The register of the discourse on Muslim women thus needs to be shifted to take into account the possibility of the operation of such a will.

Subjectivity

To counter a discourse about women that operates with the subtext "protection," we consider how a gendered subaltern subjectivity is constructed to express resistance. It is not our intention to recreate a "Shahbano" who is the origin and repository of her story, whose actions are interpretable through her motives, which in turn may be ascertained through interviews and other modes of transcription of her "inner" being. Nor do we wish to construct an individualized and individualistic "heroine" who single-handedly provoked a nation into crisis. Our mode of access to Shahbano will be through the actions she initiated in the law courts: these will be our text. Law, like language, "objectifies, typifies, anonymises."[28] Thus we move beyond a biographical dimension.

Shahbano gave two interviews, one to an Urdu newspaper *Inquilab* and the other on national television. We have not privileged these as sources of her subjectivity. Shahbano's multiple identities—as Muslim (a minority religious community), lower class (the daughter of a police constable), and woman—are severally and compositely subaltern and do not make for a symmetrical distribution of dialogue-constitutive universals.[29] In the best of circumstances, the notion of an ideal speech situation is contrafactual.[30] In the charged political and religious situation in which the media sought and were given the interviews, her freedom to apply regulative and representative speech acts was further and drastically curtailed. So that while we agree generally that speech provides an important access to self-representation, it is not always the case that "to speak

[28] Peter Berger and Thomas Luckmann, *The Social Construction of Reality* (Harmondsworth: Penguin Books, 1967), 53.

[29] Jurgen Habermas, quoted in T. A. McCarthy, "A Theory of Communicative Competence," in *Critical Sociology*, ed. Paul Connerton (Harmondsworth: Penguin, 1976), 473–78.

[30] Ibid.

is to become a subject."[31] Moreover, a direct interview with Shahbano would not have resolved this problem for us. Since she does not speak English, the politics of translation would, in any case, be deeply implicated in the "retrieval" of her speech.

In contrast, legal actions and other forms of social protest, while problematically subject to issues of mimeticism and referentiality, and still contained within discursive frames, are more "open" and recognizable as combative social action than are personal narratives. In broadly distinguishing between "speech" and "action" in this way, we hope to make the terms of our representation of Shahbano clearer. In what follows, we interpret Shahbano from the crises her legal actions produce. We create her subjectivity in terms of a series of discontinuous and exteriorized actions rather than, as in classic systems of representation, through "depth" characterization. We tentatively trace below the formation of a gendered subjectivity through its discontinuous actions and argue for a Foucauldian notion of resistance in this refusal of subjectification.

Primary socialization for an Indian is effected in terms of religion and class. Gender intersects this general ideological formation to articulate subjectivity. Shahbano's identity as Muslim and woman was gradually formed over a period of childhood. We need to distinguish this process from the violent constitution of the subject as it occurs later. Power is recognized as such only when it is exercised. When Shahbano was ejected from her home after forty years of marriage and several children, the ejection problematized the values that were embedded in the daily routines of life. And when this was followed by her husband's pronouncement of oral and unilateral divorce (as prevails in Islam), she moved to the courts. The ejection and divorce provided Shahbano with the lived experience that leads to a sharp consciousness of gender in a patriarchal culture. The litigant who approached the lower courts was a poor female Muslim subject made painfully aware of being disadvantaged by her religion and her sex and in need of economic assistance. The maintenance award of the lower court of a sum less than the daily wages of a laborer sharply constituted her economic caste identity. She appealed to the High Court in protest against this meager award. Her upper-class Muslim sisters (coreligionists) accused her of a lack of self-respect in fighting for money from a man who, by virtue of the divorce, had become a stranger. She was estranged by class division from women of her religion. We can see class and religion delicately poised in the struggle for dominance

[31] Catherine Belsey, *The Subject of Tragedy: Identity and Difference in Renaissance Drama* (London and New York: Methuen, 1985), 191.

in her response. When Hindu fundamentalists offered to "protect" her from Muslim men, her religious identity won, as her subsequent action shows. In an open letter, she denounced the Supreme Court judgment "which is apparently in my favour; but since this judgment is contrary to the Quran and the *hadith* and is an open interference in Muslim personal law, I, Shahbano, being a muslim, reject it and dissociate myself from every judgement which is contrary to the Islamic Shariat. I am aware of the agony and distress to which this judgment has subjected the muslims of India today."[32] Her apparent inconstancy or changeability must be interpreted as her refusal to occupy the subject position offered to her. When the battle was carried to Parliament and the government of India passed the bill that threw her on the mercy of the male relatives of her natal family, her gender status was again activated. She became a Muslim woman pursuing the case for the return of her *mehr* (dower) under the provisions of the new act.

It is clear that every discursive displacement is matched by a violent movement of religion/class/gender attributes to the foreground of the identity. This process of writing and erasure cannot construct that unified and freely choosing individual who is the normative male subject of Western bourgeois liberalism. The consciousness we have been describing that comes into being in response to and through the investments of a hegemonic or dominant consciousness can perhaps only be described as a subject-effect.[33] To live with what she cannot control, the female subaltern subject here responds with a discontinuous and apparently contradictory subjectivity. Shahbano's legal actions—her appeal for maintenance, her ten-year struggle in the courts, her victory, her denunciation of the judgment and renunciation of the compensation, her quest for restitution of the dower under the new act—may appear within the normative paradigm of subjectivity to conform to the male image of woman as inconstant. So deeply internalized is this notion that when Rajiv Gandhi veered around from acclaiming the judgment to supporting the Muslim Women Act, a member of the opposition attacking the bill in Parliament declaimed: "Frailty, thy name is Rajiv!"[34] But if the inconstancy that is proverbially ascribed to woman is deconstructed, we shall find not a unified, freely choosing, pur-

[32] "Open Letter to Muslims," *Inquilab* (November 13, 1985). The letter is signed by Shahbano with her thumb impression, attested by the signatures of four witnesses; trans. into English by A. Karim Shaik, in *Radiance* (November 24–30, 1985); reprinted in Asghar Ali Engineer, ed., *The Shahbano Controversy* (Hyderabad: Orient Longman, 1987), 211.

[33] Spivak, "Subaltern Studies," 341.

[34] M. S. Gurupadaswamy, "In Focus," *Sunday Observer* (May 11, 1986).

posefully changing subject, but a palimpsest of identities, now constituted, now erased, by discursive displacements.[35]

The episodic narrative of Shahbano's actions we have traced has no center and no closure. If we retraverse its trajectory, we find that for every constituted "effect" there is a simultaneous act of resistance. This for us exemplifies that refusal of subjectification that Foucault recommends, the refusal of "the simultaneous individualization and totalization of the modern power structures."[36] Shahbano's multiple identities must be read in a differential relation to each other. None of them is a positive term but exists in combination with other terms to produce meaning. We greet the resistance offered by this spacing, temporalizing self "with a certain laughter, a certain dance."[37]

The subject in law

Whether this spacing, temporalizing self is a deferral of the unified, freely choosing subject or whether the latter is itself only a metaphysic remains outside our concern here. Certainly the Constitution of India, following Western constitutional models, did envisage this unity of the Indian subject within the legal system.

While there was no specific reference to secularism in the Constitution in 1949, article 25(2) empowered the state to make laws "regulating or restricting any economic, financial, political or other secular activity which may be associated with religious practice."[38] So while the division into secular and personal law might seem to concede that the subject was split, at the time of the framing of the

[35] Palimpsest: A parchment from which writing has been partially or completely erased to make room for another text.

[36] Herbert Dreyfus and Paul Rabinow, *Michel Foucault: Beyond Structuralism and Hermeneutics* (Brighton: Harvester Press, 1982), 216.

[37] Jacques Derrida, "Difference," in *"Speech and Phenomena" and Other Essays on Husserl's Theory of Signs* (1967), trans. David B. Allison (Evanston, Ill.: Northwestern University Press, 1973), 159.

[38] When, in 1948, an attempt was made to introduce a clause to save personal law, Dr. B. R. Ambedkar, one of the framers of the Constitution, argued as follows against it: "The religious conceptions in this country are so vast that they cover every aspect of life from birth to death. There is nothing which is not religious, and, if personal law is to be saved, I am sure about it, that in social matters we shall come to a standstill. . . . After all, what are we having liberty for? We are having this liberty to reform our social system which is so full of inequalities, discriminations and other things which conflict with our fundamental rights." Ambedkar, like other liberal secularists, postulated an Indian-hood which would hold together in unity identities grounded in gender, class, language, and religion; see P. C. Chatterjee, *Secular Values for Secular India* (New Delhi: Lola Chatterjee, 1984), 13.

Constitution this division was only envisaged as a temporary accommodation of contemporary reality (the partition of the country attended by large-scale communal riots). The Constitution signals the desired coexistence of secular and personal law; and, in the hierarchical relationship between the two, we are left in no doubt that "secular" is the upper term.

This was the narrative perspective which made the telos of an eventual uniform civil code "natural," a promised goal toward which the social and legal system would evolve. Until the goal was achieved, personal law would be temporarily harbored under the overarching secular law which promises this achievement: "The State shall endeavour to secure for the citizens a Uniform Civil Code throughout the territory of India" (art. 44).

This assumption emerged unambiguously in the discussions about a comprehensive Criminal Procedure Code that was framed in 1974. When the question of the maintenance of Muslim women had similarly threatened to become an issue, the government was able to satisfy the objections of Muslims without unsettling the hierarchy of the law: "If post-divorce entitlement under personal law was realized by the divorced wife, this should be taken into account, and if maintenance had been granted earlier, it could be cancelled." In this way, Muslim personal law was given recognition at the same time that, by allowing Muslim women to have recourse to sections 125–28 of the Criminal Procedure Code, the economic, religious, and common secular identity of the female Indian subject was ensured in law.

However, with the passage of the Muslim Women Act, this ideology of the law has been jeopardized. An interesting concession in the act now makes possible the Muslim woman's continued recourse to section 125, but only with the consent of the husband: "If a divorced woman and her former husband declare by affidavit or any other declaration in writing in such form as may be prescribed, either jointly or separately, that they would prefer to be governed by the provisions of Section 125 to Section 128 of the Code of Criminal Procedure, 1973, and file such affidavit or declaration in the court hearing the application, the magistrate shall dispose of such application accordingly." That the husband's consent to such a declaration is unlikely is widely recognized. In a reversal of the previous legal hierarchy, the common Code of Criminal Procedure has now become merely an optional or special case of the personal law.

In any relationship of two terms, an implicit or explicit hierarchy prevails, where one of the terms is viewed as the "supplement."

the marginal, extraneous, gratuitous, temporary, or subsidiary element—these approximate to the terms in which personal law was viewed in the Directive Principles. But the passing of the bill has sharply illustrated the workings of "the logic of the supplement,"[39] whereby the supplement moves out of its space and deconstructs the uneasy hierarchy of the governing terms and the metaphysic of the unified subject of legal discourse that it supports. The intervention of religion in politics, or of politics in religion, exacerbates the conflict between the categories of secular and personal. Such exacerbation might eventually result in the translation of the legal division into a split in the psyche of the Indian subject.

In a climate of political and religious controversy, the progress toward a uniform civil code falters. There is a fear among minority communities that, instead of being uncompromisingly secular, a common code would only enshrine some form of codified personal law, most probably that of the majority.[40] Many conceptualizations of a common civil code are unproblematically based on a notion of modernization which, in its turn, is nothing more than a scenario of Westernization, out of keeping with the complex historical reality of the situation in India today.[41] The historical narrative of national evolution and progress, for which the uniform civil code has been projected as the "happy ending," over-simplifies. Under the pressures and exigencies of the times, we might even ask whether the attempt to exchange the present significatory function of the uniform civil code for textual status will block the accommodation of future changes.[42] The passage of the bill has vividly raised the

[39] Jacques Derrida has explained the functioning of the supplement thus: "But the supplement supplements. It adds only to replace. It intervenes or insinuates itself *in-the-place-of;* if it fills, it is as if one fills a void. If it represents and makes an image, it is by the anterior default of a presence. Compensating . . . and vicarious, the supplement is an adjunct, a subaltern instance which *takes-(the)-place*" (see *Of Grammatology,* trans. Gayatri Chakravorty Spivak [Baltimore and London: Johns Hopkins University Press, 1976], 145).

[40] As Asghar Ali Engineer points out, "Whatever the merit of a common civil code . . . when the demand for it comes from communalist Hindus, it arouses deep suspicion even among the Muslim intelligentsia and they begin to perceive it as a Hindu Code" (18).

[41] On the ideology of modernization with special reference to Islamic law, see Iqbal Masood, "Islam and 'Word Politics,' " *Express Magazine* (June 1, 1986).

[42] By "significatory function," we refer to the invocation of art. 44 as a sign: it has served until now as both threat and promise, as that which has to be fulfilled in an indeterminate future, a "deferred presence." "The circulation of signs," as Derrida points out, "defers the moment in which we can encounter the thing itself" (see *Margins of Philosophy* [Chicago: University of Chicago Press, 1982], 9). It is this free play of the sign that will be curtailed in actualizing the code.

ghosts who haunt attempts at codifications that historically have not necessarily benefited women.[43] In this case the passage of the bill has led to the collaborative hegemony of government and the Muslim Personal Law Board. For purposes of framing the law, stereotypes of the Muslim woman (and man) have been invoked and substituted for the actual socioeconomic reality of the situation of divorced Muslim women, the regional differences in *Wakf* funding, and the statistical variations in the rate of divorce. Therefore, the question of the ability of the Uniform Civil Code to (re-)construct the unified Indian subject in law is open to debate.

Nevertheless, the aim must be to close eventually the split between secular and religious law in the interests of legal equality (art. 14 of the Constitution). Perhaps reform of religious law would obviate the need for a uniform civil code.[44] Revisionary readings (similar to those already undertaken by feminist scholars in literature and the social sciences) and "interested" translations of religious texts are clearly needed. By these means, religious law may be creatively interpreted to accommodate the reality of women's contemporary situation. These are initiatives that have already begun in the wake of the Shahbano crisis. Until such a merging of the two systems takes place, the Uniform Civil Code must continue to function as the site of desire and the sign of the unified legal subject.

The identity of legal subjectivity for Indian women, even if a metaphysic, is necessary in order to counter their identity as the "protected" within the family. Accordingly, section 125 might be looked at as an enabling provision: ostensibly "negative" as to the subject position it offers, it is in practice one mode of access to a public space, a forum for combative legal action, a strategy for countering absorption and containment in the family. By being categorized as a vagrant, the destitute woman—widow, divorcee, or abandoned wife—is envisaged as a potential threat to the public peace. It would seem that ironically it is only when a woman threat-

[43] In "The Production of an Official Discourse on *Sati* in Early Nineteenth-Century Bengal," *Economic and Political Weekly,* Review of Women Studies 21, no. 17 (April 26, 1986): 32–40, Lata Mani has argued that increasing textualization of Hindu laws by colonial rulers reduced the heterogeneity, contextualization, and variety of traditional interpretations, and produced "consequences of domination" (39).

[44] The closeness of personal and secular laws already exists in some cases. Some of the personal laws of the Hindus, codified since 1955, such as the Hindu Adoption and Maintenance Act and the Hindu Marriages Act, have no specific *shastric,* i.e., religious, sanction. There exist also several uniform laws covering personal matters, such as the Special Marriage Act, 1955, the Indian Succession Act, 1875, the Guardians and Wards Act, 1890, the Indian Majority act, and the Medical Termination of Pregnancy Act, 1971; see Dhagamvar (n. 7 above), 15.

ens the public realm as an excluded figure, as criminal, prostitute, or vagrant, that she fulfills her (anti-)social role.[45] The psychological damage of potential vagrant status is partially minimized by the depersonalizing effects of legal action. Section 125 offers women a "negative" subjectivity: the new act responds by reinserting the divorcee within the family, this time as dependent on her natal family and sons.

In the ideal, subjects in law are undifferentiated, nondescript, equal, and singular. The Shahbano case points to the contradictions inherent in such "ideal" subjectification.

Resistance

Multiple intersections of power, discursive displacements, discontinuous identities refusing subjectification, the split legal subject: to read this multiple plot is to recognize that the space of the "other" has no permanent occupant. When translated into an oppositional strategy, this situation seems to lend itself to a free play of alliances between reformist groups, to a politics of association which is oriented to specific issues; and as one views the scene of resistance to the Muslim Women Bill, this possibility is confirmed. In the nationwide response first to the Supreme Court's judgment and then to the bill, the politics of coalition are most striking; there was no attempt by different groups to merge into a homogeneous oppositional identity. What one finds instead is a "multiplicity of voices of liberation [which] remain autonomous."[46]

A selective summary of events in 1985–86 shows a coming together of several feminist and reformist groups in spite of basic ideological differences among them, as well as differences on specific issues like the desirability of a common civil code, of foreign funding, of male participation, or of enactment of further reform

[45] The Supreme Court judgment makes this recategorization clear: "The liability imposed by sec. 125 to maintain close relatives who are indigent is founded upon the individual's obligation to the society to prevent vagrancy and destitution. . . . Sir James Fitz-James . . . piloted the Code of Criminal Procedure, 1872 . . . as a mode of preventing vagrancy or at least of preventing its consequences. In Jagir Kaur v. Jaswant Singh . . . Subba Rao J. speaking for the court said that [sec. 125] 'intends to serve a social purpose' " (n. 1 above). Foucault's study of a society through its procedures of exclusion is an insightful one and useful in this context; see, esp., *Madness and Civilization: A History of Insanity in the Age of Reason,* trans. R. Howard (New York: Random House, 1973), and *Discipline and Punish: The Birth of the Prison,* trans. Alan Sheridan (New York: Random House, 1979).

[46] Stanley Aronowitz, *The Crisis in Historical Materialism: Class, Politics and Culture in Marxist Theory* (New York: Praeger, 1981), 131.

(instead of implementing existing laws). That the groups shared a common platform which was open to women's wings of political parties, university teachers and lawyers' collectives, was significant.

Five organizations presented a joint memorandum to the Prime Minister: "Given the fact that the dismally low status of women is a reality for all sections of women regardless of caste or community, the necessity for affording minimum legal protection to all women is self-evident. . . . The unseemly controversy over Section 125 aims at excluding a large section of women from minimum legal protection in the name of religion." The organizations were the All India Democratic Women's Association, the National Federation of Indian Women, the All India Lawyers' Association, the Young Women's Christian Association, and the Mahila Dakshata Samiti.[47]

On January 30, 1986, the women's wing of the Rashtriya Ekjoot held a *dharna* (demonstration) in Bombay to demand a common civil code.

Between September 1985 and May 1986 Muslim women organized similar *dharnas* in all parts of the country from Darbhanga in Bihar to Pune in Maharashtra; outside the offices of the district magistrates and collectors, hundreds of Muslim divorcees supported by various organizations agitated against the bill.

A Muslim reformist organization of Maharashtra, the Muslim Satyashodak Mandal (some of whose programs are not popular with other Muslim reformists), brought a delegation of women, chiefly divorcees, to Delhi to plead their cause to the government on February 22, 1986.

About fifteen women's organizations, consisting of hundreds of women, held a rally in New Delhi on March 6, 1986, to protest the bill.

A statement published on March 8, 1986, in the journal *Mainstream* to protest the bill had 118 signatures from the Muslim intelligentsia, including eminent journalists, educationists, filmmakers, writers, and painters.

Thirty-five women's organizations joined together for a rally organized by the Women's Liberation Movement in Bombay on March 21, 1986, to demand a secular code.

Senior members of the legal profession took part in a public meeting in New Delhi in March 1986, organized by Karmikar, a women's organization.

[47] Janak Raj Jai, *Shah Bano* (New Delhi: Rajiv Publications, 1986), 119.

In West Bengal, a seminar on Women's Right of Equality before the Law was held in April 1986 and was addressed by the Marxist chief minister of the state. The Socialist leader, Raj Narain, began a seventy-two hour hunger strike to protest the bill on May 3, 1986.

On May 5, 1986, while the bill was being passed, women's organizations in the capital protested outside Parliament, chaining themselves to the iron gates of the building to symbolize their plight. Over a hundred women courted arrest.[48]

Muslim women in Delhi, including university teachers and other professionals, formed the Committee for the Protection of Rights of Muslim Women and held a convention on April 26, 1986, in New Delhi. The speakers included Asghar Ali Engineer (who led a revolt against the leadership of the Muslim Bohra community); Saifuddin Chowdhry, Muslim and leftist member of Parliament; Reshma Arif, wife of Minister Arif Mohammed Khan and an advocate (lawyer) of the Supreme Court; Shahnaz Shaikh, who challenged the Muslim personal law to obtain her divorce; Zoya Hassan, professor at Jawaharlal Nehru University; Daniel Latifi, Shahbano's counsel; and Moonis Raza, vice-chancellor of Delhi University.

A group of young women students of the Mass Communication Centre at Jamia Milia University, New Delhi, made a video film called "In Secular India." The inaugural screening was held on September 14, 1986. Calling themselves Mediastorm, the group interviewed some major figures in the controversy and also poor Muslim divorcees, and wove these interviews into the film.

The tempo was kept up in the press by articles by well-known feminist journalists like Neeraja Chowdhury, Bacchi Karkaria, Nandita Haksar, Madhu Kishwar, Vasudha Dhagamvar, and so on.[49] Women's rights activists and women lawyers

[48] These events have been listed in Engineer, ed. (no. 32 above), 237–42.

[49] In addition to articles already cited in this essay, see also Nandita Haksar, "And Justice for All," and Madhu Kishwar, "Losing Sight of the Real Issue: Another Look at the Shahbano Controversy," both in a special supplement, "Woman," *Times of India* (March 8, 1986), 1, 4; Shahida Lateef, "Indian Muslim Women: Caught in a Time Warp," *Express Magazine* (March 30, 1986); Rasheeda Bhagat, "How Poor Muslim Women Look at Maintenance" (a report from Madras), *Indian Express* (April 11, 1986); Neeraja Chowdhury, "The Communal Divide" (three-part article), in *Statesman* (April 18, 19, and 20, 1986), "Muslim Women Bill: Trail of Errors," *Statesman* (April 28, 1986), and "Shortsighted Move to Appease Communities," *Statesman* (May 1, 1986).

are actively engaged in drafting acceptable versions of a common civil code, keeping in mind the basic demand of women's equality with men.

In October 1986, the Third National Conference of Women's Studies held a session on the Shahbano case.[50]

In February 1987, the Joint Women's Programme, a national women's organization (which had earlier organized nationwide protests against the bill), collaborated with Asghar Ali Engineer, of the Institute of Islamic Studies, to publish a book, *The Shahbano Controversy*.[51]

We are well aware that the resistance initiated by the individual subject, as in Shahbano's case, can frequently move out of her control, and even out of the area of her concerns, so that any aggrandizement of her individual resistance would reduce her to a bone of contention among conflicting groups. The Shahbano crisis was not allowed to be defused in this fashion. The feminist collectivity, by embracing the individual woman's cause, converted her resistance into a significant operation within a (collective) feminist politics. We have noted how women's groups have been able to reconcile two contradictory aims: to attend to the specificity of the problem of Shahbano as a woman living in poverty, in order to focus on concrete, pragmatic, end-directed action; and also to subsume the specific issue in the larger context of Indian women's secondary social and legal status, in order to avoid the danger of isolating women of the community, of targeting their religious identity as regressive, speaking therefore on their behalf, even usurping their victim status, and ending by offering "protection." As we have detailed above, not only have women's groups formed different alliances in response to such complexities, but they have also chosen varied strategies of protest and resistance. Some groups have resorted to active consciousness-raising programs, such as demonstrations, petition drives, signature campaigns, or courting arrest. Other women have been campaigning in the press, on cinema and television, as well as in legal, religious, and academic forums.

It will be clear by now that our decentered subject is not that "poststructuralist ideal . . . the 'man without qualities' (Musil), the

[50] The National Conferences on Women's Studies are organized by the Indian Association of Women's Studies (CWDS, B-43, Panchsheel Enclave, New Delhi, 110 017). This paper, and two others on the "Shahbano" issue, were part of a workshop on religion, secularism, and women's rights convened by Uma Chakravorty and Sudesh Vaid.

[51] This book, cited in n. 32 above, is a collection of documents relating to the issue and reprints of several newspaper and periodical articles.

Reichian subject without 'character armour,' the Deleuzian schizophrenic subject."[52] Instead, by allowing a strategic redefining of her subject-position in accordance with the exigencies of the shifting political situation, she engages with the collectivity. The fragmented subject, refusing to be protected, seeks access to the public realm by erupting into its discourses, problematizing the shared assumptions across those discourses, and disrupting their harmony. "Shahbano" is to be found in the transformative power of gender operating in such analytic categories as "minorities," "citizens," and "working-classes." The contradictions of the gendered situation cease to be socially inert at historical junctures. Shahbano activated these contradictions, even as other women have pushed them toward a crisis.

It is this view of gender as social force that allows us to express an "optimism of the will" that counters the "pessimism of the intelligence"[53] inevitable in tracing a narrative that concludes with the passage of a retrogressive law. Some developments following the passing of the bill further permit a certain cautious optimism.

> The act was challenged in the Supreme Court by the *Anjuman-e-Taraqqi Pasand* Muslim group on May 22, 1986.[54]
>
> The first two legal verdicts under the new act have gone in favor of the divorced women. In January 1988, Rekha Dixit, a woman magistrate in the Lucknow court, ordered Shafat Ahmed to pay his divorced wife Fahmida Sardar Rs 30,000 as "reasonable and fair provision" plus Rs 3,000 as *iddat* (maintenance) and Rs 52,000 as *mehr* (dower). Eight days later she directed Mohammed Khalid Ahmed to pay his divorced wife Shahida Khatoon Rs 11,000 (*mehr*), Rs 1,500 (*iddat*), and Rs 69,000 as "reasonable and fair provision." In making these generous settlements, Rekha Dixit was interpreting liberally the statutory provision regarding "reasonable and fair provision" as laid down in the act.[55]
>
> There is hope that the shape of new legislation relating to women's issues, including the drafting of a uniform civil code, may show a greater awareness of the interests of women.[56]

[52] Leonard Green, Jonathan Culler, and Richard Klein, "Interview: Frederic Jameson," *Diacritics* 12 (Fall 1982): 72–91, esp. 82.

[53] Antonio Gramsci, *Selections from Prison Writings, 1910–1920*, ed. Quintin Hoare, trans. John Mathews (London: Lawrence & Wishart, 1977), 175n.

[54] Engineer, ed. (n. 32 above), 242.

[55] Minu Jain, "Curious Role Reversal," *Sunday Observer* (January 24, 1988).

[56] The three supposedly pro-women acts passed in 1987—the Dowry Amendment Act, the Prevention of Immoral Traffic Act, and the Indecent Representation of

So we read deliberately against the grain: the narrative that concludes with the Muslim Women Act is also a beginning which has opened a space in the public realm for women. It is in our attempt to retain Shahbano within the concerns of a feminist project—to ensure that the crisis initiated by her does not move away from the issue of destitute women—that the question we posed at the beginning, Where is Shahbano the woman? finds its tentative answer.

Department of English
Delhi University

Women Act—"were intended to soften the negative impact of the politically motivated Muslim Women (Protection of Rights in Divorce) Act" (see unsigned editorial, "Women versus Women," *Statesman* [September 2, 1988]). These acts have nevertheless been widely perceived not only as powerless to effect real changes but also as impinging upon civil rights. The Commission of Sati (Prevention) Act, 1987 (which bans the celebration of *Sati*), has also come in for the same criticism (see *The Current Indian Statutes,* June 1988, pt. 6, 7–12). The pressure from women's groups for effective legal reform therefore continues.

ON BEING THE OBJECT OF PROPERTY

PATRICIA J. WILLIAMS

On being invisible

Reflections

For some time I have been writing about my great-great-grandmother. I have considered the significance of her history and that of slavery from a variety of viewpoints on a variety of occasions: in every speech, in every conversation, even in my commercial transactions class. I have talked so much about her that I finally had to ask myself what it was I was looking for in this dogged pursuit of family history. Was I being merely indulgent, looking for roots in the pursuit of some genetic heraldry, seeking the inheritance of being special, different, unique in all that primogeniture hath wrought?

I decided that my search was based in the utility of such a quest, not mere indulgence, but a recapturing of that which had escaped historical scrutiny, which had been overlooked and underseen. I, like so many blacks, have been trying to pin myself down in history, place myself in the stream of time as significant, evolved, present in the past, continuing into the future. To be without documentation is too unsustaining, too spontaneously ahistorical, too dangerously malleable in the hands of those who would rewrite not merely the past but my future as well. So I have been picking through the ruins for my roots.

What I know of my mother's side of the family begins with my great-great-grandmother. Her name was Sophie and she lived in Tennessee. In 1850, she was about twelve years old. I know that she was purchased when she was eleven by a white lawyer named

This essay originally appeared in *Signs*, vol. 14, no. 1, Autumn 1988.

Austin Miller and was immediately impregnated by him. She gave birth to my great-grandmother Mary, who was taken away from her to be raised as a house servant.[1] I know nothing more of Sophie (she was, after all, a black single mother—in today's terms—suffering the anonymity of yet another statistical teenage pregnancy). While I don't remember what I was told about Austin Miller before I decided to go to law school, I do remember that just before my first day of class, my mother said, in a voice full of secretive reassurance, "The Millers were lawyers, so you have it in your blood."[2]

When my mother told me that I had nothing to fear in law school, that law was "in my blood," she meant it in a very complex sense. First and foremost, she meant it defiantly; she meant that no one should make me feel inferior because someone else's father was a judge. She wanted me to reclaim that part of my heritage from which I had been disinherited, and she wanted me to use it as a source of strength and self-confidence. At the same time, she was asking me to claim a part of myself that was the dispossessor of another part of myself; she was asking me to deny that disenfranchised little black girl of myself that felt powerless, vulnerable and, moreover, rightly felt so.

In somewhat the same vein, Mother was asking me not to look to her as a role model. She was devaluing that part of herself that was not Harvard and refocusing my vision to that part of herself that was hard-edged, proficient, and Western. She hid the lonely, black, defiled-female part of herself and pushed me forward as the projection of a competent self, a cool rather than despairing self, a masculine rather than a feminine self.

I took this secret of my blood into the Harvard milieu with both the pride and the shame with which my mother had passed it along to me. I found myself in the situation described by Marguerite Duras, in her novel *The Lover:* "We're united in a fundamental shame at having to live. It's here we are at the heart of our common fate, the fact that [we] are our mother's children, the children of a candid creature murdered by society. We're on the side of society which has reduced her to despair. Because of what's been done to our mother, so amiable, so trusting, we hate life, we hate ourselves."[3]

Reclaiming that from which one has been disinherited is a good thing. Self-possession in the full sense of that expression is the companion to self-knowledge. Yet claiming for myself a heritage

[1] For a more detailed account of the family history to this point, see Patricia Williams, "Grandmother Sophie," *Harvard Blackletter* 3 (1986): 79.

[2] Patricia Williams, "Alchemical Notes: Reconstructing Ideals from Deconstructed Rights," *Harvard Civil Rights–Civil Liberties Law Review* 22 (1987): 418.

[3] Marguerite Duras, *The Lover* (New York: Harper & Row, 1985), 55.

the weft of whose genesis is my own disinheritance is a profoundly troubling paradox.

Images

A friend of mine practices law in rural Florida. His office is in Belle Glade, an extremely depressed area where the sugar industry reigns supreme, where blacks live pretty much as they did in slavery times, in dormitories called slave ships. They are penniless and illiterate and have both a high birth rate and a high death rate.

My friend told me about a client of his, a fifteen-year-old young woman pregnant with her third child, who came seeking advice because her mother had advised a hysterectomy—not even a tubal ligation—as a means of birth control. The young woman's mother, in turn, had been advised of the propriety of such a course in her own case by a white doctor some years before. Listening to this, I was reminded of a case I worked on when I was working for the Western Center on Law and Poverty about eight years ago. Ten black Hispanic women had been sterilized by the University of Southern California–Los Angeles County General Medical Center, allegedly without proper consent, and in most instances without even their knowledge.[4] Most of them found out what had been done to them upon inquiry, after a much-publicized news story in which an intern charged that the chief of obstetrics at the hospital pursued a policy of recommending Caesarian delivery and simultaneous sterilization for any pregnant woman with three or more children and who was on welfare. In the course of researching the appeal in that case, I remember learning that one-quarter of all Navajo women of childbearing age—literally all those of childbearing age ever admitted to a hospital—have been sterilized.[5]

[4] *Madrigal v. Quilligan*, U.S. Court of Appeals, 9th Circuit, Docket no. 78-3187, October 1979.

[5] This was the testimony of one of the witnesses. It is hard to find official confirmation for this or any other sterilization statistic involving Native American women. Official statistics kept by the U.S. Public Health Service, through the Centers for Disease Control in Atlanta, come from data gathered by the National Hospital Discharge Survey, which covers neither federal hospitals nor penitentiaries. Services to Native American women living on reservations are provided almost exclusively by federal hospitals. In addition, the U.S. Public Health Service breaks down its information into only three categories: "White," "Black," and "Other." Nevertheless, in 1988, the Women of All Red Nations Collective of Minneapolis, Minnesota, distributed a fact sheet entitled "Sterilization Studies of Native American Women," which claimed that as many as 50 percent of all Native American women of childbearing age have been sterilized. According to "Surgical Sterilization Surveillance: Tubal Sterilization and Hysterectomy in Women Aged 15–44, 1979–1980," issued

As I reflected on all this, I realized that one of the things passed on from slavery, which continues in the oppression of people of color, is a belief structure rooted in a concept of black (or brown, or red) anti-will, the antithetical embodiment of pure will. We live in a society in which the closest equivalent of nobility is the display of unremittingly controlled will-fulness. To be perceived as unremittingly will-less is to be imbued with an almost lethal trait.

Many scholars have explained this phenomenon in terms of total and infantilizing interdependency of dominant and oppressed.[6] Consider, for example, Mark Tushnet's distinction between slave law's totalistic view of personality and the bourgeois "pure will" theory of personality: "Social relations in slave society rest upon the interaction of owner with slave; the owner, having total dominion over the slave. In contrast, bourgeois social relations rest upon the paradigmatic instance of market relations, the purchase by a capitalist of a worker's labor power; that transaction implicates only a part of the worker's personality. Slave relations are total, engaging the master and slave in exchanges in which each must take account of the entire range of belief, feeling, and interest embodied by the other; bourgeois social relations are partial, requiring only that participants in a market evaluate their general productive characteristics without regard to aspects of personality unrelated to production."[7]

Although such an analysis is not objectionable in some general sense, the description of master-slave relations as "total" is, to me,

---

by the Centers for Disease Control in 1983, "In 1980, the tubal sterilization rate for black women . . . was 45 percent greater than that for white women" (7). Furthermore, a study released in 1984 by the Division of Reproductive Health of the Center for Health Promotion and Education (one of the Centers for Disease Control) found that, as of 1982, 48.8 percent of Puerto Rican women between the ages of 15 and 44 had been sterilized.

[6] See, generally, Stanley Elkins, *Slavery* (New York: Grosset & Dunlap, 1963); Kenneth Stampp, *The Peculiar Institution* (New York: Vintage, 1956): Winthrop Jordan, *White over Black* (Baltimore: Penguin Books, 1968).

[7] Mark Tushnet, *The American Law of Slavery* (Princeton, N.J.: Princeton University Press, 1981), 6. There is danger, in the analysis that follows, of appearing to "pick" on Tushnet. That is not my intention, nor is it to impugn the body of his research, most of which I greatly admire. The choice of this passage for analysis has more to do with the randomness of my reading habits; the fact that he is one of the few legal writers to attempt, in the context of slavery, a juxtaposition of political theory with psychoanalytic theories of personality; and the fact that he is perceived to be of the political left, which simplifies my analysis in terms of its presumption of sympathy, i.e., that the constructions of thought revealed are socially derived and unconscious rather than idiosyncratic and intentional.

quite troubling. Such a choice of words reflects and accepts—at a very subtle level, perhaps—a historical rationalization that whites had to, could do, and did do everything for these simple, above-animal subhumans. It is a choice of vocabulary that fails to acknowledge blacks as having needs beyond those that even the most "humane" or "sentimental" white slavemaster could provide.[8] In trying to describe the provisional aspect of slave law, I would choose words that revealed its structure as rooted in a concept of, again, black anti-will, the polar opposite of pure will. I would characterize the treatment of blacks by whites in whites' law as defining blacks as those who had no will. I would characterize that treatment not as total interdependency, but as a relation in which partializing judgments, employing partializing standards of humanity, impose generalized inadequacy on a race: if pure will or total control equals the perfect white person, then impure will and total lack of control equals the perfect black man or woman. Therefore, to define slave law as comprehending a "total" view of personality implicitly accepts that the provision of food, shelter, and clothing (again assuming the very best of circumstances) is the whole requirement of humanity. It assumes also either that psychic care was provided by slave owners (as though a slave or an owned psyche could ever be reconciled with mental health) or that psyche is not a significant part of a whole human.

Market theory indeed focuses attention away from the full range of human potential in its pursuit of a divinely willed, invisibly handed economic actor. Master-slave relations, however, focused attention away from the full range of black human potential in a somewhat different way: it pursued a vision of blacks as simple-

[8] In another passage, Tushnet observes: "The court thus demonstrated its appreciation of the ties of sentiment that slavery could generate between master and slave and simultaneously denied that those ties were relevant in the law" (67). What is noteworthy about the reference to "sentiment" is that it assumes that the fact that emotions could grow up between slave and master is itself worth remarking: slightly surprising, slightly commendable for the court to note (i.e., in its "appreciation")—although "simultaneously" with, and presumably in contradistinction to, the court's inability to take official cognizance of the fact. Yet, if one really looks at the ties that bound master and slave, one has to flesh out the description of master-slave with the ties of father-son, father-daughter, half-sister, half-brother, uncle, aunt, cousin, and a variety of de facto foster relationships. And if one starts to see those ties as more often than not intimate family ties, then the terminology "appreciation of . . . sentiment . . . between master and slave" becomes a horrifying mockery of any true sense of family sentiment, which is utterly, utterly lacking. The court's "appreciation," from this enhanced perspective, sounds blindly cruel, sarcastic at best. And to observe that courts suffused in such "appreciation" could simultaneously deny its legal relevance seems not only a truism; it misses the point entirely.

minded, strong-bodied economic actants.[9] Thus, while blacks had an indisputable generative force in the marketplace, their presence could not be called activity; they had no active role in the market. To say, therefore, that "market relations disregard the peculiarities of individuals, whereas slave relations rest on the mutual recognition of the humanity of master and slave"[10] (no matter how dialectical or abstracted a definition of humanity one adopts) is to posit an inaccurate equation: if "disregard for the peculiarities of individuals" and "mutual recognition of humanity" are polarized by a "whereas," then somehow regard for peculiarities of individuals must equal recognition of humanity. In the context of slavery this equation mistakes whites' overzealous and oppressive obsession with projected specific peculiarities of blacks for actual holistic regard for the individual. It overlooks the fact that most definitions of humanity require something beyond mere biological sustenance, some healthy measure of autonomy beyond that of which slavery could institutionally or otherwise conceive. Furthermore, it overlooks the fact that both slave and bourgeois systems regarded certain attributes as important and disregarded certain others, and that such regard and disregard can occur in the same glance, like the wearing of horseblinders to focus attention simultaneously toward and away from. The experiential blinders of market actor and slave are focused in different directions, yet the partializing ideologies of each makes the act of not seeing an unconscious, alienating component of seeing. Restoring a unified social vision will, I think, require broader and more scattered resolutions than the simple symmetry of ideological bipolarity.

Thus, it is important to undo whatever words obscure the fact that slave law was at least as fragmenting and fragmented as the bourgeois worldview—in a way that has persisted to this day, cutting across all ideological boundaries. As "pure will" signifies the whole bourgeois personality in the bourgeois worldview, so wisdom, control, and aesthetic beauty signify the whole white personality in slave law. The former and the latter, the slavemaster and the burgermeister, are not so very different when expressed in those terms. The reconciling difference is that in slave law the emphasis is really

[9] "Actants have a kind of phonemic, rather than a phonetic role: they operate on the level of function, rather than content. That is, an actant may embody itself in a particular character (termed an acteur) or it may reside in the function of more than one character in respect of their common role in the story's underlying 'oppositional' structure. In short, the deep structure of the narrative generates and defines its actants at a level beyond that of the story's surface content" (Terence Hawkes, *Structuralism and Semiotics* [Berkeley: University of California Press, 1977], 89).

[10] Tushnet, 69.

on the inverse rationale: that irrationality, lack of control, and ugliness signify the whole slave personality. "Total" interdependence is at best a polite way of rationalizing such personality splintering; it creates a bizarre sort of yin-yang from the dross of an oppressive schizophrenia of biblical dimension. I would just call it schizophrenic, with all the baggage that that connotes. That is what sounds right to me. Truly total relationships (as opposed to totalitarianism) call up images of whole people dependent on whole people; an interdependence that is both providing and laissez-faire at the same time. Neither the historical inheritance of slave law nor so-called bourgeois law meets that definition.

None of this, perhaps, is particularly new. Nevertheless, as precedent to anything I do as a lawyer, the greatest challenge is to allow the full truth of partializing social constructions to be felt for their overwhelming reality—reality that otherwise I might rationally try to avoid facing. In my search for roots, I must assume, not just as history but as an ongoing psychological force, that, in the eyes of white culture, irrationality, lack of control, and ugliness signify not just the whole slave personality, not just the whole black personality, but me.

Vision

Reflecting on my roots makes me think again and again of the young woman in Belle Glade, Florida. She told the story of her impending sterilization, according to my friend, while keeping her eyes on the ground at all times. My friend, who is white, asked why she wouldn't look up, speak with him eye to eye. The young woman answered that she didn't like white people seeing inside her.

My friend's story made me think of my own childhood and adolescence: my parents were always telling me to look up at the world; to look straight at people, particularly white people; not to let them stare me down; to hold my ground; to insist on the right to my presence no matter what. They told me that in this culture you have to look people in the eye because that's how you tell them you're their equal. My friend's story also reminded me how very difficult I had found that looking-back to be. What was hardest was not just that white people saw me, as my friend's client put it, but that they looked through me, that they treated me as though I were transparent.

By itself, seeing into me would be to see my substance, my anger, my vulnerability, and my wild raging despair—and that alone is hard enough to show, to share. But to uncover it and to have it devalued by ignore-ance, to hold it up bravely in the organ of my eyes and to have it greeted by an impassive stare that passes right through all that which is me, an impassive stare that moves on and attaches itself to my left earlobe or to the dust caught in the rusty vertical geysers of my wiry hair or to the breadth of my freckled brown nose—this is deeply humiliating. It re-wounds, relives the early childhood anguish of uncensored seeing, the fullness of vision that is the permanent turning-away point for most blacks.

The cold game of equality-staring makes me feel like a thin sheet of glass: white people see all the worlds beyond me but not me. They come trotting at me with force and speed; they do not see me. I could force my presence, the real me contained in those eyes, upon them, but I would be smashed in the process. If I deflect, if I move out of the way, they will never know I existed.

Marguerite Duras, again in *The Lover,* places the heroine in relation to her family. "Every day we try to kill one another, to kill. Not only do we not talk to one another, we don't even look at one another. When you're being looked at you can't look. To look is to feel curious, to be interested, to lower yourself."[11]

To look is also to make myself vulnerable; yet not to look is to neutralize the part of myself which is vulnerable. I look in order to see, and so I must look. Without that directness of vision, I am afraid I will will my own blindness, disinherit my own creativity, and sterilize my own perspective of its embattled, passionate insight.

On ardor

The child

One Saturday afternoon not long ago, I sat among a litter of family photographs telling a South African friend about Marjorie, my godmother and my mother's cousin. She was given away by her light-skinned mother when she was only six. She was given to my grandmother and my great-aunts to be raised among her darker-skinned cousins, for Marjorie was very dark indeed. Her mother left the family to "pass," to marry a white man—Uncle Frederick, we called him with trepidatious presumption yet without his ever knowing of our existence—an heir to a meat-packing fortune. When Uncle Frederick died thirty years later and the fortune was lost, Marjorie's mother rejoined the race, as the royalty of resentful fascination—Lady Bountiful, my sister called her—to regale us with tales of gracious upper-class living.

[11] Duras, 54.

My friend said that my story reminded him of a case in which a swarthy, crisp-haired child was born, in Durban, to white parents. The Afrikaner government quickly intervened, removed the child from its birth home, and placed it to be raised with a "more suitable," browner family.

When my friend and I had shared these stories, we grew embarrassed somehow, and our conversation trickled away into a discussion of laissez-faire economics and governmental interventionism. Our words became a clear line, a railroad upon which all other ideas and events were tied down and sacrificed.

The market

As a teacher of commercial transactions, one of the things that has always impressed me most about the law of contract is a certain deadening power it exercises by reducing the parties to the passive. It constrains the lively involvement of its signatories by positioning enforcement in such a way that parties find themselves in a passive relationship to a document: it is the contract that governs, that "does" everything, that absorbs all responsibility and deflects all other recourse.

Contract law reduces life to fairy tale. The four corners of the agreement become parent. Performance is the equivalent of obedience to the parent. Obedience is dutifully passive. Passivity is valued as good contract-socialized behavior; activity is caged in retrospective hypotheses about states of mind at the magic moment of contracting. Individuals are judged by the contract unfolding rather than by the actors acting autonomously. Nonperformance is disobedience; disobedience is active; activity becomes evil in contrast to the childlike passivity of contract conformity.

One of the most powerful examples of all this is the case of Mary Beth Whitehead, mother of Sara—of so-called Baby M. Ms. Whitehead became a vividly original actor *after* the creation of her contract with William Stern; unfortunately for her, there can be no greater civil sin. It was in this upside-down context, in the picaresque unboundedness of breachor, that her energetic grief became hysteria and her passionate creativity was funneled, whorled, and reconstructed as highly impermissible. Mary Beth Whitehead thus emerged as the evil stepsister who deserved nothing.

Some time ago, Charles Reich visited a class of mine.[12] He discussed with my students a proposal for a new form of bargain by

[12] Charles Reich is author of *The Greening of America* (New York: Random House, 1970) and professor of law at the University of San Francisco Law School.

which emotional "items"—such as praise, flattery, acting happy or sad—might be contracted for explicitly. One student, not alone in her sentiment, said, "Oh, but then you'll just feel obligated." Only the week before, however (when we were discussing the contract which posited that Ms. Whitehead "will not form or attempt to form a parent-child relationship with any child or children"), this same student had insisted that Ms. Whitehead must give up her child, because she had *said* she would: "She was obligated!" I was confounded by the degree to which what the student took to be self-evident, inalienable gut reactions could be governed by illusions of passive conventionality and form.

It was that incident, moreover, that gave me insight into how Judge Harvey Sorkow, of New Jersey Superior Court, could conclude that the contract that purported to terminate Ms. Whitehead's parental rights was "not illusory."[13]

(As background, I should say that I think that, within the framework of contract law itself, the agreement between Ms. Whitehead and Mr. Stern was clearly illusory.[14] On the one hand, Judge Sorkow's opinion said that Ms. Whitehead was seeking to avoid her *obligations*. In other words, giving up her child became an actual obligation. On the other hand, according to the logic of the judge, this was a service contract, not really a sale of a child; therefore delivering the child to the Sterns was an "obligation" for which there was no consideration, for which Mr. Stern was not paying her.)

Judge Sorkow's finding the contract "not illusory" is suggestive not just of the doctrine by that name, but of illusion in general, and delusion, and the righteousness with which social constructions are conceived, acted on, and delivered up into the realm of the real as "right," while all else is devoured from memory as "wrong." From this perspective, the rhetorical tricks by which Sara Whitehead became Melissa Stern seem very like the heavy-worded legalities by which my great-great-grandmother was pacified and parted from her child. In both situations, the real mother had no say, no power; her powerlessness was imposed by state law that made her and her child helpless in relation to the father. My great-great-grandmother's

[13] See, generally, In the Matter of Baby "M," A Pseudonym for an Actual Person, Superior Court of New Jersey, Chancery Division, Docket no. FM-25314-86E, March 31, 1987. This decision was appealed, and on February 3, 1988, the New Jersey Supreme Court ruled that surrogate contracts were illegal and against public policy. In addition to the contract issue, however, the appellate court decided the custody issue in favor of the Sterns but granted visitation rights to Mary Beth Whitehead.

[14] "An illusory promise is an expression cloaked in promissory terms, but which, upon closer examination, reveals that the promisor has committed himself not at all" (J. Calamari and J. Perillo, *Contracts*, 3d ed. [St. Paul: West Publishing, 1987], 228).

powerlessness came about as the result of a contract to which she was not a party; Mary Beth Whitehead's powerlessness came about as a result of a contract that she signed at a discrete point of time—yet which, over time, enslaved her. The contract-reality in both instances was no less than magic: it was illusion transformed into not-illusion. Furthermore, it masterfully disguised the brutality of enforced arrangements in which these women's autonomy, their flesh and their blood, were locked away in word vaults, without room to reconsider—*ever.*

In the months since Judge Sorkow's opinion, I have reflected on the similarities of fortune between my own social positioning and that of Sara Melissa Stern Whitehead. I have come to realize that an important part of the complex magic that Judge Sorkow wrote into his opinion was a supposition that it is "natural" for people to want children "like" themselves. What this reasoning raised for me was an issue of what, exactly, constituted this "likeness"? (What would have happened, for example, if Ms. Whitehead had turned out to have been the "passed" descendant of my "failed" godmother Marjorie's mother? What if the child she bore had turned out to be recessively and visibly black? Would the sperm of Mr. Stern have been so powerful as to make this child "his" with the exclusivity that Judge Sorkow originally assigned?) What constitutes, moreover, the collective understanding of "un-likeness"?

These questions turn, perhaps, on not-so-subtle images of which mothers should be bearing which children. Is there not something unseemly, in our society, about the spectacle of a white woman mothering a black child? A white woman giving totally to a black child; a black child totally and demandingly dependent for everything, for sustenance itself, from a white woman. The image of a white woman suckling a black child; the image of a black child sucking for its life from the bosom of a white woman. The utter interdependence of such an image; the selflessness, the merging it implies; the giving up of boundary; the encompassing of other within self; the unbounded generosity, the interconnectedness of such an image. Such a picture says that there is no difference; it places the hope of continuous generation, of immortality of the white self in a little black face.

When Judge Sorkow declared that it was only to be expected that parents would want to breed children "like" themselves, he simultaneously created a legal right to the same. With the creation of such a "right," he encased the children conforming to "likeliness" in protective custody, far from whole ranges of taboo. Taboo about touch and smell and intimacy and boundary. Taboo about ardor, possession, license, equivocation, equanimity, indifference, intolerance, rancor, dispossession, innocence, exile, and candor. Taboo about death. Taboos that amount to death. Death and sacredness, the valuing of body, of self, of other, of remains. The handling lovingly in life, as in life; the question of the intimacy versus the dispassion of death.

In effect, these taboos describe boundaries of valuation. Whether something is inside or outside the marketplace of rights has always been a way of valuing it. When a valued object is located outside the market, it is generally understood to be too "priceless" to be accommodated by ordinary exchange relationships; when, in contrast, the prize is located within the marketplace, all objects outside become "valueless." Traditionally, the Mona Lisa and human life have been the sorts of subjects removed from the fungibility of commodification, as "priceless." Thus when black people were bought and sold as slaves, they were placed beyond the bounds of humanity. And thus, in the twistedness of our brave new world, when blacks have been thrust out of the market and it is white children who are bought and sold, black babies have become "worthless" currency to adoption agents—"surplus" in the salvage heaps of Harlem hospitals.

The imagination

"Familiar though his name may be to us, the storyteller in his living immediacy is by no means a present force. He has already become something remote from us and something that is getting even more distant. . . . Less and less frequently do we encounter people with the ability to tell a tale properly. . . . It is as if something that seemed inalienable to us, the securest among our possessions, were taken from us: the ability to exchange experiences."[15]

My mother's cousin Marjorie was a storyteller. From time to time I would press her to tell me the details of her youth, and she would tell me instead about a child who wandered into a world of polar bears, who was prayed over by polar bears, and in the end eaten. The child's life was not in vain because the polar bears had been made holy by its suffering. The child had been a test, a message from god for polar bears. In the polar bear universe, she would tell me, the primary object of creation was polar bears, and the rest of the living world was fashioned to serve polar bears. The clouds took their shape from polar bears, trees were designed to give shel-

[15] Walter Benjamin, "The Storyteller," in *Illuminations*, ed. Hannah Arendt (New York: Schocken, 1969), 83.

ter and shade to polar bears, and humans were ideally designed to provide polar bears with meat.[16]

The truth, the truth, I would laughingly insist as we sat in her apartment eating canned fruit and heavy roasts, mashed potatoes, pickles and vanilla pudding, cocoa, Sprite, or tea. What about roots and all that, I coaxed. But the voracity of her amnesia would disclaim and disclaim and disclaim; and she would go on telling me about the polar bears until our plates were full of emptiness and I became large in the space which described her emptiness and I gave in to the emptiness of words.

On life and death

Sighing into space

There are moments in my life when I feel as though a part of me is missing. There are days when I feel so invisible that I can't remember what day of the week it is, when I feel so manipulated that I can't remember my own name, when I feel so lost and angry that I can't speak a civil word to the people who love me best. Those are the times when I catch sight of my reflection in store windows and am surprised to see a whole person looking back. Those are the times when my skin becomes gummy as clay and my nose slides around on my face and my eyes drip down to my chin. I have to close my eyes at such times and remember myself, draw an internal picture that is smooth and whole; when all else fails, I reach for a mirror and stare myself down until the features reassemble themselves like lost sheep.

Two years ago, my godmother Marjorie suffered a massive stroke. As she lay dying, I would come to the hospital to give her her meals. My feeding her who had so often fed me became a complex ritual of mirroring and self-assembly. The physical act of holding the spoon to her lips was not only a rite of nurture and of sacrifice, it was the return of a gift. It was a quiet bowing to the passage of time and the doubling back of all things. The quiet woman who listened to my woes about work and school required now that I bend my head down close to her and listen for mouthed word fragments, sentence crumbs. I bent down to give meaning to her silence, her wandering search for words.

She would eat what I brought to the hospital with relish; she would reject what I brought with a turn of her head. I brought fruit

[16] For an analysis of similar stories, see Richard Levins and Richard Lewontin, *The Dialectical Biologist* (Cambridge, Mass.: Harvard University Press, 1985), 66.

and yogurt, ice cream and vegetable juice. Slowly, over time, she stopped swallowing. The mashed potatoes would sit in her mouth like cotton, the pudding would slip to her chin in slow sad streams. When she lost not only her speech but the power to ingest, they put a tube into her nose and down to her stomach, and I lost even that medium by which to communicate. No longer was there the odd but reassuring communion over taste. No longer was there some echo of comfort in being able to nurture one who nurtured me.

This increment of decay was like a little newborn death. With the tube, she stared up at me with imploring eyes, and I tried to guess what it was that she would like. I read to her aimlessly and in desperation. We entertained each other with the strange embarrassed flickering of our eyes. I told her stories to fill the emptiness, the loneliness, of the white-walled hospital room.

I told her stories about who I had become, about how I had grown up to know all about exchange systems, and theories of contract, and monetary fictions. I spun tales about blue-sky laws and promissory estoppel, the wispy-feathered complexity of undue influence and dark-hearted theories of unconscionability. I told her about market norms and gift economy and the thin razor's edge of the bartering ethic. Once upon a time, I rambled, some neighbors of mine included me in their circle of barter. They were in the habit of exchanging eggs and driving lessons, hand-knit sweaters and computer programming, plumbing and calligraphy. I accepted the generosity of their inclusion with gratitude. At first, I felt that, as a lawyer, I was worthless, that I had no barterable skills and nothing to contribute. What I came to realize with time, however, was that my value to the group was not calculated by the physical items I brought to it. These people included me because they wanted me to be part of their circle, they valued my participation apart from the material things I could offer. So I gave of myself to them, and they gave me fruit cakes and dandelion wine and smoked salmon, and in their giving, their goods became provisions. Cradled in this community whose currency was a relational ethic, my stock in myself soared. My value depended on the glorious intangibility, the eloquent invisibility of my just being *part* of the collective; and in direct response I grew spacious and happy and gentle.

My gentle godmother. The fragility of life; the cold mortuary shelf.

Dispassionate deaths

The hospital in which my godmother died is now filled to capacity with AIDS patients. One in sixty-one babies born there, as in New

York City generally, is infected with AIDS antibodies.[17] Almost all are black or Hispanic. In the Bronx, the rate is one in forty-three.[18] In Central Africa, experts estimate that, of children receiving transfusions for malaria-related anemia, "about 1000 may have been infected with the AIDS virus in each of the last five years."[19] In Congo, 5 percent of the entire population is infected.[20] The *New York Times* reports that "the profile of Congo's population seems to guarantee the continued spread of AIDS."[21]

In the Congolese city of Pointe Noir, "the annual budget of the sole public health hospital is estimated at about $200,000—roughly the amount of money spent in the United States to care for four AIDS patients."[22]

The week in which my godmother died is littered with bad memories. In my journal, I made note of the following:

> *Good Friday:* Phil Donahue has a special program on AIDS. The segues are:
>
> a. from Martha, who weeps at the prospect of not watching her children grow up
>
> b. to Jim, who is not conscious enough to speak just now, who coughs convulsively, who recognizes no one in his family any more
>
> c. to Hugh who, at 85 pounds, thinks he has five years but whose doctor says he has weeks
>
> d. to an advertisement for denture polish ("If you love your Polident Green/then gimmeeya SMILE!")
>
> e. and then one for a plastic surgery salon on Park Avenue ("The only thing that's expensive is our address")
>
> f. and then one for what's coming up on the five o'clock news (Linda Lovelace, of *Deep Throat* fame, "still recovering from a double mastectomy and complications from silicone injections" is being admitted to a New York hospital for a liver transplant)
>
> g. and finally one for the miracle properties of all-purpose house cleaner ("Mr. Cleeean/is the man/behind the

[17] B. Lambert, "Study Finds Antibodies for AIDS in 1 in 61 Babies in New York City," *New York Times* (January 13, 1988), sec. A.

[18] Ibid.

[19] "Study Traces AIDS in African Children," *New York Times* (January 22, 1988), sec. A.

[20] J. Brooke, "New Surge of AIDS in Congo May Be an Omen for Africa," *New York Times* (January 22, 1988), sec. A.

[21] Ibid.

[22] Ibid.

shine/is it wet or is it dry?" I note that Mr. Clean, with his gleaming bald head, puffy musculature and fever-bright eyes, looks like he is undergoing radiation therapy). Now back to our show.

h. "We are back now with Martha," (who is crying harder than before, sobbing uncontrollably, each jerking inhalation a deep unearthly groan). Phil says, "Oh honey, I hope we didn't make it worse for you."

Easter Saturday: Over lunch, I watch another funeral. My office windows overlook a graveyard as crowded and still as a rush-hour freeway. As I savor pizza and milk, I notice that one of the mourners is wearing an outfit featured in the window of Bloomingdale's (59th Street store) only since last weekend. This thread of recognition jolts me, and I am drawn to her in sorrow; the details of my own shopping history flash before my eyes as I reflect upon the sober spree that brought her to the rim of this earthly chasm, her slim suede heels sinking into the soft silt of the graveside.

Resurrection Sunday: John D., the bookkeeper where I used to work, died, hit on the head by a stray but forcefully propelled hockey puck. I cried copiously at his memorial service, only to discover, later that afternoon when I saw a black rimmed photograph, that I had been mourning the wrong person. I had cried because the man I *thought* had died is John D. the office messenger, a bitter unfriendly man who treats me with disdain; once I bought an old electric typewriter from him which never worked. Though he promised nothing, I have harbored deep dislike since then; death by hockey puck is only one of the fates I had imagined for him. I washed clean my guilt with buckets of tears at the news of what I thought was his demise.

The man who did die was small, shy, anonymously sweet-featured and innocent. In some odd way I was relieved; no seriously obligatory mourning to be done here. A quiet impassivity settled over me and I forgot my grief.

Holy communion

A few months after my godmother died, my Great Aunt Jag passed away in Cambridge, at ninety-six the youngest and the last of her siblings, all of whom died at ninety-seven. She collapsed on her way home from the polling place, having gotten in her vote for "yet another Kennedy." Her wake was much like the last family gathering at which I had seen her, two Thanksgivings ago. She was a little hard of hearing then and she stayed on the outer edge of the conversation, brightly, loudly, and randomly asserting enjoyment of her meal. At the wake, cousins, nephews, daughters-in-law, first wives, second husbands, great-grand-nieces gathered round her casket and got acquainted all over again. It was pouring rain outside. The funeral home was dry and warm, faintly spicily clean-smelling; the walls were solid, dark, respectable wood; the floors were cool stone tile. On the door of a room marked "No Admittance" was a sign that reminded workers therein of the reverence with which each body was held by its family and prayed employees handle the remains with similar love and care. Aunt Jag wore yellow chiffon; everyone agreed that laying her out with her glasses on was a nice touch.

Afterward, we all went to Legal Seafoods, her favorite restaurant, and ate many of her favorite foods.

On candor

Me

I have never been able to determine my horoscope with any degree of accuracy. Born at Boston's now-defunct Lying-In Hospital, I am a Virgo, despite a quite poetic soul. Knowledge of the *hour* of my birth, however, would determine not just my sun sign but my moons and all the more intimate specificities of my destiny. Once upon a time, I sent for my birth certificate, which was retrieved from the oblivion of Massachusetts microfiche. Said document revealed that an infant named Patricia Joyce, born of parents named Williams, was delivered into the world "colored." Since no one thought to put down the hour of my birth, I suppose that I will never know my true fate.

In the meantime, I read what text there is of me.

My name, Patricia, means patrician. Patricias are noble, lofty, elite, exclusively educated, and well mannered despite themselves. I was on the cusp of being Pamela, but my parents knew that such a me would require lawns, estates, and hunting dogs too.

I am also a Williams. Of William, whoever he was: an anonymous white man who owned my father's people and from whom some escaped. That rupture is marked by the dark-mooned mystery of utter silence.

Williams is the second most common surname in the United States; Patricia is *the* most common prename among women born in 1951, the year of my birth.

Them

In the law, rights are islands of empowerment. To be un-righted is to be disempowered, and the line between rights and no rights is most often the line between dominators and oppressors. Rights contain images of power, and manipulating those images, either visually or linguistically, is central in the making and maintenance of rights. In principle, therefore, the more dizzyingly diverse the images that are propagated, the more empowered we will be as a society.

In reality, it was a lovely polar bear afternoon. The gentle force of the earth. A wide wilderness of islands. A conspiracy of polar bears lost in timeless forgetting. A gentleness of polar bears, a fruitfulness of polar bears, a silent black-eyed interest of polar bears, a bristled expectancy of polar bears. With the wisdom of innocence, a child threw stones at the polar bears. Hungry, they rose from their nests, inquisitive, dark-souled, patient with foreboding, fearful in tremendous awakening. The instinctual ferocity of the hunter reflected upon the hunted. Then, proud teeth and warrior claws took innocence for wilderness and raging insubstantiality for tender rabbit breath.

In the newspapers the next day, it was reported that two polar bears in the Brooklyn Zoo mauled to death an eleven-year-old boy who had entered their cage to swim in the moat. The police were called and the bears were killed.[23]

In the public debate that ensued, many levels of meaning emerged. The rhetoric firmly established that the bears were innocent, naturally territorial, unfairly imprisoned, and guilty. The dead child (born into the urban jungle of a black, welfare mother and a Hispanic alcoholic father who had died literally in the gutter only six weeks before) was held to a similarly stern standard. The police were captured, in a widely disseminated photograph,[24] shooting helplessly, desperately, into the cage, through three levels of bars, at a pieta of bears; since this image, conveying much pathos, came nevertheless not in time to save the child, it was generally felt that the bears had died in vain.[25]

In the egalitarianism of exile, pluralists rose up as of one body, with a call to buy more bears, control juvenile delinquency, eliminate all zoos, and confine future police.[26]

[23] J. Barron, "Polar Bears Kill a Child at Prospect Park Zoo," *New York Times* (May 20, 1987), sec. A.

[24] *New York Post* (May 22, 1987), p. 1.

[25] J. Barron, "Officials Weigh Tighter Security at Zoos in Parks," *New York Times* (May 22, 1987), sec. B.

[26] Ibid.

In the plenary session of the national meeting of the Law and Society Association, the keynote speaker unpacked the whole incident as a veritable laboratory of emergent rights discourse. Just seeing that these complex levels of meaning exist, she exulted, should advance rights discourse significantly.[27]

At the funeral of the child, the presiding priest pronounced the death of Juan Perez not in vain, since he was saved from growing into "a lifetime of crime." Juan's Hispanic-welfare-black-widow-of-an-alcoholic mother decided then and there to sue.

The universe between

How I ended up at Dartmouth College for the summer is too long a story to tell. Anyway, there I was, sharing the town of Hanover, New Hampshire, with about two hundred prepubescent males enrolled in Dartmouth's summer basketball camp, an all-white, very expensive, affirmative action program for the street-deprived.

One fragrant evening, I was walking down East Wheelock Street when I encountered about a hundred of these adolescents, fresh from the courts, wet, lanky, big-footed, with fuzzy yellow crew cuts, loping toward Thayer Hall and food. In platoons of twenty-five or so, they descended upon me, jostling me, smacking me, and pushing me from the sidewalk into the gutter. In a thoughtless instant, I snatched off my brown silk headrag, my flag of African femininity and propriety, my sign of meek and supplicatory place and presentation. I released the armored rage of my short nappy hair (the scalp gleaming bare between the angry wire spikes) and hissed: "Don't I exist for you?! See Me! And deflect, godammit!" (The quaint professionalism of my formal English never allowed the rage in my head to rise so high as to overflow the edges of my text.)

They gave me wide berth. They clearly had no idea, however, that I was talking to them or about them. They skirted me sheepishly, suddenly polite, because they did know, when a crazed black person comes crashing into one's field of vision, that it is impolite to laugh. I stood tall and spoke loudly into their ranks: "I have my rights!" The Dartmouth Summer Basketball Camp raised its collective eyebrows and exhaled, with a certain tested nobility of exhaustion and solidarity.

I pursued my way, manumitted back into silence. I put distance between them and me, gave myself over to polar bear musings. I allowed myself to be watched over by bear spirits. Clean white wind and strong bear smells. The shadowed amnesia; the absence

[27] Patricia Williams, "The Meaning of Rights" (address to the annual meeting of the Law and Society Association, Washington, D.C., June 6, 1987).

of being; the presence of polar bears. White wilderness of icy meat-eaters heavy with remembrance; leaden with undoing; shaggy with the effort of hunting for silence; frozen in a web of intention and intuition. A lunacy of polar bears. A history of polar bears. A pride of polar bears. A consistency of polar bears. In those meandering pastel polar bear moments, I found cool fragments of white-fur invisibility. Solid, black-gummed, intent, observant. Hungry and patient, impassive and exquisitely timed. The brilliant bursts of exclusive territoriality. A complexity of messages implied in our being.

School of Law
City University of New York

CULTURAL FEMINISM VERSUS POST-STRUCTURALISM: THE IDENTITY CRISIS IN FEMINIST THEORY

LINDA ALCOFF

For many contemporary feminist theorists, the concept of woman is a problem. It is a problem of primary significance because the concept of woman is the central concept for feminist theory and yet it is a concept that is impossible to formulate precisely for feminists. It is the central concept for feminists because the concept and category of woman is the necessary point of departure for any feminist theory and feminist politics, predicated as these are on the transformation of women's lived experience in contemporary culture and the reevaluation of social theory and practice from women's point of view. But as a concept it is radically problematic precisely for feminists because it is crowded with the overdeterminations of male supremacy, invoking in every formulation the limit, contrasting Other, or mediated self-reflection of a culture built on the control of females. In attempting to speak for women, feminism often seems to presuppose that it knows what women truly are, but such an assumption is foolhardy given that every source of knowledge about

In writing this essay I have benefited immeasurably as a participant of the 1984–85 Pembroke Center Seminar on the Cultural Construction of Gender at Brown University. I would also like to thank Lynne Joyrich, Richard Schmitt, Denise Riley, Sandra Bartky, Naomi Scheman, and four anonymous reviewers for their helpful comments on an earlier draft of this paper.

This essay originally appeared in *Signs*, vol. 13, no. 3, Spring 1988.

women has been contaminated with misogyny and sexism. No matter where we turn—to historical documents, philosophical constructions, social scientific statistics, introspection, or daily practices—the mediation of female bodies into constructions of woman is dominated by misogynist discourse. For feminists, who must transcend this discourse, it appears we have nowhere to turn.[1]

Thus the dilemma facing feminist theorists today is that our very self-definition is grounded in a concept that we must deconstruct and de-essentialize in all of its aspects. Man has said that woman can be defined, delineated, captured—understood, explained, and diagnosed—to a level of determination never accorded to man himself, who is conceived as a rational animal with free will. Where man's behavior is underdetermined, free to construct its own future along the course of its rational choice, woman's nature has overdetermined her behavior, the limits of her intellectual endeavors, and the inevitabilities of her emotional journey through life. Whether she is construed as essentially immoral and irrational (à la Schopenhauer) or essentially kind and benevolent (à la Kant), she is always construed as an essential *something* inevitably accessible to direct intuited apprehension by males.[2] Despite the variety of ways in which man has construed her essential characteristics, she is always the Object, a conglomeration of attributes to be predicted and controlled along with other natural phenomena. The place of the free-willed subject who can transcend nature's mandates is reserved exclusively for men.[3]

Feminist thinkers have articulated two major responses to this situation over the last ten years. The first response is to claim that feminists have the exclusive right to describe and evaluate woman. Thus cultural feminists argue that the problem of male supremacist

[1] It may seem that we can solve this dilemma easily enough by simply defining woman as those with female anatomies, but the question remains, What is the significance, if any, of those anatomies? What is the connection between female anatomy and the concept of woman? It should be remembered that the dominant discourse does not include in the category woman everyone with a female anatomy: it is often said that aggressive, self-serving, or powerful women are not "true" or "real" women. Moreover, the problem cannot be avoided by simply rejecting the concept of "woman" while retaining the category of "women." If there are women, then there must exist a basis for the category and a criterion for inclusion within it. This criterion need not posit a universal, homogeneous essence, but there must be a criterion nonetheless.

[2] For Schopenhauer's, Kant's, and nearly every other major Western philosopher's conception of woman, and for an insight into just how contradictory and incoherent these are, see Linda Bell's excellent anthology, *Visions of Women* (Clifton, N.J.: Humana Press, 1983).

[3] For an interesting discussion of whether feminists should even seek such transcendence, see Genevieve Lloyd, *The Man of Reason* (Minneapolis: University of Minnesota Press, 1984), 86–102.

culture is the problem of a process in which women are defined by men, that is, by a group who has a contrasting point of view and set of interests from women, not to mention a possible fear and hatred of women. The result of this has been a distortion and devaluation of feminine characteristics, which now can be corrected by a more accurate feminist description and appraisal. Thus the cultural feminist reappraisal construes woman's passivity as her peacefulness, her sentimentality as her proclivity to nurture, her subjectiveness as her advanced self-awareness, and so forth. Cultural feminists have not challenged the defining of woman but only that definition given by men.

The second major response has been to reject the possibility of defining woman as such at all. Feminists who take this tactic go about the business of deconstructing all concepts of woman and argue that both feminist and misogynist attempts to define woman are politically reactionary and ontologically mistaken. Replacing woman-as-housewife with woman-as-supermom (or earth mother or super professional) is no advance. Using French post-structuralist theory these feminists argue that such errors occur because we are in fundamental ways duplicating misogynist strategies when we try to define women, characterize women, or speak for women, even though allowing for a range of differences within the gender. The politics of gender or sexual difference must be replaced with a plurality of difference where gender loses its position of significance.

Briefly put, then, the cultural feminist response to Simone de Beauvoir's question, "Are there women?" is to answer yes and to define women by their activities and attributes in the present culture. The post-structuralist response is to answer no and attack the category and the concept of woman through problematizing subjectivity. Each response has serious limitations, and it is becoming increasingly obvious that transcending these limitations while retaining the theoretical framework from which they emerge is impossible. As a result, a few brave souls are now rejecting these choices and attempting to map out a new course, a course that will avoid the major problems of the earlier responses. In this paper I will discuss some of the pioneer work being done to develop a new concept of woman and offer my own contribution toward it.[4] But first, I must spell out more clearly the inadequacies of the first two

[4] Feminist works I would include in this group but which I won't be able to discuss in this essay are Elizabeth L. Berg, "The Third Woman," *Diacritics* 12 (1982): 11–20; and Lynne Joyrich, "Theory and Practice: The Project of Feminist Criticism," unpublished manuscript (Brown University, 1984). Luce Irigaray's work may come to mind for some readers as another proponent of a third way, but for me Irigaray's emphasis on female anatomy makes her work border too closely on essentialism.

responses to the problem of woman and explain why I believe these inadequacies are inherent.

Cultural feminism

Cultural feminism is the ideology of a female nature or female essence reappropriated by feminists themselves in an effort to revalidate undervalued female attributes. For cultural feminists, the enemy of women is not merely a social system or economic institution or set of backward beliefs but masculinity itself and in some cases male biology. Cultural feminist politics revolve around creating and maintaining a healthy environment—free of masculinist values and all their offshoots such as pornography—for the female principle. Feminist theory, the explanation of sexism, and the justification of feminist demands can all be grounded securely and unambiguously on the concept of the essential female.

Mary Daly and Adrienne Rich have been influential proponents of this position.[5] Breaking from the trend toward androgyny and the minimizing of gender differences that was popular among feminists in the early seventies, both Daly and Rich argue for a returned focus on femaleness.

For Daly, male barrenness leads to parasitism on female energy, which flows from our life-affirming, life-creating biological condition: "Since female energy is essentially biophilic, the female spirit/body is the primary target in this perpetual war of aggression against life. Gyn/Ecology is the re-claiming of life-loving female energy."[6] Despite Daly's warnings against biological reductionism,[7] her own analysis of sexism uses gender-specific biological traits to explain male hatred for women. The childless state of "all males" leads to a dependency on women, which in turn leads men to "deeply identify with 'unwanted fetal tissue.' "[8] Given their state of fear and insecurity it becomes almost understandable, then, that men would desire to dominate and control that which is so vitally necessary to them: the life-energy of women. Female energy, conceived by Daly as a natural essence, needs to be freed from its male parasites, released for creative expression and recharged through bonding

[5] Although Rich has recently departed from this position and in fact begun to move in the direction of the concept of woman I will defend in this essay (Adrienne Rich, "Notes toward a Politics of Location," in her *Blood, Bread, and Poetry* [New York: Norton, 1986]).

[6] Mary Daly, *Gyn/Ecology* (Boston: Beacon, 1978), 355.

[7] Ibid., 60.

[8] Ibid., 59.

with other women. In this free space women's "natural" attributes of love, creativity, and the ability to nurture can thrive.

Women's identification as female is their defining essence for Daly, their haecceity, overriding any other way in which they may be defined or may define themselves. Thus Daly states: "Women who accept false inclusion among the fathers and sons are easily polarized against other women on the basis of ethnic, national, class, religious and other *male-defined differences*, applauding the defeat of 'enemy' women."[9] These differences are apparent rather than real, inessential rather than essential. The only real difference, the only difference that can change a person's ontological placement on Daly's dichotomous map, is sex difference. Our essence is defined here, in our sex, from which flow all the facts about us: who are our potential allies, who is our enemy, what are our objective interests, what is our true nature. Thus, Daly defines women again and her definition is strongly linked to female biology.

Many of Rich's writings have exhibited surprising similarities to Daly's position described above, surprising given their difference in style and temperament. Rich defines a "female consciousness"[10] that has a great deal to do with the female body.

> I have come to believe . . . that female biology—the diffuse, intense sensuality radiating out from clitoris, breasts, uterus, vagina; the lunar cycles of menstruation; the gestation and fruition of life which can take place in the female body—has far more radical implications than we have yet come to appreciate. Patriarchal thought has limited female biology to its own narrow specifications. The feminist vision has recoiled from female biology for these reasons; it will, I believe, come to view our physicality as a resource, rather than a destiny. . . . We must touch the unity and resonance of our physicality, our bond with the natural order, the corporeal ground of our intelligence.[11]

Thus Rich argues that we should not reject the importance of female biology simply because patriarchy has used it to subjugate us. Rich believes that "our biological grounding, the miracle and paradox of the female body and its spiritual and political meanings" holds the key to our rejuvenation and our reconnection with our specific female attributes, which she lists as "our great mental capacities . . . ; our highly developed tactile sense; our genius for close

[9] Ibid., 365 (my emphasis).
[10] Adrienne Rich, *On Lies, Secrets, and Silence* (New York: Norton, 1979), 18.
[11] Adrienne Rich, *Of Woman Born* (New York: Bantam, 1977), 21.

observation; our complicated, pain-enduring, multi-pleasured physicality."[12]

Rich further echoes Daly in her explanation of misogyny: "The ancient, continuing envy, awe and dread of the male for the female capacity to create life has repeatedly taken the form of hatred for every other female aspect of creativity."[13] Thus Rich, like Daly, identifies a female essence, defines patriarchy as the subjugation and colonization of this essence out of male envy and need, and then promotes a solution that revolves around rediscovering our essence and bonding with other women. Neither Rich nor Daly espouse biological reductionism, but this is because they reject the oppositional dichotomy of mind and body that such a reductionism presupposes. The female essence for Daly and Rich is not simply spiritual or simply biological—it is both. Yet the key point remains that it is our specifically female anatomy that is the primary constituent of our identity and the source of our female essence. Rich prophesies that "the repossession by women of our bodies will bring far more essential change to human society than the seizing of the means of production by workers. . . . In such a world women will truly create new life, bringing forth not only children (if and as we choose) but the visions, and the thinking, necessary to sustain, console and alter human existence—a new relationship to the universe. Sexuality, politics, intelligence, power, motherhood, work, community, intimacy will develop new meanings; thinking itself will be transformed."[14]

The characterization of Rich's and Daly's views as part of a growing trend within feminism toward essentialism has been developed most extensively by Alice Echols.[15] Echols prefers the name

[12] Ibid., 290.

[13] Ibid., 21.

[14] Ibid., 292. Three pages earlier Rich castigates the view that we need only release on the world women's ability to nurture in order to solve the world's problems, which may seem incongruous given the above passage. The two positions are consistent however: Rich is trying to correct the patriarchal conception of women as essentially nurturers with a view of women that is more complex and multifaceted. Thus, her essentialist conception of women is more comprehensive and complicated than the patriarchal one.

[15] See Alice Echols, "The New Feminism of Yin and Yang," in *Powers of Desire: The Politics of Sexuality,* ed. Ann Snitow, Christine Stansell, and Sharon Thompson (New York: Monthly Review Press, 1983), 439–59, and "The Taming of the Id: Feminist Sexual Politics, 1968–83," in *Pleasure and Danger: Exploring Female Sexuality,* ed. Carole S. Vance (Boston: Routledge & Kegan Paul, 1984), 50–72. Hester Eisenstein paints a similar picture of cultural feminism in her *Contemporary Feminist Thought* (Boston: G. K. Hall, 1983), esp. xvii–xix and 105–45. Josephine Donovan has traced the more recent cultural feminism analyzed by Echols and Eisenstein to the earlier matriarchal vision of feminists like Charlotte Perkins Gilman (Josephine Donovan, *Feminist Theory: The Intellectual Traditions of American Feminism* [New York: Ungar, 1985], esp. chap. 2).

"cultural feminism" for this trend because it equates "women's liberation with the development and preservation of a female counter culture."[16] Echols identifies cultural feminist writings by their denigration of masculinity rather than male roles or practices, by their valorization of female traits, and by their commitment to preserve rather than diminish gender differences. Besides Daly and Rich, Echols names Susan Griffin, Kathleen Barry, Janice Raymond, Florence Rush, Susan Brownmiller, and Robin Morgan as important cultural feminist writers, and she documents her claim persuasively by highlighting key passages of their work. Although Echols finds a prototype of this trend in early radical feminist writings by Valerie Solanis and Joreen, she is careful to distinguish cultural feminism from radical feminism as a whole. The distinguishing marks between the two include their position on the mutability of sexism among men, the connection drawn between biology and misogyny, and the degree of focus on valorized female attributes. As Hester Eisenstein has argued, there is a tendency within many radical feminist works toward setting up an ahistorical and essentialist conception of female nature, but this tendency is developed and consolidated by cultural feminists, thus rendering their work significantly different from radical feminism.

However, although cultural feminist views sharply separate female from male traits, they certainly do not all give explicitly essentialist formulations of what it means to be a woman. So it may seem that Echols's characterization of cultural feminism makes it appear too homogeneous and that the charge of essentialism is on shaky ground. On the issue of essentialism Echols states:

> This preoccupation with defining the female sensibility not only leads these feminists to indulge in dangerously erroneous generalizations about women, but to imply that this identity is innate rather than socially constructed. At best, there has been a curiously cavalier disregard for whether these differences are biological or cultural in origin. Thus Janice Raymond argues: "Yet there are differences, and some feminists have come to realize that those differences are important whether they spring from socialization, from biology, or from the total history of existing as a woman in a patriarchal society."[17]

Echols points out that the importance of the differences varies tremendously according to their source. If that source is innate, the cultural feminist focus on building an alternative feminist culture

[16] Echols, "The New Feminism of Yin and Yang," 441.
[17] Ibid., 440.

is politically correct. If the differences are not innate, the focus of our activism should shift considerably. In the absence of a clearly stated position on the ultimate source of gender difference, Echols infers from their emphasis on building a feminist free-space and woman-centered culture that cultural feminists hold some version of essentialism. I share Echols's suspicion. Certainly, it is difficult to render the views of Rich and Daly into a coherent whole without supplying a missing premise that there is an innate female essence.

Interestingly, I have not included any feminist writings from women of oppressed nationalities and races in the category of cultural feminism, nor does Echols. I have heard it argued that the emphasis placed on cultural identity by such writers as Cherríe Moraga and Audre Lorde reveals a tendency toward essentialism also. However, in my view their work has consistently rejected essentialist conceptions of gender. Consider the following passage from Moraga: "When you start to talk about sexism, the world becomes increasingly complex. The power no longer breaks down into neat little hierarchical categories, but becomes a series of starts and detours. Since the categories are not easy to arrive at, the enemy is not easy to name. It is all so difficult to unravel."[18] Moraga goes on to assert that "some men oppress the very women they love," implying that we need new categories and new concepts to describe such complex and contradictory relations of oppression. In this problematic understanding of sexism, Moraga seems to me light-years ahead of Daly's manichean ontology or Rich's romanticized conception of the female. The simultaneity of oppressions experienced by women such as Moraga resists essentialist conclusions. Universalist conceptions of female or male experiences and attributes are not plausible in the context of such a complex network of relations, and without an ability to universalize, the essentialist argument is difficult if not impossible to make. White women cannot be all good or all bad; neither can men from oppressed groups. I have simply not found writings by feminists who are oppressed also by race and/or class that place or position maleness wholly as Other. Reflected in their problematized understanding of masculinity is a richer and likewise problematized concept of woman.[19]

[18] Cherríe Moraga, "From a Long Line of Vendidas: Chicanas and Feminism," in *Feminist Studies/Critical Studies*, ed. Teresa de Lauretis (Bloomington: Indiana University Press, 1986), 180.

[19] See also Moraga, "From a Long Line of Vendidas," 187, and Cherríe Moraga, "La Guera," in *This Bridge Called My Back: Writings by Radical Women of Color*, ed. Cherríe Moraga and Gloria Anzaldúa (New York: Kitchen Table, 1983), 32–33; Barbara Smith, "Introduction," in *Home Girls: A Black Feminist Anthology*, ed. Barbara Smith (New York: Kitchen Table, 1983), xix–lvi; "The Combahee River Collective Statement," in Smith, ed., 272–82; Audre Lorde, "Age, Race, Class, and

Even if cultural feminism is the product of white feminists, it is not homogeneous, as Echols herself points out. The biological accounts of sexism given by Daly and Brownmiller, for example, are not embraced by Rush or Dworkin. But the key link between these feminists is their tendency toward invoking universalizing conceptions of woman and mother in an essentialist way. Therefore, despite the lack of complete homogeneity within the category, it seems still justifiable and important to identify (and criticize) within these sometimes disparate works their tendency to offer an essentialist response to misogyny and sexism through adopting a homogeneous, unproblematized, and ahistorical conception of woman.

One does not have to be influenced by French post-structuralism to disagree with essentialism. It is well documented that the innateness of gender differences in personality and character is at this point factually and philosophically indefensible.[20] There are a host of divergent ways gender divisions occur in different societies, and the differences that appear to be universal can be explained in nonessentialist ways. However, belief in women's innate peacefulness and ability to nurture has been common among feminists since the nineteenth century and has enjoyed a resurgence in the last decade, most notably among feminist peace activists. I have met scores of young feminists drawn to actions like the Women's Peace Encampment and to groups like Women for a Non-Nuclear Future by their belief that the maternal love women have for their children can unlock the gates of imperialist oppression. I have great respect for the self-affirming pride of these women, but I also share Echols's fear that their effect is to "reflect and reproduce dominant cultural assumptions about women," which not only fail to represent the variety in women's lives but promote unrealistic expectations about "normal" female behavior that most of us cannot satisfy.[21] Our gender categories are positively constitutive and not mere hindsight descriptions of previous activities. There is a self-perpetuating circularity between defining woman as essentially peaceful and nur-

---

Sex: Women Redefining Difference," in her *Sister Outsider* (Trumansburg, N.Y.: Crossing, 1984), 114–23; and bell hooks, *Feminist Theory: From Margin to Center* (Boston: South End, 1984). All of these works resist the universalizing tendency of cultural feminism and highlight the differences between women, and between men, in a way that undercuts arguments for the existence of an overarching gendered essence.

[20] There is a wealth of literature on this, but two good places to begin are Anne Fausto-Sterling, *Myths of Gender: Biological Theories about Women and Men* (New York: Basic, 1986); and Sherrie Ortner and Harriet Whitehead, eds., *Sexual Meanings: The Cultural Construction of Gender and Sexuality* (New York: Cambridge University Press, 1981).

[21] Echols, "The New Feminism of Yin and Yang," 440.

turing and the observations and judgments we shall make of future women and the practices we shall engage in as women in the future. Do feminists want to buy another ticket for women of the world on the merry-go-round of feminine constructions? Don't we want rather to get off the merry-go-round and run away?

This should not imply that the political effects of cultural feminism have all been negative.[22] The insistence on viewing traditional feminine characteristics from a different point of view, to use a "looking glass" perspective, as a means of engendering a gestalt switch on the body of data we all currently share about women, has had positive effect. After a decade of hearing liberal feminists advising us to wear business suits and enter the male world, it is a helpful corrective to have cultural feminists argue instead that women's world is full of superior virtues and values, to be credited and learned from rather than despised. Herein lies the positive impact of cultural feminism. And surely much of their point is well taken, that it was our mothers who made our families survive, that women's handiwork is truly artistic, that women's care-giving really is superior in value to male competitiveness.

Unfortunately, however, the cultural feminist championing of a redefined "womanhood" cannot provide a useful long-range program for a feminist movement and, in fact, places obstacles in the way of developing one. Under conditions of oppression and restrictions on freedom of movement, women, like other oppressed groups, have developed strengths and attributes that should be correctly credited, valued, and promoted. What we should not promote, however, are the restrictive conditions that gave rise to those attributes: forced parenting, lack of physical autonomy, dependency for survival on mediation skills, for instance. What conditions for women do we want to promote? A freedom of movement such that we can compete in the capitalist world alongside men? A continued restriction to child-centered activities? To the extent cultural feminism merely valorizes genuinely positive attributes developed under oppression, it cannot map our future long-range course. To the extent that it reinforces essentialist explanations of these attributes, it is in danger of solidifying an important bulwark for sexist oppression: the belief in an innate "womanhood" to which we must all adhere lest we be deemed either inferior or not "true" women.

[22] Hester Eisenstein's treatment of cultural feminism, though critical, is certainly more two-sided than Echols's. While Echols apparently sees only the reactionary results of cultural feminism, Eisenstein sees in it a therapeutic self-affirmation necessary to offset the impact of a misogynist culture (see Eisenstein [n. 15 above]).

Post-structuralism

For many feminists, the problem with the cultural feminist response to sexism is that it does not criticize the fundamental mechanism of oppressive power used to perpetuate sexism and in fact reinvokes that mechanism in its supposed solution. The mechanism of power referred to here is the construction of the subject by a discourse that weaves knowledge and power into a coercive structure that "forces the individual back on himself and ties him to his own identity in a constraining way."[23] On this view, essentialist formulations of womanhood, even when made by feminists, "tie" the individual to her identity as a woman and thus cannot represent a solution to sexism.

This articulation of the problem has been borrowed by feminists from a number of recently influential French thinkers who are sometimes called post-structuralist but who also might be called post-humanist and post-essentialist. Lacan, Derrida, and Foucault are the front-runners in this group. Disparate as these writers are, their (one) common theme is that the self-contained, authentic subject conceived by humanism to be discoverable below a veneer of cultural and ideological overlay is in reality a construct of that very humanist discourse. The subject is not a locus of authorial intentions or natural attributes or even a privileged, separate consciousness. Lacan uses psychoanalysis, Derrida uses grammar, and Foucault uses the history of discourses all to attack and "deconstruct"[24] our concept of the subject as having an essential identity and an authentic core that has been repressed by society. There is no essential core "natural" to us, and so there is no repression in the humanist sense.

There is an interesting sort of neodeterminism in this view. The subject or self is never determined by biology in such a way that

[23] Michel Foucault, "Why Study Power: The Question of the Subject," in *Beyond Structuralism and Hermeneutics: Michel Foucault*, ed. Hubert L. Dreyfus and Paul Rabinow, 2d ed. (Chicago: University of Chicago Press, 1983), 212.

[24] This term is principally associated with Derrida for whom it refers specifically to the process of unraveling metaphors in order to reveal their underlying logic, which usually consists of a simple binary opposition such as between man/woman, subject/object, culture/nature, etc. Derrida has demonstrated that within such oppositions one side is always superior to the other side, such that there is never any pure difference without domination. The term "deconstruction" has also come to mean more generally any exposure of a concept as ideological or culturally constructed rather than natural or a simple reflection of reality (see Derrida, *Of Grammatology*, trans. G. Spivak [Baltimore: Johns Hopkins University Press, 1976]; also helpful is Jonathan Culler's *On Deconstruction* [Ithaca, N.Y.: Cornell University Press, 1982]).

human history is predictable or even explainable, and there is no unilinear direction of a determinist arrow pointing from some fairly static, "natural" phenomena to human experience. On the other hand, this rejection of biological determinism is not grounded in the belief that human subjects are underdetermined but, rather, in the belief that we are overdetermined (i.e., constructed) by a social discourse and/or cultural practice. The idea here is that we individuals really have little choice in the matter of who we are, for as Derrida and Foucault like to remind us, individual motivations and intentions count for nil or almost nil in the scheme of social reality. We are constructs—that is, our experience of our very subjectivity is a construct mediated by and/or grounded on a social discourse beyond (way beyond) individual control. As Foucault puts it, we are bodies "totally imprinted by history."[25] Thus, subjective experiences are determined in some sense by macro forces. However, these macro forces, including social discourses and social practices, are apparently not overdetermined, resulting as they do from such a complex and unpredictable network of overlapping and crisscrossing elements that no unilinear directionality is perceivable and in fact no final or efficient cause exists. There may be, and Foucault hoped at one point to find them,[26] perceivable processes of change within the social network, but beyond schematic rules of thumb neither the form nor the content of discourse has a fixed or unified structure or can be predicted or mapped out via an objectified, ultimate realm. To some extent, this view is similar to contemporary methodological individualism, whose advocates will usually concede that the complex of human intentions results in a social reality bearing no resemblance to the summarized categories of intentions but looking altogether different than any one party or sum of parties ever envisaged and desired. The difference, however, is that while methodological individualists admit that human intentions are ineffective, post-structuralists deny not only the efficacy but also the ontological autonomy and even the existence of intentionality.

Post-structuralists unite with Marx in asserting the social dimension of individual traits and intentions. Thus, they say we cannot understand society as the conglomerate of individual intentions but, rather, must understand individual intentions as constructed within a social reality. To the extent post-structuralists emphasize social explanations of individual practices and experiences I find their work illuminating and persuasive. My disagreement occurs,

[25] Michel Foucault, "Nietzsche, Genealogy, History," in *The Foucault Reader*, ed. Paul Rabinow (New York: Pantheon, 1984), 83.

[26] This hope is evident in Michel Foucault's *The Order of Things: An Archaeology of the Human Sciences* (New York: Random House, 1973).

however, when they seem totally to erase any room for maneuver by the individual within a social discourse or set of institutions. It is that totalization of history's imprint that I reject. In their defense of a total construction of the subject, post-structuralists deny the subject's ability to reflect on the social discourse and challenge its determinations.

Applied to the concept of woman the post-structuralist's view results in what I shall call nominalism: the idea that the category "woman" is a fiction and that feminist efforts must be directed toward dismantling this fiction. "Perhaps . . . 'woman' is not a determinable identity. Perhaps woman is not some thing which announces itself from a distance, at a distance from some other thing. . . . Perhaps woman—a non-identity, non-figure, a simulacrum—is distance's very chasm, the out-distancing of distance, the interval's cadence, distance itself."[27] Derrida's interest in feminism stems from his belief, expressed above, that woman may represent the rupture in the functional discourse of what he calls logocentrism, an essentialist discourse that entails hierarchies of difference and a Kantian ontology. Because woman has in a sense been excluded from this discourse, it is possible to hope that she might provide a real source of resistance. But her resistance will not be at all effective if she continues to use the mechanism of logocentrism to redefine woman: she can be an effective resister only if she drifts and dodges all attempts to capture her. Then, Derrida hopes, the following futuristic picture will come true: "Out of the depths, endless and unfathomable, she engulfs and distorts all vestige of essentiality, of identity, of property. And the philosophical discourse, blinded, founders on these shoals and is hurled down these depths to its ruin."[28] For Derrida, women have always been defined as a subjugated difference within a binary opposition: man/woman, culture/nature, positive/negative, analytical/intuitive. To assert an essential gender difference as cultural feminists do is to reinvoke this oppositional structure. The only way to break out of this structure, and in fact to subvert the structure itself, is to assert total difference, to be that which cannot be pinned down or subjugated within a dichotomous hierarchy. Paradoxically, it is to be what is not. Thus feminists cannot demarcate a definitive category of "woman" without eliminating all possibility for the defeat of logocentrism and its oppressive power.

Foucault similarly rejects all constructions of oppositional subjects—whether the "proletariat," "woman," or "the oppressed"—as

[27] Jacques Derrida, *Spurs*, trans. Barbara Harlow (Chicago: University of Chicago Press, 1978), 49.

[28] Ibid., 51.

mirror images that merely recreate and sustain the discourse of power. As Biddy Martin points out, "The point from which Foucault deconstructs is off-center, out of line, apparently unaligned. It is not the point of an imagined absolute otherness, but an 'alterity' which understands itself as an internal exclusion."[29]

Following Foucault and Derrida, an effective feminism could only be a wholly negative feminism, deconstructing everything and refusing to construct anything. This is the position Julia Kristeva adopts, herself an influential French post-structuralist. She says: "A woman cannot be; it is something which does not even belong in the order of being. *It follows that a feminist practice can only be negative*, at odds with what already exists so that we may say 'that's not it' and 'that's still not it.' "[30] The problematic character of subjectivity does not mean, then, that there can be no political struggle, as one might surmise from the fact that post-structuralism deconstructs the position of the revolutionary in the same breath as it deconstructs the position of the reactionary. But the political struggle can have only a "negative function," rejecting "everything finite, definite, structured, loaded with meaning, in the existing state of society."[31]

The attraction of the post-structuralist critique of subjectivity for feminists is two-fold. First, it seems to hold out the promise of an increased freedom for women, the "free play" of a plurality of differences unhampered by any predetermined gender identity as formulated by either patriarchy or cultural feminism. Second, it moves decisively beyond cultural feminism and liberal feminism in further theorizing what they leave untouched: the construction of subjectivity. We can learn a great deal here about the mechanisms of sexist oppression and the construction of specific gender categories by relating these to social discourse and by conceiving of the subject as a cultural product. Certainly, too, this analysis can help us understand right-wing women, the reproduction of ideology, and the mechanisms that block social progress. However, adopting nominalism creates significant problems for feminism. How can we seriously adopt Kristeva's plan for only negative struggle? As the Left should by now have learned, you cannot mobilize a movement that is only and al-

[29] Biddy Martin, "Feminism, Criticism, and Foucault," *New German Critique* 27 (1982): 11.

[30] Julia Kristeva, "Woman Can Never Be Defined," in *New French Feminisms*, ed. Elaine Marks and Isabelle de Courtivron (New York: Schocken, 1981), 137 (my italics).

[31] Julia Kristeva, "Oscillation between Power and Denial," in Marks and Courtivron, eds., 166.

ways against: you must have a positive alternative, a vision of a better future that can motivate people to sacrifice their time and energy toward its realization. Moreover, a feminist adoption of nominalism will be confronted with the same problem theories of ideology have, that is, Why is a right-wing woman's consciousness constructed via social discourse but a feminist's consciousness not? Post-structuralist critiques of subjectivity pertain to the construction of all subjects or they pertain to none. And here is precisely the dilemma for feminists: How can we ground a feminist politics that deconstructs the female subject? Nominalism threatens to wipe out feminism itself.

Some feminists who wish to use post-structuralism are well aware of this danger. Biddy Martin, for example, points out that "we cannot afford to refuse to take a political stance 'which pins us to our sex' for the sake of an abstract theoretical correctness. . . . There is the danger that Foucault's challenges to traditional categories, if taken to a 'logical' conclusion . . . could make the question of women's oppression obsolete."[32] Based on her articulation of the problem with Foucault we are left hopeful that Martin will provide a solution that transcends nominalism. Unfortunately, in her reading of Lou Andreas-Salome, Martin valorizes undecidability, ambiguity, and elusiveness and intimates that by maintaining the undecidability of identity the life of Andreas-Salome provides a text from which feminists can usefully learn.[33]

However, the notion that all texts are undecidable cannot be useful for feminists. In support of his contention that the meaning of texts is ultimately undecidable, Derrida offers us in *Spurs* three conflicting but equally warranted interpretations of how Nietzsche's texts construct and position the female. In one of these interpretations Derrida argues we can find purportedly feminist propositions.[34] Thus, Derrida seeks to demonstrate that even the seemingly incontrovertible interpretation of Nietzsche's works as misogynist can be challenged by an equally convincing argument that they are not. But how can this be helpful to feminists, who need to have their accusations of misogyny validated rather than rendered "undecidable"? The point is not that Derrida himself is antifeminist, nor that there is nothing at all in Derrida's work that can be useful for feminists. But the thesis of undecidability as it is applied in the case of Nietzsche sounds too much like yet another version of the antifeminist argument that our perception of sexism is based on a skewed, limited perspective and that what we take to be misogyny is in reality helpful rather than hurtful to the cause of women. The

[32] Martin, 16–17.
[33] Ibid., esp. 21, 24, and 29.
[34] See Derrida, *Spurs*, esp. 57 and 97.

declaration of undecidability must inevitably return us to Kristeva's position, that we can give only negative answers to the question, What is a woman? If the category "woman" is fundamentally undecidable, then we can offer no positive conception of it that is immune to deconstruction, and we are left with a feminism that can be only deconstructive and, thus, nominalist once again.[35]

A nominalist position on subjectivity has the deleterious effect of de-gendering our analysis, of in effect making gender invisible once again. Foucault's ontology includes only bodies and pleasures, and he is notorious for not including gender as a category of analysis. If gender is simply a social construct, the need and even the possibility of a feminist politics becomes immediately problematic. What can we demand in the name of women if "women" do not exist and demands in their name simply reinforce the myth that they do? How can we speak out against sexism as detrimental to the interests of women if the category is a fiction? How can we demand legal abortions, adequate child care, or wages based on comparable worth without invoking a concept of "woman"?

Post-structuralism undercuts our ability to oppose the dominant trend (and, one might argue, the dominant danger) in mainstream Western intellectual thought, that is, the insistence on a universal, neutral, perspectiveless epistemology, metaphysics, and ethics. Despite rumblings from the Continent, Anglo-American thought is still wedded to the idea(l) of a universalizable, apolitical methodology and set of transhistorical basic truths unfettered by associations with particular genders, races, classes, or cultures. The rejection of subjectivity, unintentionally but nevertheless, colludes with this "generic human" thesis of classical liberal thought, that particularities of individuals are irrelevant and improper influences on knowledge. By designating individual particularities such as subjective experience as a social construct, post-structuralism's negation of the authority of the subject coincides nicely with the classical liberal's view that human particularities are irrelevant. (For the liberal, race, class, and gender are ultimately irrelevant to questions of justice and truth because "underneath we are all the same." For the post-

[35] Martin's most recent work departs from this in a positive direction. In an essay coauthored with Chandra Talpade Mohanty, Martin points out "the political limitations of an insistence on 'indeterminacy' which implicitly, when not explicitly, denies the critic's own situatedness in the social, and in effect refuses to acknowledge the critic's own institutional home." Martin and Mohanty seek to develop a more positive, though still problematized, conception of the subject as having a "multiple and shifting" perspective. In this, their work becomes a significant contribution toward the development of an alternative conception of subjectivity, a conception not unlike the one that I will discuss in the rest of this essay ("Feminist Politics: What's Home Got to Do with It?" in Lauretis, ed. [n. 18 above], 191–212, esp. 194).

structuralist, race, class, and gender are constructs and, therefore, incapable of decisively validating conceptions of justice and truth because underneath there lies no natural core to build on or liberate or maximize. Hence, once again, underneath we are all the same.) It is, in fact, a desire to topple this commitment to the possibility of a worldview—purported in fact as the best of all possible worldviews—grounded in a generic human, that motivates much of the cultural feminist glorification of femininity as a valid specificity legitimately grounding feminist theory.[36]

The preceding characterizations of cultural feminism and post-structuralist feminism will anger many feminists by assuming too much homogeneity and by blithely pigeonholing large and complex theories. However, I believe the tendencies I have outlined toward essentialism and toward nominalism represent the main, current responses by feminist theory to the task of reconceptualizing "woman." Both responses have significant advantages and serious shortcomings. Cultural feminism has provided a useful corrective to the "generic human" thesis of classical liberalism and has promoted community and self-affirmation, but it cannot provide a long-range future course of action for feminist theory or practice, and it is founded on a claim of essentialism that we are far from having the evidence to justify. The feminist appropriation of post-structuralism has provided suggestive insights on the construction of female and male subjectivity and has issued a crucial warning against creating a feminism that reinvokes the mechanisms of oppressive power. Nonetheless, it limits feminism to the negative tactics of reaction and deconstruction and endangers the attack against classical liberalism by discrediting the notion of an epistemologically significant, specific subjectivity. What's a feminist to do?

We cannot simply embrace the paradox. In order to avoid the serious disadvantages of cultural feminism and post-structuralism, feminism needs to transcend the dilemma by developing a third course, an alternative theory of the subject that avoids both essentialism and nominalism. This new alternative might share the post-structuralist insight that the category "woman" needs to be theorized through an exploration of the experience of subjectivity, as opposed to a description of current attributes, but it need not concede that such an exploration will necessarily result in a nominalist position on gender, or an erasure of it. Feminists need to explore

[36] A wonderful exchange on this between persuasive and articulate representatives of both sides was printed in *Diacritics* (Peggy Kamuf, "Replacing Feminist Criticism," *Diacritics* 12 [1982]: 42–47; and Nancy Miller, "The Text's Heroine: A Feminist Critic and Her Fictions," *Diacritics* 12 [1982]: 48–53).

the possibility of a theory of the gendered subject that does not slide into essentialism. In the following two sections I will discuss recent work that makes a contribution to the development of such a theory, or so I shall argue, and in the final section I will develop my own contribution in the form of a concept of gendered identity as positionality.

Teresa de Lauretis

Lauretis's influential book, *Alice Doesn't,* is a series of essays organized around an exploration of the problem of conceptualizing woman as subject. This problem is formulated in her work as arising out of the conflict between "woman" as a "fictional construct" and "women" as "real historical beings."[37] She says: "The relation between women as historical subjects and the notion of woman as it is produced by hegemonic discourses is neither a direct relation of identity, a one-to-one correspondence, nor a relation of simple implication. Like all other relations expressed in language, it is an arbitrary and symbolic one, that is to say, culturally set up. The manner and effects of that set-up are what the book intends to explore."[38] The strength of Lauretis's approach is that she never loses sight of the political imperative of feminist theory and, thus, never forgets that we must seek not only to describe this relation in which women's subjectivity is grounded but also to change it. And yet, given her view that we are constructed via a semiotic discourse, this political mandate becomes a crucial problem. As she puts it, "Paradoxically, the only way to position oneself outside of that discourse is to displace oneself within it—to refuse the question as formulated, or to answer deviously (though in its words), even to quote (but against the grain). The limit posed but not worked through in this book is thus the contradiction of feminist theory itself, at once excluded from discourse and imprisoned within it."[39] As with feminist theory, so, too, is the female subject "at once excluded from discourse and imprisoned within it." Constructing a theory of the subject that both concedes these truths and yet allows for the possibility of feminism is the problem Lauretis tackles throughout *Alice Doesn't.* To concede the construction of the subject via discourse entails that the feminist project cannot be simply "how to make visible the invisible" as if the essence of gender were

[37] Teresa de Lauretis, *Alice Doesn't* (Bloomington: Indiana University Press, 1984), 5.

[38] Ibid., 5–6.

[39] Ibid., 7.

out there waiting to be recognized by the dominant discourse. Yet Lauretis does not give up on the possibility of producing "the conditions of visibility for a different social subject."[40] In her view, a nominalist position on subjectivity can be avoided by linking subjectivity to a Peircean notion of practices and a further theorized notion of experience.[41] I shall look briefly at her discussion of this latter claim.

Lauretis's main thesis is that subjectivity, that is, what one "perceives and comprehends as subjective," is constructed through a continuous process, an ongoing constant renewal based on an interaction with the world, which she defines as experience: "And thus [subjectivity] is produced not by external ideas, values, or material causes, but by one's personal, subjective engagement in the practices, discourses, and institutions that lend significance (value, meaning, and affect) to the events of the world."[42] This is the process through which one's subjectivity becomes en-gendered. But describing the subjectivity that emerges is still beset with difficulties, principally the following: "The feminist efforts have been more often than not caught in the logical trap set up by [a] paradox. Either they have assumed that 'the subject,' like 'man,' is a generic term, and as such can designate equally and at once the female and male subjects, with the result of erasing sexuality and sexual difference from subjectivity. Or else they have been obliged to resort to an oppositional notion of 'feminine' subject defined by silence, negativity, a natural sexuality, or a closeness to nature not compromised by patriarchal culture."[43] Here again is spelled out the dilemma between a post-structuralist genderless subject and a cultural feminist essentialized subject. As Lauretis points out, the latter alternative is constrained in its conceptualization of the female subject by the very act of distinguishing female from male subjectivity. This appears to produce a dilemma, for if we de-gender subjectivity, we are committed to a generic subject and thus undercut feminism, while on the other hand if we define the subject in terms of gender, articulating female subjectivity in a space clearly distinct from male subjectivity, then we become caught up in an oppositional dichotomy controlled by a misogynist discourse. A gender-bound subjectivity seems to force us to revert "women to the body and to sexuality as an immediacy of the biological, as nature."[44] For all her insistence on a subjectivity constructed through practices, Lauretis is clear

[40] Ibid., 8–9.
[41] Ibid., 11.
[42] Ibid., 159.
[43] Ibid., 161.
[44] Ibid.

that *that* conception of subjectivity is not what she wishes to propose. A subjectivity that is fundamentally shaped by gender appears to lead irrevocably to essentialism, the posing of a male/female opposition as universal and ahistorical. A subjectivity that is not fundamentally shaped by gender appears to lead to the conception of a generic human subject, as if we could peel away our "cultural" layers and get to the real root of human nature, which turns out to be genderless. Are these really our only choices?

In *Alice Doesn't* Lauretis develops the beginnings of a new conception of subjectivity. She argues that subjectivity is neither (over)determined by biology nor by "free, rational, intentionality" but, rather, by experience, which she defines (via Lacan, Eco, and Peirce) as "a complex of habits resulting from the semiotic interaction of 'outer world' and 'inner world,' the continuous engagement of a self or subject in social reality."[45] Given this definition, the question obviously becomes, Can we ascertain a "female experience"? This is the question Lauretis prompts us to consider, more specifically, to analyze "that complex of habits, dispositions, associations and perceptions, which en-genders one as female."[46] Lauretis ends her book with an insightful observation that can serve as a critical starting point:

> This is where the specificity of a feminist theory may be sought: not in femininity as a privileged nearness to nature, the body, or the unconscious, an essence which inheres in women but to which males too now lay a claim; not in female tradition simply understood as private, marginal, and yet intact, outside of history but fully there to be discovered or recovered; not, finally, in the chinks and cracks of masculinity, the fissures of male identity or the repressed of phallic discourse; *but rather in that political, theoretical, self-analyzing practice* by which the relations of the subject in social reality can be rearticulated from the historical experience of women. Much, very much, is still to be done.[47]

Thus Lauretis asserts that the way out of the totalizing imprint of history and discourse is through our "political, theoretical self-

[45] Ibid., 182. The principal texts Lauretis relies on in her exposition of Lacan, Eco, and Peirce are Jacques Lacan, *Ecrits* (Paris: Seuil, 1966); Umberto Eco, *A Theory of Semiotics* (Bloomington: Indiana University Press, 1976), and *The Role of the Reader: Explorations in the Semiotic of Texts* (Bloomington: Indiana University Press, 1979); and Charles Sanders Peirce, *Collected Papers*, vols. 1–8 (Cambridge, Mass.: Harvard University Press, 1931–58).

[46] Lauretis, *Alice Doesn't* (n. 37 above), 182.

[47] Ibid., 186 (my italics).

analyzing practice." This should not be taken to imply that only intellectual articles in academic journals represent a free space or ground for maneuver but, rather, that all women can (and do) think about, criticize, and alter discourse and, thus, that subjectivity can be reconstructed through the process of reflective practice. The key component of Lauretis's formulation is the dynamic she poses at the heart of subjectivity: a fluid interaction in constant motion and open to alteration by self-analyzing practice.

Recently, Lauretis has taken off from this point and developed further her conception of subjectivity. In the introductory essay for her latest book, *Feminist Studies/Critical Studies*, Lauretis claims that an individual's identity is constituted with a historical process of consciousness, a process in which one's history "is interpreted or reconstructed by each of us within the horizon of meanings and knowledges available in the culture at given historical moments, a horizon that also includes modes of political commitment and struggle. . . . Consciousness, therefore, is never fixed, never attained once and for all, because discursive boundaries change with historical conditions."[48] Here Lauretis guides our way out of the dilemma she articulated for us in *Alice Doesn't*. The agency of the subject is made possible through this process of political interpretation. And what emerges is multiple and shifting, neither "prefigured . . . in an unchangeable symbolic order" nor merely "fragmented, or intermittent."[49] Lauretis formulates a subjectivity that gives agency to the individual while at the same time placing her within "particular discursive configurations" and, moreover, conceives of the process of consciousness as a strategy. Subjectivity may thus become imbued with race, class, and gender without being subjected to an overdetermination that erases agency.

Denise Riley

Denise Riley's *War in the Nursery: Theories of the Child and Mother* is an attempt to conceptualize women in a way that avoids what she calls the biologism/culturalist dilemma: that women must be either biologically determined or entirely cultural constructs. Both of these approaches to explaining sexual difference have been theoretically and empirically deficient, Riley claims. Biological deterministic accounts fail to problematize the concepts they use, for example, "biology," "nature," and "sex" and attempt to reduce

[48] Lauretis, ed. (n. 18 above), 8.
[49] Ibid., 9.

"everything to the workings of a changeless biology."[50] On the other hand, the "usual corrective to biologism"[51]—the feminist-invoked cultural construction thesis—"ignores the fact that there really is biology, which must be conceived more clearly" and moreover "only substitutes an unbounded sphere of social determination for that of biological determination."[52]

In her attempt to avoid the inadequacies of these approaches, Riley states: "The tactical problem is in naming and specifying sexual difference where it has been ignored or misread; but without doing so in a way which guarantees it an eternal life of its own, a lonely trajectory across infinity which spreads out over the whole of being and the whole of society—as if the chance of one's gendered conception mercilessly guaranteed every subsequent facet of one's existence at all moments."[53] Here I take Riley's project to be an attempt to conceptualize the subjectivity of woman as a gendered subject, without essentializing gender such that it takes on "an eternal life of its own"; to avoid both the denial of sexual difference (nominalism) and an essentializing of sexual difference.

Despite this fundamental project, Riley's analysis in this book is mainly centered on the perceivable relations between social policies, popularized psychologies, the state, and individual practices, and she does not often ascend to the theoretical problem of conceptions of woman. What she does do is proceed with her historical and sociological analysis *without ever losing sight of the need to problematize her key concepts*, for example, woman and mother. In this she provides an example, the importance of which cannot be overestimated. Moreover, Riley discusses in her last chapter a useful approach to the political tension that can develop between the necessity of problematizing concepts on the one hand and justifying political action on the other.

In analyzing the pros and cons of various social policies, Riley tries to take a feminist point of view. Yet any such discussion must necessarily presuppose, even if it is not openly acknowledged, that needs are identifiable and can therefore be used as a yardstick in evaluating social policies. The reality is, however, that needs are terribly difficult to identify, since most if not all theories of need rely on some naturalist conception of the human agent, an agent who either can consciously identify and state all of her or his needs or whose "real" needs can be ascertained by some external process

[50] Denise Riley, *War in the Nursery: Theories of the Child and Mother* (London: Virago, 1983), 2.

[51] Ibid., 6.

[52] Ibid., 2, 3.

[53] Ibid., 4.

of analysis. Either method produces problems: it seems unrealistic to say that only if the agent can identify and articulate specific needs do the needs exist, and yet there are obvious dangers to relying on "experts" or others to identify the needs of an individual. Further, it is problematic to conceptualize the human agent as having needs in the same way that a table has properties, since the human agent is an entity in flux in a way that the table is not and is subject to forces of social construction that affect her subjectivity and thus her needs. Utilitarian theorists, especially desire and welfare utilitarian theorists, are particularly vulnerable to this problem, since the standard of moral evaluation they advocate using is precisely needs (or desires, which are equally problematic).[54] Feminist evaluations of social policy that use a concept of "women's needs" must run into the same difficulty. Riley's approach to this predicament is as follows: "I've said that people's needs obviously can't be revealed by a simple process of historical unveiling, while elsewhere I've talked about the 'real needs' of mothers myself. I take it that it's necessary both to stress the non-self-evident nature of need and the intricacies of its determinants, and also to act politically as if needs could be met, or at least met half-way."[55] Thus Riley asserts the possibility and even the necessity of combining decisively formulated political demands with an acknowledgment of their essentialist danger. How can this be done without weakening our political struggle?

On the one hand, as Riley argues, the logic of concrete demands does not entail a commitment to essentialism. She says: "Even though it is true that arguing for adequate childcare as one obvious way of meeting the needs of mothers does suppose an orthodox division of labor, in which responsibility for children is the province of women and not of men, nevertheless this division is what, by and large, actually obtains. Recognition of that in no way commits you to supposing that the care of children is fixed eternally as female."[56] We need not invoke a rhetoric of idealized motherhood to demand that women here and now need child care. On the other hand, the entire corpus of Riley's work on social policies is dedicated to demonstrating the dangers that such demands can entail. She explains these as follows: "Because the task of illuminating 'the needs of mothers' starts out with gender at its most decisive and inescapable point—the biological capacity to bear children—

[54] For a lucid discussion of just how difficult this problem is for utilitarians, see Jon Elster, "Sour Grapes—Utilitarianism and the Genesis of Wants," in *Utilitarianism and Beyond*, ed. Amartya Sen and Bernard Williams (Cambridge: Cambridge University Press, 1982), 219–38.

[55] Riley, 193–94.

[56] Ibid., 194.

there's the danger that it may fall back into a conservative restating and confirming of social-sexual difference as timeless too. This would entail making the needs of mothers into fixed properties of 'motherhood' as a social function: I believe this is what happened in postwar Britain."[57] Thus, invoking the demands of women with children also invokes the companion belief in our cultural conception of essentialized motherhood.

As a way of avoiding this particular pitfall, Riley recommends against deploying any version of "motherhood" *as such.* I take it that what Riley means here is that we can talk about the needs of women with children and of course refer to these women as mothers but that we should eschew all reference to the idealized institution of motherhood as women's privileged vocation or the embodiment of an authentic or natural female practice.

The light that Riley sheds on our problem of woman's subjectivity is three-fold. First, and most obviously, she articulates the problem clearly and deals with it head on. Second, she shows us a way of approaching child-care demands without essentializing femininity, that is, by keeping it clear that these demands represent only current and not universal or eternal needs of women and by avoiding invocations of motherhood altogether. Third, she demands that our problematizing of concepts like "women's needs" coexist alongside a political program of demands in the name of women, without either countermanding the other. This is not to embrace the paradox but, rather, to call for a new understanding of subjectivity that can bring into harmony both our theoretical and our political agendas.

Denise Riley presents a useful approach to the political dimension of the problem of conceptualizing woman by discussing ways to avoid essentialist political demands. She reminds us that we should not avoid political action because our theory has uncovered chinks in the formulation of our key concepts.

A concept of positionality

Let me state initially that my approach to the problem of subjectivity is to treat it as a metaphysical problem rather than an empirical one. For readers coming from a post-structuralist tradition this statement will require immediate clarification. Continental philosophers from Nietzsche to Derrida have rejected the discipline of meta-

[57] Ibid., 194–95.

physics in toto because they say it assumes a naive ontological connection between knowledge and a reality conceived as a thing-in-itself, totally independent of human practices and methodology. Echoing the logical positivists here, these philosophers have claimed that metaphysics is nothing but an exercise in mystification, presuming to make knowledge claims about such things as souls and "necessary" truths that we have no way of justifying. Perhaps the bottom line criticism has been that metaphysics defines truth in such a way that it is impossible to attain, and then claims to have attained it. I agree that we should reject the metaphysics of transcendent things-in-themselves and the presumption to make claims about the noumena, but this involves a rejection of a specific ontology of truth and particular tradition in the history of metaphysics and not a rejection of metaphysics itself. If metaphysics is conceived not as any particular ontological commitment but as the attempt to reason through ontological issues that cannot be decided empirically, then metaphysics continues today in Derrida's analysis of language, Foucault's conception of power, and all of the post-structuralist critiques of humanist theories of the subject. Thus, on this view, the assertion that someone is "doing metaphysics" does not serve as a pejorative. There are questions of importance to human beings that science alone cannot answer (including what science is and how it functions), and yet these are questions that we can usefully address by combining scientific data with other logical, political, moral, pragmatic, and coherence considerations. The distinction between what is normative and what is descriptive breaks down here. Metaphysical problems are problems that concern factual claims about the world (rather than simply expressive, moral, or aesthetic assertions, e.g.) but are problems that cannot be determined through empirical means alone.[58]

In my view the problem of the subject and, within this, the problem of conceptualizing "woman," is such a metaphysical problem. Thus, I disagree with both phenomenologists and psychoanalysts who assert that the nature of subjectivity can be discovered via a certain methodology and conceptual apparatus, either the epoche or the

[58] In this conception of the proper dimension of and approach to metaphysics (as a conceptual enterprise to be decided partially by pragmatic methods), I am following the tradition of the later Rudolf Carnap and Ludwig Wittgenstein, among others (Rudolf Carnap, "Empiricism, Semantics, and Ontology," and "On the Character of Philosophical Problems," both in *The Linguistic Turn*, ed. R. Rorty [Chicago: University of Chicago Press, 1967]; and Ludwig Wittgenstein, *Philosophical Investigations*, trans. G. E. M. Anscombe [New York: Macmillan, 1958]).

theory of the unconscious.[59] Neurophysiological reductionists likewise claim to be able to produce empirical explanations of subjectivity, but they will by and large admit that their physicalist explanations can tell us little about the experiential reality of subjectivity.[60] Moreover, I would assert that physicalist explanations can tell us little about how the concept of subjectivity should be construed, since this concept necessarily entails considerations not only of the empirical data but also of the political and ethical implications as well. Like the determination of when "human" life begins—whether at conception, full brain development, or birth—we cannot through science alone settle the issue since it turns on how we (to some extent) choose to define concepts like "human" and "woman." We cannot discover the "true meaning" of these concepts but must decide how to define them using all the empirical data, ethical arguments, political implications, and coherence constraints at hand.

Psychoanalysis should be mentioned separately here since it was Freud's initial problematizing of the subject from which developed post-structuralist rejection of the subject. It is the psychoanalytic conception of the unconscious that "undermines the subject from any position of certainty" and in fact claims to reveal that the subject is a fiction.[61] Feminists then use psychoanalysis to problematize the gendered subject to reveal "the fictional nature of the sexual category to which every human subject is none the less assigned."[62] Yet while a theorizing of the unconscious is used as a primary means of theorizing the subject, certainly psychoanalysis alone cannot provide all of the answers we need for a theory of the gendered subject.[63]

As I have already stated, it seems important to use Teresa de Lauretis's conception of experience as a way to begin to describe the features of human subjectivity. Lauretis starts with no given biological or psychological features and thus avoids assuming an

[59] I am thinking particularly of Husserl and Freud here. The reason for my disagreement is that both approaches are in reality more metaphysical than their proponents would admit and, further, that I have only limited sympathy for the metaphysical claims they make. I realize that to explain this fully would require a long argument, which I cannot give in this essay.

[60] See, e.g., Donald Davidson, "Psychology as Philosophy," in his *Essays on Actions and Interpretations* (Oxford: Clarendon Press, 1980), 230.

[61] Jacqueline Rose, "Introduction II," in *Feminine Sexuality: Jacques Lacan and the Ecole Freudienne*, ed. Juliet Mitchell and Jacqueline Rose (New York: Norton, 1982), 29, 30.

[62] Ibid., 29.

[63] Psychoanalysis must take credit for making subjectivity a problematic issue, and yet I think a view that gives psychoanalysis hegemony in this area is misguided, if only because psychoanalysis is still extremely hypothetical. Let a hundred flowers bloom.

essential characterization of subjectivity, but she also avoids the idealism that can follow from a rejection of materialist analyses by basing her conception on real practices and events. The importance of this focus on practices is, in part, Lauretis's shift away from the belief in the totalization of language or textuality to which most antiessentialist analyses become wedded. Lauretis wants to argue that language is not the sole source and locus of meaning, that habits and practices are crucial in the construction of meaning, and that through self-analyzing practices we can rearticulate female subjectivity. Gender is not a point to start from in the sense of being a given thing but is, instead, a posit or construct, formalizable in a nonarbitrary way through a matrix of habits, practices, and discourses. Further, it is an interpretation of our history within a particular discursive constellation, a history in which we are both subjects of and subjected to social construction.

The advantage of such an analysis is its ability to articulate a concept of gendered subjectivity without pinning it down one way or another for all time. Given this and given the danger that essentialist conceptions of the subject pose specifically for women, it seems both possible and desirable to construe a gendered subjectivity in relation to concrete habits, practices, and discourses while at the same time recognizing the fluidity of these.

As both Lacan and Riley remind us, we must continually emphasize within any account of subjectivity the historical dimension.[64] This will waylay the tendency to produce general, universal, or essential accounts by making all our conclusions contingent and revisable. Thus, through a conception of human subjectivity as an emergent property of a historicized experience, we can say "feminine subjectivity is construed here and now in such and such a way" without this ever entailing a universalizable maxim about the "feminine."

It seems to me equally important to add to this approach an "identity politics," a concept that developed from the Combahee River Collective's "A Black Feminist Statement."[65] The idea here is that one's identity is taken (and defined) as a political point of departure, as a motivation for action, and as a delineation of one's

[64] See Juliet Mitchell, "Introduction I," in Mitchell and Rose, eds., 4–5.

[65] This was suggested to me by Teresa de Lauretis in an informal talk she gave at the Pembroke Center, 1984–85. A useful discussion and application of this concept can be found in Elly Bulkin, Minnie Bruce Pratt, and Barbara Smith, *Yours in Struggle: Three Feminist Perspectives on Anti-Semitism and Racism* (Brooklyn, N.Y.: Long Haul Press, 1984), 98–99. Martin and Mohanty's paper (n. 35 above) offers a fruitful reading of the essay in *Yours in Struggle* by Minnie Bruce Pratt entitled "Identity: Skin Blood Heart" and brings into full relief the way in which she uses identity politics. See also "The Combahee River Collective" (n. 19 above).

politics. Lauretis and the authors of *Yours in Struggle* are clear about the problematic nature of one's identity, one's subject-ness, and yet argue that the concept of identity politics is useful because identity is a posit that is politically paramount. Their suggestion is to recognize one's identity as always a construction yet also a necessary point of departure.

I think this point can be readily intuited by people of mixed races and cultures who have had to choose in some sense their identity.[66] For example, assimilated Jews who have chosen to become Jewish-identified as a political tactic against anti-Semitism are practicing identity politics. It may seem that members of more easily identifiable oppressed groups do not have this luxury, but I think that just as Jewish people can choose to assert their Jewishness, so black men, women of all races, and other members of more immediately recognizable oppressed groups can practice identity politics by choosing their identity as a member of one or more groups as their political point of departure. This, in fact, is what is happening when women who are not feminists downplay their identity as women and who, on becoming feminists, then begin making an issue of their femaleness. It is the claiming of their identity as women as a political point of departure that makes it possible to see, for instance, gender-biased language that in the absence of that departure point women often do not even notice.

It is true that antifeminist women can and often do identify themselves strongly as women and with women as a group, but this is usually explained by them within the context of an essentialist theory of femininity. Claiming that one's politics are grounded in one's essential identity avoids problematizing both identity and the connection between identity and politics and thus avoids the agency involved in underdetermined actions. The difference between feminists and antifeminists strikes me as precisely this: the affirmation or denial of our right and our ability to construct, and take responsibility for, our gendered identity, our politics, and our choices.[67]

Identity politics provides a decisive rejoinder to the generic human thesis and the mainstream methodology of Western political

[66] This point has been the subject of long, personal reflection for me, as I myself am half Latina and half white. I have been motivated to consider it also since the situation is even more complicated for my children, who are half mine and half a Jewish father's.

[67] I certainly do not believe that most women have the freedom to choose their situations in life, but I do believe that of the multiple ways we are held in check, internalized oppressive mechanisms play a significant role, and we can achieve control over these. On this point I must say I have learned from and admired the work of Mary Daly, particularly *Gyn/Ecology* (n. 6 above), which reveals and describes these internal mechanisms and challenges us to repudiate them.

theory. According to the latter, the approach to political theory must be through a "veil of ignorance" where the theorist's personal interests and needs are hypothetically set aside. The goal is a theory of universal scope to which all ideally rational, disinterested agents would acquiesce if given sufficient information. Stripped of their particularities, these rational agents are considered to be potentially equally persuadable. Identity politics provides a materialist response to this and, in so doing, sides with Marxist class analysis. The best political theory will not be one ascertained through a veil of ignorance, a veil that is impossible to construct. Rather, political theory must base itself on the initial premise that all persons, including the theorist, have a fleshy, material identity that will influence and pass judgment on all political claims. Indeed, the best political theory for the theorist herself will be one that acknowledges this fact. As I see it, the concept of identity politics does not presuppose a prepackaged set of objective needs or political implications but problematizes the connection of identity and politics and introduces identity as a factor in any political analysis.

If we combine the concept of identity politics with a conception of the subject as positionality, we can conceive of the subject as nonessentialized and emergent from a historical experience and yet retain our political ability to take gender as an important point of departure. Thus we can say at one and the same time that gender is not natural, biological, universal, ahistorical, or essential and yet still claim that gender is relevant because we are taking gender as a position from which to act politically. What does position mean here?

When the concept "woman" is defined not by a particular set of attributes but by a particular position, the internal characteristics of the person thus identified are not denoted so much as the external context within which that person is situated. The external situation determines the person's relative position, just as the position of a pawn on a chessboard is considered safe or dangerous, powerful or weak, according to its relation to the other chess pieces. The essentialist definition of woman makes her identity independent of her external situation: since her nurturing and peaceful traits are innate they are ontologically autonomous of her position with respect to others or to the external historical and social conditions generally. The positional definition, on the other hand, makes her identity relative to a constantly shifting context, to a situation that includes a network of elements involving others, the objective economic conditions, cultural and political institutions and ideologies, and so on. If it is possible to identify women by their position within this network of relations, then it becomes possible to ground a feminist argument for women, not on a claim that their innate capacities are being stunted, but that their position within the network lacks power and mobility and requires radical change. The position of women is relative and not innate, and yet neither is it "undecidable." Through social critique and analysis we can identify women via their position relative to an existing cultural and social network.

It may sound all too familiar to say that the oppression of women involves their relative position within a society; but my claim goes further than this. I assert that the very subjectivity (or subjective experience of being a woman) and the very identity of women is constituted by women's position. However, this view should not imply that the concept of "woman" is determined solely by external elements and that the woman herself is merely a passive recipient of an identity created by these forces. Rather, she herself is part of the historicized, fluid movement, and she therefore actively contributes to the context within which her position can be delineated. I would include Lauretis's point here, that the identity of a woman is the product of her own interpretation and reconstruction of her history, as mediated through the cultural discursive context to which she has access.[68] Therefore, the concept of positionality includes two points: first, as already stated, that the concept of woman is a relational term identifiable only within a (constantly moving) context; but, second, that the position that women find themselves in can be actively utilized (rather than transcended) as a location for the construction of meaning, a place from where meaning is constructed, rather than simply the place where a meaning can be *discovered* (the meaning of femaleness). The concept of woman as positionality shows how women use their positional perspective as a place from which values are interpreted and constructed rather than as a locus of an already determined set of values. When women become feminists the crucial thing that has occurred is not that they have learned any new facts about the world but that they come to view those facts from a different position, from their own position as subjects. When colonial subjects begin to be critical of the formerly imitative attitude they had toward the colonists, what is happening is that they begin to identify with the colonized rather than the colonizers.[69] This difference in positional perspective does not necessitate a change in what are taken to be facts, although new facts may come into view from the new position, but it does ne-

[68] See Teresa de Lauretis, "Feminist Studies/Critical Studies: Issues, Terms, Contexts," in Lauretis, ed. (n. 18 above), 8–9.

[69] This point is brought out by Homi Bhabha in his "Of Mimicry and Man: The Ambivalence of Colonial Discourse," *October* 28 (1984): 125–33; and by Abdur Rahman in his *Intellectual Colonisation* (New Delhi: Vikas, 1983).

cessitate a political change in perspective since the point of departure, the point from which all things are measured, has changed.

In this analysis, then, the concept of positionality allows for a determinate though fluid identity of woman that does not fall into essentialism: woman is a position from which a feminist politics can emerge rather than a set of attributes that are "objectively identifiable." Seen in this way, being a "woman" is to take up a position within a moving historical context and to be able to choose what we make of this position and how we alter this context. From the perspective of that fairly determinate though fluid and mutable position, women can themselves articulate a set of interests and ground a feminist politics.

The concept and the position of women is not ultimately undecidable or arbitrary. It is simply not possible to interpret our society in such a way that women have more power or equal power relative to men. The conception of woman that I have outlined limits the constructions of woman we can offer by defining subjectivity as positionality within a context. It thus avoids nominalism but also provides us with the means to argue against views like "oppression is all in your head" or the view that antifeminist women are not oppressed.

At the same time, by highlighting historical movement and the subject's ability to alter her context, the concept of positionality avoids essentialism. It even avoids tying ourselves to a structure of gendered politics conceived as historically infinite, though it allows for the assertion of gender politics on the basis of positionality at any time. Can we conceive of a future in which oppositional gender categories are not fundamental to one's self-concept? Even if we cannot, our theory of subjectivity should not preclude, and moreover prevent, that eventual possibility. Our concept of woman as a category, then, needs to remain open to future radical alteration, else we will preempt the possible forms eventual stages of the feminist transformation can take.

Obviously, there are many theoretical questions on positionality that this discussion leaves open. However, I would like to emphasize that the problem of woman as subject is a real one for feminism and not just on the plane of high theory. The demands of millions of women for child care, reproductive control, and safety from sexual assault can reinvoke the cultural assumption that these are exclusively feminine issues and can reinforce the right-wing's reification of gender differences unless and until we can formulate a political program that can articulate these demands in a way that challenges rather than utilizes sexist discourse.

Recently, I heard an attack on the phrase "woman of color" by a woman, dark-skinned herself, who was arguing that the use of this phrase simply reinforces the significance of that which should have no significance—skin color. To a large extent I agreed with this woman's argument: we must develop the means to address the wrongs done to us without reinvoking the basis of those wrongs. Likewise, women who have been eternally construed must seek a means of articulating a feminism that does not continue construing us in any set way. At the same time, I believe we must avoid buying into the neuter, universal "generic human" thesis that covers the West's racism and androcentrism with a blindfold. We cannot resolve this predicament by ignoring one half of it or by attempting to embrace it. The solution lies, rather, in formulating a new theory within the process of reinterpreting our position, and reconstructing our political identity, as women and feminists in relation to the world and to one another.

Department of Philosophy
Kalamazoo College

KNOWERS, KNOWING, KNOWN: FEMINIST THEORY AND CLAIMS OF TRUTH

MARY E. HAWKESWORTH

Despite a growing philosophical movement away from preoccupations with epistemology in general, and foundationalism in particular, feminist theorists continue to explore theories of knowledge.[1] Recurrent tendencies within the dominant disciplines to marginalize feminist scholarship as a subject of interest to "women only"

I would like to thank Philip Alperson, Frank Cunningham, Judith Grant, and three anonymous reviewers for their helpful comments on an earlier version of this paper.

[1] For general arguments against an excessive philosophical preoccupation with epistemology, see Jacques Derrida, *Dissemination* (Chicago: University of Chicago Press, 1981); John Gunnell, *Between Philosophy and Politics* (Amherst: University of Massachusetts Press, 1986); Mark Krupnick, ed., *Displacement* (Bloomington: University of Indiana Press, 1983); Paul Kress, "Against Epistemology," *Journal of Politics* 41, no. 2 (May 1979): 526–42. For specific arguments against foundationalism, see Richard Rorty, *Philosophy and the Mirror of Nature* (Princeton, N.J.: Princeton University Press, 1979); Richard Bernstein, *Beyond Objectivism and Relativism* (Philadelphia: University of Pennsylvania Press, 1983); Don Herzog, *Without Foundations: Justification in Political Theory* (Ithaca, N.Y.: Cornell University Press, 1985). It is worth noting the irony that even those most intent on repudiating epistemology on the grounds that traditional epistemological concerns involve claims altogether beyond the possibilities for human knowledge are themselves advancing epistemological claims.

This essay originally appeared in *Signs*, vol. 14, no. 3, Spring 1989.

inspire a quest for an epistemological foundation that can rescue feminist claims from trivialization by demonstrating their truth and importance.[2] The discovery of a pervasive androcentrism in the definition of intellectual problems as well as in specific theories, concepts, methods, and interpretations of research fuels efforts to distinguish between knowledge and prejudice.[3] The recognition that epistemological assumptions have political implications stimulates efforts to attain theoretical self-consciousness concerning the intellectual presuppositions of feminist analysis.[4] Dissatisfaction with paternalistic politics premised on malestream conceptions of "women's nature" sustains feminist epistemological challenges to men's claims to "know" women's nature or what constitutes "women's best interests."[5] Objections raised by Third World women and women of color to the political priorities of white, Western feminists generate profound skepticism about the ability of any particular group of women to "know" what is in the interest of all women.[6]

[2] Sandra Harding and Merrill Hintikka, eds., *Discovering Reality: Feminist Perspectives on Epistemology, Metaphysics, Methodology and Philosophy of Science* (Dordrecht: D. Reidel, 1983); Dale Spender, ed., *Men's Studies Modified: The Impact of Feminism on the Academic Disciplines* (Oxford: Pergamon, 1981).

[3] In addition to the works of Harding and Hintikka, eds., and Spender, ed. (*Men's Studies Modified*) mentioned above, see also Sandra Harding, *The Science Question in Feminism* (Ithaca, N.Y.: Cornell University Press, 1986); Carol Pateman and Elizabeth Gross, eds., *Feminist Challenges* (Boston: Northeastern University Press, 1986); Marion Lowe and Ruth Hubbard, eds., *Women's Nature: Rationalizations of Inequality* (New York: Pergamon, 1983); Evelyn Fox Keller, *Reflections on Gender and Science* (New Haven, Conn.: Yale University Press, 1984); and Jean Grimshaw, *Philosophy and Feminist Thinking* (Minneapolis: University of Minnesota Press, 1986).

[4] Nancy Hartsock, "The Feminist Standpoint: Developing a Ground for a Specifically Feminist Historical Materialism," in Harding and Hintikka, eds., 283–310, and *Money, Sex and Power: Towards a Feminist Historical Materialism* (Boston: Northeastern University Press, 1985); Alison Jaggar, *Feminist Politics and Human Nature* (Totowa, N.J.: Rowman & Allanheld, 1983); and Rita Mae Kelly, Bernard Ronan, and Margaret Cawley, "Liberal Positivistic Epistemology and Research on Women and Politics," *Women and Politics* 7, no. 3 (Fall 1987): 11–27.

[5] Such challenges of men's claims to "know" women's nature have been a staple of feminist criticism since its inception. For examples of early critiques, see Christine de Pisan's fifteenth-century treatise, *The Book of the City of the Ladies*, trans. Earl Jeffrey Richards (New York: Persea, 1982); Mary Wollstonecraft, *Vindication of the Rights of Women*, ed. Charles Hagelman (New York: Norton, 1967); and John Stuart Mill, *The Subjection of Women* (Cambridge, Mass.: MIT Press, 1970). For more recent criticisms, see Mary Daly, *Gyn/Ecology: The Metaethics of Radical Feminism* (Boston: Beacon, 1978); Dale Spender, ed., *Women of Ideas and What Men Have Done to Them* (London: Ark Paperbacks, 1983).

[6] Angela Davis, *Women, Race and Class* (New York: Random House, 1981); Gloria Joseph and Jill Lewis, *Common Differences: Conflicts in Black and White Feminist Perspectives* (New York: Anchor Press/Doubleday, 1981); Paula Giddens, *When and Where I Enter: The Impact of Black Women on Race and Sex in America* (New York: Bantam, 1984).

The identification of conflicts experienced by many women between the contradictory demands of "rationality" and "femininity" stimulate a search for theoretical connections between gender and specific ways of knowing.[7]

The various issues that have inspired feminist interest in theories of knowledge have also produced divergent arguments concerning the premises of a "feminist epistemology." Three models for a feminist theory of knowledge surface with great regularity: feminist empiricism, feminist standpoint theories, and feminist postmodernism.[8]

Feminist empiricism accepts the tenets of philosophical realism (which posit the existence of the world independent of the human knower) and empiricist assumptions about the primacy of the senses as the source of all knowledge about the world. Feminist empiricists maintain that sexism and androcentrism are identifiable biases of individual knowers that can be eliminated by stricter application of existing methodological norms of scientific and philosophical inquiry. From this view, the appropriate method for apprehending the truth about the world involves a process of systematic observation in which the subjectivity of the observer is controlled by rigid adherence to neutral procedures designed to produce identical measurements of the real properties of objects. The eradication of misogynist bias is compatible with, indeed, is a necessary precondition for, the achievement of objective knowledge, for it promotes the acquisition of an unmediated truth about the world; it frees substantive knowledge about reality from the distorting lenses of particular observers.[9]

[7] Genevieve Lloyd, *The Man of Reason: Male and Female in Western Philosophy* (London: Methuen, 1984); Carol McMillan, *Women, Reason and Nature* (Oxford: Basil Blackwell, 1982); Helen Weinrich-Haste, "Redefining Rationality: Feminism and Science" (guest lecture presented at the Ontario Institute for Studies in Education, Toronto, Ontario, October 9, 1986).

[8] This characterization of the alternatives is developed most clearly by Sandra Harding in *The Science Question in Feminism* (n. 3 above). For alternative characterizations of the options available to feminism, see Jaggar; Eloise Buker, "Hermeneutics: Problems and Promises for Doing Feminist Theory" (paper presented at the Annual Meeting of the American Political Science Association, New Orleans, August 30, 1985); and Susan Hekman, "The Feminization of Epistemology: Gender and the Social Sciences," *Women and Politics* 7, no. 3 (Fall 1987): 65–83.

[9] For examples of feminist empiricist arguments, see Janet Richards, *The Skeptical Feminist* (London: Penguin, 1982); S. C. Bourque and J. Grossholtz, "Politics an Unnatural Practice: Political Science Looks at Female Participation," *Politics and Society* 4, no. 2 (Winter 1974): 225–66; M. Goot and E. Reid, "Women and Voting Studies: Mindless Matrons or Sexist Scientism," Sage Professional Papers in Comparative Political Sociology (Newbury Park, Calif.: Sage, 1975); Jill McCalla Vickers, "Memoirs of an Ontological Exile: The Methodological Rebellions of Feminist Research," in *Feminism in Canada*, ed. Geraldine Finn and Angela Miles (Montreal: Black Rose, 1982).

Drawing on historical materialism's insight that social being determines consciousness, feminist standpoint theories reject the notion of an "unmediated truth," arguing that knowledge is always mediated by a host of factors related to an individual's particular position in a determinate sociopolitical formation at a specific point in history. Class, race, and gender necessarily structure the individual's understanding of reality and hence inform all knowledge claims. Although they repudiate the possibility of an unmediated truth, feminist standpoint epistemologies do not reject the notion of truth altogether. On the contrary, they argue that while certain social positions (the oppressor's) produce distorted ideological views of reality, other social positions (the oppressed's) can pierce ideological obfuscations and attain a correct and comprehensive understanding of the world. Thus, feminist analysis grounded on the privileged perspective that emerges from women's oppression constitutes the core of a "successor science" that can replace the truncated projects of masculinist science with a more systematic and sophisticated conception of social and political life.[10]

Taking the perspectivism intimated by standpoint epistemologies to its logical conclusion, "feminist postmodernism" rejects the very possibility of *a* truth about reality. Feminist postmodernists use the "situatedness" of each finite observer in a particular sociopolitical, historical context to challenge the plausibility of claims that any perspective on the world could escape partiality. Extrapolating from the disparate conditions that shape individual identities, they raise grave suspicions about the very notion of a putative unitary consciousness of the species. In addition, the argument that knowledge is the result of invention, the imposition of form on the world rather than the result of discovery, undermines any belief that the Order of Being could be known even if it exists. As an alternative to the futile quest for an authoritative truth to ground feminist theory, feminist postmodernists advocate a profound skepticism regarding universal (or universalizing) claims about the existence, nature, and powers of reason.[11] Rather than succumb to the authoritarian impulses of the will to truth, they urge instead the

[10] For examples of feminist standpoint arguments, see Hartsock, "The Feminist Standpoint," and *Money, Sex and Power;* Jaggar; Mary O'Brien, *The Politics of Reproduction* (London: Routledge & Kegan Paul, 1981); Hilary Rose, "Hand, Brain and Heart: A Feminist Epistemology for the Natural Sciences," *Signs: Journal of Women in Culture and Society* 9, no. 1 (Autumn 1983): 73–90; Dorothy Smith, "Women's Perspective as a Radical Critique of Sociology," *Sociological Inquiry* 44, no. 1 (1974): 7–13.

[11] Jane Flax, "Gender as a Social Problem: In and For Feminist Theory," *American Studies/Amerika Studien* 31, no. 2 (1986): 193–213.

development of a commitment to plurality and the play of difference.[12]

Even so brief a summary of the alternative epistemologies currently vying for feminist allegiance indicates that no single contender can address all of the concerns that have fueled feminists' turn to epistemology. The elements of feminist empiricism and feminist standpoint epistemologies that sustain feminist claims concerning a privileged perspective on the world are at odds with the insight generated by the long struggle of women of color within the feminist movement, that there is no uniform "women's reality" to be known, no coherent perspective to be privileged. Yet the feminist postmodernists' plea for tolerance of multiple perspectives is altogether at odds with feminists' desire to develop a successor science that can refute once and for all the distortions of androcentrism. So intractable is the pull of these competing demands that it has led one of the most astute feminist scholars to recommend that feminists simply recognize and embrace the tensions created by these alternative insights. As Sandra Harding puts it: "Feminist analytical categories *should* be unstable at this moment in history. We need to learn how to see our goal for the present moment as a kind of illuminating 'riffing' between and over the beats of the various patriarchal theories and our own transformations of them, rather than as a revision of the rhythms of any particular one (Marxism, psychoanalysis, empiricism, hermeneutics, postmodernism . . .) to fit what we think at the moment we want to say. The problem is that we do not know and we should not know just what we want to say about a number of conceptual choices with which we are presented—except that the choices themselves create no-win dilemmas for our feminisms."[13]

[12] For additional examples of feminist postmodernism, see Jane Flax, "Postmodernism and Gender Relations in Feminist Theory," *Signs* 12, no. 4 (Summer 1987): 621–43; Donna Haraway, "A Manifesto for Cyborgs: Science, Technology and Socialist Feminism in the 1980s," *Socialist Review* 80 (March/April 1985): 65–107; Claudine Hermann, "The Virile System," in *New French Feminisms*, ed. Elaine Marks and Isabelle de Courtivron (New York: Schocken, 1981); Hekman, "The Feminization of Epistemology," and Susan Hekman, "Derrida, Feminism and Epistemology" (paper presented at the Annual Meeting of the American Political Science Association, Washington, D.C., September 2, 1988); Luce Irigaray, *Speculum of the Other Woman*, trans. Gillian Gill (Ithaca, N.Y.: Cornell University Press, 1985), and *This Sex Which Is Not One*, trans. Catherine Porter (Ithaca, N.Y.: Cornell University Press, 1985).

[13] Harding (n. 3 above), 244; see also 194–96. This ambivalence is also apparent in Jane Flax's article, "Postmodernism and Gender Relations in Feminist Theory," which categorizes feminist theory as a "a type of postmodern philosophy" (624) while simultaneously illuminating some of the deficiencies of postmodernism for

Has feminism arrived at such an impasse that its best hope with respect to epistemological issues is to embrace incompatible positions and embed a contradiction at the heart of its theory of knowledge? There is an alternative approach to epistemological questions that can avoid this unhappy resolution. The purpose of this paper is to explore certain troublesome shifts in feminist arguments about knowledge that lead to the no-win dilemmas outlined by Harding. By changing the focus of feminist epistemological investigations from questions about knowers to claims about the known, feminism can both preserve important insights of postmodernism and serve as a corrective to a variety of inadequate conceptions of the world. By adopting a conception of cognition as a human practice, a critical feminist epistemology can identify, explain, and refute persistent androcentric bias within the dominant discourses without privileging a putative "woman's" perspective and without appealing to problematic conceptions of "the given."

Knowers

Both in academic institutions and in interpersonal interactions, feminists often become acquainted with the claims of established knowledge from the underside. The classic texts of Western history, philosophy, literature, religion, and science, riddled with misinformation about women, are handed down as sacred truths. When individual women attempt to challenge the adequacy of such misogynist accounts, they are frequently informed that their innate inabilities preclude their comprehension of these classic insights. Hence it is not surprising that brilliant feminists have agreed that reason has served as a weapon for the oppression of women, that it has functioned as "a kind of gang rape of women's minds,"[14] that "in masculine hands, logic is often a form of violence, a sly kind of tyranny."[15]

In response to such widespread abusive intellectual practices, feminist analysis often shifts very subtly from a recognition of misinformation about women to a suspicion concerning the dissemi-

---

feminists committed to human emancipation. Thus Flax concludes that "the relation of feminist theorizing to the postmodern project of deconstruction is necessarily ambivalent" (625).

[14] Mary Daly, *Beyond God the Father* (Boston: Beacon, 1973), 9.

[15] Simone de Beauvoir, *The Second Sex*, trans. and ed. H. M. Parshley (New York: Bantam, 1960), 201.

nation of disinformation about women. The fact that the Western intellectual tradition has been conceived and produced by men is taken as evidence that this tradition exists to serve the misogynist interests of men. The existence of the misinformation is taken as evidence of "sexual ideology, a set of false beliefs deployed against women by a conscious, well-organized male conspiracy."[16] The slide from misinformation to disinformation has a number of dire consequences for feminist approaches to epistemology. In focusing attention on the source of knowledge, that is, on men, rather than on the validity of specific claims advanced by men, the terms of debate are shifted toward psychological and functionalist analyses and away from issues of justification. This in turn allows a number of contested epistemological assumptions about the nature of knowledge, the process of knowing, standards of evidence, and criteria of assessment to be incorporated unreflectively into feminist arguments.

In feminist treatments of knowledge one frequently encounters the curious claim that reason is gendered.[17] The claim takes a variety of different forms. It is said that rationality, a tough, rigorous, impersonal, competitive, unemotional, objectifying stance, "is inextricably intertwined with issues of men's gender identities" such as obsession with separation and individuation.[18] It is said that "distinctively (Western) masculine desires are satisfied by the preoccupation with method, rule and law-governed behavior and activity."[19] It is said that the connections between masculinization, reification, and objectification are such that should women attempt to enter the male realm of objectivity, they have only one option: to deny their female nature and adopt the male mode of being.[20] It is said that all dichotomies—objective/subjective, rational/irrational, reason/emotion, culture/nature—are a product of the basic male/

[16] Toril Moi traces this subtle shift in the work of a number of contemporary French feminists and offers an insightful critique of this slide (see *Sexual/Textual Politics: Feminist Literary Theory* [New York: Methuen, 1985], 28).

[17] For a detailed and illuminating discussion of the arguments that sustain this claim, see Judith Grant, "I Feel Therefore I Am: A Critique of Female Experience as a Basis for Feminist Epistemology," *Women and Politics* 7, no. 3 (Fall 1987): 99–114.

[18] Harding, 63. For similar claims, see Susan Bordo, "The Cartesian Masculinization of Thought," *Signs* 11, no. 3 (Spring 1986): 439–56; Kathy Ferguson, "Male Ordered Politics: Feminism and Political Science" (paper presented at the Annual Meeting of the American Political Science Association, New Orleans, August 30, 1985).

[19] Harding (n. 3 above), 229. See also Isaac Balbus, *Marxism and Domination* (Princeton, N.J.: Princeton University Press, 1982); Keller (n. 3 above).

[20] For a sustained consideration of the possibility that the "ideals of reason have incorporated an exclusion of the feminine," see Genevieve Lloyd, *The Man of Reason* (London: Methuen, 1982), 8.

female hierarchy that is central to patriarchal thought and society.[21] It is said that reason is morphologically and functionally analogous to the male sex organ, linear, hard, penetrating but impenetrable.[22] And it is said that representational conceptions of knowledge that privilege evidence based on sight/observation/"the gaze" are derived from men's need to valorize their own visible genitals against the threat of castration posed by women's genitalia, which exist as "nothing to be seen."[23]

Underlying all these claims are speculative psychological notions about a fragile, defensive male ego that impels men constantly to "prove" their masculinity by mastering women, to affirm their own value by denigrating that which is "other."[24] Whether one wishes to defend these psychological claims or to attack them, it is important to note that at issue are certain psychological theories, particular conceptions of psychosexual development, specific notions about the role of the body and of sexuality in the formation of individual identity, and speculations about the relationship between personal identity and sociability. While all of these questions are important and worthy of systematic investigation, they are not epistemological questions per se. The slide from consideration of claims about knowledge and about the truth of certain propositions about women contained in classical texts to concerns about the "will to power" embodied in the claims of "male reason" moves feminist inquiry to a set of highly complex psychological issues that in principle could be completely irrelevant to the resolution of the initial epistemological questions.

[21] Elizabeth Fee, "Whither Feminist Epistemology?" (paper presented at Beyond the Second Sex Conference, Philadelphia, University of Pennsylvania, 1984). Hekman discusses a number of feminist works that link dichotomous thinking to gender hierarchy in "The Feminization of Epistemology" (n. 8 above).

[22] Irigaray, *Speculum of the Other Woman* (n. 12 above), and *This Sex Which Is Not One* (n. 12 above); Hélène Cixous, "Le rire de la Méduse," *L'Arc* 61 (1975): 39–54, trans. Keith Cohen and Paula Cohen, "The Laugh of the Medusa," *Signs* 1, no. 4 (Summer 1976): 875–93, and "Le sexe ou la tête," *Les Cahiers du GRIF* 13 (1976): 5–15, trans. Annette Kuhn, "Castration or Decapitation?" *Signs* 7, no. 1 (Autumn 1981): 41–55; and Ferguson.

[23] Irigaray, *Speculum of the Other Woman,* 48.

[24] Whether these contentious claims are drawn directly from the theories of Freud or indirectly from Freud by means of Klein, Winnicott, and Chodorow, or by means of Lacan and Irigaray, the ultimate blame for the fragility of male identity is attributed to women qua mothers. Despite their theoretical complexities, the various interpretations of the "oedipal conflict" manage to insinuate that it is women-only childcare practices that are the cause of psychic needs to oppress women. That a good deal of feminist theorizing should be premised on such "blame the victim" assumptions is itself very puzzling.

Feminist discussions of epistemology often devolve into modes of functionalist argument. Unlike psychological arguments that attempt to explain phallocentric claims in terms of the psychic needs of male knowers, functionalist arguments focus attention on the putative "interests" served by particular beliefs, whether they be the interests of discrete individuals, groups, classes, institutions, structures, or systems.[25] Thus it is said that "male reason" promotes the interests of men as a sex-class by securing women's collusion in their own oppression, transforming each woman from a forced slave into a willing one.[26] It is said that sexist beliefs serve the interests of individual men, for each man reaps psychological, economic, and political advantages in a society organized according to patriarchal imperatives.[27] It is said that sexist ideology serves the interests of capitalism, for it reproduces the relations of dominance and subordination required by capitalist production; it facilitates the reproduction of labor power on a daily as well as a generational basis; it creates a marginal female labor force willing to work for less than subsistence wages; and it creates divisions within the working class on the basis of gender that thwart the development of unified class consciousness and revolutionary action.[28] And it is said that "male rationality," functioning in accordance with the "logic of identity," operates as a mechanism of social control. In the interests of unrelenting domination, "thought seeks to have everything under control, to eliminate all uncertainty, unpredictability, to eliminate otherness."[29] Authoritarian reason imposes conformity

[25] For the purposes of developing a logical taxonomy, it might be preferable to identify psychological arguments as one form of functionalism, a form that emphasizes the psychological needs and interests served by particular ideas. Because of the frequency with which psychological claims surface in feminist epistemology, in the foregoing analysis I have treated psychological claims independently, but they are also vulnerable to the kinds of problems associated with functionalism.

[26] Mill (n. 5 above); Germaine Greer, *The Female Eunuch* (London: St. Albans, 1971).

[27] Sara Ann Ketchum and Christine Pierce, "Separatism and Sexual Relationships" in *Philosophy and Women,* ed. Sharon Bishop and Marjorie Weinsweig (Belmont, Calif.: Wadsworth Press, 1979), 163–71.

[28] Wally Seccombe, "The Housewife and Her Labour under Capitalism," *New Left Review* 83 (January–February 1973): 3–24; John Berger and Jean Mohr, *A Seventh Man* (London: Harmondsworth, 1975); Victoria Beechey, "Some Notes on Female Wage Labour in the Capitalist Mode of Production," *Capital and Class* 3 (Fall 1977): 45–64, and "Women and Production," in *Feminism and Materialism,* ed. Annette Kuhn and Ann Marie Wolpe (London: Routledge & Kegan Paul, 1978).

[29] Iris Young, "Impartiality and the Civic Public: Some Implications for Feminist Critiques of Moral and Political Theory," *Praxis International* 5, no. 4 (1986): 381–401, esp. 384.

by policing thoughts, purging from the realm of the thinkable all that differs from its own narrow presuppositions.

Functionalist arguments are frequently offered as causal explanations for the existence of particular ideas on the assumption that the function served constitutes the raison d'être for the belief; for example, misogynist notions were/are invented precisely to serve as mechanisms of social control. Yet this teleological assumption, which equates function with first and final cause, overlooks the possibility that the origin of an idea may be totally unrelated to specific uses made of the idea.[30] Functionalist explanations also tend to gloss over complex sociological, political, and historical issues that arise when one attempts to demonstrate that a particular idea or belief actually serves the latent or manifest functions attributed to it in a contemporary setting and that it served this function in a variety of different historical epochs. As feminists pursue the intractable problems associated with functionalist explanations, they are once again carried away from questions concerning the validity of particular claims about women. In the search for the putative purposes served by androcentric notions, arguments concerning the merits of these claims are abandoned.

Feminist analyses that focus on men as the source of knowledge and on the psychological needs and social purposes served by androcentric rationality as *the* central epistemological issues are premised on a number of highly problematic assumptions about the nature of reason and the process of knowing. Rather than acknowledging that reason, rationality, and knowledge are themselves essentially contested concepts that have been the subject of centuries of philosophical debate, there is a tendency to conflate all reasoning with one particular conception of rationality, with instrumental reason.[31] Associated with Enlightenment optimism about the possibility of using reason to gain technical mastery over nature, with rigorous methodological strictures for controlled observation and experimentation, with impartial application of rules to ensure replicability, with the rigidity of the fact/value dichotomy and means-ends analysis that leave crucial normative questions unconsidered, with

[30] For critiques of functionalist arguments within feminism, see Richards (n. 9 above); and Michèle Barrett, *Women's Oppression Today: Problems in Marxist Feminist Analysis* (London: Verso, 1980).

[31] Feminist approaches to epistemology are not alone in reducing a variety of theoretical conceptions of reason to a monolithic notion of instrumental rationality. Richard Bernstein has argued that this is a problem in a number of postmodern theories (see "The Rage against Reason," *Philosophy and Literature* 10, no. 2 [October 1986]: 186–210). For an insightful critique of this tendency within feminism, see Grimshaw (n. 3 above).

processes of rationalization that threaten to imprison human life in increasingly dehumanized systems, and with the deployment of technology that threatens the annihilation of all life on the planet, instrumental reason makes a ready villain.[32] When this villain is in turn associated with uniquely male psychological propensities, it is all too easy to assume that one comprehends not only that men have gotten the world wrong but also why they have gotten it wrong. The supposition that error is the result of willful deception dovetails patly with uncritical notions about unrelenting male drives for dominance and mastery.

The notion that instrumental reason is essentially male also sustains the appealing suggestion that the deployment of a uniquely female knowledge—a knowledge that is intuitive, emotional, engaged, and caring—could save humanity from the dangers of unconstrained masculinism.[33] To develop an account of this alternative knowledge, some feminists have turned to the body, to sexed embodiedness, to thinking in analogy with women's sexuality, to eros, and to women's psychosexual development.[34] Some have focused on the rich resources of women's intuition.[35] Others draw on insights from historical materialism, from theories of marginalization, and from the sociology of knowledge in an effort to generate an account of experiences common to all women that could provide a foun-

[32] For critiques of instrumental reason, see Max Weber, *The Protestant Ethic and the Spirit of Capitalism*, trans. Talcott Parsons (New York: Charles Scribner's Sons, 1958); Hans-Georg Gadamer, "Historical Transformations of Reason," in *Rationality Today*, ed. Theodore Geraets (Ottawa: University of Ottawa Press, 1979); Max Horkheimer and Theodore Adorno, *The Dialectic of Enlightenment* (New York: Herder & Herder, 1972); and Jurgen Habermas, "Dialectics of Rationalization," *Telos* 49 (Fall 1981): 5–31.

[33] See, e.g., Daly, *Gyn/Ecology* (n. 5 above); Marilyn French, *Beyond Power: On Women, Men and Morals* (New York: Summit, 1985); Sara Ruddick, "Maternal Thinking," *Feminist Studies* 6, no. 2 (1980): 342–67, and "Pacifying the Forces: Drafting Women in the Interests of Peace," *Signs* 8, no. 3 (Spring 1983): 471–89. Several feminist scholars have recently noted the irony that this oppositional conception of male and female reason reproduces the caricatures of masculine and feminine that have marked patriarchal social relations (see Grant [n. 17 above]; and Hekman, "The Feminization of Epistemology" [n. 8 above]).

[34] Consider Lorraine Code, "Is the Sex of the Knower Epistemologically Significant?" *Metaphilosophy* 12, nos. 3/4 (July/October 1981): 267–76; Cixous, "Le rire de la Méduse" (n. 22 above), and "Le sexe ou la tête" (n. 22 above); Irigaray, *Speculum of the Other Woman* (n. 12 above); H. K. Trask, *Eros and Power: The Promise of Feminist Theory* (Philadelphia: University of Pennsylvania Press, 1986); and Jane Flax, "Political Philosophy and the Patriarchal Unconscious: A Psychoanalytic Perspective on Epistemology and Metaphysics," in Harding and Hintikka, eds. (n. 2 above).

[35] Compare Daly's *Gyn/Ecology*, French's *Beyond Power*, and Susan Griffin's *Woman and Nature: The Roaring Inside Her* (New York: Harper Colophon, 1980).

dation for a women's standpoint or perspective.[36] The unification of manual, mental, and emotional capacities in women's traditional activities, the sensuous, concrete, and relational character of women's labor in the production of use-values and in reproduction, and the multiple oppressions experienced by women that generate collective struggles against the prevailing social order have all been advanced as the grounds for women's privileged epistemological perspective.[37] In appealing to certain physical, emotional, psychological, and social experiences of women, all of these approaches attempt to solve the problem of the source of knowledge and the validity of knowledge claims simultaneously by conflating the disparate issues of knower and known. They suggest that women's unique experience of reality enables them to pierce ideological distortions and grasp the truth about the world. Where men have gotten it wrong, women will get things right.

When stated so baldly, the claim that women will produce an accurate depiction of reality, either because they are women or because they are oppressed, appears to be highly implausible. Given the diversity and fallibility of all human knowers, there is no good reason to believe that women are any less prone to error, deception, or distortion than men. Appeals to the authority of the female "body" to substantiate such claims suffer from the same defects as the appeals to the authority of the senses so central to the instrumental conception of reason that these feminists set out to repudiate. Both fail to grasp the manifold ways in which all human experiences, whether of the external world or of the internal world, are mediated by theoretical presuppositions embedded in language and culture.[38]

[36] It is important to note that in contrast to claims concerning the immediate apprehension of reality characteristic of discussions of women's embodiedness and intuition, standpoint theories emphasize that a "privileged" standpoint is "achieved rather than obvious, a mediated rather than an immediate understanding . . . an achievement both of science (analysis) and of political struggle" (Hartsock, "The Feminist Standpoint" [n. 4 above], 288). Thus standpoint theories are far more sophisticated in their analysis of knowledge than feminist intuitionists and feminist empiricists. But standpoint theories still suffer from overly simplistic conceptions of the self and of science, which sustain problematic claims concerning the "universal" experiences of women that afford a foundation for a "privileged" standpoint.

[37] On the unification of capacities, see Rose (n. 10 above); the character of women's labor is examined in Hartsock "The Feminist Standpoint," and *Money, Sex and Power* (n. 4 above); and the multiple oppressions of women come under scrutiny in Jaggar (n. 4 above).

[38] In an effort to illuminate the extent to which conceptions of the "body" are socially mediated, Monique Wittig has noted that "in our [women's] case ideology goes far since our bodies as well as our minds are the product of this manipulation. We have been compelled in our bodies and our minds to correspond, feature by feature, with the idea of nature that has been established for us. Distorted to such

Both adhere to notions of transparency and a "natural" self who speaks a truth free of all ambiguity. Both adhere to the great illusion that there is one position in the world or one orientation toward the world that can eradicate all confusion, conflict, and contradiction.

These problems are not eliminated by moving from embodiedness to intuition. The distrust of the conceptual aspects of thought, which sustains claims that genuine knowledge requires immediate apprehension, presumes not only that an unmediated grasp of reality is possible but also that it is authoritative. Moreover, appeals to intuition raise the specter of an authoritarian trump that precludes the possibility of rational debate. Claims based on intuition manifest an unquestioning acceptance of their own veracity. When one assertion informed by the immediate apprehension of reality confronts another diametrically opposed claim also informed by the immediate apprehension of reality, there is no rational way to adjudicate such a dispute. Of course, one might appeal to a notion of adjudication on "intuitive" grounds, but this is the beginning of a vicious regress. Thus, intuition provides a foundation for claims about the world that is at once authoritarian, admitting of no further discussion, and relativist, since no individual can refute another's "immediate" apprehension of reality. Operating at a level of assertion that admits of no further elaboration or explication, those who abandon themselves to intuition conceive and give birth to dreams, not to truth.[39]

The theoretical monism that informs claims of truth rooted in the "body" and in intuition also haunts the arguments of feminist standpoint epistemologies. Although proponents of feminist standpoint theories are careful to note that conceptions of knowledge are historically variable and contestable, certain aspects of their arguments tend to undercut the force of that acknowledgment. For to claim that there is a distinctive women's "perspective" that is "privileged" precisely because it possesses heightened insights into the nature of reality, a superior access to truth, is to suggest that there is some uniform experience common to all women that generates this univocal vision. Yet if social, cultural, and historical differences

---

an extent that our deformed body is what they call 'natural,' is what is supposed to exist as such before oppression. Distorted to such an extent that at the end oppression seems to be a consequence of this 'nature' in ourselves (a nature which is only an idea)" (*Feminist Frameworks*, ed. Alison Jaggar and Paula Rothenberg [New York: McGraw Hill, 1984], 148–52, esp. 148).

[39] G. W. F. Hegel advances a detailed critique of intuitionism in his preface to the *Phenomenology of Spirit* (trans. J. B. Baillie [New York: Harper Colophon, 1967], 73–75).

are taken seriously, the notion of such a common experience becomes suspect. In the absence of such a homogeneous women's experience, standpoint epistemologies must either develop complicated explanations of why some women see the truth while others do not, a strategy that threatens to undermine the very notion of a "women's standpoint," or collapse into a trivial and potentially contradictory pluralism that conceives of truth as simply the sum of all women's partial and incompatible views.[40] It might be suggested that this problem could be avoided by substituting the notion of a "feminist perspective" for that of a "women's perspective." Such a move could then account for the fact that some women grasp the truth while others do not by appealing to the specific experiences that make one a feminist. This move would also create the possibility that some men—those who are feminists—could also grasp the truth, thereby freeing this claim from the specter of biologism. But this strategy encounters other problems by assuming that there is some unique set of experiences that create a feminist. The rich and diverse histories of feminism in different nations and the rivalry among competing feminist visions within contemporary American society (e.g., liberal feminism vs. radical feminism vs. marxist feminism vs. socialist feminism vs. psychoanalytic feminism) raise serious challenges to the plausibility of claims concerning a uniform mode of feminism or an invariant path to feminist consciousness.

Starting from a subjectivist approach to epistemology that focuses on issues pertaining to the faculties and sentiments of knowers as the source of knowledge, feminist inquiry arrives at an impasse. Presuppositions concerning a "natural" subject/self capable of grasping intuitively the totality of being, and a homogeneous women's experience that generates a privileged view of reality, fail to do justice to the fallibility of human knowers, to the multiplicity and diversity of women's experiences, and to the powerful ways in which race, class, ethnicity, culture, and language structure individuals' understandings of the world. Claims concerning diverse and incompatible intuitions about the essential nature of social reality premised on immediate apprehensions of that reality overlook the theoretical underpinnings of all perception and experience and consequently devolve into either authoritarian assertion or uncritical relativism. Moreover, the pervasive tolerance for and indulgence in "gender symbolism" within feminist discussions of epistemology reproduce patriarchal stereotypes of men and women—

[40] This problem has been noted by Alan Soble, "Feminist Epistemology and Women Scientists," *Metaphilosophy* 14, nos. 3/4 (July/October 1983): 291–307; Grant (n. 17 above); and Harding (n. 3 above).

flirting with essentialism, distorting the diverse dimensions of human knowing, and falsifying the historical record of women's manifold uses of reason in daily life.[41]

Knowing

If the complex epistemological problems that confront feminist theory cannot be resolved by appeals to the authority of the body, intuition, or a universal Woman's experience, neither can they be solved by reference to a neutral scientific or philosophical method. Feminist empiricism, in its reliance on scientific techniques designed to control for subjectivity in the process of observation, and feminist standpoint theories that rely on historical/dialectical materialism as a method for achieving an objective grasp of reality depend on problematic conceptions of perception, experience, knowledge, and the self. An alternative account of human cognition can illuminate the defects of these conceptions. Critiques of foundationalism have emphasized that the belief in a permanent, ahistorical, Archimedean point that can provide a certain ground for knowledge claims is incompatible with an understanding of cognition as a human practice.[42] They have suggested that the belief that particular techniques of rational analysis can escape finitude and fallibility and grasp the totality of being misconstrues both the nature of subjective intellection and the nature of the objective world. Attacks on foundationalism therefore raise questions concerning specific forms of knowing, particular conceptions of subjectivity, and various theories of the external world. Insights drawn from these works can delineate the contours of a critical feminist epistemology, which avoids the limitations of feminist empiricism and feminist standpoint theories.

Standard critiques of foundationalism impugn deductive and inductive logic as the ground of objective knowledge. To challenge rationalists' confidence in the power of logical deduction as a method for securing the truth about the empirical world, critics typically point out that the truth of syllogistic reasoning is altogether dependent on the established truth of the syllogism's major and minor

[41] In *The Science Question in Feminism*, Harding defines gender symbolism in terms of the attribution of dualistic gender metaphors to distinctions that rarely have anything to do with sex differences, e.g., "male" reason vs. "female" intuition (17).

[42] See, e.g., Hans Albert, *Treatise on Critical Reason*, trans. Mary Varney Rorty (Princeton, N.J.: Princeton University Press, 1985); Bernstein, *Beyond Objectivism and Relativism* (n. 1 above); Stanley Cavell, *The Claim of Reason* (New York: Oxford University Press, 1979); Rorty (n. 1 above).

premises. Yet when one moves from relations of ideas governed by logical necessity to a world of contingency, the "established truth" of major and minor premises is precisely what is at issue. Thus, rather than providing an impeccable foundation for truth claims, deduction confronts the intractable problems of infinite regress, the vicious circle, or the arbitrary suspension of the principle of sufficient reason through appeals to intuition or self-evidence.[43]

Attacks on empiricist exuberance have been equally shattering. It has been repeatedly pointed out that inductive generalizations, however scrupulous and systematic, founder on a host of problems: observation generates correlations that cannot prove causation; conclusions derived from incomplete evidence sustain probability claims but do not produce incontestable truth.[44] Moreover, where rationalism tends to overestimate the power of theoretical speculation, empiricism errs in the opposite extreme by underestimating the role of theory in shaping perception and structuring comprehension.[45] Thus, the "objectivity" of the empiricist project turns on the deployment of an untenable dichotomy between "facts" and "values"—a dichotomy that misconstrues the nature of perception, fails to comprehend the theoretical constitution of facticity, and uncritically disseminates the "myth of the given."[46]

As an alternative to a conception of knowledge that is dependent on the existence of an unmediated reality that can be grasped directly by observation or intellection, antifoundationalists suggest a conception of cognition as a human practice.[47] In this view, "knowing" presupposes involvement in a social process replete with rules of compliance, norms of assessment, and standards of excellence that are humanly created. Although humans aspire to unmediated knowledge of the world, the nature of perception precludes such direct access. The only possible access is through theory-laden con-

[43] These arguments were developed forcefully by David Hume in his *Enquiry concerning Human Understanding* (Oxford: Clarendon, 1975). For more recent treatment of the issues, see Albert.

[44] For a review of these arguments, see Albert; and Karl Popper, *Conjectures and Refutations* (New York: Basic, 1962).

[45] Albert.

[46] The "myth of the given" is discussed in Wilfred Sellars, *Science, Perception and Reality* (New York: Humanities Press, 1963), 64. For helpful introductions to Sellars's work, see Gibson Winter, *Elements for a Social Ethic: Scientific and Ethical Perspectives on Social Process* (New York: Macmillan, 1966), 61–166; Richard Bernstein, *The Restructuring of Social and Political Theory* (Philadelphia: University of Pennsylvania Press, 1976), 121–35; and Gunnell (n. 1 above), 68–90.

[47] For a detailed discussion of the conception of practice invoked here, see Alasdair MacIntyre, *After Virtue* (Notre Dame, Ind.: University of Notre Dame Press, 1981), 174–89.

ventions that organize and structure observation by according meanings to observed events, bestowing relevance and significance on phenomena, indicating strategies for problem solving, and identifying methods by which to test the validity of proposed solutions. Knowledge, then, is a convention rooted in the practical judgments of a community of fallible inquirers who struggle to resolve theory-dependent problems under specific historical conditions.

Acquisition of knowledge occurs in the context of socialization and enculturation to determinate traditions that provide the conceptual frameworks through which the world is viewed. As sedimentations of conventional attempts to comprehend the world correctly, cognitive practices afford the individual not only a set of accredited techniques for grasping the truth of existence but also a "natural attitude," an attitude of "suspended doubt" with respect to a wide range of issues based on the conviction that one understands how the world works. In establishing what will be taken as normal, natural, real, reasonable, expected, and sane, theoretical presuppositions camouflage their contributions to cognition and their operation on the understanding. Because the theoretical presuppositions that structure cognition operate at the tacit level, it is difficult to isolate and illuminate the full range of presuppositions informing cognitive practices. Moreover, any attempt to elucidate presuppositions must operate within a "hermeneutic circle." Any attempt to examine or to challenge certain assumptions or expectations must occur within the frame of reference established by mutually reinforcing presuppositions. That certain presuppositions must remain fixed if others are to be subjected to systematic critique does not imply that individuals are "prisoners" trapped within the cognitive framework acquired through socialization.[48] Critical reflection on and abandonment of certain theoretical presuppositions is possible within the hermeneutic circle; but the goal of transparency, of the unmediated grasp of things as they are, is not, for no investigation, no matter how critical, can escape the fundamental conditions of human cognition.

Thus, the conception of cognition as a human practice challenges the possibility of unmediated knowledge of the world, as well as notions such as "brute facts," the "immediately given," "theory-free research," "neutral observation language," and "self-evident truths," which suggest that possibility. Because cognition is always theoretically mediated, the world captured in human knowledge and designated "empirical" is itself theoretically constituted. Divergent

[48] In *Beyond Objectivism and Relativism,* Bernstein characterizes this erroneous conclusion as the "myth of the framework" (84).

cognitive practices rooted in conventions such as common sense, religion, science, philosophy, and the arts construe the empirical realm differently, identifying and emphasizing various dimensions, accrediting different forms of evidence, different criteria of meaning, different standards of explanation, different tokens of truthfulness. Such an understanding of the theoretical constitution of the empirical realm in the context of specific cognitive practices requires a reformulation of the notion of "facts." A fact is a theoretically constituted proposition, supported by theoretically mediated evidence and put forward as part of a theoretical formulation of reality. A fact is a contestable component of a theoretically constituted order of things.[49]

The recognition that all cognition is theory-laden has also generated a critique of many traditional assumptions about the subject/self that undergird rationalist, empiricist, and materialist conceptions of knowing. Conceptions of the "innocent eye," of the "passive observer," of the mind as a "tabula rasa" have been severely challenged.[50] The notion of transparency, the belief that the individual knower can identify all his/her prejudices and purge them in order to greet an unobstructed reality has been rendered suspect.[51] Conceptions of an atomistic self who experiences the world independent of all social influences, of the unalienated self who exists as potentiality awaiting expression, and of a unified self who can grasp the totality of being have been thoroughly contested.[52] The very idea of the "subject" has been castigated for incorporating assumptions about the "logic of identity" that posit knowers as undifferentiated, anonymous, and general, possessing a vision independent of all identifiable perspectives.[53] Indeed, the conception of the knowing "subject" has been faulted for failure to grasp that rather than being the source of truth, the subject is the product of particular

[49] For an intriguing discussion of some of the most fundamental presuppositions that have shaped Western cognitive practices since the seventeenth century, see Michel Foucault, *The Order of Things: An Archaeology of the Human Sciences* (New York: Vintage, 1973).

[50] See Popper; Harold Brown, *Perception, Theory and Commitment: The New Philosophy of Science* (Chicago: Precedent, 1977); and Norman Stockman, *Anti-Positivist Theories of Science: Critical Rationalism, Critical Theory and Scientific Realism* (Dordrecht: D. Reidel, 1983).

[51] Albert (n. 42 above); Popper (n. 44 above); Brown; and Stockman.

[52] Seyla Benhabib, *Critique, Norm and Utopia* (New York: Columbia University Press, 1986); Charles Taylor, "Foucault on Freedom and Truth," *Political Theory* 12, no. 2 (1984): 152–83; William E. Connolly, "Taylor, Foucault and Otherness," *Political Theory* 13, no. 3 (1985): 365–76.

[53] See, e.g., Alan Megill, *Prophets of Extremity: Nietzsche, Heidegger, Foucault, Derrida* (Berkeley and Los Angeles: University of California Press, 1985); Young (n. 29 above), 381–401.

regimes of truth.[54] In postmodernist discourses, the notion of a sovereign subject who possesses unparalleled powers of clairvoyance affording direct apprehension of internal and external reality has been supplanted by a conception of the self as an unstable constellation of unconscious desires, fears, phobias, and conflicting linguistic, social, and political forces.

In addition to challenging notions of an unmediated reality and a transparent subject/self, the conception of cognition as a human practice also takes issue with accounts of reason that privilege one particular mode of rationality while denigrating all others. Attempts to reduce the practice of knowing to monadic conceptions of reason fail to grasp the complexity of the interaction between traditional assumptions, social norms, theoretical conceptions, disciplinary strictures, linguistic possibilities, emotional dispositions, and creative impositions in every act of cognition. Approaches to cognition as a human practice emphasize the expansiveness of rationality and the irreducible plurality of its manifestations within diverse traditions. Perception, intuition, conceptualization, inference, representation, reflection, imagination, remembrance, conjecture, rationalization, argumentation, justification, contemplation, ratiocination, speculation, meditation, validation, deliberation—even a partial listing of the many dimensions of knowing suggests that it is a grave error to attempt to reduce this multiplicity to a unitary model. The resources of intellection are more profitably considered in their complexity, for what is involved in knowing is heavily dependent on what questions are asked, what kind of knowledge is sought, and the context in which cognition is undertaken.[55]

The conception of cognition as a human practice has a great deal to offer feminist analysis, for it provides an explanation of androcentric bias within dominant discourses that is free of the defects of psychological and functionalist arguments. Rather than imputing contentious psychological drives to all males or positing speculative structural interests for all social formations, feminists can examine the specific processes by which knowledge has been constituted within determinate traditions and explore the effects of the exclusion of women from participation in those traditions. Feminists can investigate the adequacy of the standards of evidence, criteria of relevance, modes of analysis, and strategies of argumentation privileged by the dominant traditions. By focusing on the theoretical constitution of the empirical realm, feminists can illuminate the presuppositions that circumscribe what is believed to exist and

[54] Michel Foucault, *Discipline and Punish* (New York: Vintage, 1977), and *The History of Sexuality* (New York: Vintage, 1980), vol. 1.

[55] Cavell (n. 42 above).

identify the mechanisms by which facticity is accredited and rendered unproblematic. In raising different questions, challenging received views, refocusing research agendas, and searching for methods of investigation adequate to the problems of feminist scholarship, feminists can contribute to the development of a more sophisticated understanding of human cognition.

The conception of cognition as a human practice suggests that feminist critique is situated within established traditions of cognition even as it calls those traditions into question. Thus feminists must deal deftly with the traditions that serve both as targets of criticism and as sources of norms and techniques essential to the critical project. Moreover, the conception of cognition as a human practice suggests that feminist analysis itself can be understood as a rich and varied tradition. To build feminist epistemology on an understanding of cognition as a human practice, then, requires careful consideration of the diverse cognitive practices that already structure feminist inquiry. Rather than privileging one model of rational inquiry, feminists must first consider the level of analysis, the degree of abstraction, the type of explanation, the standards of evidence, the criteria of evaluation, the tropes of discourse, and the strategies of argumentation that would be appropriate to feminist investigations of concrete problems. Awareness of the structuring power of tacit theoretical presuppositions requires detailed investigation of the political implications of determinate modes of inquiry. The politics of knowledge must remain a principle concern of feminist analysis, not only in the course of examining malestream thought but also in determining the most fruitful avenues for feminist research. For the analytic techniques developed in particular cognitive traditions may have unfortunate political implications when applied in different contexts. Cognitive practices appropriate for psychological analysis may not be appropriate for political and sociological analysis; hermeneutic techniques essential for an adequate interpretation of human action may be wholly inadequate to the task of structural analysis; statistical techniques crucial for the illumination of discrimination may be powerless to address problems relating to ideological oppression; semiotic analyses central to the development of feminist literary criticism may be insufficient to the task of feminist historical investigations; hormonal and endocrinological studies necessary for the creation of feminist health care may be altogether inapplicable as accounts of motivation or explanations of action. Causal, dialectical, genealogical, hermeneutic, psychological, semiotic, statistical, structural, and teleological explanations may all be important to specific aspects of feminist inquiry. But knowing which mode of analysis is appropriate in specific problem situations is an issue that feminist epistemology has not yet adequately addressed.

Feminist epistemology must be sufficiently sophisticated to account for the complexity and for the political dimensions of diverse cognitive practices. To equate feminist epistemology with any particular technique of rationality is to impose unwarranted constraints on feminist inquiry, impairing its ability to develop and deploy an arsenal of analytic techniques to combat the distortions that permeate the dominant malestream discourses. Neither feminist empiricism nor feminist standpoint theories afford an adequate framework for addressing these difficult issues. Feminist empiricism is committed to untenable beliefs about the nature of knowledge and process of knowing that render it unable to explain the persistence of sexist bias within established disciplines and unable to grasp the politics of knowledge. Feminist standpoint theories are far more attuned to the ideological dimensions of knowledge, yet they remain committed to an overly simplistic model of knowledge that tends to assume a "collective singular subject," to posit a false universality, to neglect the multiplicity of structuring processes that shape cognitive practices, and to underestimate the disjuncture between problems of oppression and questions of truth.[56] The conception of cognition as a human practice provides a context for the development of a critical feminist epistemology that can transcend these limitations.[57]

Known

Understanding cognition as a human practice does not, in itself, resolve the question of what, if anything, can be known. Skeptics, relativists, deconstructivists, structuralists, hermeneuticists, and

[56] For a detailed discussion of the problem of assuming a collective singular subject, see Benhabib.

[57] In suggesting that an understanding of cognition as a human practice can help feminist analysis avoid the problems of feminist empiricism and feminist standpoint theories while simultaneously illuminating fruitful strategies of inquiry, I do not mean to suggest that the notion of cognition as a human practice itself could or should supplant feminist investigations of knowledge claims. Feminist inquiry remains as important in the field of epistemology as in any other traditional academic area of investigation, precisely because most contemporary practitioners in these fields, like their predecessors in the Western tradition, suffer from a peculiar form of gender blindness. Even those most sensitive to the politics of knowledge in contexts involving race and class remain remarkably unaware of the unique issues raised by the problem of gender. Feminist analysis serves as a crucial corrective for this acute and pervasive form of masculinist myopia.

critical theorists might all concur about the social construction of cognition, yet come to different conclusions about the nature of truth claims. Within the context of feminist approaches to epistemology, many of the critiques of traditional conceptions of reason have been voiced by feminist postmodernists. Thus it is important to consider whether feminist postmodernism constitutes an adequate epistemology for feminist theory. Such an assessment requires an examination of the theoretical and political implications of postmodernism, as well as a discussion of the light that postmodernism sheds on the question of what can be known.

Discussions of the "situatedness" of knowers suggest that the claims of every knower reflect a particular perspective shaped by social, cultural, political, and personal factors and that the perspective of each knower contains blind spots, tacit presuppositions, and prejudgments of which the individual is unaware.[58] The partiality of individual perspectives in turn suggests that every claim about the world, every account, "can be shown to have left something out of the description of its object and to have put something in which others regard as nonessential."[59] Recognition of the selectivity of cognitive accounts, in terms of conscious and unconscious omission and supplementation, has led some postmodern thinkers to characterize the world in literary terms, to emphasize the fictive elements of "fact," the narrative elements of all discourse—literary, scientific, historical, social, political—and the nebulousness of the distinction between text and reality. The move to intertextuality suggests that the world be treated as text, as a play of signifiers with no determinate meaning, as a system of signs whose meaning is hidden and diffuse, as a discourse that resists decoding because of the infinite power of language to conceal and obfuscate.[60] Postmodernist discourses celebrate the human capacity to misunderstand, to universalize the particular and the idiosyncratic, to privilege the ethnocentric, and to conflate truth with those prejudices that advantage the knower. Postmodernist insights counsel that Truth be abandoned because it is a hegemonic and, hence, destructive illusion.

Postmodernism has much to commend it. Its sensitivity to the hubris of scientific reason has illuminated the manifold ways in which scientism sustains authoritarian tendencies. Its merger of the horizons of philosophical and literary discourses has loosened the

58 See, e.g., Buker (n. 8 above); and Moi (n. 16 above).

59 Hayden White, *Tropics of Discourse* (Baltimore: Johns Hopkins University Press, 1978), 3.

60 For a helpful introduction to and critique of the postmodern shift from world to text, see Megill (n. 53 above).

disciplinary strictures of both traditions and produced creative deconstructions of the tacit assumptions that sustain a variety of unreflective beliefs. Its attentiveness to discourse has heightened our understanding of the integral relations between power and knowledge, and of the means by which particular power/knowledge constellations constitute us as subjects in a determinate order of things. Its refusal to validate univocal interpretations has generated a new appreciation of plurality and has stimulated creative thinking about ways to value difference.

But postmodernism also has a number of defects that militate against the uncritical adoption of all of its tenets into feminist epistemology. Indeed, crucial social and political insights of a critical feminist theory should serve as a corrective to some of the excesses of postmodernism.

The undesirable consequences of the slide into relativism that results from too facile a conflation of world and text is particularly evident when feminist concerns are taken as the starting point. Rape, domestic violence, and sexual harassment (to mention just a few of the realities that circumscribe women's lives) are not fictions or figurations that admit of the free play of signification. The victim's account of these experiences is not simply an arbitrary imposition of a purely fictive meaning on an otherwise meaningless reality. A victim's knowledge of the event may not be exhaustive; indeed, the victim may be oblivious to the fact of premeditation, may not comprehend the motive for the assault, may not know the identity of the assailant. But it would be premature to conclude from the incompleteness of the victim's account that all other accounts (the assailant's, defense attorney's, character witnesses' for the defendant) are equally valid or that there are no objective grounds on which to distinguish between truth and falsity in divergent interpretations. The important point here is not that it is easy to make these determinations or that they can always be made in particular cases but that standards related to the range of human cognitive practices allow us to distinguish between partial views (the inescapable condition of human cognition) and false beliefs, superstitions, irrebuttable presumptions, willful distortions. Although it is often extraordinarily difficult to explicate the standards of evidence, the criteria of relevance, paradigms of explanation, and norms of truth that inform such distinctions, the fact that informed judgments can be made provides sufficient ground to avoid premature plunges into relativism, to insist instead that there are some things that can be known.

The world is more than a text. Theoretical interpretations of the world must operate within different parameters than those of literary criticism. Although both theories of life and theories of literature are necessarily dependent on conceptual schemes that are themselves structured by language and, hence, contestable and contingent, theories of life must deal with more than the free play of signifiers. There is a modicum of permanence within the fluidity of the life-world: traditions, practices, relationships, institutions, and structures persist and can have profound consequences for individual life prospects, constraining opportunities for growth and development, resisting reconstitution, frustrating efforts toward direction and control. It is a serious mistake to neglect the more enduring features of existing institutional structures and practices while indulging the fantasies of freedom afforded by intertextuality. Contentment with relativist perspectivism does not do justice to the need for systematicity in analyses of the structural dimensions of social and political life. Although much can be gained from the recognition that there are many sides to every story and many voices to provide alternative accounts, the escape from the monotony of monologue should not be at the expense of the very notion of truth. The need to debunk scientistic assumptions about the unproblematic nature of the objective world does not require the total repudiation of either external reality or the capacity for critical reflection and rational judgment.[61]

A critical feminist epistemology must avoid both the foundationalist tendency to reduce the multiplicity of reasons to a monolithic "Reason" and the postmodernist tendency to reject all reasons *tout court*. Keenly aware of the complexity of all knowledge claims, it must defend the adoption of a minimalist standard of rationality that requires that belief be apportioned to evidence and that no assertion be immune from critical assessment. Deploying this minimalist standard, feminist analysis can demonstrate the inadequacies of accounts of human nature derived from an evidentiary base of only half the species; it can refute unfounded claims about women's "nature" that are premised on an atheoretical naturalism; it can identify androcentric bias in theories, methods, and concepts and show how this bias undermines explanatory force; it can demonstrate that the numerous obstacles to women's full participation in social, political, and economic life are humanly created and hence

[61] The conception of cognition as a human practice requires a coherence theory of truth. Due to the limitations of space, it is not possible to explore the dimensions of this conception in detail here; nor is it possible to provide a systematic defense of this conception of truth against the charge of relativism. For works that do undertake both those tasks, see Bernstein, *Beyond Objectivism and Relativism* (n. 1 above); Cavell (n. 42 above); Herzog (n. 1 above); and William E. Connolly, *Appearance and Reality in Politics* (Cambridge: Cambridge University Press, 1981).

susceptible to alteration. In providing sophisticated and detailed analyses of concrete situations, feminists can dispel distortions and mystifications that abound in malestream thought.

Based on a consistent belief in and acceptance of fallibility as inescapable and consonant with life in a world of contingencies, feminists need not claim universal, ahistorical validity for their analyses. They need not assert that theirs is the only or the final word on complex questions. In the absence of claims of universal validity, feminist accounts derive their justificatory force from their capacity to illuminate existing social relations, to demonstrate the deficiencies of alternative interpretations, to debunk opposing views. Precisely because feminists move beyond texts to confront the world, they can provide concrete reasons in specific contexts for the superiority of their accounts. Such claims to superiority are derived not from some privileged standpoint of the feminist knower nor from the putative merits of particular intuitions but from the strength of rational argument, from the ability to demonstrate point by point the deficiencies of alternative explanations. At their best, feminist analyses engage both the critical intellect and the world; they surpass androcentric accounts because in their systematicity more is examined and less is assumed.

Postmodernism's retreat to the text has a political dimension not altogether consonant with its self-proclaimed radicalism. There is an unmistakable escapist tendency in the shift to intertextuality, in the move from fact to fiction. The abandonment of reason(s) is accompanied by a profound sense of resignation, a nihilist recognition that there is nothing to do because nothing can be done. At a moment when the preponderance of rational and moral argument sustains prescriptions for women's equality, it is a bit too cruel a conclusion and too reactionary a political agenda to accept that reason is impotent, that equality is impossible. Should postmodernism's seductive text gain ascendancy, it will not be an accident that power remains in the hands of the white males who currently possess it. In a world of radical inequality, relativist resignation reinforces the status quo. For those affronted by the arrogance of power, there are political as well as intellectual reasons to prefer a critical feminist epistemology to a postmodernist one. In confrontations with power, knowledge and rational argumentation alone will not secure victory, but feminists can use them strategically to subvert male dominance and to transform oppressive institutions and practices.

Department of Political Science
University of Louisville

ABOUT THE CONTRIBUTORS

LESLIE A. ADELSON is associate professor of German at Ohio State University. Her publications include "Der arme Mann und 'diese solidarischen Löcher': Zu Begriff und Funktion von Weiblichkeit bei Botho Strauss," in *Weiblichkeit und Avantgarde,* ed. Inge Stephan and Sigrid Weigel (Berlin: Argument, 1987), 165–86, and "The Bomb and I: Peter Sloterdijk, Botho Strauss, and Christa Wolf," *Monatshefte* 78, no. 4 (Winter 1986): 500–513. Her research interests include contemporary West German prose, feminist aesthetics, the "new subjectivity," and the relationship between history and aesthetic production.

LINDA ALCOFF is assistant professor of philosophy at Syracuse University. She is author of "Justifying Feminist Social Science," *Hypatia* 2, no. 3 (1987): 107–27, and she is writing an article about Foucault's influence upon feminism as well as writing a book-length manuscript about coherence and truth.

CAROL COHN is a senior research scholar at the Center for Psychological Studies in the Nuclear Age and a research associate in the Department of Psychiatry at Harvard Medical School. She attended the Harvard/MIT Nuclear Weapons, Technology, and Arms Control Summer Program and spent a year as a visiting scholar in the Defense and Arms Control Studies Program at MIT's Center for International Studies. She is currently writing a book about the specialized language and thinking of nuclear defense intellectuals and their influence on American political culture.

MARILYN R. FARWELL is associate professor of English at the University of Oregon. Her research focuses on the relations between contemporary literary theory and women's literature, especially as these relations resonate with lesbian topics. She has published essays on Virginia Woolf, Milton, and Adrienne Rich and is currently working on a series of essays about the ways in which current lesbian theory permits a new reading of women's contemporary fiction and poetry.

JANE FLAX is associate professor of political science at Howard University and a practicing psychotherapist in Chevy Chase, Maryland. She is author of *Thinking Fragments: Psychoanalysis, Feminism, and Postmodernism in the Contemporary West* (Berkeley: University of California Press, 1989) and is currently working on a paper about the possibilities of postmodernist-feminist theories of justice.

THOMAS FOSTER is a Ph.D. candidate in the English department at the University of Wisconsin—Madison. He is currently writing a dissertation on oppositional practices and modern women's writing, including the work of H. D., Marianne Moore, Gertrude Stein, Sylvia Townsend Warner, Virginia Woolf, Nella Larsen, and Zora Neale Hurston.

CHRISTINE FROULA is associate professor of English and comparative literature and theory at Northwestern University. Her research interests include women and the Western literary tradition, modern literature, and feminist and literary theory. Recently, she has completed a book on gender and literary authority (New York: Columbia University Press, forthcoming).

SANDRA HARDING is professor of philosophy and director of women's studies at the University of Delaware. She is the author of *The Science Question in Feminism* (Ithaca, N.Y.: Cornell University Press, 1986), which won the Jessie Bernard Award of the American Sociological Association in 1987. She edited *Feminism and Methodology: Social Science Issues* (Bloomington: Indiana University Press, 1987); and coedited *Sex and Scientific Inquiry* (Chicago: University of Chicago Press, 1987), with Jean O'Barr.

MARY E. HAWKESWORTH is associate professor of political science at the University of Louisville. Her interests include contemporary political philosophy, feminist theory, and policy analysis. She is the author of *Theoretical Issues in Policy Analysis* (Albany: State University of New York Press, 1988), and editor of the *Encyclopaedia of Government and Politics* (London: Routledge, 1990). Currently, she is writing a book about feminist theory and political life.

DEBORAH K. KING is associate professor of sociology at Dartmouth College. Her research primarily concerns the development of an Afrocentric perspective on race, class, and gender in black women's political consciousness and activism. She is completing a book that examines the enforcement of affirmative action employment policies in higher education.

MICHELINE RIDLEY MALSON is an assistant professor in Public Policy at Duke University. Her interests include black single-parent families headed by women, black women and gender roles, and social policy and social programs. She is author of "Black Women's Sex Roles: The Social Context for a New Ideology," *Journal of Social Issues* 39, no. 3 (1983): 101–14, and "The Social Support Systems of Black Families," *Marriage and Family Review* 5, no. 4 (1983): 37–58. Currently she is completing a book describing the dynamics of black single-parent households.

JEAN F. O'BARR is director of Women's Studies at Duke University, where she teaches in the political science department. Her interests focus on contemporary feminism and women in higher education. She is the editor of *Women and a New Academy: Gender and Cultural Contexts* (Madison: University of Wisconsin Press, 1989), *Reconstructing the Academy: Women's Education and Women's Studies* (Chicago: University of

Chicago Press, 1988), with Elizabeth Minnich and Rachel Rosenfeld, and *Sex and Scientific Inquiry* (Chicago: University of Chicago Press, 1987), with Sandra Harding. She currently serves as editor of *Signs*.

ZAKIA PATHAK is a senior lecturer in English at Miranda House at Delhi University. Her research interests include theory and its uses and the female as subject. She is author of "Drabble's *Waterfall*: An Appropriation of Eliot's *Mill*," in *Woman/Image/Text: Feminist Readings of Literary Texts*, ed. Lola Chatterjee (New Delhi: Trianka, 1986).

SUSAN RUBIN SULEIMAN is professor of romance and comparative literatures at Harvard University. She is the author of *Authoritarian Fictions: The Idealogical Novel as a Literary Genre* (New York: Columbia University Press, 1983), and editor of *The Female Body in Western Culture: Contemporary Perspectives* (Cambridge, Mass.: Harvard University Press, 1986).

RAJESWARI SUNDER RAJAN is a lecturer in English in the Miranda House at Delhi University. Her research interests include feminist theory and Third World politics. She is author of "Male Mentors and the Female Imagination: George Eliot's Intellectual Background," and "Katherine Mansfield and the Question of Women's Writing," in *Women/Image/Text: Feminist Readings of Literary Texts*, ed. Lola Chatterjee (New Delhi: Trianka, 1986).

SARAH WESTPHAL-WIHL is assistant professor and Canada Research Fellow in the comparative literature program at McGill University. She is coeditor of the *Signs* special issue "Sisters and Workers: Medieval Perspectives on Women's Communities," 14, no. 2 (Winter 1989), and author of "The Ladies Tournament: Marriage, Sex, and Honor in Thirteenth-Century Germany," *Signs* 14, no. 2 (Winter 1989): 371–88. Currently, she is working on a book about the social and symbolic power of the representation of women in medieval literature.

PATRICIA J. WILLIAMS is associate professor of law in the City University of New York Law School at Queens College. She teaches commercial and consumer law and jurisprudence and is currently working on a book that examines the intersection of constitutional rights and commercial interests.

MARY WYER is managing editor of *Signs*. She was associate acquisitions editor at the University of Wisconsin Press, 1980–82, and administrative coordinator of the Women's Studies Program at MIT, 1983–85. She is currently teaching a course at Duke University on feminist editing practices.

ELISABETH YOUNG-BRUEHL is professor of letters at Wesleyan University. She is the author of *Hannah Arendt: For Love of the World* (New Haven, Conn.: Yale University Press, 1982), *Anna Freud: A Biography* (New York: Summit, 1988), and *Freud on Women* (New York: Norton, 1989).

INDEX